West Malaysia

0   50   100

Kilometers

LEGEND

▬▬ Major Road	◯ Village	🛕 Chinese Temple	
═══ Through Road	◎ Town	Ψ Hindu Temple	
—— Tertiary Road	◉ Major Town	⊥ Church	
▪▪▪ Int'l Boundary	☐ CITY	Mosque	
▪▪▪ Provincial Boundary	■ CAPITAL	✈ Airport	
▬▬ Railway	✛ Hospital	Museum	
▬▬ Park Boundary	★ Police	★ Place of interest	
▲ Mountain	■ Hotel	Reserve	
↑ Direction to another town	▲ Shops/Banks	Ⓒ Telekoms	
🚌 Bus Station	● Restaurant	⊠ Post Office	

WEST MALAYSIA

and Singapore

Edited by
WENDY MOORE

PASSPORT BOOKS
a division of *NTC Publishing Group*
Lincolnwood, Illinois USA

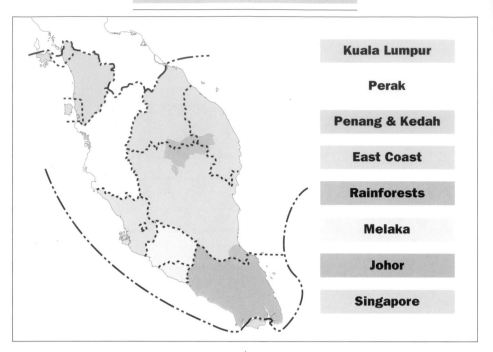

Kuala Lumpur

Perak

Penang & Kedah

East Coast

Rainforests

Melaka

Johor

Singapore

This edition first published by Passport Books, a division of NTC Publishing Group, 4255 West Touhy Avenue, Lincolnwood (Chicago), Illinois 60646-1975 U.S.A. Originally published by Periplus Editions (HK) Ltd. Copyright © 1993 Periplus Editions (HK) Ltd. All rights reserved.

Publisher: Eric Oey

Managing Editor: Mike Cooper

Production: Sue Bowles, Mary Chia

Cartography: Regina Wong, Kathy Wee, Violet Wong

Printed in the Republic of Singapore
ISBN: 0-8442-9891-3

Cover: *Hamzah, one of Kota Bharu's top dalang, or shadow-puppeteers. Photo by Radin Moh'd Noh Saleh.*
Page 1: *A Malay girl dressed for a celebration at Kuala Terengganu. Photo by Alain Evrard.*
Pages 4-5: *In the shade of "chick" shopfront blinds. Photo by Alain Evrard.*
Pages 6-7: *A young Hindu penitent during the Thaipusam festival in Penang. Photo by Jean Leo Dugast.*
Frontispiece: *Young members of a tambourine band. Photo by Alain Evrard.*

Passport's Regional Guides

BALI
The Emerald Isle

NEW GUINEA
Journey into the Stone Age

SPICE ISLANDS
Exotic Eastern Indonesia

JAVA
Garden of the East

BORNEO
Journey into the Tropical Rainforest

SULAWESI
Island Crossroads of Indonesia

SUMATRA
Island of Adventure

EAST OF BALI
From Lombok to Timor

UNDERWATER INDONESIA
A Guide to the World's Best Diving

EAST MALAYSIA
and Brunei

WEST MALAYSIA
and Singapore

The Passport Regional Guides of Indonesia and Malaysia offer an in-depth, region by region look at this diverse and fascinating corner of the globe. Each volume contains over 150 stunning color photographs, as well as authoritative essays on history and culture. Comprehensive, up-to-date travel information round out these books, making them the most practical travel guides available on the region.

Contents

12 CONTENTS

CONTENTS   **13**

PART I

Land Where the Winds Meet

Dangling like a pendant from the tip of continental Asia, Peninsular Malaysia lies at the heart of Southeast Asia. Bordered in the north by Thailand, this verdant, tropical land stretches southwards 740km (460mi) to end at the Straits of Johor which seperate the Peninsula from the neighboring island republic of Singapore. Malaysia's Borneo states of Sarawak and Sabah lie to the east, 530km (329mi) across the China Sea.

The peninsula has been well known since antiquity as it is straddled by the vital sea routes between India, the Middle East and China. It is also at the nexus of the monsoons. Ptolemy, the Greek astronomer, called it "The Golden Chersonese"; ancient mariners dubbed it "The Land Where the Winds Meet."

Early traders were lured by the products of the rainforests, the green mantle which still covers much of the country's mountainous interior, shrouding its elusive abundance of wildlife. The natural beauty of Peninsular Malaysia is one of the principal attractions for visitors today.

Inland from the popular coastal islands with their white sand beaches and aquamarine seas, are fertile alluvial plains punctuated by limestone hills containing ancient cave dwellings. The granite mountains of the Main Range, Banjaran Titiwangsa, form the peninsula's spine, splitting it into the culturally distinct regions of east and west.

While the west flourished during the tin mining and rubber booms, and economic migrants created an ethnically diverse population, the east kept its Malay identity and evolved in relative isolation from economic and colonial pressures.

The east thus retained many of the customs, crafts, arts and beliefs now hardly found in the west. These ancient traditions are actually on the increase in certain areas. Nowadays the west is connected to the east by new highways and access is no longer the month-long elephant trek it once was.

The peninsula's "golden age" occcured in the 15th century, when the great empire of Melaka was at its zenith. Much of modern-day Malaysia's political, religious and legal systems have their origins in that time. The empire fell to the Portuguese in 1511, then to the Dutch in the mid 17th century. But it was the British, from their strongholds in Penang and Singapore, who dominated the peninsula from the late 19th century.

Concrete evidence of the colonial era is found throughout the country in architectural form but most poignantly at the hill resorts of the Cameron Highlands and Fraser's Hill, where the cultural anachronism of afternoon tea in the gardens of a Malaysian mock-Tudor house becomes especially odd at 3,000 feet amid the rainforests.

Since independence in 1957 Malaysia has seen steady economic growth and a much higher standard of living following a number of industrialization programs aimed ultimately at gaining the country "developed nation" status by 2020.

Peninsular Malaysia's natural and ethnic diversity, coupled with the hospitable nature of its people and the efficient transportation infrastructure make traveling not only visually and culturally enriching but also socially stimulating and extremely easy.

Singapore, Peninsular Malaysia's dynamic southern neighbor, has seen phenomenal change over the past 25 years. Renowned for its airport, shopping and cuisine, the city state has a lot more than might initially meet the eye. Beneath a high tech Western veneer there lies a vibrant and unique society and the city state invariably rewards those who take the time to appreciate it fully.

Opposite: Celebrating her nation's independence from the British on Merdeka Day, a Malay girl holds a traditional decoration which derives from the flowering coconut palm. Photo by Radin Moh'd Noh Salleh.

GEOGRAPHY

Peninsula at the Tip of Mainland Asia

Malaysia's geography is characterized by stability and gentleness. None of the tectonic violence found in the neighboring regions occurs here. Earth tremors are rare and insignificant, there are no volcanoes, and typhoons and monsoons peter out before they reach the country's shores.

As if to emphasize this, forests cover the rugged hills of the interior with a lush blanket of foliage, softening harsh outlines and smoothing out rough edges. Even the land's major cash crops (rubber and oil palm) are trees, and it is this rich vegetation which invariably has the greatest impact on visitors.

The Malay Peninsula is a long and slender, slightly bulbous strip of land that extends southward from mainland Southeast Asia to the equator. The upper portion of the peninsula belongs to Thailand; the southerly half is known as Peninsular Malaysia, to distinguish it from the eastern Malaysian states of Sabah and Sarawak in Borneo. At the narrow Isthmus of Kra in Thailand, the peninsula's northernmost point, less than 50km (31mi) of land separates the Indian Ocean from the Gulf of Thailand and the South China Sea.

Ridges, domes, peaks and plains

A ridge of granite mountains forms the peninsula's north-south backbone. This is known as the Main Range, or more poetically in Malay as Banjaran Titiwangsa. Many of the range's peaks reach above 1,800m (6,000ft), including Gunung Korbu, the peninsula's second highest at 2,183m (7,160ft), as well as the hill stations at Cameron Highlands, Fraser's Hill and Genting Highlands.

At the northern end of Peninsular Malaysia, near the Thai border, other granite ranges and extensive hill country occurs. Towards the east coast is an H-shaped range of sandstone mountains, most of which lie within Taman Negara National Park, including the peninsula's highest peak, Gunung Tahan 2,191m (7,186ft). These sandstone mountains are generally steeper than the granite domes of the Main Range, with knife-edge ridges that jut upward sharply.

Extensive alluvial plains surround the mountains, and it is here that most agricultural settlements have developed. The materials forming these expanses of fertile land have resulted from the erosion of hill

R. MOH'D NOH SALLEH

slopes over the centuries, and the accumulation of marine sediments and sand created by the action of the ocean. Along the west coast, the trapping of silt by mangrove trees has created a natural landfill which has moved the coastline outward. Ptolemy recorded that in his day the coastal plain of the peninsula joined Sumatra, closing the Melaka Straits, but geological research indicates that this is not true.

The west coast plain is by far Peninsular Malaysia's most important economic region.

Tin has been mined extensively in Perak and Selangor for a century and a half, accounting in the late-19th century for more than a third of all colonial revenues. Timber is also a significant resource, and more recently the west coast plains have been the site of Malaysia's major rubber and oil palm estates. All of these have provided new jobs and created an infrastructure which is now developing at a rapid pace.

At scattered locations on the peninsula, especially where the foothills meet the coastal plains, clusters of limestone karst hills protrude like giant fingers from the earth. These curious topographical features, with vertical and overhanging cliff faces, are often depicted in traditional Chinese paintings, and it can come as a surprise to visitors that they also occur in Malaysia. Such tower karst formations do not have simple drainage from peak to base, but contain networks of sinkholes and channels, enabling water to flow in several directions. Examples of these clusters can be seen in Perak and Kelantan, Perlis and Kedah, including the Langkawi islands.

Rock lifestyles

Limestone is soft, which accounts for the existence of bottom cliffs. Through weathering, a block of rock will fall and leave a bare new face which in turn may be affected by water seepage, not just on the surface but up to 3m (10ft) or more into what looks like solid rock. These hills are often unstable due to such erosion.

They are nevertheless attractive places to live. The soft limestone also results in caves, carved out by the action of water over the millennia. The overhanging cliffs, which form the cave mouths, provide dry homes that have been exploited by man since prehistory. Many of the most famous archaeological sites in Malaysia occur in such surroundings, and today groups of squatters and smallholders live in similar dwellings; a way of life not without risk. In 1972, near Ipoh, 30 people living in shanties were killed by a rockfall.

The caves not only provide a home for man, but for a host of bats, insects and other animal life. Although Peninsular Malaysia also has some coastal caves in sandstone and other rock these are insignificant in comparison with the richness and abundance of the limestone caves.

The combination of tree cover, mountain ranges and the peripheral influence of continental monsoons govern a complex water regime. On the west coast there tend to be two peaks of rainfall a year, usually from April-May and October-December. On the east coast there is a much stronger, more dependable single wet season around October-January. These wet seasons are not monsoons, but occur during the turbulent inter-monsoon period when the wind changes direction from northeast to southwest.

On the west coast storms can be accompanied by sudden strong winds known as Sumatras. These build up under the influence of the southwest monsoon in the afternoon or evening over the coast of Sumatra, reaching

Opposite: Limestone hills pitted with caves are a distinctive feature of rural Perlis. **Above, left:** *Rainforest covers the foothills of the Banjaran Titiwangsa in Negeri Sembilan.* **Above, right:** *These fruiting* pandanus *thrive in the salty, sandy soils of the East Coast.*

the Malaysian coast early the following day. Elsewhere on the peninsula violent winds are rare and short-lived, generally blowing for the few minutes before a thunderstorm breaks.

Vegetation and precipitation

Montane forest above 900m (3,000ft) is typically cloud-covered and trees play a major role in stripping water from the atmosphere as the clouds sweep past. It is said that ten times as much water can be trapped by condensation than is gathered as rainfall. If so, montane forest must contribute disproportionately to the amount of water flowing down catchments.

Studies in Malaysia have shown that reduced tree cover can increase the amount of water flowing downstream. Because the loss of lowland trees reduces the leaf surface-area for evapo-transpiration, less water therefore re-evaporates into the atmosphere. This has been supported by similar research in many other countries. The neglected factor is that the amount of rainfall itself depends on vegetation cover. Although fewer trees in a small area increases water flow downstream—because overall rainfall is not affected—widespread loss of trees can prevent precipitation in the first place.

Mountains also contribute to rainfall, most of which is orographic, resulting in the typical rain shadows often seen behind them. The central peninsula from Jerantut south to

Kuala Pilah is one of the driest regions in terms of total annual rainfall, both here and in Kedah/Perlis there can be periods of over a month with no rain at all.

The peninsula's main rivers are the Perak—which flows from near the Thai border, down through the west coast plain to the Melaka Straits—and the Kelantan, the Terengganu and the Pahang in the east, which flow into the South China Sea. It has been suggested that the east-flowing Pahang River once flowed westwards, along the course of the present day Muar River, into the Melaka Straits. This change is thought to have occurred in the low-lying south of Pahang, in the peninsula's largest natural lake system—Tasek Bera—which is in fact a very slow-flowing complex of blackwater creeks.

Ancient riverine trading routes

Until at least the 19th century the peninsula's rivers provided the only efficient thoroughfares for long-distance inland transport and trade. The route along the Muar, through Tasek Bera and eastwards down the Pahang, provided the main means of crossing the peninsula. Another such ancient course traversed the south, following the Muar and Semberong rivers across Johor. While another led far up the Pahang river and out through Dungun in Terengganu. Although these routes were principally used for trade, they also served as military conduits during

R. MOH'D NOH SALLEH

civil conflicts between states.

Throughout the world there have been major changes in sea levels and these are traced largely by geographical features. Approximately 7,000 years ago the sea is thought to have been some 20m (66ft) below its present level. This would probably not have been low enough to join Malaysia to Sumatra, but there was certainly such a link during the more remote past. In the Pliocene period, over a million years ago, Malaysia, Sumatra, Java and Borneo were one single land mass.

Although there is some disagreement among geologists over higher levels, it is now generally accepted that by 5,000 years ago the sea had risen to 6m (20ft) above its present level in this part of the world. On some limestone hills in Kedah a shelf of undercut rock can be seen several meters above the ground where, in the prehistoric past, waves eroded the soft limestone. Sand dunes can also be found at several sites along the peninsula's east and west coasts up to 15km (9mi) inland.

As well as redefining the landscape, these geographical shifts contributed to the formation of resources such as tin and petroleum, and thus helped to enhance the country's economic well-being. While tin became a major source of revenue during the colonial era, the turbulence of the international tin market since the 1970s has resulted in many former tin mining companies turning to limestone quarrying. The Kinta Valley in Perak, once the hub of the world's tin industry, is now a major production center for cement, road chippings, marble and even the calcium which goes into toothpaste.

Although the presence of gold provided inspiration for the evocative titles of early travel books such as the *Golden Chersonese* (*see Further Reading p. 280*), it is present in such small quantities that it is seldom exploited. But the black gold, petroleum, is now a major revenue earner.

Despite the fact that Malaysia's first oil well, "The Old Lady," is onshore in East Malaysia, most of the current reserves lie far out to sea. Clusters of rigs can be seen off the coast of Terengganu and other big fields further north have yet to be opened up. Whereas it used to be normal practice to burn off the gas which escapes when oil is extracted, this too is now put to use in the colossal pipeline projects which will eventually link Malaysia, Singapore and Thailand in a regional energy network.

—*Geoffrey Davison*

Opposite: *Seen from the ground, this rainforest canopy displays "crown-shyness," where each tree-canopy is distinct from that of its neighbor.*
Above: *A flowering ginger plant.*
Below: *Carnivorous pitcher plants, thrive in the montane forests above 1,000m.*

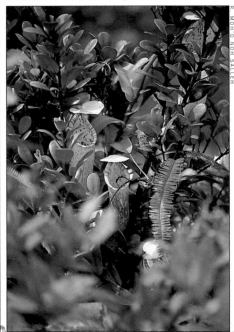

WILDLIFE

Biological Riches of the Rainforest

In the evergreen jungles of Peninsular Malaysia, snakes seldom hang from branches awaiting innocent passers-by, and the tiger's roar or the trumpeting of elephants is a rare treat even for the seasoned explorer.

Yet the richness of the fauna which inhabits this small peninsula is statistically impressive. In a total area of only 132,828km^2 (51,285mi^2) there are over 203 species of mammal, 638 resident and migrant bird species, over 200 varieties of lizards and snakes, 92 species of amphibian and some 200 different types of freshwater fishes. The insect count is phenomenal: there are over 1,032 different butterflies, and an educated estimate of the moth species numbers 8,000. The numbers of beetles, stick insects, grasshoppers, cicadas, ants, termites and others has yet to be assessed.

Much of the wildlife—60 to 70%—lives in

the humid evergreen rainforest and looking for these animals can pose a challenge to the uninitiated. You need to tune your eyes and ears to see and hear them. Many creatures are easier heard than seen, and can be readily detected by their distinctive songs and calls.

Tigers and panthers can sometimes be spotted or heard in Taman Negara and Endau Rompin where reasonable populations still exist. Elephants can occasionally be seen along the East-West Highway and in the wildlife reserves and national park. The Sumatran rhino—the world's most endangered animal—lingers on in Endau Rompin where there is a population of about 20 individuals.

The *seladang*, or wild ox, grazes in small clearings in Taman Negara, and a few remote wildlife reserves. To see any of these rare animals, special expeditions usually need to be mounted, yet with a bit of luck they may also be glimpsed in the wildlife parks.

The incredible diversity and richness of the rainforest is illustrated by the different species of plant life found in a small area. Two hectares of rainforest can house over 200 species of trees, and together with epiphytes, climbers, shrubs, herbs, fungi, and mosses, the number can exceed 1,000 species.

This range of plant life is the main factor determining the diversity of animal life. Plants not only generate a variety of foods for specific animals, but also provide a variety of microhabitats. Nooks and crannies are used by smaller invertebrates for shelter, and the hunting of these small creatures by insectivores generates a need for specialization and evolution which results in a corresponding richness in predator species.

Basic rules of survival

For most forest animals, being found in large concentrations spells trouble: they are more easily located by predators and the spread of disease in the population often results in epidemics. The solution of wildlife survival is to live scattered as individuals, and to meet occasionally to breed during favorable times when food is abundant.

The struggle for survival is never-ending, and the law of the jungle always in full operation. The fittest survive, while the weak and obvious get eaten. For those that are not swift and agile, there is a pressing need to hide and be unseen. Camouflage is the trick, stillness the key.

Insects often take on the form and shape of leaves, stick insects and inch worms resemble branches and twigs, and even their stationary postures mimic the host plant. Spiders that live on the tree trunks have mottled patterns and crouch to resemble the nodules on the bark.

Most animals in the forest are brown, enabling them to blend in with the tree trunks and leaf litter on the forest floor. Others, such as the tiger, make use of its black stripes to break its well-known form among the grass and reeds. The tapir, with its distinct black and white patches, matches the forest in the moonlight with a mosaic pattern of light and dark, while squirrels and tree shrews dart and freeze in their forage for food to evade detection.

Watching them, watching you

By behavior, pattern and color, the animals in the forest conceal themselves from observers and predators alike. Watching wildlife demands immense patience and time. To see wildlife in the rainforest is to be part of the rainforest yourself.

Despite the development in the cities and along the coast, Peninsular Malaysia still has 59% forest cover and there are numerous wildlife areas. At hill stations such as Fraser's Hill and Genting Highlands, gibbons can be readily heard and squirrels and monkeys easily observed. At Taman Negara, deer, wild pigs, mousedeer, monkeys and monitor lizards can be sighted at the Park Headquarters at Kuala Tahan. Around the overnight hides, civet cats, tigers, wild cattle, tapirs, or other rare animals are sometimes sighted by the nearby salt-licks.

Endau Rompin State Park, although less accessible, provides similar adventure opportunities. Leaf monkeys are easily observed at the Kuala Selangor Nature Park just outside Kuala Lumpur, and the world's largest living turtle, the giant leatherback, comes ashore to nest at Rantau Abang in Terengganu between May and August. Singapore also has wildlife refuges, including the Bukit Timah Forest Reserve in the heart of the island.

In Peninsular Malaysia most wildlife is protected by law although hunting of some wild animals is allowed and regulated by the Department of Wildlife and National Parks. Malaysia and Singapore are both signatories to CITES, and trade in endangered species is strictly prohibited. Development has been rapid in recent years and the wildlife in most lowland forest areas is in retreat. Only gazetted conservation areas ensure the perpetuation and survival of this rich and unique fauna for the future.

—*Kiew Bong Heang*

Opposite: This Malayan elephant was one of a trio which swam across the Johor Straits to an island off Singapore. They were returned to the Peninsula by the elephant-relocation unit.
Below: The diminutive mousedeer is not a deer, but a distant relation of the camel.

WWF MALAYSIA

BIRDS

Paradise for the Serious Ornithologist

Peninsular Malaysia's lowland tropical rainforest is the oldest and richest biological environment on earth. Over half of the 460 resident bird species are found mainly or exclusively in these forests. Their habitats have remained unchanged for millions of years, and the forest birds who inhabit them have evolved into many closely-related species. For example, there are 19 different bulbuls and 47 species of babblers.

Forest birds are typically sedentary, especially the insectivorous species such as babblers, flycatchers and woodpeckers. Males and females often pair for life and stay in a small area that constitutes their feeding ground and nesting territory. Only breeding once a year, they have much smaller clutches than similar birds in temperate lands.

Fruit-eating birds like hornbills, pigeons and barbets are more dynamic and often move up to the lower montane habitat to find fruiting trees. A fig tree in fruit is one of Malaysia's great wildlife spectacles, for 20-30 bird species may visit in a single morning, together with numerous mammals, including squirrels and monkeys.

No bird moves across the rainforests' entire vertical plane. Leafbirds and minivets stay high up in the canopies, trogons and broadbills perch at midstorey level, and pheasants and pittas rarely leave the forest floor. There are no hummingbirds, but keep an eye out for nectar-eaters like sunbirds, spiderhunters and flowerpeckers.

In the forest, birdwatchers have to be constantly alert. Often a bird appears briefly and there are only a few seconds in which to see it and make an identification before it disappears into the dense greenery. Knowing the calls of the birds is a great advantage.

The great diversity of species makes the Malaysian rainforest one of the best places in the world for serious ornithologists. At Taman Negara many lowland birds come out in the open at Kuala Tahan, and there is good viewing from trails and elevated hides. Other notable areas include Endau-Rompin, Templer Park near Kuala Lumpur, and the Pantai Forest Reserve in Johor.

Peninsular Malaysia is part of the Oriental zoogeographical region stretching from the Indian subcontinent to Wallace's Line east of Borneo and Bali. There are very few endemic

MORTON STRANGE

species in Peninsular Malaysia because it is part of the Sunda subregion which includes Thailand's far south, and the islands of Sumatra, Java and Borneo. During the last Ice Age, when sea levels were much lower than today, this area was joined, and as a result most of the fauna is shared with these surrounding areas. In Peninsular Malaysia only two species, the Malayan Whistling Thrush and the Mountain Peacock Pheasant, are considered true endemic species.

With rapid economic growth and development much of the lowland rainforest has been cleared, and birds have declined in numbers. In a 1988 world survey of threatened birds, Peninsular Malaysia had 12 resident species listed, and 10 were lowland rainforest birds. Four of the sensitive pheasants are in danger of extinction and others are very rare and seldom seen. Asian hornbills are also becoming harder to see and the Helmeted Hornbill is regarded as threatened with extinction. Other endangered birds include the Giant and Fairy Pitta, the Giant Swift and the peculiar Masked Finfoot that can still be seen near the Tahan River inside Taman Negara.

Hill stations and bird waves

In the montane rainforest the avifauna is so different that the birdwatcher might as well have traveled to a different continent. More than 70 bird species in Peninsular Malaysia are exclusively found between 1,000-1,500m (3,300-5,00ft), and a handful of upper montane specialists are found only between 1,300-2,100m (4,300-7,000ft).

Birdwatching at the hill stations, particularly Fraser's Hill, is an enjoyable and highly rewarding experience. The birds are easy to see because you are at eye-level with the low tree tops in the hilly terrain, and they are often colorful and vocal and seem to be more confiding than lowland forest birds.

All rainforest birds form "bird waves" but this phenomenon is especially typical of the montane regions. The forest appears to be quiet and devoid of avifauna, and then suddenly it comes alive with birds like orioles, nuthatches and many different babblers.

Mangroves form another ecosystem of special interest to the birdwatcher. Johor still has some large expanses which are easily accessed from Kukup on the southwest coast. At Kuala Selangor near Kuala Lumpur, and at Kuala Gula in Perak there are protected patches of mangroves and also visitor's facilities. On the nearby mudflats, herons, storks

and migratory shorebirds feed at low tide. Most of these are widely distributed Palaearctic species. Including migrants, visitors and vagrants, 623 different species have been spotted in Peninsular Malaysia.

Birds seen around gardens and parks often originate from mangroves and coastal scrub. They are adaptable species and once they make the transition they become very numerous. Open-country birds which often visit gardens include munias, bee-eaters, starlings, kingfishers and shrikes.

Singapore's avifauna, listed at 326 species, is no different than Malaysia's, apart from a few species which are vagrants, or have escaped captivity, but it is a convenient place to birdwatch. Beautiful garden birds like the Black-naped Oriole and Crimson Sunbird are more widespread, and along the north coast near Serangoon, Mandai and Sungei Buloh estuaries, shorebirds and other migratory species can be easily spotted. Rainforest birds can be seen at Bukit Timah Nature Reserve and the Watercatchment Forest where trails lead in from Lornie Road, Upper Thomson Road and Mandai Road, but the species diversity cannot compare with that of Malaysia.

—Morton Strange

__Opposite:__ A female Olive-Backed Sunbird sips nectar from a bottle-brush flower. __Above, left:__ The Thick-billed Pigeon. __Above, right:__ The Asian Fairy Bluebird is often spotted at Fraser's Hill.

PREHISTORY

Cave Dwellers and Forest Foragers

Through both prehistoric and historic time, Peninsular Malaysia has witnessed the presence of many different layers of human culture. Initially, early hominids of the species *Homo erectus* may have passed through here as they migrated to Java about one million years ago.But no traces of these early humans have been found in the peninsula and scholars are still divided as to whether the Chinese and Javan populations were the ancestors of modern East Asians and Australasians, or an extinct side line of evolution.

Our first clear evidence for human activity dates from perhaps 35,000 years ago, when makers of stone tools left their cores, flakes and hammerstones of quartzite at the site of Kota Tampan, near Lenggong in the Perak Valley (*see Kota Tampan, p. 87*). This site was probably on a lake shoreline when it was occupied and subsequently sealed under an

MUZIUM NEGARA

ash fall from a massive eruption of the Toba volcano in Sumatra about 31,000 years ago. At this time, the sea's surface was about 50m (164ft) below its present level owing to the trapping of water in the high latitude ice sheets. Kota Tampan was thus probably located much further inland than today, and perhaps in drier and open forest conditions.

By about 10,000 years ago the climate was warming to present temperatures and the Malaysian rainforests were becoming more equatorial. From this time until the appearance of agricultural populations in the peninsula about 4000 years ago, we find traces of hunting and gathering activities in limestone rock shelters right across the country, and in a few surviving shell mounds on the western coast. Archaeologists refer to this period as the "Hoabinhian" named after cave sites in northern Vietnam.

About ten rock shelters and two shell middens have produced good evidence for Hoabinhian living and dying; perhaps the best is Gua Cha in inland Kelantan which was occupied by Hoabinhians between about 10,000 and 3,000 years ago. The 2m (6.5ft) thickness of Hoabinhian layers at Gua Cha revealed many flaked pebble tools, riverine shellfish, and bones of cooked and eaten forest animals such as cattle, deer, pig, monkey and squirrel. The people also buried their dead in flexed postures in the cave floor, as they also did about 9,000 years ago in the cave of Gua Gunung Runtuh in Perak.

They came from the north

By 2000BC the peninsula had witnessed important economic changes; new populations with agriculture (probably rice and millet) and sedentary villages moved southwards from today's Thailand into Peninsular Malaysia. These people made burnished and cord-marked pottery, similar to that found in sites as far north as Kanchanaburi in central Thailand. They used polished stone adzes and spears with bone points, and wore stone bracelets, shell bead necklaces, and clothing of beaten barkcloth.

Large and wealthy burial grounds with fully-extended burials have been found on sites dating from this period in central Thailand, where there is also clear evidence of rice cultivation. Direct evidence for rice growing in Peninsular Malaysia has yet to be found, perhaps because most archaeological sites concentrate on rock shelters, away from likely early rice-growing areas. One such shelter is again Gua Cha where the

Hoabinhians were succeeded about 3,000 years ago by people who buried their dead with very finely crafted pots, stone adzes and stone bracelets. More finds from around 2,000BC have also been recently reported from Jenderam Hilir in Selangor.

People who made burnished and cord-marked Neolithic pottery like that discovered in Gua Cha continued to occupy the peninsula until around 500BC, if not later. Between 500BC and 500AD the archaeological record illustrates major changes. Bronze drums of Vietnamese manufacture ("Dongson" drums), bronze bells and a broad range of iron tools have been found across northern and central Peninsular Malaysia. Clearly, the ethnic patterning was tranforming rapidly. The Malays, documented in Sumatra by 7th-century Srivijayan inscriptions, had perhaps arrived on the coasts of the Malay Peninsula with their interest in sea-borne trade. But if Malays were settling the coasts as early as 2,000 years ago, who was there before them?

The great ethnogenesis debate

Questions of ethnicity are hard to answer from the record of prehistoric archaeology. Prehistoric records in the southern peninsula are almost non existent; almost all our knowledge comes from the north and central regions and from southern Thailand. But even with this restriction we can still ask whose ancestors made the archaeological record over the past 10,000 years.

Ethnolinguistically, there are today three major population groupings; the Semang Negrito foragers of the northern interior rainforests, the Senoi cultivators of the southern interior (both the Semang and Senoi are known as Orang Asli and speak Austroasiatic languages in the Mon-Khmer subgroup, which also includes Khmer of Cambodia and Vietnamese), and the Austronesian-speaking groups in coastal districts and the far south of whom the Malays are the most numerous and widespread. The Austronesians are today one of the most widely dispersed major ethnolinguistic groups on earth, including populations as far apart geographically as the peoples of Madagascar, Aboriginal Taiwan, Indonesia, the Philippines, and all of Oceania beyond western Melanesia.

Although archaeologists and anthropologists like to disagree over questions of ethnogenesis, my own opinion is that the Semang forest foragers are the fairly direct descendants of the Hoabinhians, whereas the slightly more Mongoloid Senoi represent the

descendants of both the Hoabinhians and the Neolithic cultivators who entered the Malay Peninsula around 2,000BC from southern Thailand. The Malays and their Austronesian-speaking relatives (the speakers of so-called "Aboriginal Malay" or Orang Asli Melayu dialects) probably migrated into the peninsula from an original homeland in western Borneo between 2,000 and 3,000 years ago.

After their arrival it seems that many previously Austroasiatic-speaking groups adopted Austronesian languages. Malay linguistic origins are closely tied to related languages such as Iban and Selako in western Borneo. It is thus clear that the original direction of Malayic migration was from Indonesia into the Malay Peninsula, perhaps via eastern Sumatra, and not vice-versa. Malay proper—the language associated with Hindu Srivijaya and subsequent Muslim sultanates in Island Southeast Asia—perhaps only replaced the Mon language in the northern peninsular after the 12th century.

The Malay Peninsula has been a region which people have entered rather than left in prehistoric times, and it has absorbed its migrants and forged them into one of modern Southeast Asia's most diversified societies.

—*Peter Bellwood*

Opposite: A Hoabinhian burial site at the Gua Cha, a rock shelter in inland Kelantan. *Above:* Prehistoric cave drawings in Gua Badak, Perak.

EARLY HISTORY

Melaka and the Legendary Kingdoms

Due to a lack of documentation it is difficult to reconstruct with any real certainty the history of Peninsular Malaysia prior to the 15th century. Consequently, the centuries before 1400—the "pre-Melakan period"—are usually considered as being relatively less important in the evolution of modern Malaysia. Historians have tended to regard the rise of the great entrepôt of Melaka, on the west coast, as the starting point for Malay history.

Cultural foundations

However, the growth of Melaka from a quiet fishing village to a world-renowned emporium and center of Malay culture cannot be understood without knowing that beneath the splendor of its court and the vigor of its commerce was a strong foundation of governmental traditions that must have taken centuries to evolve. Malaysia's civilization does not begin at Melaka, but instead stretches much deeper into the past.

Before the 7th century the empire of Funan—located in the Menan basin of the Indo-Chinese Peninsula near today's Kampuchea—was the first great power in Southeast Asian history. Smaller states in the Malay Peninsula showed support to this kingdom, but around the 6th century these mainland states, as well as other island states throughout Southeast Asia, liberated themselves and Funan started to decline in power.

Early powers in Southeast Asia

Political power then shifted from the Asian mainland to the islands of the Malay Archipelago. During the Funan supremacy the most popular crossing between the Indian Ocean and South China Sea was an overland route across the narrow isthmus of Kra in today's southern Thailand.

The rise of maritime empires meant sea routes via the Straits of Melaka became more popular and this contributed greatly to the development of ports in Sumatra and Java.

By the mid-7th century, two states emerged in Sumatra—Melayu (situated on the mouth of the Batang Hari) and Srivijaya. Inscriptions dated 686 to 688AD suggest that during this time Srivijaya was gaining power, and soon its influence swept across the straits to the Malay Peninsula.

The exact extent of Srivijaya's imperial

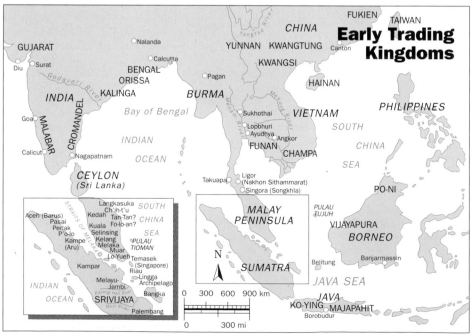

Early Trading Kingdoms

control is still vague and historians are also uncertain as to where it was situated, although it was most probably on the east coast of Sumatra.

The rise of Srivijaya

Srivijaya sent envoys to China bearing gifts, for Chinese friendship was crucial as Srivijaya depended upon the China trade. By 900AD Srivijaya's power in Southeast Asia was unchallenged and small states in Sumatra, the Malay Peninsula and Western Java were subjected to its maritime supremacy. Occasional threats to the empire included the attack on its capital by Dharmavansa, King of Java in the 990s, but these were easily handled by Srivijaya's massive counter attacks.

In its heyday Srivijaya commanded the entire East-West trade, and was so powerful that ships were forced to sail through the Straits of Melaka and call on its ports to pay toll and tribute. As late as the 13th century, Chua Ju-kua, the Chinese Inspector of Foreign Trade, wrote that all foreign ships passing the Straits were forced to pay toll under threat of outright destruction.

So what happened to Srivijaya? There is no single answer, but the erosion of friendly relations with China and India contributed to its fall. India's most powerful maritime power during this time was the Cholas, who were greatly interested in the China and Southeast Asian trade.

It is likely that the expansion of Srivijaya's power in Indonesian waters caused friction between the two maritime powers. The Cholas clearly envied Srivijaya's success and were essentially determined to get a piece of the action.

A crippling naval attack

In 1025AD, the Cholas launched a naval attack on all Srivijaya's major trading stations which certainly weakened the empire and following this many states attempted to free themselves from Srivijaya's control.

During later Sung times and in the Mongol period (1279-1368) the Chinese found that Siam offered better products that were much in demand, and gradually shifted focus away from Srivijaya. According to Marco Polo's reports, China then shifted its interests within Sumatra from Srivijaya to Melayu, which consequently became a more important trading center.

Gradually, the name Srivijaya lost its impact. A new star, the Majapahit empire, rose in Java and together with the Siamese

empire undermined the remaining power of Srivijaya

During this time, there were also other smaller empires on the Malay Peninsula such as Chih Tu, Langkasuka, and Tan Tan. Their exact dates are still unknown, but historians believe that they emerged roughly around the same time as Srivijaya, which overshadowed these smaller trading ports.

Envoys on elephant back

Most of these legendary kingdoms were nevertheless "civilized," with their own forms of government, and ceremonies which included those for welcoming visitors from abroad which showed that they had already made contact with other states. Historical records mention that envoys from China were treated with respect and that the messengers were carried about on elephants.

From the 5th century onwards, there also existed a renowned power called the Government of Old Kedah (Kerajaan Kedah Tua) situated at Lembah Bujang in the north of the peninsula (*see story "Lembah Bujang," p. 106*). Despite challenges from its neighbors, especially Siam, it continued expanding until its zenith during the 14th century.

Above: Evidence of the Peninsular's pre-Islamic era, this Buddha statue was found at Lembah Bujang in southern Kedah, the site of Old Kedah, a Hindu-Buddhist kingdom.

Another important regional administrative center and port of the time was Pengkalan Bujang, and merchant ships from India, West Asia and China stopped over at this well-known trading hub until the emergence of Melaka as the regon's major entrepôt.

Malaka: the origins

There are two main versions on the origins of Melaka. The most popular being that found in Sejarah Melayu, the court annals of the Melakan Sultanate. It begins with an impressive genealogy tracing the line of Melaka kings back to Alexander the Great—described as a Muslim king, Raja Iskandar—then follows the fortunes of his dynastic line in India and the Malay world until three of his descendants miraculously appear on Bukit Si Guntang in Palembang, Sumatra.

One of them, Sri Tri Buana, was made ruler and later left Palembang in the hands of his brothers and went in search of new lands. Their fleet first arrived at Bintan in the Riau-Lingga archipelago, and subsequently moved to the island of Temasek where Sri Tri Buana established Singapura or the "Lion City," named after a strange lion-like beast he sighted there. His descendants ruled Singapore for five generations, until the last ruler, Parameswara, was forced to flee to Muar when the Javanese attacked.

The account has it that one day while hunting north of Muar one of Parameswara's hounds was kicked by a white mousedeer. The ruler exclaimed, "This is a good place, where even the mousedeer are full of fight!" Because he was standing under a Melaka tree, he decided that the new settlement should bear that name.

China's powerful protection

In 1403, a Chinese fleet under Admiral Yin Chi'ng, arrived at the settlement on the Melaka River and brought Parameswara presents of silk woven with golden flowers and other valuable gifts, and asked him to pay tribute to their Emperor. Melaka's ruler saw China as a powerful protector against Siam and accordingly sent envoys with tribute to China in 1405.

The Emperor spoke in praise of him, appointed him King of Melaka and sent him a commission, a seal, a suit of silk clothes and a yellow umbrella, which were delivered to Parameswara in 1406. This event was the turning point in Melaka's history. From this point on it started to establish itself as an important trading port for China and traders began to flock there.

Once Melaka embraced Islam in the early 15th century, the kingdom became transformed. The Sejarah Melayu regards the acceptance of Islam as a watershed in Melaka's history, an event which confirmed the kingdom's superior status.

As Melaka expanded territorially, it persuaded or compelled its vassals in the Straits area to accept Islam, and its growing prestige and commercial success also reinforced the process of Islamization throughout the archipelago. Muslim traders from abroad preferred to stop over at Melaka because of the protection they could expect from fellow Muslims, and the presence of a mosque meant that they could pray without outside interference.

Omnipotent sultans

The life of Melaka's people was centered around the royal court. The sultan had no council of advisors, and was totally free to declare war or peace on anybody, but he did, however, have informal consultations with those he chose. His main source of income came from taxes paid by foreign traders, and he also obtained wealth through conquests and tributes from vassal states.

Melaka was visited by merchants from all over the world who came to trade mainly in spices, silk, and tea. Since Melaka was recognized by China as the "sole distributor" for China's goods in Asia, it attracted an ever-expanding population. Most of them communicated in the Malay language and even today Melaka's Straits-born Chinese still speak a special form of Malay. Melaka's native population consisted of the Orang Laut (Sea People)—who lived on the coast and derived their income from fishing—and the Minangkabau from Sumatra who functioned as middlemen, buying native goods and then reselling them.

Laws and loyalty

The Sejarah Melayu hardly refers to the daily life of the people although there is mention of offences committed. However, the laws of that time provide an insight into the activities of ordinary folk during the 15th century. Basically there were two major laws.

The Hukum Kanun Melaka dealt solely with aspects of the agrarian society, and also recognized the status of slaves who had their own rights and were not to be treated harshly by their masters. The Undang-Undang Laut Melaka related to maritime rights like the power of a ship's captain, and the rights of his crew members.

Despite these laws, rulers enjoyed almost absolute power as the Malay masses generally accorded the ruler total loyalty. This was based on the concepts of *daulat* (sovereignty) and *derhaka* (disobedience). *Daulat* provided the ruler with power and privileges which placed him above society and criticism, and entitled him to undivided loyalty from his subjects. Meanwhile *derhaka* placed fear in the subjects if they were disloyal. If a subject rebelled against a ruler this would be considered *derhaka* and the culprit would be severely punished.

Zenith of the empire

During Sultan Mansur Syah's reign Melaka reached its peak and, according to the *Sejarah Melayu*, envoys were sent to Sumatra, Pahang, Minangkabau, Siak, Siam and Kampar. It also mentions that even though China was a very powerful country, it still had to bow to Melaka's greatness, and that when China's emperor suffered an incurable disease, he was advised by the medicine-man to drink and bathe with water that had been used to wash Sultan Mansur Syah's leg.

Mansur Syah's predecessor, Muzaffar Syah, established Islam as the state religion and defeated Siam in a battle near Muar with the help of his able *bendahara* (similar to a Prime Minister), Tun Perak and the leg-endary warrior Hang Tuah. The former was renowned for his administrative and diplomatic skills, and was regarded as the power behind the throne responsible for the defence and expansion of Melaka.

A sultan goes undercover

A later ruler, Sultan Alauddin Riayat Syah also strengthened Melaka as an empire after Sultan Mansur Syah had laid the foundation. He tightened up security by building more "police stations" and this brave ruler also disguised himself as a thief and went undercover to solve the town's robbery problems.

After the death of Bendahara Tun Perak, his position was taken over by his cousin, Sri Maharaja, a very able man of whom it was said that Melaka would not fall to any power as long as he was alive. However, he was not appreciated by Sultan Mahmud who had him and his family executed.

One account states that Sri Maharaja was better known to the foreign merchants than the Sultan himself. Not long after this incident, the Portuguese attacked Melaka, and the fall of the empire in 1511 marked the beginning of Western domination in the Malay archipelago.

—Zuraina Majid

Below: *British officers meet with a Perak chieftain at his Kuala Kangsar home in this mid-19th century etching.*

COLONIAL HISTORY

The Impact and Aftermath of the West

In August 1511 Melaka, the famed center for archipelago trade, was captured by the Portuguese in an effort to control the sea routes to the spice islands and to spread Christianity. They then proceeded to destroy Melaka's great mosque, drive out Muslim traders, build churches and a formidable new fort, while encouraging missionary activity.

The Portuguese had assumed they would inherit Melaka's former prosperity, but without Muslim patronage it never regained its former prestige. Meanwhile, the heirs of the former dynasty fled to the Riau-Lingga archipelago in the southern Melaka Straits, from where they repeatedly yet unsuccessfully sought to re-capture their previous capital. Despite their hold on the town, the Portuguese had no hope of dominating the Malay peninsula and their influence was largely confined to the area around Melaka.

With Melaka in non-Malay hands, new trading centers emerged along the Melaka Straits. From its capital, alternatively in the Riau-Lingga archipelago and along the Johor River, the former Melaka dynasty attempted to reassert its old hegemony, but it now faced competition from the Portuguese as well as the aggressive new Sumatran state of Aceh. From 1619 the Acehnese made a number of raids on Malay states. Pahang's previously flourishing trade was destroyed and for many years the tin-producing state of Perak was an Acehnese vassal.

At the beginning of the 17th-century, the arrival of the Dutch East India Company (VOC) seemed to offer Malays the hope of new allies against the Portuguese. But although Johor assisted the Dutch to take Melaka from Portugal in January 1641, the town did not return to Malay hands.

Like the Portuguese, the Dutch hoped to conclude monopoly agreements with Malay rulers which would give them exclusive access to lucrative products such as tin. Kedah and Perak's rulers entered into such contracts in expectation of Dutch help against Aceh and Siam, which had ambitions to extend its suzerainty down the peninsula. However, the VOC did not want to become involved in expensive wars, and hopes of assistance soon faded.

At the end of the 17th century Johor was clearly the most powerful Malay state, con-

R. MOH'D NOH SALLEH

trolling Pahang, Terengganu, Selangor and Siak in Sumatra. Aceh's power had fallen, and Perak was again independent. Meanwhile Kedah, Patani, and Kelantan acknowledged Siam's authority while still recognizing that they were part of the Malay world. In 1699, however, Malay respect for Johor as the heir to Melaka was shaken when the ruler was murdered by his nobles. Though the Bendahara (Prime Minister) assumed power, many condemned the regicide as a heinous crime and refused to accept the new order.

Demographic flux

The demise of the prestigious Melaka line coincided with large movements of non-Malays into the region. Minangkabau groups from Sumatra had earlier settled in modern-day Negeri Sembilan, but there had been no conflict with existing Malay polities. Chinese and Indians were present in small numbers, but remained confined to coastal settlements under the authority of Malay rulers. Bugis and Makassarese from Sulawesi, fleeing from prolonged wars in their homeland, proved less easy to absorb.

Malaya's sparsely populated lands were an open invitation to these refugees and by the first decade of the 18th-century numerous communities had appeared, particularly in Selangor. Well known as traders, the Bugis also had a formidable reputation as warriors. When a Minangkabau prince, claiming to be the son of the murdered ruler, seized control of Johor in 1717 it was a group of Bugis who ousted him.

Meanwhile, Terengganu, previously a Johor vassal, became independent, and in 1766 the Bugis of Selangor established a separate state outside Johor's authority. Further afield, the wars between Siam and Burma allowed Patani, Kedah, and Kelantan a new degree of independence.

Singapore and the British

The decline of the Dutch East India Company during the 18th-century was accompanied by the emergence of England as the world's foremost commercial power. Concerned with developing the China trade, the English had already occupied the island of Penang, previously under Kedah, in 1786. In 1819 Stamford Raffles, vehemently opposed to the extension of Dutch authority in the east, made an agreement with Johor permitting the English to establish a trading post on Singapore island. As momentous as the fall of Melaka, this event changed the course of Malay history.

Although the British never set out to colonize the peninsula, once established in Singapore it was regarded as lying within their "sphere of influence."

After this, British involvement in the Malay Peninsula increased. In 1826 Melaka, Penang, Singapore and Province Wellesley (a strip of land along the Kedah coast) were incorporated as the Straits Settlements. Population increased rapidly, especially in Singapore, which became a linchpin of English trade with China. Its prosperity attracted large numbers of Chinese migrants, fleeing from poverty and civil unrest. Soon they began to move into the peninsula, developing agricultural plantations and tin mines.

As Chinese and British economic involvement was increasing, a series of succession disputes broke out among Malay ruling families. Chinese secret societies and, indirectly, British financiers became caught up in these struggles as they backed one or another contender, hoping for favored treatment.

Conflict, intervention and treaties

But such assistance tended to prolong the conflicts, in turn encouraging British merchants in the Straits Settlements to appeal for British political intervention to restore order to trade. This was a persuasive argument because industrializing Britain needed tin which the Malay Peninsula provided.

In 1874, when one contender for the Perak throne asked for British help, the Straits Settlements Governor seized the opportunity to move in. The Perak prince gained British support in the form of the Pangkor Engagement in return for accepting a resident whose advice he was required to accept on all matters "except religion and custom."

By 1888 similar treaties had been signed with Selangor, Negeri Sembilan, and Pahang—and in 1896 they became the Federated Malay States (FMS) with Kuala Lumpur as the capital. Johor, because of its links with Singapore, was also closely tied to British economic interests, although the adroitness of its ruler meant it retained its independence until 1914.

Change came less quickly along the east coast. In Pahang a major rebellion against the British occurred in 1891, led by district chiefs protesting against a lessening of their former privileges. Colonial ambitions meant that

Opposite: *This mid-19th century watercolor of Melaka's Town Square with the Stadthuys (to the right) and Christ Church (center)*

YU CHEE CHONG FINE ART, LONDON

Siam was under increasing pressure to relinquish its Malay vassals—Patani, Kelantan, and Terengganu—and in 1909 all except Patani were surrendered to the British in return for diplomatic privileges. However, in economic terms the east coast lagged behind the west, attracting less Chinese migrants and remaining more "Malay" in character.

By 1919 "British Malaya" was complete. Fundamental in the formulation of colonial government was the British view that although the Malays were likeable people, they were ill inclined to do the backbreaking work of developing tin mines and rubber estates. This was left to immigrant labor from China and India which doubled Malaya's population during the early 20th century.

In the process the Malays were locked out of the export-oriented sector of the colonial economy, and with the exception of the ruling elite, were denied opportunities for economic advancement. Despite lip service to the notion that Malays were the rightful political heirs, they received little training in government and civil servants were rarely given responsible positions.

Another colonial assumption which had far-reaching implications was that the Chinese and Indians were itinerants, and there was no need to provide a common school system for all. A small number of upper-class Malays, Chinese and Indians did receive an English education, but the majority acquired only basic schooling in the vernacular. Thus the opportunity to bridge differences between ethnic groups among the mass of the population was lost.

Ethnic divisions were further encouraged by the revolutionary movements in China which excited the Chinese community, and a number joined the Malayan Communist Party (MCP), formed in 1930. Indians took similar pride in the developing Indian independence movement, while Malays were caught up by the call for Islamic reform which urged Muslims to modernize education in order to compete with the West. Largely concerned with developing a unified economy and administration, the British gave little thought to the possibility of Malayan independence, and how a new nation would deal with deepening ethnic distinctions.

World War II and independence

Malaya's independence was precipitated by the outbreak of World War II. Japan attacked the peninsula in late 1941, and by February 1942 Malaya and Singapore were in Japanese hands. All British officials were imprisoned, and towards the end of the war there were hints that Japan might grant Malaya independence. Anxious to win local support, the Japanese generally treated Malays and Indians lenietly but because of Japan's conflict with China, the Chinese met systematic discrimination. It was therefore Chinese groups, dominated by the MCP, which led wartime resistance against the Japanese.

As a result, when the war ended many British thought the Chinese should be rewarded with full citizenship. But it was difficult to erradicate suspicions resulting from years of separate ethnic development. The British government's proposal of a "Malayan Union" which would make Chinese and Indians citizens thus aroused unprecedented opposition among the Malays.

In 1946, a group of leading Malays formed the United Malays National Organization (UMNO). Basic to UMNO's platform was the upholding of "special privileges" which Malays should enjoy as the original occupants of the land, and the status of Malay Sultans. The Malayan Union was revoked in February 1948 and replaced by the Federation of Malaya which united the peninsula under one government. Singapore, heavily Chinese, was excluded because its incorporation would mean Malays would be outnumbered.

The Federation was seen as a victory for the Malays, and many Chinese became sympathetic towards the MCP's aim of establishing a Malayan republic. Mid 1948 marked the beginning of the Malayan Emergency, when the MCP embarked on a systematic campaign of violence directed against European interests. Since the communists were mainly Chinese, they received substantial help from their rural compatriots. From 1950 British forces gained control by resettling these communities into "New Villages"—thus denying the MCP access to supplies. The Emergency officially ended in 1960.

A prime reason for the ultimate failure of the communist insurrection was a new political alliance between Malay and Chinese leaders and Britain's commitment to Malaya's independence. The formation of the Alliance, consisting of UMNO, the Malayan Chinese party (MCA) and later the Malayan Indian Association (MIA) gave hope for multi-cultural politics.By 1955 the Alliance and its call for independence had overwhelming support. A constitution was developed for the new nation which created a federation of states with a strong central government, retaining certain privileges for Malays. Singapore was again not included because of continuing fears of ethnic imbalance.

On 15 August 1957, under its first Prime Minister Tunku Abdul Rahman, Malaya was declared independent; two years later Singapore became internally self-governing. Both looked towards increasing prosperity, but still faced the problem of replacing ethnic loyalties by a common allegiance to a modern state.

—*Barbara Watson Andaya*

Opposite: *A colonial tin mine boss poses with his coolies at a Perak tin mine in the 1880s.*
Above: *Rubber planters dressed in amateur dramatics costumes, at Seremban in the 1880s.*

MODERN HISTORY

Independence and the Road to Tomorrow

The orderly transition to independence allowed the government under Tengku Abdul Rahman to turn its attention immediately to economic development. The new leadership avoided espousing radical economic and social change; the existing free market economy was maintained, and foreign investments encouraged. At the same time new federal programs were implemented to promote development in poorer rural areas which were largely Malay.

The first five years after independence were marked by impressive gains; schools and clinics were built while basic transport and communications infrastructure expanded across the country. The fight against the communist insurgency was slowly being won, and in 1960 the Emergency was officially ended.

Inter-ethnic cooperation within the Alliance was severely tested by the competing demands and expectations of its constituent communities. In 1959, UMNO and MCA (Malayan Chinese party) disputed over parliamentary seat allocation and education policy. The Alliance system of political accommodation survived when the Tengku stood firm and MCA backed down. In the national elections the Alliance retained power but the opposition made gains.

In early September 1963 Singapore, Sabah, and Sarawak joined Malaya to form Malaysia—twice the land area of Malaya. The multi-racial and multi-cultural character of the country became even more diverse with the inclusion of other distinctive indigenous groups from Sabah and Sarawak.

The formation led to regional tension. The Philippines insisted Sabah was part of the Sulu sultanate, while Indonesia interpreted the move as a new colonial manoeuver. Relations were severed on September 17th 1963 and Indonesia under Sukarno launched a campaign of confrontation (*Konfrontasi*) against Malaysia. The conflict came dangerously close to war as Indonesia infiltrated commandos into Malaysia.

Within Malaysia, differences between the Kuala Lumpur and Singapore leaders surfaced. The PAP (People's Action Party) under Lee Kuan Yew insisted on a more equalitarian policy, but the Alliance maintained that preferential provisions in government policies were necessary for the disadvantaged Malay

ARKIB NEGARA

community to progress.

The dispute worsened when the PAP contested the 1964 pariamentary elections. Two racial riots in Singapore in early 1965 convinced the Tengku that the island state had to leave the federation to avoid dangerous inter-ethnic conflicts. Singapore separated from Malaysia in August 1965 to become an independent republic. Two months later, a failed coup d'etat in Indonesia led to the phasing out of Sukarno and the confrontation against Malaysia came to an end.

Restructuring society

Within Malaysia, the debate on communally-related issues intensified as the 1969 parliamentary elections approached. The Alliance was returned but lost parliamentary seats and control of two states. Racial violence broke out a few days later resulting in heavy casualties. Parliament was suspended and the country was placed under emergency rule. The National Operations Council with Tun Abdul Razak as director virtually ruled the country between May 1969 and February 1971.

Parliament was reconvened in 1971 and Tun Abdul Razak became the new Prime Minister. Under him two important changes took place. Firstly, consensus politics within the ruling coalition, now renamed Barison Nasional, was broadened to include parties from Sabah and Sarawak as well as three others which previously were in the opposition. Secondly, a 20-year New Economic Policy was introduced aimed at eradicating poverty and restructuring society to eliminate identification of race with economic functions.

The government set targets using strategies of positive discrimination to increase Malay participation in the corporate sector, employment, and higher education. A national educational policy with Malay as the main language of instruction was begun at all levels of education. The implementation of NEP witnessed a significant social transformation as a rural to urban population shift took place.

A vision of the future

Dato Hussein Onn succeeded as Prime Minister when Tun Abdul Razak died in 1976 and the new Prime Minister maintained existing policies and direction. Increased revenue from oil ensured continued high economic growth. The ruling coalition retained commanding majorities in elections and coped effectively with emerging social and political problems such as state rights, religious extremism, student and peasant agitations, and intra-party factionalism.

In 1981, Dato Sri Dr. Mahathir Mohammed became Malaysia's fourth Prime Minister. Non-aristocratic in background and once sacked from the party for harshly criticising the Tengku, Mahathir set agendas to take the nation to new economic and political status. His style was regarded as authoritarian by critics as he sought to enhance power and influence of the political executive and to define more strictly those of the traditional rulers, the judiciary, the unions, and various non-governmental organizations. In 1987 he narrowly survived a bitterly-contested challenge to his leadership of UMNO.

The winning of the 1990 general elections has greatly strengthened Mahathir's political position. Impressive economic performance and foreign investments have lent weight to Malaysia's projection of achieving developed country status by the year 2020. Vision 2020 has became a goal and a symbol as the country shifts slowly but perceptibly from narrow communal concerns and rhetorics of the past to seek a broader international role.
—*Lee Kam Hing*

Opposite: Tunku Abdul Rahman (far left), the King and his consort escort the outgoing British Governor at independence. Below: The playing fields in Kuala Lumpur; the official venue for national celebrations, since independence was proclaimed here in 1957.

ALAIN EVRARD

PEOPLES

Asia's Cultural Crossroads

At the center of the maritime trade routes between India, the Middle East and China, the Malay Peninsula has always been a cultural crossroads. In Melaka's heyday, the cosmopolitan port attracted an extraordinary diversity of merchants: chronicles of those times record that over sixty different languages were spoken in the streets. The current richness of Malaysia's cultural traditions has been influenced over the centuries by a combination of trade, religion, education, and colonialism.

The present population stands at some 17.5 million. The Malays form the majority at 52%, the Chinese number around 37%, the Indians 10% and the remaining 1% comprises the aboriginal Orang Asli, Eurasians and Europeans.

Who are the Malays? The Federal constitution defines the Malays as *bumiputra*, or "sons of the soil," who speak Malay, profess Islam as their religion and adopt the Malay culture as their way of life. The bond with Islam is an integral part of the Malay personality; all Malays are Muslim and it is forbidden by law to convert them to other religions.

Although Muslim, the Malays retain certain animistic and Hindu beliefs. Some Malays believe in spirits and ghosts, make sacrificial offerings to appease the spirits, and use amulets for protection against evil deeds. Some Hindu marriage and birth rituals have also been assimilated into the Malay way of life and are now part and parcel of their cultural traditions.

Hindu heritage at the royal court

The Malay court and its regalia, which uses yellow as the royal color, are also remnants of their former Hindu heritage, as are some of the rituals performed during the installation of a sultan. Furthermore, the *pawang* or *dukun*, traditional magicians, are still popular even though Malay society is rapidly assimilating modern values and is exposed to an increasing amount of scientific knowledge. The Perak court retains a royal *pawang* who is said to possess the spiritual powers that safeguard the royal lineage and the throne.

Of the ancient Malay states which survive today, Kedah, Perak, Selangor, Johor, Pahang, Terengganu, Kelantan, Perlis and Negeri Sembilan still maintain the position and status

R. MOH'D NOH SALLEH

of a sultan or raja. The constitution also provides for the appointment of a paramount ruler or King. Every five years, depending on their tenure on the thrones of their respective states, one of the nine Malay rulers is instated as the Yang di-Pertuan Agung.

His Majesty Sultan Azlan Shah, the present king, is the last of the first rotation. Though the position of the Malay rulers and King is merely ceremonial according to the Federal Constitution, they are still looked upon as the custodians and protectors of Malay culture, customs and Islam in their respective states.

The new dynamic renaissance in Islam has, to a certain extent, transformed the thinking of most Malays to be more "Islamic," but not fanatical. The current multi-racial fabric of Malaysian society with its divergent traditions and different religious roots have more or less checked extremism from various racial quarters.

Assimilated influences

In a context of modern development the Malays still cherish their great cultural attachments to Islam as a way of life (*addin*), their language (Bahasa Melayu), their culture and their sultan. These are important attributes in the make-up of the Malay personality which are often incomprehensible to others.

Culturally speaking, the Malays have assimilated traits from Hinduism, Islam and to a certain extent from the West, but they have also inherited the influences of the Minangkabau from West Sumatra (especially the people of Negeri Sembilan), the Javanese, the Achinese, the Bugis, and in Kelantan, Perlis and Kedah, the Thai influence is obvious in traditional dances and the shadow-puppet play.

Islam nevertheless remains the dominant feature in the lives of most Malays. Education and practice have formed a strong foundation in establishing an Islamic heritage that governs their lives. Traders and missionaries brought Arabic script, the language of the Koran, to the shores of the Malay world. This in turn gave rise to the Jawi script which is used by Malays to this day, in addition to the more recent use of roman script.

Language and privileges

Bahasa Malayu is the official language of Malaysia but English is widely spoken and an important second language. Although Bahasa Malayu has been spoken throughout the Malay world for centuries, it unfortunately became less significant as a medium of

Opposite: A school excursion to Kuala Kedah's historical fort is a happy occasion for these schoolgirls from Kedah state. *Below:* Although these Indian women are Malaysians by birth they still wear the saree, follow the Hindu religion and preserve many cultural traditions.

R IAN LLOYD

instruction during the British colonial period, when the school system emphasized English as the vehicle of instruction and government. However, after Merdeka (independence), Malay replaced English as the official language, and today it is an important tool for retaining national unity.

Together with the indigenous peoples of Sarawak and Sabah, and the Orang Asli, the Malays are classed as *bumiputra*, who share special privileges laid down in the Federal constitution. These privileges were formulated to assist the *bumiputra* to compete with the other more advanced races—in particular the Chinese—in the fields of economy and education.

Legacy of colonial division

The relative backwardness of the Malays and other indigenous peoples was mainly due to the British colonial policy of "divide and rule" when the Malays were entrenched as poor peasants, fishermen and minor civil servants; the Chinese dominated the business world, and the Indians were mainly laborers in rubber estates, roadworks and railways.

However, the New Economic Policy adopted by the Malaysian government after the race riots of May 13th, 1969, greatly helped the *bumiputras*. Today the Malays are moving into the formerly Chinese bastions, and now play an important role in sectors such as banking, commerce, industry, education, sci-

ence and technology.

The ancestors of the second largest group of peninsular peoples—the Chinese—mainly arrived as immigrants from southern China in search of greener pastures from the late 19th century onwards. Many started as laborers, small shopkeepers and merchants in Penang, Melaka, Taiping, Kuala Lumpur, and other tin mining towns. The influx of Chinese into the country introduced new cultural traits alien to the Malays. Chinese temples and rituals, dragon and lion dances and other festivals became part of the Malaysian cultural scene.

The concentration of Chinese in certain urban areas led to the formation of Chinatowns which can still be seen in practically every large town on the peninsula, including Malay-dominated states such as Alor Setar in Kedah, Kota Bharu in Kelantan, and Kuala Terengganu in Terengganu. These urban centers still reflect the cultural heritage of the country of their forebears.

Straits Chinese

There is little cultural assimilation of Malay culture into the mainstream of Malaysian Chinese heritage, with the exception of the Baba and Nonya (*see Babas and Nonyas, p. 168*) culture of Melaka, Penang and Singapore. These people, also known as the Straits Chinese or the *peranakan*, which means "born here" in Malay, speak a distinct Malay dialect among themselves and have no knowledge of Chinese languages.

In dress as well as in diet they have adopted the culture of the Malays. Most still follow Chinese religions however, and some are Christians. According to the *Sejarah Melayu,* "The Malay Annals," Sultan Mansur Shah, the Sultan of Melaka in the 15th century, married a Chinese princess, Hang Li Po. The princess and her entourage of 500 handmaidens sailed to Melaka, and their descendants are the present-day Babas and Nonyas.

Roots of Malaysia's Indians

The third-largest racial group, the Indians, were brought into Malaya, mostly from southern India, as contract laborers on the European rubber estates, railways and telecommunications works in the 19th century. Others established themselves as small traders and merchants, setting up business ventures in Penang, Singapore and other peninsula towns.

Since most of these traders were Muslim they found it relatively easy to assimilate into the Malay community through marriage as well as other religious activities. The descendants of these mixed marriages known as the *mamak* can be found mostly in Penang and Singapore. One of the most famous families of these mixed marriages is the Merican family of Penang whose descendants are spread all over Malaysia and Singapore. Even the Prime Minister, Datuk Seri Dr Mahathir Muhammad is of mixed blood, with an Indian Muslim father and a Malay mother.

The majority of the Indians, who are mostly Hindus, brought with them all the religious and cultural traits of Hinduism including the caste system. Although they make up only 10% of the population, their festival of Deepavali is a national holiday, and some states also have a public holiday on Thaipusam, when tranced penitents pierce their bodies with iron hooks and undergo a pilgrimage to their holy temples.

The celebrations symbolize the victory of good over evil and candles decorate every Hindu home during this festival. Like the Malays who celebrate their Hari Raya with open houses for visitors, the Hindus do the same for Deepavali.

"The Original People"

Besides the three major races there are also the Orang Asli, or the peninsular aboriginal peoples, known as the Senoi, Jakun, Negritos and other splinter groups which live mainly in the mountainous interior (*see story Orang Asli, p. 152*). Most of the Orang Asli settlers are agriculturists, while others work in the jungle collecting rattan and other forest products. A number of them work with the Aboriginal Department while others find employment as soldiers of the Senoi Praak, the nation's best jungle trackers. Others in Cameron Highlands work as laborers in the tea plantations and vegetable gardens.

Cultural values retained

Some of the Orang Asli have converted to Islam, while others have become Christians, but many remain animists. They still maintain the *tok batin* as the leader of their tribe, and traditional medicine men also play an important role. Many continue use the blowpipe and are skilled hunters, while others are creative craftsmen producing fine wood carvings (*see Mah Meri p. 69*).

Although those who live near Malay villages have adopted much of the Malay way of life and their children are educated in Bahasa Melayu, they nevertheless continue to cherish their own culture.

—*Yahaya Ismail*

Opposite: Schoolgirls of Malay, Chinese and Indian parentage join together to celebrate their nation's Independence Day.
Below: These three schoolboys are part of the Peninsular's growing youth population.

RELIGION

The World's Great Faiths in Unison

Walk down any street in Peninsular Malaysia, or drive through the countryside and it is apparent that religion is very much part of everyday life.

From the tiny village *surau* to the tiled halls of the National Mosque, the amplified voice of the muezzin calls Muslims to prayer five times a day. Every morning, candles and joss-sticks are lit at the altars outside thousands of Chinese shops, flowers and fruit are presented at ancestral shrines, and the tinkling of bells signifies that the *puja* is about to begin at the neighborhood Indian temple.

Devotional diversity

Although Islam is the national faith, freedom to worship according to the religion of your choice is preserved in the constitution. The devotional make-up of Malaysia is as diverse as its population and all the world's great religions are represented throughout the peninsula.

An old saying has it that "tradition comes down from the mountains, but religion comes from the sea," and this in part explains why Malaysia's apparently devout Muslims still cling to traditions that are obvious remnants of pantheist, or pre-Islamic, times.

The spirit world

In the beginning, spirits were everywhere. They inhabited rocks, trees, mountains, seas, rivers and lakes and had to be appeased for they were in control of all the natural forces. In agricultural societies it was a disaster if the rains failed to come, and traditional medicine men, known as *bomoh*, are still called upon to invoke the rains in remote villages during droughts. Their spells are preceded with Koranic verses, but their chants are still addressed to the nature spirits.

Some aboriginal Negrito and Orang Asli tribes have embraced Islam, yet many still practice the earth religion of their ancestors. The Negrito, for instance, believe it is dangerous to laugh at butterflies as these are often spirits of the dead. Even the Malays have a code of conduct for entering the jungle, or putting to sea, which ensures that the spirits are appeased.

Animist religions, however, only survived deep inland for when other religions came to the region it was "from the sea." Hinduism

R IAN LLOYD

arrived first, brought by Indian traders at least a millennium ago, and spread rapidly throughout the coastal ports which the merchants frequented.

Influences from abroad

India was then at its cultural zenith, and Malay sailors who had ventured across the Bay of Bengal brought back wondrous tales. Sanskrit texts in the Malay language show that astronomy, textile dyeing, the potter's wheel, monumental architecture, glass, and wet-rice agriculture all came to Malaysia from India. But most influential of all was Hindu philosophy and the concept of a god-like ruler possessing absolute power. Remnants of this era are still seen in the royal courts, in wedding ceremonies and shadow-puppet plays.

Buddhism was the second of the world's great religions to arrive on Malaysian shores. Although little lasting influence remains, tangible evidence survives in the 10th-century temple mounts at Kedah's Bujang Valley where the inhabitants' curious religion was a mixture of Shiva and Vishnu cults combined with Mahayana Buddhism, similar to other communities in Sumatra and Sarawak.

Islam moved across the Melaka Straits from Sumatra to the Malay Peninsula and was by far the most successful of the new faiths. In 1411, Parameswara, Melaka's ruler, embraced the faith, and the Malay population quickly followed suit, although historical evidence records that Islam was already established in Terengganu during the 14th century, predating the Melakan conversion. The faith of Mohammad didn't reach Southeast Asia on the blade of a sword, but was a peaceful conversion initiated by wealthy Arab and Indian traders. Psychologically it had great attractions; its revolutionary concepts freed men from the Hindu feudal bondage.

The celebrated Arab traveler Ibn Battuta visited Sumatra in 1323 and wrote of its rich trading kingdoms. He noted that the Muslim ruler was a "humble-hearted man who walks on foot to the Friday prayer."

Islam—the national religion

Six hundred years later the Malays are still fervent about their faith, and to be Malay is synonomous with being a Muslim. So intertwined are the two that when a person of another race converts to Islam they are said to have *masuk Melayu*, or "become Malay" which is synonymous with *masuk Islam*, "become a Muslim."

From the dawn call of the muezzin to the sonorous Allah hu-Akbar, "God is Great," of the evening prayer, Islam pervades all of

Opposite: *Dressed in sarongs and* songkok hats, *Malay men relax after Friday prayers outside a Malaka mosque.*
Below: *Smoke from joss-sticks fills the air at this temple in Georgetown, Penang.*

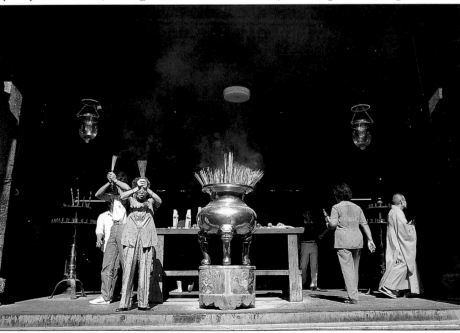

JEAN-LÉO DUGAST

Malay life. At birth, the *kalimah shahadah,* the first principle of Islam—"There is no god but Allah and Mohammad is the messenger of Allah"—is whispered in the baby's ear. The other four principles, namely, to pray five times a day, to fast during the month of Ramadan, to pay the *zakat*—a charitable tax for the poor—and to make the pilgrimage to Mecca, are the pillars of the faith and form the basis of most Malays' lives.

Although Malaysia has its fundamentalists, Islam here is tempered with tradition. A BMW-driving executive still goes to the village healer for those ailments that the doctor can't cure. And before docking his boat at a popular holiday island, the Malay boatman mouths a silent prayer, asking permission from the island spirits to enter their domain.

A multitude of deities

It is a tribute to the racial tolerance of Malaysian peoples that such differing religions can survive side by side, for the Chinese and Indian faiths embody everything that is condemned by Islam. They worship more than one god and a multitude of idols, and eat pork which is forbidden to Muslims but there are few incidents sparked by religious difference.

Small Chinese and Indian communities have existed in the Malay Peninsula for centuries, notably in Melaka where some 300-year-old temples still survive, but the majority

arrived during the British colonial period as plantation workers and traders.

Malaysian Chinese can be Taoists, Buddhists, Confucianists, or usually a mixture of all of these. Their festivals are among the most exciting events of the calendar. Spirits must be propitiated in order to bring good luck. Elaborate offerings are burnt at the Hungry Ghost Festival to ensure the ghosts are appeased.

Superstition and symbolism pervade all aspects of life. At the Lunar New Year, red—signifying prosperity—is lavishly splashed everywhere. Banners inscribed with good luck slogans are draped across houses, hotels and shopfronts. Lengthy noodles are eaten to ensure long life, and spectacular lion dances are staged to expel evil spirits.

Hinduism is the principal religion of Malaysia's Indians who form 10% of the population. Many were originally from Tamil Nadu in southern India, and this is reflected in their temples with magnificent towering archways, known as *gopuram*, which are lavishly decorated with human and animal deities.

The culmination of the Malaysian Hindu festival calendar is Thaipusam, held to celebrate Subramaniam's victory over evil forces. Penitents shoulder massive *kavadis*—frames decorated with peacock feathers attached with hooked chains to their chests—and pierce their flesh with skewers to gain favor with the gods.

There are famous processions in Singapore and Penang, but the most spectacular is staged at Kuala Lumpur's Batu Caves where the penitents climb 272 stairs up a limestone cliff-face to a sacred shrine deep inside a vast cavern. It may look painful to some of the 800,000 onlookers, but the participants deny there is any pain attached.

Conquistadores and the cross

Christianity, the last major religion to reach the peninsula, arrived with the Portuguese when they conquered Melaka in 1511. They only held power for little over a century but the enclaves of Catholicism they left behind are still firmly entrenched. At Easter and Christmas time when the Portuguese Eurasians of Melaka open their homes for feasting and celebrations, their traditions, food, dances, and even their language form archaic remnants of their Portuguese past.

Left: *Seated on a decorated dais, in front of an "eternal flame" this Hindu couple are blessed by a priest on their wedding day.*

BOMOH

Magic and Traditional Healing

Being a Malay, a devout Muslim and a *bomoh*, Haji Osman believes that for every illness there must be an agent responsible for it, and that for all these sicknesses there must be a cure. Consequently, it is necessary to continuously seek ways and means to free oneself from the illness, a process known as *ikhtiar*.

In common with other *bomoh*—which loosely translates as a medicine-man cum magician—Haji Osman believes that everything derives from God, but that human beings are nevertheless responsible for the illnesses that befall them. People can become sick through irresponsible behavior, for example, which can be avoided by behaving properly. However, supernatural forces such as evil spirits—locally known as *hantu* or *penunggu*—can possess an individual whose soul is weak. Illness can also be caused by sorcery, which used to be rampant, but rare today.

A *bomoh* uses various healing techniques, the most popular being his ability to heal fractured bones. Many Malaysians believe that modern medicine is no match for treating fractures, and even those who have undergone western medical treatment often seek further help from a traditional healer. *Bomohs* are also well versed in the art of curing with herbal medicines.

Only a Malay who has received the calling can become a real *bomoh*, and he usually learns his art by serving as an apprentice to a well-known master. An individual can also become a *bomoh* through inheritance, and often the master will choose one of his siblings to learn his art. The chosen one can be any of his children, but to be eligible an individual must have certain physical and mental characteristics.

One specific requirement is the ability to remember and recite long incantations. This is extremely important because in every form of healing there are various mantras that need to be recited. Even medicine has its own incantations so as to ensure its effectiveness.

If a *bomoh* forgets his words this would ruin the healing process.

Incantations can be magical words or verses chosen from the Koran. However, most mantras begin with the name of God and end with the mention of the holy prophet Mohammad. This is to ensure that what is being done is always accomplished with the help of God.

Some *bomoh* treat a wide range of ailments, others specialize in healing certain illnesses, and some, like the *pawang* don't even involve themselves in healing. The *pawang hujan*, performs rituals to prevent rain, and the *pawang buaya* is called upon to catch crocodiles. Besides these, there is also the *bidan*—a female *bomoh* whose speciality is childbirth.

Although many *bomoh* are still active they are a dying breed. The aging specialist is often unwilling to hand over his secrets because he believes that today's youth lack the strong self-discipline that is needed to strictly observe the many taboos and prohibitions. Without this inner strength they may endanger their lives if they attempt to practice the *bomoh's* esoteric knowledge.

—*Hashim bin Awang A.R.*

Below: *Surrounded by ritual paraphenalia and an absorbed, usually predominantly male audience, streetside medicine-men are a common sight in the Peninsula's major towns.*

JEAN-LEO DUGAST

ADAT

Ancient Ways Passed Down Generations

To orthodox Malays it is important that the practice of *adat*, or traditional custom, is upheld at all times, for this is an essential part of life, a sentiment reflected in the old proverb, "*biar mati anak, jangan mati adat*," which translates literally as "lose a child rather than lose a custom."

The practice of traditional custom begins from before birth and culminates with death, and even though *adat* varies from state to state, and even from village to village, the following examples are basic customs which, with slight variations, occur acorss the peninsula.

Childbirth and circumcision

In most villages and rural areas, the seventh month of pregnancy is when the rocking of the abdomen, *lenggang perut,* is carried out. Certain materials are gathered and prepared, including seven different colored sarongs,

one *gantang* (about three kilos) of rice, a ripe unhusked coconut, cotton yarn, resinous *damar*, seven white candles, a betel-nut box, and lastly some massage oil. When these are ready the midwife invites the mother-to-be to lie down on a mattress over which the colored sarongs have been arranged.

After gently massaging her with the oil, the midwife takes the peeled coconut and rolls it seven times across the abdomen. On the last roll she allows it to fall to the floor. If it stops with the "eye" facing upwards it is believed the child will be a boy. To conclude the ceremony, the midwife grasps both ends of all the seven *sarongs* to form a cradle, and then rocks the woman a couple of times before pulling the *sarongs* out.

Hours before the child is born, the husband cuts a bunch of thorny *pandanus* leaves and hangs them beneath the house to trap any evil spirits that might harm the mother and her newborn baby.

Immediately after the seventh day, a feast is held during which time it is also customary to shave the baby's head, and give the child a name. The newborn is passed around to the guests who bless it with scented water before the head is shaved. The hair is then put into a young coconut filled with water and buried alongside a coconut seedling planted near the house, to serve as a reminder of the birth.

Another important *adat* which is still observed, is the *bertindek telinga*, or piercing

R IAN LLOYD

of a girl's ear lobes—when she is between five and 10 years old—and the *bersunat*, the boy's circumcision, when he is between eight and 12. On the auspicious day the boy is dressed in fine clothes, and carried around the village on a special dais. Before the ceremony begins, a few things are prepared for the arrival of the *mudin* who will perform the operation. These include about three yards of white cloth, one live rooster, a bowl of water, a banana stem, and a betel-nut box.

Once the boy has been prepared by the *mudin* and certain incantations or spells have been read, he is washed and then seated on the banana stem. After the lightning-quick operation, the *mudin* takes the live rooster, holds it above the boy and notes its response by looking at its feathers.

From this ritual, the *mudin* is supposed to be able to judge the boy's sexual prowess in the future. Thereafter, for the following three mornings, the *mudin* will dress the boy's wound until he is satisfied that he has recovered. Today, many parents take their sons to a clinic where the circumcision is performed by a doctor.

The wedding

By far the most popular *adat* is the marriage ceremony and customs. Although traditions differ from state to state, there are certain basic practices which most Malays adhere to, regardless of whether they come from rural or urban society. Parents go to great lengths to spend time and money on making the occasion a memorable one, and to ensure that the marriage ceremony and all the *adat* involved meets the expectations of their community.

The basic rules and customs of a marriage can be divided into three stages. Firstly, the parents will deputize a close relative as their representative to select a suitable partner for their son. When a bride has been chosen the engagement or betrothal takes place, when the go-between approaches the girl's parents for their consent.

Once the decision has been made, a ring and other gifts are sent to the bride, followed by a ceremonial feast. In a case of breach of promise by the man the gifts are all forfeited, but if the bride changes her mind then she has to return twice the number of gifts or double their value. This *adat* has been followed for generations, although many Malays these days pick their own partners.

Apart from agreeing on the dowry and wedding expenses, other items exchanged on the wedding day have to be agreed upon by both parties. These include a ring, a complete bridal attire, good quality cloth (usually pure silk), a complete betel-nut set, cakes and fruits, and others. These are carried at the head of the procession accompanying the ceremonially-dressed bridegroom, to the bride's house, where the marriage is solemnised.

Before the *bersanding*, there are other minor rituals like hair-trimming and teeth-filing, as well as staining of the fingers with henna. After this comes the finale where the bride and groom are seated on a specially decorated *pelamin*, or dais.

Family elders and friends bless the couple by ceremonially feeding them yellow rice, and sprinkling them with *tepung tawar* (rice flour mixed with water), sliced petals and scented water. Having done this the guest is presented with a decorated egg symbolizing sincerity, purity and fertility.

There are numerous other customs, including traditional funeral *adat* which is still followed by all Malays; customs which relate to occupations, for example fishermen; and a wealth of traditions and customs observed by the royal families.

—*Mohd. Kassim Haji Ali*

Opposite: *At a Melakan Malay wedding feast, guests given red-dyed eggs—a symbol of fertility.* **Above:** *The bride and groom perform the* bersanding, *a traditional "sitting in state" which derives from pre-Islamic times.*

LITERATURE

Adventures, Epics and a New Identity

It was just after dark. The village folk started to gather around a thatched hut—a theatre stage of sorts. Flame flickered from bamboo torches, illuminating the stage, and the audience settled themselves on mats or on the ground while the storyteller began tuning his instrument.

For this particular tale, the *rebab*—a three-stringed upright fiddle—provided the accompaniment for the main characters who journey across rivers, hills and jungle, through romance, battles and intrigues, to at last arrive at their rightful kingdoms with stunning brides or miraculous magical potions.

Such was the mood and climate of traditional folklore—the root of the Malay literary tradition. In a society of limited literacy, storytelling was the norm. People with exceptional memory, wit, and the ability to render tales with intonation and rhythm, interspursed by poetry and punchlines, could make a decent living and acquire renown.

Fairy tales, fables and comedy

The vast repertoire of these local geniuses, included fairy-tales, adaptations of Hindu epics, local humor and fables. Malay fairy tales, known as *penglipur lara,* usually center around the journey of a prince in quest of love, truth, justice or miracles. The prince often leaves the comfort of his palace to suffer through difficult terrain, battling ogres, *jinns,* multiple-headed beasts and supernatural villains.

A favorite version involves a prince unaware, or robbed of his royal status. After almost unending ordeals he is rewarded with his bride, his rightful heritage, or the once elusive throne. The names of these popular fairy tales are always preceded by the word *hikayat,* meaning tale or romance, for example Hikayat Malim Deman, "The Tale of Deman the Navigator."

As Peninsular Malaysia was originally an animistic society influenced to some degree by Hindiusm, before the advent of Islamization in the 15th century, adaptations of the Hindu epics *Ramayana* and *Mahabhrata,* including the *Hikayat Seri Rama,* became part of traditional Malay literature.

In humorous tales—another traditional genre—we meet idiotic simpletons such as Pak Pandir, and Mat Jenin. These characters

MAULID NABI NATIONAL LIBRARY

are commoners with simple minds and their endless misfortunes never ceased to provide amusement. Characters such as Si Luncai and Pak Belalang are also commoners, but they were smart and scheming, outwitting even kings.

Malay literature also features animal characters. Apart from local adaptions of Aesop's fables, the Malays have their distinctive beast epic in the Hikayat Sang Kancil. Sang Kancil is a dimunitive mousedeer, commonly known among the Malays as *pelanduk*. The antics of Sang Kancil include outwitting bigger beasts such as crocodiles and even humans. These fables, animal epics and humorous stories served to educate as well as entertain their peasant audiences.

An Islamic heritage

The coming of Islam brought two of the biggest treasures to Malay literary tradition: the rich collections of folk tales from Arabia and Persia, and the Arabic script, which was adopted and adapted to the Malay language. The effect of the latter phenomenon was the enrichment and enhancement of the Malay language itself. Arabic and Persian words were progressively Malayanized and remain part of the language today.

As the sultans were the first to embrace Islam their palaces (*istana*) became centers for Islamic knowledge and writings. Ministers and noblemen became literate and several writers of exceptional perception emerged. Written works on royal geneology, history and law evolved from this tradition.

Almost all the Malay kingdoms had a *hikayat* that depicted the history and tradition of their kings, and the code of law that governed the affairs of state. The most well-known is *Sejarah Melayu*, the so-called Malay Annals, which chronicles the Melakan Sultanate; others include the *Tuhfat al-Nafis* (for Riau), *Hikayat Merong Mahawangsa* (for Kedah), and *Misa Melayu* (for Perak).

European literary genres

As early as the 1500s, the Malay Archipelago came into contact with the formidable European powers of Portugal, Holland and England. The fall of Malaka in 1511 to the Portuguese marked a slow and steady change among the Malay people. When the Dutch and English demarcated their sphere of influence on the Malay world in the mid 1800s, the Malay Peninsula happened to be for the English, who proceeded to gain political and economic control over the Malays.

The social system changed and eventually English became the dominant language. One indirect effect of this was the introduction of western literary genres—novels, short stories and poetry. The British also established a formal education system, published newspapers, and encouraged the use of Roman alphabets in written Malay. Consequently the Malay language is among the few languages in the world that can be written in two different scripts—Arabic and Roman.

The pre-war period

The beginning of the 20th century, saw the emergence of Malay novels, starting with *Hikayat Faridah Hanum*, and followed by *Kawan Benar* and others. Also dubbed as Pre-War novels, these books were didactic and very moralistic. The writing style was very much influenced by traditional genres, thus the word "hikayat" was still appended to earlier titles. Women's emancipation and freedom to choose one's life partner were the mainstay of pre-war literary themes, be it in the novels or short stories.

The turn of the century also marked the transition and change in form, style and purpose of Malay literature. Writing became the mouthpiece for the observant to voice their concerns over social ills and injustice.

Post independence to present day

Then came World War II and the Japanese occupation. The emergence of this Asian power gave impetus to the craving for independence, and via the circulation of newspapers, the written word became the vehicle of social reorientation. Short stories, poetry and novels gave a new sense of direction, identity and self-esteem to the Malays. Historians agree that the press and literature played a crucial part in bringing about awareness among the Malays.

Even after independence, Malay writers had to battle for supremacy and recognition due to the overwhelming influence of English in Malaysian social and commercial life. However, due to the implementation of National Education Policy and the National Language Policy by the government, plus the enthusiasm of local writers and publishing houses, Malay literature is currently undergoing a popular revival.

—*Said Halim*

Opposite: *This hand-written* Maulud Nabi, *a book of songs in praise of Prophet Muhammad, on display at Kuala Lumpur's National Library.*

MUSIC & DANCE

Percussion, Puppets and Trance Dance

Malaysian music and dance is remarkably diverse due to the cosmopolitan nature of the population. Typical genres range from traditional Malay folk-dance dramas like *Mak Yong* to the *ngajat* dances from Malaysian Borneo. Choreogaphed movements also vary from simple steps and tunes in Dikir Barat to the complicated moves in Joget Gamelan.

Traditional Malaysian music is basically percussive. Gongs of various kinds provide the beat for many dances, and entire gong ensembles from the huge *kenong* to the small *bonang* are used in *gamelan* orchestras to accompany the graceful dance of Joget Gamelan. Besides gongs, there are drums of various sizes, from the large *rebana ubi* used to punctuate important events to the small *jingled-rebana* (frame drums) used as an accompaniment to vocal recitations in religious ceremonies.

The peninsular aborigines, known as Orang Asli (*see Orang Asli p.152*), have a great variety of tribal or ethnic music. Similar to other tribal groups in Southeast Asia, they use materials from their surroundings to create musical instruments like gourd and cane mouth organs, mouth and nose-blown flutes, wooden xylophones, and bamboo stamping tubes. They also use the knobbed gong characteristic throughout Southeast Asia.

Malaysian traditional music is functional and music-making is an inherent part of religious rituals, court ceremonies, and life-cycle celebrations. The solemn *nobat* court music serves the function of upholding the sovereignty of Malaysian kings and legitimizing their power or *daulat*.

Nobat originated from the Middle East and became part of the royal regalia when Islam was first introduced into the Malay Peninsula in the 13th century. Gracing the courts of Kedah, Perak, Selangor and Terengganu, *nobat* is only performed at ceremonies such as the ruler's installation, weddings or funerals. Its orchestra includes the *nehara* (kettledrum), *gendang* (double-headed drums), *nafiri* (silver trumpet), and an oboe. These instruments are considered sacred by Malaysian society and are highly revered.

Hinduism and Islam have also influenced dance and music in Malaysia. Stories from the Hindu epics, Ramayana and Mahabharata, form the main repertoire for several

R. MOH'D NOH SALLEH

dian, guitar and maracas. Like Nobat, Ghazal came from the Middle East and became an instant hit with the locals especially so because of its Arabic/Persian melody and the romantic lyrics. Today, it is performed at weddings, fun fairs, festivals, royal birthdays and other functions.

Malaysia is also renowned for its traditional dance. The repertoire is endless and includes many graceful dances including Joget Gamelan and Asyik which both originated from the court tradition and became popular

types of shadow–puppet plays—*wayang kulit*. The most popular being the Wayang Siam, performed in Kelantan on the East Coast. The epic Ramayana is about the adventures of Prince Rama, his beautiful wife, Siti Dewi, and the villainous rival, Maharaja Rawana, the ogre king. Nowadays these classical stories are seldom performed as puppeteers tend to prefer the diversions, or *ranting* (branches) of stories in which the principal characters encounter different hazards and enemies.

Accompanied by an ensemble of musicians who play three kinds of drums, a pair of small knobbed gongs, a pair of hanging gongs, a pair of small hand cymbals and *serunai* or reed oboe, the puppeteer, or *dalang*, stirs up great excitement and enthusiasm during his performances. The *dalang* is the sole pupeteer and his skills are enormous. His expertise includes the adept handling of all puppets, voice imitations for 40 to 50 different characters, cuing his musicians; singing and comedy; and creating the right sound effects for all scenes.

Music of the shamans

Besides accompanying puppet theaters and dance dramas such as *mak yong*, traditional music is also used in spiritualism. A shaman without music and sound is one without power. On the East Coast, Main Puteri is a popular trance-dance accompanied by a makyong ensemble which consists of a *rebab* (fiddle), two *gendang* (double-headed drums), and a pair of gongs known as *tetawak*. The chief performer, Tok Puteri, entranced by the music of the *rebab,* communicates with the spirits. Aided by his attendant, Tok Minduk, who is also the rebab player, he "sucks out" evil spirits from afflicted patients.

A popular form of folk singing is Ghazal, found mostly in Johor. Ghazal is the vocal rendition of love poems, known as *pantun,* to the accompaniment of various musical instruments such as the *gambus*, tabla, violin, accor-

folk performances once royal patronage ceased to exist. Joget Gamelan is a Malay folk dance accompanied by a *gamelan* ensemble which includes various kinds of gongs, xylophones, and drums.

These dances depict certain episodes of stories relating to the royal household. The costumes are elaborate and include a decorated headdress, a silk blouse, and an ankle-length skirt. Their accessories include a narrow belt with a large gilded buckle known as a *pending*, and a long silk scarf tied behind the buckle. The dancers hold the ends of the scarf with their fingertips and make graceful gestures as they dance.

Asyik, the oldest and most prestigious court dance was usually performed in the palace's inner private hall for exclusive ceremonies. The dancers were beautiful young girls who were trained from an an early age in the palace compound and the dances imitated their daily activities like weaving silk thread, and winding yarn. Today, Asyik and Joget Gamelan have transcended the palace boundaries to become popular entertainments.

—Ku Zam Zam

Opposite: In Kelantan during festival times, teams compete on the rebana ubi*, a large decorated drum. **Above, left:** Subtle hand moves are an essential part of Malay dance. **Above, right:** Gongs, drums and* serunai *accompanying a* silat *performance in Kelantan.*

ARCHITECTURE

The Timeless Kampung Home

In the 15th century, Ma Huan and Fei Hsin, a couple of Chinese travelers, described the Malay house, and although it has evolved through the centuries to suit changing lifestyles, the basic shape and construction remains much the same. Perched on stilts, surrounded by rice-fields, and shaded by tropical fruit trees, these unique wooden structures merge aesthetically with the scenery throughout the country.

Wooden *kampung* houses are still numerous, but they are being threatened by architectural ideas alien to the Malaysian climate and way of life. Formerly, excellent building timber was easily obtainable from the jungle. Thatched roofs, known as *attap*, were made from *nipah* palm fronds which grew beside the rivers, and flooring was made by splitting the tough nibung palms. Today, agriculture and development encroach into the rain-forests and riverbanks and these materials are becoming harder to obtain and more expensive, forcing rural dwellers to turn to cheaper, less-suitable concrete homes.

Traditional wooden homes, with long windows open to the floor are ventilated by the slightest breeze. By contrast, windows in modern concrete homes are set too high for proper ventilation. The new houses are also built in rows which inhibits the airflow, unlike the kampung where homes are arranged so the breeze can circulate around them.

At the entrance of most traditional homes is a covered porch known as an *anjung*, often decorated with elaborate wood carvings, where guests are greeted. From here, stairs lead to a long covered verandah, known as the *serambi* where close friends and relatives are entertained, and where the family rest in the heat of the afternoon. Leading off the *serambi* is the *rumah ibu*, literally the "mother house," and the main living area. Often poorer families build this core house first and then add the *dapur* (kitchen) and other rooms later as the family prosper. Over generations, a small house can evolve into a mansion.

Evolving to suit the climate

Houses were built for the Malay lifestyle which centers around Islam and community life. Privacy was not high priority, in fact, there is no equivalent in the Malay language. Interiors are open with only a few partitions and the full-length windows provide an easy view of the house interior. Inside older homes there is a sense of space and coolness; woven *pandanus* mats cover the wooden floors and furniture is minimal.

Furniture arrived with the Portuguese in 16th-century Melaka and their words *almari* for cupboard and *meja* for table still survive. Except in the houses of the nobility, furniture was scarce until the British colonial era, when it became more popular. Following this trend, house shapes changed and hipped roofs

appeared as higher headroom was needed for the European-style furniture.

Local influences also shaped the traditional house. In Perak and Kedah, homes are raised even higher than in the south. This was to be above flood levels, but also to protect from tiger attacks, a very real danger well into this century. Outside influences have also played their part in the different regional designs. Around Melaka, where 100-year-old homes are no rarity, there are architectural variations that occur nowhere else in the peninsula. Courtyards and curved, tiled staircases show Chinese and European influences—remnants of Melaka's rich cosmopolitan past.

In adjoining Negeri Sembilan, settled in the 16th century by the matriarchal Minangkabau from Sumatra, homes have curved roof ridges emulating the horns of the water buffalo, or *kabau*, which symbolizes Minangkabau culture. Along the upper East Coast, which for centuries paid tribute to the Thai court, gable roof ends and wall panelling are similar to traditional Thai styles.

House-building rituals

Village life was, and in many places still is, a communal affair, with the entire kampung often participating in house-building. Certain rituals are observed before construction commences. A house site is carefully selected, for an inauspicious site may bring ruin to the

family. The *bomoh* chants and burns incense, and then the woman of the house measures a stick and a string of rattan to the length of her outstretched arms. The *bomoh* then ties the rattan to the stick and plants it at the site beside a full bucket of water.

The next morning they are measured. If they have shrunk the site is no good, but if they have grown it is suitable. Similarly, if the water has overflowed it is a good omen, but if it has lessened it is a negative sign. If one test proves positive then it is here that the *tiang seri,* the main column of the house, will be placed. The site is then cleared, but the surrounding trees and shrubs are left intact—the reason why traditional homes fit in so well with their surroundings.

The second ceremony is the raising of the *tiang seri,* or central column. All the components are prepared beforehand as the Malay house is a pre-fabricated structure first made on the ground, and later assembled on site. A rice-flour mixture, believed to frustrate evil, is sprinkled on the columns, and pieces of white, black, and red cloth, known as *bunga halang,* are placed atop the columns to ward off ghosts and malicious spirits. Coins are buried under the *tiang seri* to help ensure a prosperous future for the inhabitants, and to appease the *semangat,* or house spirit.

Although many Malays are urban dwellers, the kampung is where their heart really belongs. Many of them feel a special attachment to their ancestral homes where so many generations have lived and died, and hopefully these traditional homes will continue to adorn the Malaysian countryside for many more generations to come.

Opposite: *The tiled front staircase of Melaka's old houses is a feature unique to the state.*
Above, left: *An elaborately-carved* tiang seri *column, the central support of the Malay house.*
Above right: *Art nouveau tiles, imported from Europe, are found on many Melaka houses*

FOOD

A Spicy Cultural Heritage

Peninsular Malaysia is a food-lovers dream, both in terms of value for money and variety. The most renowned culinary centers are Penang, Kuala Lumpur, Melaka and Ipoh, although many other towns, including Kota Bharu and Johor Bahru, specialize with their own regional cuisines.

On the road

Food from roadside stalls is still some of the best Malaysia can offer, despite the urban trend towards Singapore-style air-conditioned food centers.

Malayanized "Nonya" and various Chinese provincial cuisines are abundantly available—Penang and Melaka being the Nonya and Eurasian food centers—as well as Southern Indian food, but traditional Malay cooking is found throughout the peninsula.

Some Malay food is hot (*pedas*), but most is not, thanks to the extensive use of cooling, cholesterol-rich coconut milk (*santan*) in Malay curries—this gives them their typically *lemak* (milky, coconutty) appearance, texture and flavor. But the vital companion condiments are consistently spicy: no Malaysian meal is complete without *sambals*.

Hot stuff

There is a great variety of these hot sauces, ranging from the straight chilli-*sambal* to *sambal-belacan* (pronounced "blachan"), a potent and odorous dark red-brown paste of chilli and fermented shrimps (while not for the faint-hearted, it grows on you). Other accompaniments include sharp pickles, known as *acar* (pronounced "achar").

Further light and shade is added to Malay cuisine with the use of *assam* (sour) ingredients such as *serai* (lemon-grass) and *assam* itself, the tamarind fruit, besides the subtler, dusky-lemon flavours emanating from aromatic leaves such as the pandanus leaf, *daun ketumbar* (coriander), *daun limau perut* (lime leaves), or *daun kesom* leaves. Ginger and *lengkuas* (galangal) root, together with bawang *puteh* (garlic), give yet more depth.

Chicken, fish and prawns are the staple meats in the Malay diet, with beef (*lembu*) and lamb or goat (*kambing*) seen less often. (*Kangkong* greens, water convolvulus, traced with *sambal belacan* make an excellent side-dish complementing fish or prawn curries.)

One meat you will never see on a Malay table is pork (*babi*), taboo (*haram*) to all Muslims. However, both the Buddhist-Taoistic Nonya Chinese and the Christian Portuguese Eurasians of Malaysia have married pork with Malay cooking styles, creating unique dishes.

The glue that sticks all this good stuff together is of course rice (*nasi*). There are many interesting dishes which feature rice as their centrepiece—for example, *nasi lemak*, a simple but superb breakfast dish comprising coconut-and-pandan-leaf cooked rice; *sambal ikan bilis* (tiny crisp-fried *ikan bilis* fish, similar to anchovies, in a hot chilli paste), fried peanuts, strips of fried egg, sometimes a small fried salted fish, and cucumber.

Other rice-based dishes include *nasi kunyit*, a yellow rice—named after the *kunyit,* turmeric powder, coloring—cooked with coconut and *pandan*; and *nasi biryani*, a spicy rice usually served with chicken.

Graduating to the malodorous

Aficionados quickly graduate from easy-to-love standards—coconut-curry coated, tender beef *rendang*; *longtong*, a vegetable stew with rice-cake squares in coconut soup; and barbecued shashlik-like sticks of *satay* meats dipped in peanut-chilli sauce—to exotica such as the foul-smelling Durian, prickly of exterior but creamy-marshmallow inside, or the broad-bean-like green *petai* bean, a known kidney-cleanser (and wind-maker), eaten either raw with *samban belacan* or chopped and fried with chilli, sliced small red onions (*bawang merah*) and *ikan bilis*.

Laksa is a meal in itself, so don't bother to order anything else. There are two kinds, *laksa lemak* or *laksa assam*, the latter being a Thai-influenced Penang speciality. Both feature a thick coconut-chilli soup over a noodle and seafood base It is the wonderful convergence of flavors—lemon grass and pineapple, peppercorns with mint and lime leaves, chilli and coconut—that gives this dish its special character. In *laksa assam* the lemony tang is highlighted.

Battered bananas for breakfast

For a breakfast snack, sample *roti kaya*: pancake-like bread (*roti*) spread with egg-and-coconut jam (*kaya*). Similarly delicious are *pisang goreng*, or deep-fried battered bananas. Another snack or appetising side-dish, is the nearest Malaysian equivalent to pate, *otak-otak*, a pungent spiced fish paste neatly stapled inside banana-leaf wrappings.

Malay desserts are extremely creamy and sweet. *Cendol* (pronounced "Chendole"), and *bubur cha cha* are both coconut-milk based concoctions with the addition of *gula melaka*, (dark brown Melaka palm-sugar laced with coconut), green *agar-agar* (seaweed jelly "worms"), sweet potato and yam chunks, with red beans. *Pulut hitam* falls into the same category this gooey black rice porridge is served with *gula melaka* and coconut milk. *Gula melaka* itself is the name of a favorite sweet—a small pearl-sago pudding drowned in *gula melaka* sugar and coconut milk.

A grand finale

Ice kacang is a truly spectacular dessert—a veritable mountain of ice shavings streaked with violently red, green and brown syrups and laced with condensed milk. This heap hides a treasure-trove base of sweet beans, *agar-agar* sweet potato, sweet corn kernels and attap chee, the crunchy jelly-like fruit of a mangrove palm.

One Malay word you're guaranteed to need after your feast is *Sedap!*—delicious.

—*Ilsa Sharp*

Opposite: Dominated by women traders, Kota Bharu's Central Market showcases the fantastic array of fruits, vegetables and herbs that are the mainstay of Malaysian cuisine. **Below:** Rich and spicy meat and vegetable dishes on display at a Kelantan foodstall.

R. MOH'D NOH SALLEH

PART II

Introducing Kuala Lumpur

At dusk, when the domes and cupolas of the Moorish-style railway station are silhouetted against a golden tropical sunset, and the muezzin's sonorous call to prayer of "Allah-hu-Akbar" drifts from the minaret of the National Mosque, Kuala Lumpur looks and feels like a truly ancient city.

But KL, as Malaysia's largest city is fondly known, is in fact the youngest of Southeast Asia's booming capitals, its scant history spanning less than 150 years since the earliest-known settlement. Most Malaysian cities and major towns can boast older pedigrees, but none can match Kuala Lumpur's remarkable success. This rapidly-expanding, cosmopolitan city, home to 1.5 million, is the hub of the nation, and worthy of its nickname *Ibu Kota*—the "mother city."

Against a background of soaring office towers an Arabian-style mosque shaded by coconut palms now straddles the historic promontory at the confluence of the Klang and Gombak Rivers, the *kuala lumpur*, or "muddy estuary," where the city first began.

Mining, malaria and civil war

In 1857, a party of Chinese tin-miners who had poled upstream from Klang on the Melaka Straits, decided to set up camp where the rivers met, as the waters beyond were too shallow for easy navigation. The 87 pioneers unloaded their supplies on the riverbank, now known as Benteng, and their shanty town quickly expanded into the area of Medan Pasar, now a bustling banking hub.

The miners had been lured upriver by reports of prolific tin deposits in the upper Klang Valley and although the mineral riches were there, malaria took its toll. Mosquitoes bred rampantly in the stagnant waters of mining holes and after the first month only 18 of the original party survived.

Upstream at Ampang, an old Malay district, the mines were thriving. Lured by the luck of a few, and despite the horrific odds,

immigrants arrived in droves. Having escaped a life of grinding poverty in their native China there was little to lose and all to gain in the Nanyang—the southern land of promise.

Chinese secret societies operated as benefactors offering the immigrants a measure of security in return for a portion of their wages. Intense rivalry built up between these groups over the running of lucrative brothels and opium and gambling dens which dominated the leisure hours of the male-dominated shanty town. Two major groups, the Hai San and Ghee Hin were constantly waging gang wars, and coupled with the devastating epidemics and fires that periodically razed the fledgling town, the economic stability of the region was threatened.

Discontent among the Malay rulers over control of the lucrative mining revenues came to a head in 1867 when Raja Mahdi of Klang refused to remit his dues to Sultan Abdul Samad, ruler of Selangor. The Sultan enlisted the aid of his son-in-law, Tengku Kudin, a landless prince from Kedah, and also formed alliances with local chiefs.

Seizing the opportunity to exploit the differences between the secret societies, Abdul Samad appointed Yap Ah Loy, a tough, charismatic Hakka as the Kapitan Cina, the Chinese Headman of Kuala Lumpur. Yap pledged support with his powerful Hai San society. Their most bitter rivals, the Ghee Hin, sided with Raja Mahdi and the Selangor Civil War began.

The fighting was initially evenly matched, but as hostilities continued Tunku Kudin's group gained the advantage by securing the backing of the colonial government in

Overleaf: Malaysia's highest-priced property overlooks the glittering thoroughfare of Jalan Sultan Ismail. Photo by Alain Evrard. Opposite: Her face framed by a telekung headscarf, this Malay girl takes part in the Independence Day celebrations in KL. Photo by Alain Evrard.

Singapore which was keen to see the area return to economic prosperity

In 1871 when Raja Mahdi's men pirated a Chinese Penang vessel off Kuala Selangor, this was all the excuse the British needed to intervene. Gunboat diplomacy thus turned the war in Tunku Kudin's favor. Raja Mahdi, an esteemed warrior, was much more popular with the Malays than his rival, but as historian Barbara Watson Andaya writes; "The outcome of the Selangor wars demonstrated to Malays that even an unpopular or weak prince could gain power with British assistance."

From chaos to growth

After the war, with Kuala Lumpur in shambles, many Chinese were ready to quit, but

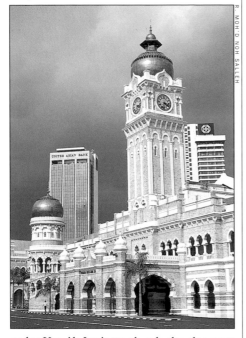

R. MOH'D NOH SALLEH

under Yap Ah Loy's tough rule the clan wars were quelled, the mines restarted, and the town boomed when tin prices doubled in 1878.

The British were eager to get their piece of the action and in 1880 Selangor's British Resident moved the state capital from Klang to the riverbank opposite Yap Ah Loy's Chinatown.

With the arrival of Frank Swettenham, who later became the Resident General of the Federated Malay States (FMS), the town underwent a transformation. Thatched huts were replaced by brick buildings and less than 40 years after the pioneering miners stepped ashore, Kuala Lumpur became the

capital of the FMS.

The next two decades witnessed a farsighted building spree that gave the city its enduring Moorish influenced architecture which owes its existence to C.E. Spooner, the state engineer, who talked the architect, A.C. Norman, out of his planned Renaissance style as he felt it was not a fitting design for a Muslim country.

As the hub of British power on the peninsula, Kuala Lumpur continued to grow rapidly. The city was unaffected by World War I, but when Malaya was invaded by the Japanese on December 8th, 1941, Kuala Lumpur soon fell. However, its architecture escaped major bomb damage as the British retreated further south.

Surrender and freedom

On returning three years later, the English encountered a different mood. The educated Malays wanted nothing less than independence. Nationalism had been steadily growing throughout the century, but had been given extra impetus by the humiliating surrender of the British. Finally, on August 31st, 1957, the Union Jack was hauled down for the last time and the capital resounded to the cheers of *merdeka* —"freedom".

Thirty five years have passed since Independence and although the city has changed beyond belief, KL still retains a colonial feel. At the Royal Selangor Club there are BMWs in the car park and members stroll around with cellular phones, but cricket is still played every Sunday. Out along Jalan Ampang, notorious for its traffic jams, huge old raintrees still shade 19th-century tin-baron's mansions that survive between the mushrooming condominiums.

KL also shares problems inherent to any rapidly developing third-world nation. Suburbs carve up the surrounding hills, roads are clogged with 10 times more traffic than they were designed for, and in the windless season before the monsoon, the city gasps under a haze that rivals Los Angeles'. But when the rains descend the city is reborn. The winds blow the smog out across the Melaka Straits and you can see the rainforested hills looming above the city like a primeval backdrop.

Right: The copper-domed, Moorish-inspired, Sultan Abdul Samad Building was the colonial government's power base for the Federated Malay States.

Kuala Lumpur

Tasek Titiwangsa

JL. IPOH
JL. TUN ISMAIL
JL. TUN RAZAK
JL. TUN RAZAK
JL. PAHANG

Pekeliling Bus Station

General Hospital

Ipoh

JL. RAJA MUDA

Putra World Trade Centre
Pan Pacific
JL. PUTRA
JL. CHOW KIT
Tourist Promotion Board
The Mall
Putra Bus Station
JL. RAJA LAUT

Asia
Chow Kit Market

Kuala Lumpur International

JL. RAJA UDA

JL. RAJA MUDA MUSA

S. Klang

JL.
Pasar Minggu (Weekend Market)

Plaza Grand Continental

Holiday Inn City Centre

JL. KUCHING

JL. TUANKU ABDUL RAHMAN

JL. SULTAN ISMAIL
JL. RAJA ABDULLAH

JL. YAP KWAN SENG

Wisma Loke
MEDAN TUANKU

JL. AMPANG
Le Coq D'Or
Zoo Negara

JL. DANG WANGI

JL. RAJA INDIA
JL. MASJID INDIA

(MATIC)
Malaysian Tourist Information Centre

Concorde Hotel & Hard Rock Cafe
JL. P. RAMLEE
JL. PINANG

Coliseum Restuarant
Eastern

JL. AMPANG

Shangri La
Holiday Inn On The Park

India Mosque

Bukit Nanas Forest Reserve

Equatorial
Kuala Lumpur Hilton
JL. KIA PENG

Lake Gardens & Parliament House
JL. PARLIMEN

St. Mary's Church
Royal Selangor Club
Merdeka Square

JL. RAJA

JL. BEN TENG

Wisma Batik
Masjid Jame

The Weld
The Lodge

Hotel Istana
Foodstalls

JL. RAJA CHULAN

Sultan Abdul Samad Building

JL. HISHAMUDDIN
JL. SULTAN MOHD

Infokraf
Dayabumi Complex

Central Market

JL. TUN PERAK
JL. SILANG
JL. HANG KASTURI
JL. CHENG LOCK
JL. BANDAR

Menara Maybank

Town House
Regent
JL. BUKIT BINTANG
Kuala Lumpur Plaza
Lot 10
Bukit Bintang Plaza

JL. PUDU

Puduraya Taxi & Bus Station
JL. SULTAN

S. Wang Plaza
Malaysia
Parkroyal
Plaza Imbi

Malaya

Sri Mahamariamman Temple
Masjid Negara

JL. SULTAN HISHAMUDDIN

JL. KINABALU

JL. PETALING
JL. SULTAN

Chinatown
Klang Bus Station

Furama

Federal
JL. IMBI

JL. HANG JEBAT

National Art Gallery
Kuala Lumpur Visitors Centre

JL. PERDANA

Railway Station

Chan See Shu Yuen Temple
Merdeka Stadium
Victoria Institution

Stadium Negara

JL. HANG TUAH

N

JL. DAMANSARA
JL. SYED PUTRA
JL. MAHARAJALELA
JL. ISTANA
JL. LAPANGAN TERBANG
JL. LOKE YEW

YMCA
Istana Negara

0   2   4   6 km

0   2 mi

Airport

Seremban

KL SIGHTS

Walking Tours Around the Mother City

With its ever-changing skyline and constant traffic jams, Kuala Lumpur can initially appear a difficult city to get around. Yet at its very heart there is a plethora of sights easily circumnavigated on foot. More convenient and infinitely preferable to crawling through the stop-start traffic cocooned in a taxi, walking about the city center also immediately immerses the traveler in the sounds, smells, sights and sensations of life in this unique equatorial capital.

Historically, the city was bisected by the Klang River, with the colonial administrative hub centered around Merdeka Square (Dataran Merdeka) on the west bank, and the commercial region (Chinatown) on the east side. North of the confluence of the rivers is the Jalan Masjid India area, a multi-cultural district known as "Little India". East of the central district is the "Golden Triangle,"

renowned for its luxury hotels and shopping complexes, and in the wooded hills to the west of downtown are the Lake Gardens (Taman Tasek Perdana).

A swathe of green playing fields formerly known as the *Padang*, and now revamped as **Merdeka Square**, is a fitting place to begin a tour of KL. Not only was it the apex of British life in the tropics, but it has remained very much at the center of city life ever since.

The colonial hub

On Saturday nights when the road is closed to traffic, the square is a favorite venue for KL's youth who flirt by the colonial fountain under the world's tallest flagpole. Nearby, Arabic script flickers from a massive television screen as the famous Koran teacher Datuk Haji Hassan does his evening show on how best to recite the holy book. No one views this scene as a paradox, however, for it is all part and parcel of the relaxed approach that the Malays have to life and religion.

Overlooking the square is the copper-domed **Sultan Abdul Samad Building,** the forerunner of the capital's unique Moorish-style architecture which flourished between the 1890s and 1920s. A 41-meter-high clock tower and arched colonnades characterize this former Secretariat building, now the High Court, built between 1894 and 1897. To the left is old City Hall with its black domes in the same architectural style, and to the right

R. MOH'D NOH SALLEH

is yet another Moorish-style building, featuring striped brickwork and keyhole archways, now the home of Infokraf, a permanent exhibition of modern Malaysian handicrafts.

A *stengah* at the Spotted Dog

On the far side of the square is the black-and-white Tudor-style **Royal Selangor Club**, commonly known as the "Spotted Dog," the favorite watering-hole of the colonial era. The nickname either refers to the mixed-race membership or to a dalmatian which a former member used to tie up at the steps, but no one knows for sure. On the spacious verandahs you can still sip a *stengah* , half whiskey and water, and enjoy a curry tiffin lunch; but only if you're lucky enough to know a member.

Directly behind the Club on Jalan Tangsi is the beautifully restored PAM (Malaysian Institute of Architects) Building which was once the townhouse of Loke Chow Kit, a department store baron. Later it functioned as the Kuala Lumpur Resthouse. Fittingly, this colonial gem built in 1907 also houses the Heritage Trust, which spearheads the struggle to preserve the nation's architectural legacy.

Other important buildings around Merdeka Square include the Gothic-style St. Mary's Church (1907) designed by A. C. Spooner, the versatile architect famed for his Moorish style; and the neo-Renaissance style KL Memorial Library opposite Infokraf.

Architectural landmarks

Dominating the landscape to the south is the elegant, glistening-white Dayabumi Complex, a dramatic Islamic-inspired skyscraper. Beside it is the General Post Office. Further down Jalan Sultan Hishamuddin is another prominent landmark, the **National Mosque** (Masjid Negara). Built in contemporary style in 1965 it features a massive, umbrella-shaped dome and a 73-meter minaret.

On any Friday, the Muslim prayer day, thousands of KL's faithful shed their work clothes and don a *songkok*, the velvet, fez-like cap and checkered sarongs to give thanks to Allah in the marble-floored Great Hall. Visitors can also take time out to admire the aesthetic architecture of the nearby Islamic Center, which houses an impressive collection of ancient Muslim manuscripts.

From here, walk back down Jalan Perdana to the roundabout. The grandiose stone building on the right is the Railway Administration Headquarters, built in 1917—the last of the glorious Moorish government offices to be constructed. Plans are afoot to revamp these

offices into a luxury colonial-style hotel.

Directly ahead is its even more impressive neighbor, the **Kuala Lumpur Railway Station,** an architectural smorgasbord of domes, cupolas, and colonnaded archways. Travelers have waxed lyrical of its charms since its completion in 1911. Paul Theroux called it "the grandest station in Southeast Asia", but Cuthbert Woodville Harrison, writing in the 1920s was not so impressed, saying that "if not too late, the Federated States railway department ought to deal severely with the architect!"

Renowned cultural collections

Past the Railway Headquarters is the National Art Gallery, formerly the Majestic Hotel, which now houses the country's art treasures, and further down on Jalan Damansara is the **National Museum** (Muzium Negara) characterized by its sweeping Minangkabau-style roofs. Its predecessor was destroyed by badly-aimed Allied bombs meant to hit the nearby railway yards. The present museum, renowned as one of Southeast Asia's best, opened in 1963. As well as rich ethnographic

Opposite: Unusual pediments and wrought-iron balustrades decorate the early-20th century PAM Building, once a Chinese tycoon's mansion. Above: Youthful participants in a Chinese fan-dance apply last-minute make-up in front of the Tudor-style Royal Selangor Club.

and archaeological collections, Muzium Negara is best known for its colorful dioramas depicting cultural events, including a Straits Chinese wedding and a Malay circumcision ceremony.

KL's largest park

From here, a walkway leads under Jalan Damansara to **Taman Tasek Perdana,** formerly known as the Lake Gardens. KL's most popular and largest green-lung (173 acres) provides a welcome respite from the equatorial heat and boasts an excellent Bird Park with vast walk-through aviaries including a hornbill enclosure complete with rainforest trees.

Other attractions include an Orchid Gardens and a Deer Park where visitors can glimpse the diminutive mousedeer renowned in Malay fairy tales. Overlooking the gardens is Carcosa Seri Negara, an elegant colonial mansion once the home of the colonial governors and now refurbished into Malaysia's most expensive hotel.

Chinatown

Since the city's founding, the center of commercial activity has always been the grid of streets which evolved around where Yap Ah Loy, the charismatic Chinese master of KL, held sway in the late 19th-century. Roughly bordered by Jalan Petaling and Medan Pasar, Chinatown is an eclectic collection of southern-Chinese style shophouses, coffee-shops and temples overshadowed by looming high-rises.

Vendors spill out onto the sidewalks, motorcyclists weave crazily through the honking traffic, and the pedestrian crowds bare witness to Kuala Lumpur's multi-cultural population. Family businesses still flourish in turn-of-the-century shops decorated with plaster bas-reliefs of flowers, birds and dragons. Chinese druggists—*sinseh*—weigh up seeds and barks to cure everything from acne to flagging sexual powers; grocers do a roaring trade in oriental delicacies like sharks' fins,

sea slugs, and edible swallow s' nests.

Prophets of the future—an indispensable adjunct to Asian life—abound. Under the arches of the five-foot-ways which shade shoppers from the heat, you can take your pick of traditional Chinese fortune tellers or Indian palmists.

For those concerned with more earthly occupations there are a host of eating houses. Dim Sum breakfasts here are authentic, as is the chicken rice, *nasi ayam*, at Kim Hong's, one of the many tile-floored, marble-tabled

coffee shops in Jalan Bandar (Jalan Tun H.S.Lee) where the working-class patrons still wear singlets and wooden clogs.

Nearby, is the **Sri Mahamariamman Temple**, KL's oldest Hindu shrine. Outside the entrance arch, elaborately decorated with dozens of deities, women deftly thread jasmine flowers into garlands which serve as offerings to the gods. Sari-draped Indian girls file inside to the sound of bells as the Brahmin priest conducts the morning *puja*.

Hidden behind Jalan Bandar, is the Tze Ya Temple built by Yap Ah Loy who was himself added as an additional deity on his death in 1885. Its unusual location is apparently in accordance with auspicious *feng sui*—geomancic principles.

A fine temple and a notorious murder

At the Jalan Kinabalu end of Petaling Street is the city's most elaborate Chinese temple, the Chan See Shu Yuen. Built in 1906 it features a pottery, Kwangtung-style roof profusely adorned with terra-cotta figures from Chinese mythology. Nearby, next to the Traffic Police Headquarters, is the **Victoria Institution**, KL's oldest school (built in 1894) where a celebrated murder took place in 1911. The headmaster's wife claimed the victim was a rapist, but he later turned out to be her lover. Somerset Maugham used the tale for his short story "The Letter," which was made into a movie starring Bette Davis.

Come evening, Jalan Petaling metamorphoses into an open-air night market. Under a ceiling of striped umbrellas, pedestrian hordes jostle past cassette hawkers and porkfloss vendors—the night air pungent with cooking aromas and filled with a cacophony of sounds. Blind buskers on Yamaha organs compete with Malaysian heavy-metal and Cantonese opera. Here, you can score fake Rolex watches and Gucci T-shirts, as well as bargain-basement clothes and footwear.

On the edge of Chinatown, fronting the Klang River, is KL's most popular hang-out, the Art Deco-style **Central Market**. Built in the 1920s, this pastel-colored edifice was once the capital's "wet" market, haunt of fruit-sellers and fishmongers. Saved from demolition by some forward-thinking bureaucrats, the market has been refurbished into a lively maze of shops and restaurants.

Artistic enclave

The city's artists and craftsmen have congregated here, and at any given time shoppers can watch glass-blowers, batik-painters, portraitists, fortune-tellers and even catch a traditional dance performance or a shadow-puppet play. There are dozens of food stalls on the mezzanine and top floors, but for a regional treat, join the crowds and head for Abdul Majeed Khan's Kampung Pandan Restaurant for the specialty of the house: fish head curry. After dark, the Riverbank Restaurant and Bar

plays host to the best of regional jazz.

At the back entrance, past where beret-clad artists immortalize their customers in oils, a walkway connects with the colorful new Central Square, which houses local designer boutiques specializing in batik and casual wear, an American-style ice-cream parlor and an upstairs cinema.

Around Jalan Masjid India

Follow the riverbank upstream, cross Leboh Pasar Besar, formerly Market Street, venture out across the old metal bridge and look upriver. It is a rewarding vista, for here, astride the promontory where the Klang and Gombak Rivers meet, is one of Asia's most aesthetic buildings, the **Jame Mosque**. Three silver domes, pink and white-banded minarets, and graceful arched colonnades adorn this turn-of-the-century edifice which, until the opening of the National Mosque, was the principal place of worship for the city's Muslims.

Visitors are welcome except at prayer times, and travelers dressed immodestly can

Opposite left: A 19th-century fountain, adds a colonial touch to Merdeka Square.
Oppostie right: The former home of Malaysia's first prime minister now houses a tourist information office and theater.
Below: Space is at a premium in this cupboard-sized mamak shop.

don a robe for a small donation. To the left of the mosque is Batik Malaysia which specializes in hand-drawn and traditional stamped batik. Opposite here, follow Jalan Melaka to Jalan Masjid India, a lively hub of shops and restaurants dominated by traders from the Indian sub-continent. Like Aladdin's cave, glittering saris drape from the ceilings of the shops crammed with a dazzling array of brassware and stainless-steel cooking utensils. Roadside vendors selling snacks and cakes jostle for position along with flower hawkers, garland makers, buskers, and traditional medicine men.

Clothing and food

Opposite the Masjid India mosque is a row of Malay shops specializing in traditional clothing; the silky pantsuits called *baju Melayu*, white prayer veils for women, traditional *jamu* medicine from Java, prayer rugs from Turkey, and a fantastic array of headgear ranging from Mujahiddin-styles from Pakistan to PLO-style red-and-white turbans. Some of KL's best and cheapest food is found in this area where outdoor eating stalls specialize in buffet-style "pay for what you take" Malaysian curries with *ulam*, traditional herbal salads.

Take any of the side lanes to Jalan Tuanku Abdul Rahman, one of the city's busiest trading streets well-known for its department stores, fabric shops, cheap hotels, and the

famed Coliseum Restaurant; with its smoky bar and sizzling steaks it which was once the haunt of Somerset Maugham.

Further along, turn into Jalan Medan Tuanku for Wisma Loke, a baroque-style mansion which is now an art and antique gallery. Once the home of Loke Yew, a business baron, it was the first private residence in KL to be lit with electric light.

Mansions of the Golden Triangle

Outside downtown, bordered by Jalan Ampang, Jalan Tun Razak and Jalan Imbi is the area known as the "Golden Triangle" where most of the luxury hotels, shopping complexes and embassies are situated. Around the turn of the century Jalan Ampang was where the rich *towkays* (business bosses) built their mansions, and some still survive.

The most famous is Le Coq D'Or, a palatial residence, now a restaurant, which was built by a lovesick tin baron to impress his neighbors who had denied him marriage to their daughter because of his early poverty. Another beautifully-restored mansion is the former Tuanku Abdul Rahman Hall now housing the Malaysian Tourist Information Centre (MATIC) where traditional dance performances are staged.

Heading Northeast

On the corner of Jalan Tun Razak, is one of KL's most unusual contemporary structures, the unique Tabung Haji—a skyscraper shaped like an hour-glass which is the center for organizing pilgrimages to Mecca. From Jalan Ampang follow Jalan Ulu Klang to Zoo Negara for a look at Malaysia's indigenous wildlife in a parkland setting. The elephant and seal shows are very popular with children. Another park good for jogging and taking it easy is Taman Tasek Titiwangsa off Jalan Tun Razak. The trails wind around a lake and on weekends, citysiders practice *silat*—traditional self-defence, and hold top-spinning contests.

On the southern fringe of the city, off Jalan Syed Putra, is Istana Negara, a white-domed palace surrounded by spacious lawns which is the home of Malaysia's King, the Yang Di Pertuan Agung. This is a rotating position taken on a five-year basis by each of the state rulers and is currently held by Sultan Azlan Shah of Perak.

Left: *A Muslim shopkeeper sells alcohol-free perfumes used before worship at the mosque. on Jalan Masjid India*

PASAR MALAM

Shopping Under the Stars

The movies, pubs, and discos may draw a sizable evening crowd, but by far the most popular night-time amusement, not only in Kuala Lumpur but throughout the country, is the *pasar malam*, or "night market". At dusk, streets are closed to vehicular traffic, hawkers set up their stalls on the pavements, and the fun begins.

At these nocturnal bazaars, vendors sell an incredible array of ready-cooked food, fruit and vegetables, meat and fish, household goods, clothing, shoes, cassettes, tools, hardware, dry-goods, watches and electronics. In fact, the range is so extensive, that many locals do all their necessary shopping at the *pasar malam*.

A venerable social institution

Don't be fooled into thinking that purchasing is the only reason why Malaysians flock to the night markets, for it is just as much a place to socialize, pick up a girl, show off your latest dress, or just hang out and watch the action. Parents with half a dozen pyjama-clad kids in tow are not an unusual sight. For locals, the *pasar malam* is practically a sacred institution, and for travelers, it is the best introduction there is to real, unadulterated Malaysian life.

One of the great attractions to night shopping is that the equatorial climate is not conducive to strolling around the streets by day. Housewives usually go to the market early-morning. As the day heats up, smartly-dressed businesspeople head for the air-conditioned supermarkets, but the most serious shoppers save themselves for the balmy evenings when they can shop in earnest at the *pasar malam*. These days, an increasing percentage of city women work, and the night markets are perfect for working mums who have no time in the day to shop.

Pasar malam are only held in the same place one night a week, but there is at least one happening every night of the week in the Kuala Lumpur city area. An exception to this rule is the street market in Jalan Petaling, Chinatown, an exciting, noisy affair which is held every night of the week. But, markets in the Malay-dominated areas, or even in the suburbs are the most authentic, and have the best variety of food.

Sunday market on a Saturday night

The most famous is the **Pasar Minggu**, also known as the Sunday Market, which is held along Jalan Raja Muda Musa in Kampung Bahru, the oldest Malay *kampung* in the inner city. Don't be fooled into thinking that this market is held on Sunday: Malays follow the Islamic system which marks sunset as the end of the day. So the Sunday Market is actually on Saturday night.

Jalan Tuanku Abdul Rahman in the heart of downtown also closes to traffic on Saturday night and the sidewalks are lined with hawker stalls. Other locations are Jalan Angsana, off Jalan Tun Sambanthan on Wednesday night, Kampung Datuk Keramat on Friday night, and Taman Tun Dr. Ismail on Sunday night. However, there are dozens of other locations which often change nights so it is best to check with the tourist information offices who keep up to date on the venues.

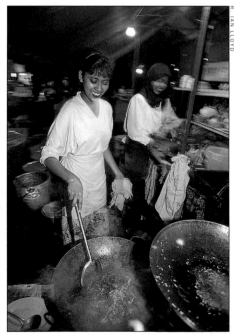

Below: *At the night market, Malaysian-style "fast food" is stir-fried in large convex frying pans known as kuali.*

R. IAN LLOYD

SIDETRIPS

Old Royal Forts and Hill Resorts

Selangor, the state which surrounds the Federal Territory of Kuala Lumpur, is often overlooked by travelers, but in the rugged northern mountains and the populous western plains are a wealth of interesting places to visit. Some, like Batu Caves with its cliffside temple, and the hill resorts of Fraser's Hill and Genting Highlands, are well known, but others, like the old royal capital of Jugra, and the hilltop fort at Kuala Selangor are far off the beaten tourist tracks.

By car, the western excursions can all be done as day trips. Fraser's Hill, however, with its bracing climate and colonial ambiance is an ideal spot to spend a few days recuperating from the often stifling heat of the lowlands.

To a cave shrine and forest reserves

Approached by climbing 272 steps up the side of a limestone massif, **Batu Caves**, 13km (8mi) north of the city, is the site of a century-old Hindu shrine. Located inside the cavernous Temple Cave, where stalactites drip from the 100-meter-high (328ft) ceiling.

The sacred shrine is a favorite venue for devout Indians particularly at the annual Thaipusam festival held in February, when 100,000 pilgrims make the arduous ascent. Thousands of devotees, in penance for past sins, enter a trance state and shoulder massive *kavadi*—symbolic frames with metal spikes attached to their flesh—and some penitents even pierce their tongues and cheeks with trident-shaped skewers.

North from Batu Caves, the Main Trunk Road climbs out of the Klang Valley through a pass to Templer Park. This forest reserve is popular with picnickers and offers excellent rock-climbing on Bukit Tahan, a solitary limestone peak. Recent construction work for a country club has somewhat spoiled the park's quietude, but the neighboring Kanching Forest Reserve (Hutan Lipur Kanching), 1km (0.6mi) further on, is still peaceful. Trails wind through the dense rainforest beside the scenic Kanching Falls which cascade from the mountains in a series of tiers.

Turn off at Kuala Kubu Bahru, 62km (38mi) north of Kuala Lumpur, for Fraser's Hill (Bukit Fraser), an old colonial retreat, 39km (24mi) further on. An alternative route to the lorry-clogged main road is the recently-built road from Batu Caves to Ulu Yam

R. MOH'D NOH SALLEH

other getaway hill resort, renowned for its casino, night-life and luxury hotels, is a total contrast to Fraser's vestiges of colonialism, for except for its stunning mountain-top location and surrounding jungle-covered hills it feels more like an Asian-style Las Vegas. Visitors either love it or hate it.

To reach Genting, 50km (31mi) northeast of KL, take the Karak Highway and turn off at Genting Sempah for the dual carriageway which winds up to the 1,800-meter-high (5,905 ft) resort. An alternative route, and one that offers a more in-depth look at the countryside is the Old Pahang Road, the original road across the mountains leading to the East Coast.

Just outside Kuala Lumpur at Gombak, a picturesque village at the foot of the mountains, is Mimaland, a hilltop resort with a boating lake and the region's largest swimming pool. The Orang Asli Museum, 1km (0.6mi) further on, has an excellent collection of tools and handicrafts of Malaysia's indigenous "original people," some of whom live in the surrounding villages.

From here, the road climbs through a series of hairpin bends to the Genting Highlands turnoff on the left. Continue along

Opposite: Middle Eastern and European architectural influences combine in the eclectic Istana Bandar, a royal palace at the former Selangor capital of Jugra.

Bahru which skirts the edges of a man-made lake and winds through rainforested hills.

Once on the old British-built Gap Road which snakes up the ranges to the top of the watershed, the traffic is left behind. Giant bamboo and tree-ferns overshadow the road, and a wraith-like mist enshrouds the forested hills. At the top of the pass, is the Tudor-style Gap Resthouse, an isolated remnant of the colonial era. From The Gap, an 8km (4.9mi) single track one-way road, which operates 40 minutes in each direction, connects with Fraser's Hill. Travelers can await the gate change while enjoying tea and cakes in the Resthouse dining room.

Colonial remnants and Vegas glitz

Perched on a series of seven hills, a cool 1,524m (5,000 ft) above sea level, **Fraser's Hill** is named after its first European resident, a hermit muleteer who mysteriously disappeared. Visitors can stay at English-style stone bungalows complete with ivy-covered walls and gardens of chrysanthemums, and even enjoy tea and scones in front of a log fire—a paradox in these equatorial realms.

Bird life is prolific along the forest trails, and once a year a bird spotting contest is held which attracts an international following. Other attractions include tennis courts, and a 9-hole golf course—one of the few public ones in Malaysia.

Genting Highlands, Kuala Lumpur's

the old road on the right for Janda Baik, a serene valley retreat popular for picnics, or follow the road to Bentong past a roadside waterfall and a stream with steaming hot springs.

Westward to Klang

The Federal Highway west of KL leads past the satellite town of Petaling Jaya and its vast industrial sprawl to Shah Alam, the new state capital of Selangor, some 20km (12.4mi) from the capital.

Dominating the landscape is the spectacular, blue and white State Mosque (Masjid Sultan Salahuddin) featuring a massive, computer-designed dome and reputedly the world's highest minarets. Continue past the mosque for the Malaysian Agricultural Park at Bukit Cerakah where local crops are exhibited and children can enjoy the suspended rope walk through the jungle.

Ever since the state capital shifted to Shah Alam, the old river port of Klang—12km (7.4mi) further down the Federal Highway— has languished in a time warp. In the town's old quarter is the Gedung Raja Abdullah, an old tin warehouse built in 1856 which was besieged and overtaken by Raja Mahdi during the Selangor Civil War.

Recently, while the building was being renovated for its new role as the Tin Museum, some early drawings were discovered beneath the old limewash. Other sights around the historic town include the Istana Alam Shah, an old palace; the Art Deco-style Sultan Sulaiman Mosque on Jalan Raja Timur; and the neo-classical government offices on Jalan Istana.

Along Route 5

South of Klang (17km/10.5mi) on Route 5, turn off at Teluk Panglima Garang for Carey Island, home of the Mah Meri wood-craftsmen, (*see page 69*). Further on, a scenic *kampung* road links Jenjarum with Jugra, the old 19th-century royal capital of Selangor.

At the hilltop Makam di Raja (Royal Mausoleum) are the graves of past sultans, and at nearby Bandar, amongst the coconut palms, is the exquisite Istana Bandar, the former palace of Sultan Alauddin Shah, which has been recently restored to its turn-of-the-century glory. This creative ruler, who apparently worked on the palace's original decorations, was also responsible for the elegant, Moorish-style mosque which bears his name, just down the road from the palace.

Follow Route 5, 46km (28.5mi) north of Klang for Kuala Selangor, another old royal capital beside the estuary of the Selangor River. Strategically sited on Bukit Melawati, a hill overlooking the town, are the ruins of Kota Melawati, originally an 18th-century fortress built by the Dutch in an ineffectual bid to control the tin trade, and later taken over by the pioneering Bugis for Sulawesi who used the fort as a base to establish the first Sultanate of Selangor.

Bugis graves and wildlife watching

Also on the hill, shaded by magnificent rain-trees, is a royal mausoleum containing the graves of the first three Bugis sultans; the original execution block; a lighthouse; and some old cannon which overlook the expansive wetlands at the base of the hill which is now the Kuala Selangor Nature Park. Home to leaf-monkeys, herons, and sea-eagles, the mangrove forest is also a favored stopover for migratory birds which can be easily viewed from observation hides.

To avoid the often horrendous traffic on the Federal Highway, return to Kuala Lumpur via Sungai Buloh to Kepong where there is the beautifully-maintained forest of FRIM (Forest Research Institute of Malaysia), and the Forest Museum.

Below: One of the many cascades at the Kanching Forest Reserve, a rainforest retreat on Kuala Lumpur's outskirts.

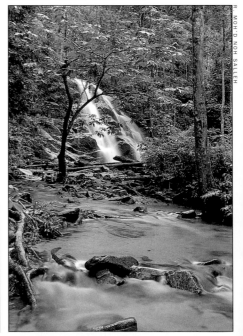

R MOH D NOH SALLEH

MAH MERI

Creators of Ancestor Carvings

Dominated by a vast oil-palm plantation, Carey Island in Selangor, 60 km west of KL, is home to a group of Orang Asli craftsmen. Apart from the Jahut people of Pahang the Orang Asli are the only other aboriginals in Peninsular Malaysia who create traditional wooden carvings.

Ethnographically, little is known of the Mah Meri, a sub-branch of the Senoi who speak a Mon-Khmer language and number around 1,400. However, elders at Kampung Sungai Bumbon, where most of the craftsmen live, maintain that their ancestors migrated to their present island home from either Johor or the islands near Singapore.

Pion anak Bumbon, the best-known wood carver, spends most days at the back of his house, sitting cross-legged on a carpet of rose-colored wood chips, quietly working on his sculptures. "Our pregnant women are not allowed to walk here," he remarks, "for the old people believe this may cause the child to be born with features resembling the spirit from which the chips are carved."

With a curved *parang* (machete) he hacks off pieces of the reddish wood which is soft to carve, but turns hard when it dries. He then selects a chisel from the array at his feet and using a hand-hewn mallet, shapes out the features of a *moyang*—literally "ancestor"—and the generic name for all the spirit images.

Well over a hundred *moyang,*, each representing a different spirit, encompass the gamut of Mah Mehri animist beliefs. Famous examples include Moyang Bahai, a demonic-looking dragon with a young girl swinging from its jaw; the spiral-shaped Moyang Puting Beliong, the spirit of the waterspout, who assists those who need water; and a powerful frog holding an evil scorpion aloft—the Moyang Katak dan Kala—which illustrates an ancient Mah Meri tale.

There are also dozens of different *topeng*, or masks, which are also *moyang*, and each has a different legend. These stories are

invariably bound up in the natural arena of swamp, jungle and sea—the Mah Meri world.

Using sandpaper—quicker than the traditional palas leaf—Pion's wife, Kantar anak Kassim, smooth-finishes a magnificent Moyang Tenong Jerat Harimau. This legendary tiger can only be seen by people with the power to see the unknown, such as a *bomoh*, a traditional medicine man, who formerly used the *moyang* for curing sickness.

The *bomoh* would go into trance in order to pick the most appropriate *moyang*, and after receiving enlightenment, would instruct the carver to make an appropriate small image. Ritual offerings of eggs, rice and a chicken were then presented, while he called on the spirit to help him cure the patient. After the ceremony the *moyang* was thrown away for it was believed to have removed the sickness and was therefore contaminated. This is the major reason why few carvings of this type remain.

Today, the craftsmen carve for collectors of primitive art and there is no lack of orders. Some scholars are skeptical of tourism and the negative effects it has on indigenous peoples, however the carvers themselves enjoy their work and feel that they arefulfilling a vital function by preserving their cutural traditions in the face of social change.

Below: Pion anak Bumbon, a Mah-Mcri master-craftsman, roughs out a "monkey in chains."

R. MOH'D NOH SALLEH

PART III

Introducing Perak

Translated in Malay, Perak's name means "silver," however Peninsular Malaysia's second largest state, which sprawls over 21,000 square kilometers of the northwest, has always been associated not with silver, but with tin. During the 1890s when the Kinta Valley reached its zenith as one of the economic jewels in the British Empire's crown, this region possessed the richest alluvial tin deposits in the world.

The tin ore originated from the granite ranges of the Barisan Titiwangsa, the mountainous chain that forms the state's eastern border. Over the ages these deposits were washed down to the valley floor. There's still plenty of mineral wealth under the ground but these days, with tin prices in the doldrums, many mines have closed down and Perak's economy has diversified.

Surrounded by curious, loaf-shaped limestone peaks pitted with Buddhist cave temples, Ipoh, the capital—"the city that tin built"—is now a thriving industrial hub. It still retains much of its colonial architecture however, as does Batu Gajah to the south.

Recent archaeological discoveries at Kota Tampan, near Lenggong in Upper Perak, confirm that man has lived there since the Stone Age. The limestone caves provided shelter beside the 400km (248mi) long Sungai Perak, the peninsula's second longest river, which has always been the state's major artery.

Legends tell of a Hindu Malay kingdom called Gangga Negara which thrived near Bruas in the northeast, however, the state's recorded history stems from the founding of its sultanate by Sultan Muzaffar Syah, a son of the last ruler of Melaka, in around 1528. The sultans set up court in their wooden palaces along the riverbank, and graves of past sultans can been seen near Kampung Gajah. The present sultanate still resides in the royal capital of Kuala Kangsar renowned for its gold-domed Ubudiah Mosque.

Control of the river trade which plied to the mining lands upriver had always been lucrative, and throughout history there were always outsiders looking for a slice of the action. During the turbulent 17th and 18th centuries, local Malays warred with the Achehnese, Bugis, Thais and the Dutch. From the early 19th century, the first Chinese miners filtered into the state, starting a wave of economic migration that would ultimately change the entire face and fortunes of the region.

In 1862 Chinese gang wars broke out in the troubled mines of Taiping and by the 1870s when a succession dispute to the throne added to the region's woes, the British had an excuse to intervene. The hastily-signed and misunderstood Pangkor Treaty saw a British Resident being installed, then promptly assassinated. However, following the execution of the Malay ringleaders, who later became heroes of nationalism, the state had no choice but to buckle down under the colonial thumb, and in 1896 became one of the four Federated Malay States.

Today, Perak's multi-cultural population stands at just over 2 million—an ethnic mix of 45% Malays, 40% Chinese, and 14% Indians whose descendants arrived as laborers during the rubber boom.

Perak is slowly realizing the potential of tourism, but in Ipoh's old Chinatown; in the royal capital of Kuala Kangsar; and in Taiping's serene Lake Gardens, meeting up with other travelers is still a novelty. It's more likely, however, in the cool Cameron Highlands, which although in Pahang, is included in this chapter as the only approach is by road from Perak.

Overleaf: Taiping's Lake Gardens, a former tin mine, transformed during colonial days into Malaysia's loveliest public gardens. Photo by Radin Moh'd Noh Salleh. Opposite: Midday prayers at Kuala Kangsar's celebrated Masjid Ubudiah. Photo by Radin Moh'd Noh Salleh.

IPOH & KINTA VALLEY

Time-Capsule Towns that Tin Built

Although Ipoh, Perak's capital city, owes its existence to the profitable tin deposits of the surrounding Kinta Valley, the city's unusual name derives from its earlier existence as a river landing for traders dealing in jungle produce. The *ipoh* or *upas* is a tree which yields a poisonous sap used by the Orang Asli on their blowpipe darts. One such tree still survives in the railway station gardens.

From village to mining hub

Cave drawings found at nearby Tambun indicate that the valley has been home to man since prehistoric times. Written history records that a village existed here in the 15th-century when a Sumatran sea captain ventured upriver to a place called Gunung Ceroh, the highest navigable point on the Kinta River, probably near where Ipoh now stands.

When the British first intervened in 1874, the valley was under the rule of the Dato' Panglima Kinta, one of the eight territorial chieftains under the umbrella of the Perak Sultanate. De Morgan, a French tin prospector, published his Kinta Valley map in 1886, and marked Ipoh as a "Malay village" with a population of a few hundred. By 1890, following a massive influx of immigrants, it had become the largest town in the Kinta Valley, the colonial administration hub and the center for tin-collecting and smelting.

Today Ipoh, with 420,000 inhabitants, sprawls into the surrounding limestone hill-country. However, much of its industry and new suburbs are on the outskirts, leaving the old center with many colonial buildings and the original Chinatown relatively untouched.

A tour of the colonial heart

An obvious starting point for a walking tour of the old town is the Moorish-style **Ipoh Railway Station**, built in 1917 with silver domes on its rooftop and colonnaded archways. Upstairs at the Station Hotel, once a favored hostelry for colonial planters and tin barons, a 183-meter-long (600ft) verandah affords marvellous views of the city against a backdrop of limestone hills.

Opposite the railway station is the elegant **City Hall** (Dewan Bandaran) built in neo-classical style, and beside it the High Court; both were built in the late 19th-century. In the back of City Hall is the Perak Tourist Information Center, and opposite is Gerai Nasi Kandar Hussein, a food center specializing in Indian-Muslim curry and rice dishes.

On the adjacent grassy square is the **J.W.W. Birch Clock Tower** built in 1917 to honor Perak's first British Resident, assassinated in 1875. Around the tower, a formerly controversial frieze illustrating the growth of civilization shows how insensitive the colonial administrators were to local culture; likenesses of prophets, forbidden in Islam, are among the depicted figures.

Further down Jalan Panglima Bukit Gantang Wahab is the Tudor-style **Royal Ipoh Club**. The club overlooks the tree-lined Padang, the playing fields which were an indispensable part of British life in the tropics. These days, early-morning footballers and joggers work out accompanied by the whirr of grass cutters.

Across the road, flanked by Royal Cuban Palms, is the imposing facade of **St. Michael's School**, a turn-of-the-century mission school. Pigeons roost in alcoves above the plaster statues of saints and at feeding time flock to the courtyard of nearby Masjid India, a North Indian-style mosque with scalloped archways.

On the far side of the Padang is the old Hong Kong and Shanghai Bank featuring Corinthian columns and a circular rooftop gazebo. Nearby, on Jalan Sultan Yusof is the FMS Bar—short for Federated Malay States—a favorite drinking haunt of the colonial era which still survives in almost original condition.

Old Chinatown

Follow Jalan Sultan Yusof up to Jalan Dato Maharaja Lela: the grid of streets around here comprise the first Chinatown which evolved from the 1880s when the district chieftain sold lots of land to Chinese merchants at $M25 a block. The old Georgetown Dispensary here is only one of at least 40, late-19th and early-20th century shophouses now listed as historical buildings.

Traditional split-bamboo blinds, known as *chiks*, colorfully painted with the shops' products and names, shade the "five-foot-ways" (covered sidewalks). Behind the *chiks* are dry goods shops selling grains displayed in rattan baskets, Chinese medicine shops which store herbs and roots in wooden drawers painted with calligraphy, and at the Star Printing Works old hand-operated printing presses are still in use. Along Jalan Leech, coffee shops with marble-topped tables

***Opposite:** Old-fashioned barbershops, usually run by Indians, are a popular and necessary adjunct of Ipoh's social life.*
***Below:** Paintings of mythical dragons and Taoist deities adorn the limestone walls, and gilded Buddhas preside over altars at the Perak Tong cave temple.*

abound, selling Ipoh chicken koay teow, curry mee, and other noodle dishes that Ipoh is famous for throughout Malaysia.

Cave temples

In the suburbs and countryside surrounding Ipoh the limestone hills are pitted with dozens of Buddhist shrines and temples, some dating from the 19th century. Six kilometers (3.7mi) south on the Kuala Lumpur trunk road at Gunung Rapat is **Sam Po Kong**, the region's biggest and oldest cave temple. Founded by a Buddhist monk in the 1890s it has landscaped gardens with symbolic statuary and a traditional Chinese archway lead to the cathedral-sized cave chamber famed for its Buddha statues and sacred tortoise pond.

Just before Gunung Rapat, with its large Mercedes Benz symbol on the summit—a gift from the German car-makers in appreciation of record-breaking sales to Ipoh's tin millionaires—turn into Jalan Raja Musa Mahadi. Follow the signs to **Gua Kek Look Tong**, the newest and most meditative of the cave temples. Set in a spectacular limestone cliff face, this massive cave is also known as the Brass Temple after its gleaming deities. A pot-bellied Laughing Buddha sits framed in the back entrance of the cave gazing out at a panorama of forested limestone hills, green valleys and a lotus-covered pond. The calm of this particular temple is enhanced by cool breezes, and

stalactites and limestone formations left in their natural state.

Beside the old Kuala Kangsar road, 6km (3.7mi) north of Ipoh is the lavish **Perak Tong** where huge wall paintings of Chinese deities have given rise to the nickname "The Tunghuang of the Peninsula" after the famed cave paintings in China. Built in 1926 by a Chinese Buddhist monk, Perak Tong also features a 15-meter-high (49ft) Buddha statue and a staircase which climbs 385 steps to the top of the cave; sadly the view of the surrounding countryside is spoiled by nearby industrial sites.

Life after tin

A 1910 guidebook described the Kinta Valley as "practically one huge tin mine," but travelers these days would be hard-pressed to find an operational tin mine in the region. There is, however, plenty of evidence of the valley's past riches: the sand hills and lakes of former workings scar much of the landscape.

While Ipoh's future without the mines was always assured, there are many old mining towns scattered throughout the valley—such as Kampar, Gopeng, Papan and Batu Gajah—which just went to sleep after the mines closed down. Consequently several of these towns continue to survive as time capsules from the turn of the century.

Few visitors ever reach little-known Papan just off Route 5, 13km (8mi) south of Ipoh, a perfectly-preserved mining town which has recently come into the spotlight. Conservationists want Papan to be designated as a historical site to save it from a zealous mining group which has plans to demolish the entire town to exploit the mineral riches beneath it. But the conservationists have time on their hands: the present depressed value of tin doesn't make this a viable proposition.

In this semi ghost town on a road to nowhere—which was probably what saved it from modernization—is a main street of original shop houses built around the turn of the century, their pastel-colored stucco walls faded from decades under the tropical sun. Except for the odd coffee shop, hardly any commercial activity disturbs the town's somnolence.

Raja Bilah's Istana, Papan's most historic building, is behind the shophouses on the right as you come into town. An entrance archway with the date 1896 leads through a walled garden to this original two-storey mansion built of brick and wood. Beautifully-carved barge boards hang from a Chinese-

When building ceased the jungle soon took over. A rooftop courtyard for parties, an underground wine cellar, and a lift were all planned for the palatial Moorish-style home. Nowadays banyan roots encircle the columns, woodpeckers nest in the recesses, masonry capitals lie abandoned like ancient Greek ruins, and graffiti from decades ago adorns the plaster walls of the bedrooms.

Wearing a solar-topee, spats, a planter's jacket, and his pistol by his side, Kellie is immortalised on a rooftop freize on the nearby **Sri Maha Mariamman** Temple, easily recognizable among the Hindu deities. One story relates that he built the temple after a number of his labourers mysteriously died while building his house.

Another version tells that Kellie donated a substantial sum towards construction after his prayers for a child were answered. The current watchman at the temple has added his own bizarre twist to the legends by claiming that Tuan Kellie was in fact given poison by his dissatisfied construction workers and that this, not pnuemonia, was the real cause of his death.

tiled roof and a peek through the windows reveals an original interior complete with antique art nouveau furniture. The house is still owned by the Raja's descendants but is only opened by prior arrangement.

Turn off at Pusing for **Batu Gajah**, a former colonial administration center 20km (12.4mi) from Ipoh. The main street is typical of Perak's tin-mining towns: rows of old Chinese shophouses with decorated *chik* blinds line the road, and women dressed in sarongs bicycle home from the market with baskets full of fresh vegetables.

The English always favored building on higher ground and a road winds to the top of a nearby hill, past old colonial bungalows and century-old tropical trees to the regal **District Courthouse**, built in 1892 during the reign of Sultan Idris. The Palladian facade painted in striking black and white, features plaster bas-reliefs of strange eye-like shapes, decorated gables, and a covered walkway.

A planter's folly

Outside of Batu Gajah on the road to Gopeng is an even more impressive building, the mysterious, unfinished folly of William Kellie Smith, known as **Kellie's Castle**. A four-storey tower dominates the massive brick mansion which would have been Malaya's most ambitious planter's home if it had ever been completed. But Kellie died while on holiday in Europe in 1926.

Above: Young Muslim girls dressed in their school uniforms take a rest under the pastel-colored archways of Ipoh's Masjid India.
Below: Abandoned before its completion, Kellie's Castle, near Batu Gajah, was the folly of a rich English rubber planter.

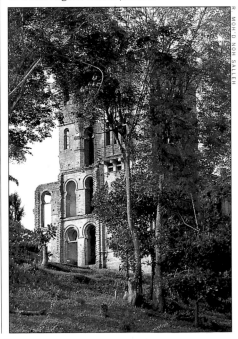

PULAU PANGKOR

Emerald Bays, White Sand Beaches

Over a century ago, Isabella Bird, a most adventurous writer, sailed up the west coast of Peninsular Malaysia, venturing into spots that Westerners had barely glimpsed—let alone a single white woman. One evening her motor launch dropped anchor off the coast of Perak beside The Dindings, the British colonials' name for the Pangkor Island group. At that time the islands were notorious because of the recent murder of an Englishman, but even this sinister event didn't cloud Miss Bird's evocative description of these isles in her book *The Golden Chersonese*:

"The sun was low and the great heat past, the breeze had died away, and in the dewy stillness the largest of the islands looked unspeakably lovely as it lay in the golden light between us and the sun, forest-covered to its steep summit, its rocky promontories running out into calm, deep, green water, and forming almost landlocked bays, margined by shores of white coral sand backed by dense groves of coco-palms whose curving shadows lay dark upon the glassy sea."

From east to west

Since those days Pulau Pangkor, and all of Malaysia, has changed beyond belief, but there is something about this Victorian description, a feeling, a mood, that still lingers on Pangkor's quiet northwestern shores and its offshore islets.

Lumut, an easy-going riverside town is the jump-off spot for Pulau Pangkor, and also offers a colonial-style Resthouse, and a country resort. Despite the presence of Malaysia's largest naval base, the town has a relaxed ambience. From here it's a half-hour ferry ride past the navy docks and across the Manjung Straits to Pangkor, the main settlement on the island.

In Pangkor everyone eats in the seafood restaurants, and this is also where to hire motorbikes and bicycles. However, most visitors overnight at Pasir Bogak, 1km (0.6mi)

across the island on the western shores where all the best beaches and accommodation are found. Facing the white sand beach is a range of lodgings from smart hotels to little thatched-roof chalets. Throughout the week the beach is quiet and pleasant, one can bathe in the green waters and sunbake on the sands in peace, but on weekends it seems like half of Perak has flocked to the seashore and that's the time to escape to the quieter shores of the northwest.

Deserted shores

Bicycles are a popular form of transport, but the island is deceptively large and the roads in the north are hilly and rugged, so if you're not physically fit it's better to hire a motorbike. North from Pasir Bogak the road winds around the coast to Teluk Nipah, a pretty bay with shaded and usually deserted beaches. Tucked into the northern corner is Coral Bay which is popular with snorkelers, although Isabella Bird's experience of "watching scarlet fish playing in the coral forests" is little but a dream these days in the islands of the Melaka Straits.

Further northward the road heads inland through the jungle. In the early morning, monkeys swing through the treetops and hornbills can be seen gliding above the rainforest canopy. Pangkor's most famous beach, Pantai Puteri Dewi—"The Beach of the Fairy Princess"—is now off limits to the public and forms part of the luxury Pan Pacific Resort in the far northwest of the island.

According to local legend the name derives from the fate of a Sumatran princess. Worried because her betrothed had failed to return home from battle, she sent out a search party which discovered his grave on Pulau Pangkor. She leapt to her death from the nearby cliff on hearing the news.

Boat builders and Dutch history

When one tires of too much sun and sea, the east coast provides plenty of interesting diversions beside its excellent seafood restaurants. At Sungai Pinang Kecil, boat-builders still make wooden fishing boats in traditional style. Further south, along the prettiest kampung road on the island, just past Kampung Teluk Kecil where gaily-painted wooden houses stand on stilts above the sands, is a 300-year-old Dutch fort.

Kota Belanda, was built by the Dutch as a foothold in their bid to monopolize the rich Perak tin trade. Restored by the National Museum in 1973, this brick bastion surrounded by coconut palms, was the scene of many fierce battles between the Dutch, the Malays and the Bugis from Sulawesi.

At Teluk Gedung, just past Kota Belanda is a large boulder known as the Batu Bersurat—"The Inscribed Stone." Carved on it are the words "Ifcralo 1743," various initials, and a picture of a child being attacked by a tiger. According to local folklore the soldiers stationed at Kota Belanda carved the inscription on the stone as a memorial to a Dutch boy who disappeared and was believed to have been eaten by a tiger.

Offshore isles

On Pulau Pangkor Laut is scenic Emerald Bay where Spencer Chapman in his book *The Jungle is Neutral* made his submarine getaway during the Japanese Occupation. The beach is now the exclusive domain of the Pansea Pangkor Laut Resort. This idyllic resort island off the southwest tip of Pulau Pangkor is reached by ferry from either Pasir Bogak or direct from Lumut. Two other isles, Pulau Mentagor and Pulau Giam, both off the west coast, are good for snorkeling and escaping the crowds.

The offshore islets are seen at their best when silhouetted by Pangkor's magnificent sunsets—conveniently viewed from Pasir Bogak Beach. Sitting on the shoreline at dusk brings to mind Isabella Bird's final thoughts on Pulau Pangkor: "Peace brooded over the quiet shores, heavy aromatic odors of night-blooming plants wrapped us round, the sun sank suddenly, the air became cool, it was a dream of tropic beauty."

Above: The firey sea and sky of a Melaka Straits sunset silhouettes a deserted islet, viewed from Pulau Pangkor's western shore.

CAMERON HIGHLANDS

Tea Estates and Colonial Retreats

Bamboo thickets and towering tree ferns arch overhead giving the serpentine road a tunnel-like appearance as it climbs out of the sultry lowlands. From above the rainforest canopy, the tree-tops look like bunches of green broccoli. Thatched-roof huts perch at the roadside and sometimes you can glimpse their inhabitants—the indigenous Orang Asli—going hunting with their blowpipes.

Ascending Malaysia's spine, the Titi-wangsa Range, the cloying equitorial heat is replaced by coolness. As the road crosses into Pahang state, the somber green of the rainforest gives way to bright green hedgerows of manicured tea bushes which characterize the Cameron Highlands, Malaysia's premier hill station.

Perched at an altitude of between 1,500 and 1,800m (4,921-5,905ft) the region was first discovered by its namesake, William Cameron, a government surveyor, in 1885.

In 1925, an official decision was made to develop the highlands. Lured by the cool climate, colonial government administrators, planters and businessmen built fashionable retreats while farmers began clearing the land. This all came to an untimely halt, however, during World War II when the Europeans were forced to return home. After the war, just as the region was getting back on its feet, the 12-year Emergency against the communist insurgents intervened: the highlands were declared a "black" zone and off limits to the public. But since the 1960s the highlands have steadily increased in popularity and tourists—domestic and international alike—now flock here to wear sweaters, sit by log fires, go for bracing walks, and most of all to escape the lowland temperatures.

From Tapah, 59km (36mi) from Ipoh, it's a winding 46km (28.5mi) climb to Ringlet, the first and lowest highlands town. Just north of here beside the Sultan Abu Bakar Dam is the Tudor-style Lakehouse Hotel. Another 14km (8.7mi) further and 305m (1,000ft) higher is Tanah Rata, the hub of the highlands, where old country homes snuggle against the hillsides. Many of the town's old grocery shops, with gold lettering on their stained glass windows advertising long-obsolete wares, are still run by Indian shopkeepers whose descendants first made their way to the Highlands 60 years ago to work on the planta-

JILL GOCHER

tions. Beyond Tanah Rata, trails wind out into the surrounding hills. Half-hour strolls lead to Robinson and Parit Falls where the famed butterfly—Raja Brooke's Birdwing—is often spotted. Other treks range from two-hour hikes to grueling all day mountain climbs, but whatever your level of fitness the cooler temperatures make any jungle walk a joy instead of an ordeal.

Further north, **Ye Olde Smokehouse** a 50-year-old Tudor-style hotel is the ultimate retreat, with its ivy-covered stone walls and English-style gardens. Inside are cosy fireplaces, overstuffed chintz lounges and a reading room full of back copies of England's *Country Life* magazine. Rooms are expensive here, but if you want to experience the life of a colonialist in the tropics this is the place to do it. The next best thing to taking a room is to treat yourself to a Devonshire tea in the garden restaurant.

North of Brinchang, the highlands' highest town, is the Sungai Palas Tea Estate, where bonsai tea bushes cover the hills, and Indian girls snip the tiny shoots on near-vertical slopes. Both Sungai Palas and Boh Estates are still run by descendants of J.A. Russell, an Englishman who took a gamble during the 1930's Depression and applied for a land grant to start a tea plantation. These estates were carved from the jungle and some towering rainforest trees still remain, like giants from the past. Just before the northeast monsoon blows up around November there is a so-called "dry" season when the roses bloom and the skies turn a deep cornflower blue. This is the best time to visit Robertson's Rose Gardens to view their flowers and stock up on homemade rose jam.

Past Sungai Palas, on the way to Gunung Brinchang along Peninsular Malaysia's highest road, a lookout provides a sweeping vista of tea plantations on one side and jungle-clad hills on the other. Further up, the forest changes to oak and laurel and mosses cover the trees and ground. At the summit, vegetation is stunted and matted by the force of the wind, but hardy rhododendrons with spotted pitcher plants hanging from them thrive. The mountain sides drop away almost vertically, but the thick vegetation below gives an illusion of cushioning safety.

The curious case of Jim Thompson

Although much has been cleared since the 1950s when Spenser Chapman wrote of "the terrifying vastness of the Malayan jungle," in his book *The Jungle is Neutral,* there are still tracts of primeval wilderness which could swallow a man without trace.

The Cameron Highlands' most celebrated mystery involves just such an incident. In 1967 the American "Thai-silk King," Jim Thompson, disappeared after retiring to his room for a nap. The event prompted the biggest search in Malaysia's history. Moonlight Cottage, the bungalow he stayed at on his ill-fated holiday still survives above Tanah Rata. No one knows what happened. Theories include a jungle suicide, communist kidnapping, a CIA hit job (Thompson had earlier ties with them), or a tiger attack, but no clues have ever come to light to confirm any of these.

In the bracing air of this region temperate vegetables, flowers and fruit thrive, and around the hills north of Brinchang are valleys of intricately-terraced and beautifully kept market gardens. Mountain springs are tapped and gravity fed through the terraces to water the spring onions, cabbages and other vegetables that can't survive on the lowlands. Further north, the hills are lined with flower and cabbage farms all the way to Blue Valley, a remote tea plantation, far off the normal tourist trail.

Opposite: Over-stuffed chairs, European bric-a-brac, and open log fires maintain the colonial ambience at Ye Olde Smokehouse, which overlooks the golf course at Tanah Rata.

PERAK RIVER

Through the Valley of the Kings

The Perak River Valley, known in Malay as Hilir Perak, is a traditional rural area with many unspoilt villages, little-known historic sites and peaceful riverine scenery little changed for decades, as well as Malaysia's answer to the Leaning Tower of Pisa.

Leaving Kuala Lumpur for Teluk Intan (166km/103mi), travelers can either turn off at Bidor on the main north road, or take the coastal route via Kuala Selangor.

The tilting tower of Teluk Intan

Formerly known as Teluk Anson (after an officious colonial public servant) this riverine town reverted to its Malay name of Teluk Intan after independence, although some still refer to it by the old title through force of habit. Teluk Intan thrived in the days when river travel was the only means of access to the rich upstream tin-mining fields. But since

road and rail took over, this town, like so many others on the river, was left behind.

The centre of Teluk Intan is dominated by a pagoda-shaped clock tower which tilts—proof that the low-lying town is sinking. Built by a rich Chinese contractor in 1885, the quaint 27-meter-high (88ft) tower is a curious mixture of oriental and colonial architectural styles. The eight-tiered roof is decked with Chinese tiles and the very English-looking clock often shows the wrong time. There are carved gables and a winding staircase that leads to a metal tank on the seventh tier which used to serve as the town's water supply.

Around the streets that encircle the clock tower are century-old shophouses with rows of verandah columns inscribed with Chinese calligraphy. On Jalan Pasar there's a bustling covered market, and colorful statues of Hindu deities adorn the Chettiar Temple behind the clock tower.

One block towards the river from the clocktower is the ageless Restoran Yussoffia, a Muslim-Indian restaurant in a pastel-colored old shophouse decorated with bas reliefs of Arabic writing and Islamic symbols. Their cuisine is as memorable as the decor—try the delicious mutton *murtabah*—Indian pancakes with a spicy meat filling served with curry sauce. There are also good Malay food stalls beside the river, a favorite place to watch the sun go down. Downstream from the town the Sungai Perak lazily loops its way to the estuary at Bagan Datuk and out into the Melaka Straits.

Elephant village and royal graves

Out of town, cross the Sungai Bidor for Kampung Gajah (26km/16mi), passing rice paddies where wooden homes perch above the flooded fields and pink lotus bloom in the canals. Kampung Gajah means "the elephant village" and in the old days was heavily-populated with *Elephas maximus*. They were a favored method of transport throughout the Lower Perak district, especially among the ruling class, and historical photos show parties fording the Perak River, and prospecting for tin on elephant back. In the swampy forests to the east, an isolated herd still survives, far from their more numerous kin in the central ranges.

Nicknamed "**The Valley of the Kings**," the region between Kampung Gajah and Parit, 65km (40mi) to the north, is the original home of the Perak Sultanate. Dozens of old royal graves dating from the 16th century are found along here, indicated by distinctive road signs, painted royal yellow and bearing the name of each sultan and his number in the dynastic line. Sultan Muzaffar Syah, the founder of the Perak Sultanate, and his wife, are buried at Teluk Bakong, 11km (6.8mi) south of Bota Kanan, and their graves are marked with intricately-carved headstones known as *batu nisan*.

Death of an Englishman

There are other important tombs at Pulau Tiga, Kampung Jawa, Kampung Melayu and Pulau Besar. At the latter village is also another famous grave, that of J.W.W. Birch, the first British Resident of Perak, murdered in 1875 while using a bath house at Pasir Salak, further north.

Birch's assassination was condemned by the colonial government, but later historians are of the opinion that Birch was a tactless administrator who had little regard for Malay laws and religion. He was posting signs of controversial new laws which limited the local chiefs' powers when he was killed.

Just after Kampung Gajah, turn left across the Sungai Perak, and immediately left again along a tiny road which winds past traditional Malay homes made of oiled wood with long shuttered windows, scalloped and latticed eaves and rising-sun carvings on the gables. At Pasir Salak, 2km (1.2mi) along the road, is a historical complex with a reconstructed 120-year-old Rumah Kutai—traditional Perak

house. A memorial marks where Birch met his fate, and a monument in the form of a *kris* dagger commemorates Datuk Maharaja Lela, Datuk Sagor and their followers who lead the uprising against the British and who have since been established as heroes of Malaysian nationalism.

Just before Bota Kanan is the Pusat Pembiakan Tuntung Perak, a center for breeding river turtles which is open to the public. From the crossroads, Route 5 goes to Ipoh (east) or Pulau Pangkor (west). Continue north up the river valley for Parit past traditional houses shaded by orchards of durian trees.

The prickly "queen of fruits" is also favorite fare for tigers and it's said that this is why Parit houses were built so high off the ground. Huge raintrees shade this former royal town where a wooden Malay-style Resthouse overlooks the river, and a footbridge spans the Sungai Perak to a recreational park on an island.

From Parit, travelers can go to Ipoh (31km/19mi) or head to Kuala Kangsar, Perak's current royal capital, by taking the winding, less popular route through rubber estates and sleepy villages along the west bank of the river.

Opposite: Cats, village women and schoolgirls take advantage of this resting spot outside a sundry store in Teluk Intan.

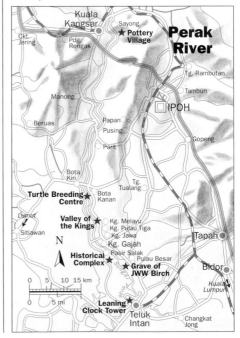

KUALA KANGSAR

Perak's Riverside Royal Capital

Ever since the 1740s when Sultan Muzaffar Syah III quarrelled with his brother and moved his court upriver, Kuala Kangsar has been the royal capital of Perak. Overlooking a bend of the languid Sungai Perak, against a distant backdrop of purple mountains, this picturesque town with its golden-domed mosque and royal palaces still retains much of the tropical ambience that moved a Victorian writer to admit that "I like Kwala Kangsa better than any place that I have been at in Asia..."

In those days the royal town was a few days journey on elephant-back over the mountains to Ipoh, but now travelers either arrive by train or via the 42-km (26mi) expressway which climbs out of the Kinta Valley, tunnels through a rainforested mountain and descends into the Perak River Valley.

Straddling the Kangsar River, which emp-ties into the Perak, the town's administrative and commercial hub is sited on the north bank, and the royal residences on the south. Chinese and Indian businesses prevail, and the English have also left their mark in the town's many colonial-style buildings, but all these influences have scarcely touched the Malay essence of Kuala Kangsar.

For all the royal sights follow Jalan Istana south along the riverbank. Rambling, tropical trees bedecked with birds'-nest ferns, shade the riverside park—a relaxing spot for watch-ing the wooden ferryboats ply back and forth across the river to Sayong, a kampung re-nowned for its distinctive pottery (*see p. 86*). In the windy season, boys fly large moon-shaped kites from the sandbanks on the opposite side of the river.

The turn-of-the-century mansion across from the park was formerly the British Resident's home, but is now a girl's school. This building replaced the old wooden bunga-low where Hugh Low, the British Resident, together with his pet apes, entertained Isabella Bird, author of *The Golden Chersonese*. This book makes fascinating reading for travelers intending to visit Kuala Kangsar (*see Further Reading, p. 280*).

A fine mosque

Downriver is the Resthouse, where the views from the dining-room verandah are much the same as in 19th-century etchings. From here,

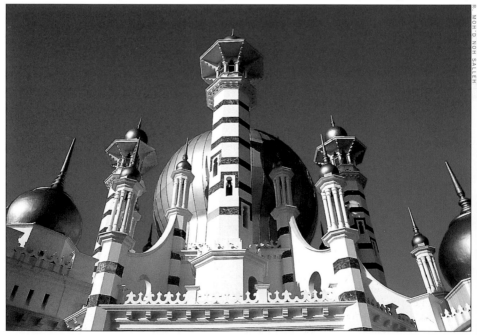

R. MOH'D NOH SALLEH

Jalan Istana winds up a rise, past neo-classical Istana Hulu, the former palace of Perak's 28th sultan, built in 1898. Kuala Kangsar's famed **Masjid Ubudiah** now comes into view, its golden onion domes gleam in the sunlight atop an "Arabian Nights"mosque of white and black marble. Sultan Idris laid the foundation stone in 1913 , but construction was delayed because World War I slowed up imports of the Italian marble which had had to be reordered after the first shipment was destroyed by the sultan's elephants who ran amok while in rut.

When the mosque was eventually finished six years later, Sultan Idris had died and it was opened by his successor, Sultan Abdul Jalil. Nowadays young girls chant from their Korans on the cool marble floors; boys play rounders on the verandah; and at prayer times, sarong-clad villagers wander informally in to pay their respects to Allah. Beside the mosque is the Makam Diraja, the royal mausoleum, and across the road is a well-known *madrasah*, a religious school which specializes in teaching Arabic. Many students go on to study at Middle Eastern Universities.

Regal residences

Continue along Jalan Istana for the grandiose Istana Iskandariah, the official home of the Perak Sultanate, currently occupied by Sultan Azlan Shah. Commanding a hilltop position overlooking the river, the 1930s palace is a combination of Saracenic and Art Deco styles. Viewed from the town jetty upstream, the palace's white towers topped with golden mosaic domes look fantastically mediaeval looming above the tropical greenery.

Beyond the Iskkana Iskandariah is yet another royal residence, the Istana Kenangan, now the **Royal Museum**. This whimsical palace is one of the few remaining royal residences built in traditional style. Early craftsmen used no nails, and this gem of Malay woodwork features carved panels, friezes and barge-boards, and woven wall panels of split bamboo. Open every day except Friday, the museum houses royal regalia and heirlooms. An interesting collection of historical photographs shows royalty on elephant back, and moustachioed British gents sternly posing beside sultans dressed in brocade sarongs with *kris* daggers in their waistbands.

In the past, the villages around the royal palaces were where the royal artisans lived and worked, and past Istana Kenangan, at Kampung Padang Changkak, a few blacksmiths using traditional methods still forge

parang (machetes), and *kris*. Kuala Kangsar is also famous for its gold-thread embroidery on velvet, called *tekatan*, and although some village women are still adept at this needle-craft, they usually only work on commissions. However, at the Kraftangan complex at Enggor, 20km (12.4mi) before Kuala Kangsar on the old Ipoh road, *tekatan* and many other traditional Perak crafts are still being practised and are on sale at the showroom.

On the north side of town, schoolboys play rugby on the spacious Padang of the prestigious **Malay College**, where the register reads like a "*Who's Who*"of Malay public life. Built by the British in 1905 to train royal offspring, the residential college is now open to all academically-qualified boys.

Opposite, is the Pavilion Polo Iskandar, an unusual octagonal tower built of wood and supported by brick columns, where Sultan Iskandar (1918-1938) used to relax between chukkas of polo. Continue along Jalan Tun Abdul Razak, past the hawker selling delicious *rojak petis*—fruit salad with peanut sauce—to the District Offices. The large rubber tree here is one of the first experimental trees planted over a century ago and a forerunner of the crop that changed the face and fortunes of Malaya.

Opposite: Minarets striped in black marble surround the glowing main dome of the celebrated Masjid Ubudiah at Kuala Kangsar.

Kuala
Kangsar

SAYONG

1 Istana Kenangan   7 Former British Residency
2 Istana Iskandaria   8 Rubber Tree
3 Masjid Ubudiah   9 Polo Pavilion
4 Royal Mausoleum   10 Malay College
5 Istana Hulu   11 Railway Station
6 Resthouse   12 Bus Station

N

not to scale

TAIPING

"Town of Everlasting Peace"

At mid-morning in the coffee shops of Taiping customers fervently place bets: not on horse-races or "four-digit" lotteries, but on a game of chance peculiar to this town. The local gamblers are putting money on what time the afternoon rain will begin. That it will arrive is a virtual certainty for Taiping lays claim to being the wettest town in Peninsular Malaysia. This daily shower makes for cool nights and fresh mornings, and also provides another reason to hang about the town coffee shops which serve up some of the country's tastiest and cheapest cuisine.

Tin and opium gang wars

Located 36km (22mi) north of Kuala Kangsar, the "Town of Everlasting Peace" as Taiping's name translates, was anything but peaceful in the mid-19th century when it was at the center of gang wars between rival Chinese clans fighting over tin holdings. Their bitter feuds, known as the Larut Wars, seriously affected the region's lucrative tin and opium production and eventually led to British interference and the inevitable appointment of a Resident. The clans were split up—the Hai San to Taiping and the Ghee Hin to neighboring Kamunting.—and after that calm prevailed.

From 1848, when Long Jaafar, the district Malay chieftain, had started giving the Chinese mining rights, the population expanded rapidly. A few decades later a traveler remarked that Taiping was "an important Chinese town, with a street about a mile long, with large bazaars and shops making a fine appearance, being much decorated in Chinese style."

Approaching Taiping today, much still rings true from this Victorian description. Mauve-colored hills rise abruptly behind the still-predominantly Chinese town which has some fine 19th-century architecture, the scenic Lake Gardens, and Malaysia's oldest railway station, museum, and hill resort.

Taiping is an easy and absorbing town to wander around, with many decorative old shops and houses adorned with art nouveau tiles, plaster bird and flower reliefs, and wooden nameboards painted in gold calligraphy. The original Town Market on Jalan Pasar is one of the last wood and wrought-iron markets still functioning on the peninsula. On the market's perimeter are hawker stalls which

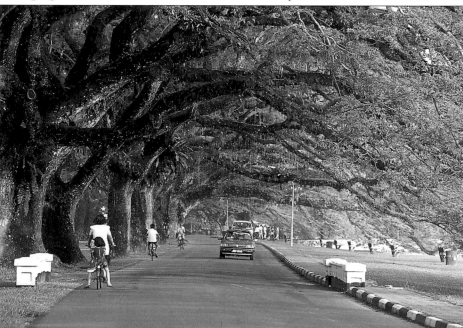

offer cheap and tasty noodle dishes. Opposite, on the walls of an old Indian restaurant an antique clock proclaims "Bismillah Eating House Established 1900." This traditional establishment on Jalan Besar serves excellent *murtabah* and *roti canai.*

Taiping's multi-cultural population worships along Jalan Kota where within two blocks are the Old Taiping Town Mosque, the Sri Nagamuthu (Hindu) temple, Seng Tong Chinese Temple and the Indian Mosque. On Jalan Stesen is the old zinc-roofed railway station, which retains a steam-train water pump, signs hung in wrought-iron brackets, and wooden swing doors on the Station Master's Office. Further along Jalan Stesen, shaded by huge raintrees, is the King Edward VII School built in 19th-century colonial style.

Back on Jalan Kota, are the **District Offices**, another architectural gem built in 1879, which feature a distinctive Palladian facade and rooftop pediments. The offices were designed by Francis Caulfield, who was also the architect of the similar-styled Batu Gajah Courthouse. Further north on Jalan Taming Sari is another fine example of colonial architecture: the Muzium Perak, Malaysia's oldest museum built in 1886. Its fascinating displays include an elephant's skull, a tapir's skeleton, stuffed mousedeers, a rattan elephant *howdah*, Malay weapons and coats of mail, and traditional crafts and costumes.

Lake Gardens and Bukit Larut

Opposite the museum, follow the walls of Malaysia's oldest jail and turn right for the renowned Lake Gardens, a chain of lakes and lotus ponds with islands of palms and feathery bamboo. These century-old parklands, created from abandoned tin-mines, are at their best at dawn and dusk when *tai-chi* exponents exercise on the spacious lawns, and joggers and walkers take to the canopied roads shaded by the peninsula's most magnificent raintrees. On the massive, moss-covered branches grow orchids, creepers and at least 15 different fern species.

Follow Jalan Air Terjun through the Lake Gardens for Bukit Larut, formerly called Maxwell's Hill after the British Resident who first proposed the idea of a hilltop retreat in the late-19th century. Early visitors made their ascent in chairs carried by coolies. These days, land rovers climb the winding 9km (5.6mi) road through towering rainforest to the 1,035-meter-high (3,395ft) resort which has changed little since colonial days. Old-style wooden resthouses provide basic fare

and accomodation amongst terraced lawns, pine trees and dahlia gardens. There's not much to do here, but that's part of the attraction. Early morning, before haze envelops the coast, the view spans from Pulau Pangkor in the south to Penang in the north. The nearby forests offer good opportunities for watching birds and spotting gibbon and wild boar.

Outside Taiping

Kuala Sepetang, formerly Port Weld, 11 km (6.8 mi) west of Taiping, is a bustling fishing port in the midst of a mangrove forest which can be viewed from a wooden walkway built above the wetlands at the Forest Park. Matang, a picturesque kampung on the way to Kuala Sepetang, is a traditional Malay stronghold where an old walled enclosure is all that remains of Kota Ngah Ibrahim, a fort which figured prominently during the Larut Wars of the 1860s.

Ngah Ibrahim was later exiled to the Seychelles by the British for his involvement in the killing of the British Resident J.W.W. Birch. Maharaja Lela, one of the other conspirators, and later a hero of Malay nationalists, was hung from a tree that still stands in the fort grounds.

Opposite: Draped in ferns and mosses, these century-old raintrees planted during the British colonial days, form an arch over the road at Taiping's Lake Gardens.

N

Taiping

not to scale

Muzium Perak

Rest-house

Bukit Larut

Railway Station

Zoo

Lake Gardens

❶ Post Office
❷ Town Market
❸ Clocktower
❹ District Offices
❺ King Edward VII Sch.
❻ Indian Mosque
❼ Bus Station
❽ Hotel Panorama & Berkat Supermarket
❾ Pusat Penjaja
❿ Bismillah Rest.

PART IV

Introducing Penang & Kedah

An elderly tourist overheard mentioning that "after I visited Penang I also went to Malaysia," may have got his geography muddled up, but such is the fame of the nation's best-known destination that he can be forgiven his blunder. Located off the northwest coast, this turtle-shaped island, a mere 24km (15mi) long by 12km (7.5mi) wide, is renowned for its beaches, spicy cuisine, elegant colonial architecture, bazaars and temples, as well as its independent-minded, multi-cultural population.

Penang has long inspired travelers to wax lyrical of its charms. In the 1930s, a fastidious New Yorker appalled by other Asian cities noticed that in Penang, "Europeans lived by choice" and that the island "by virtue of its climate, its scenery, its inhabitants, its many amenities, is livable and human." Later, Penang gained fame as a favorite stopover on the Asia hippy trail. Today, although "The Pearl of the Orient" has lost a little of its lustre through rampant urbanization it still has a magnetic appeal.

In 1786, Captain Francis Light, an adventurous English trader in the service of the East India Company, persuaded the Sultan of Kedah to sign over Pulau Pinang, "The Isle of Betel-nut Palms" in return for protection against enemies. This promise was never honored, but there was little Kedah could do against the might of the British Empire.

Penang thrived as an entrepôt for the lucrative tea and opium trade between India and China. Georgetown port was crammed with *praus*, junks, and steamers bringing the Chinese, Burmese, Javanese, Arabs, Malays, Sikhs, Madrassees, and Klings: the ancestors of today's cosmopolitan population. Penang's importance declined with the rise of Singapore, but it boomed again during the tin rush of the 1850s and the turn-of-the-century rubber boom. The island continues to dominate the economy of the northwest today.

Kedah, "The Nation's Rice Bowl," and pocket-sized Perlis, the two northwestern states which border Thailand, are as unknown as Penang is famed, although the idyllic isles of Pulau Langkawi are currently the rising stars of Malaysian tourism. Compared to Penang, and especially Georgetown, a very Chinese city, the northwest states are still largely agricultural and Malay-dominated.

Traditional villages are surrounded by paddy fields, and life still follows the rhythm of the harvest. Few tourists ever spend time exploring the northwest—except for Pulau Langkawi—and this region is a delight for travelers who enjoy being a novelty.

Kedah lays claim to being Malaysia's oldest state. The present royal family trace their roots back to pre-Islamic times, and in the south at Lembah Bujang are remains of 7th century Hindu/Buddhist temples. In 1821, Kedah was conquered by the Thais who ruled the state for the next 25 years.

Remnants of those times linger in the state capital of Alor Star, where 19th-century royal palaces show distinctive Thai architectural influences. The Sultan was later reinstated, but the region was under Thai suzerainty until 1909 when Kedah was transferred to Britain. However, they successfully controlled their own affairs and British influence was minimal.

Limestone massifs pitted with caves, loom above the rice paddies and sugarcane fields of tiny Perlis, Malaysia's smallest state. Originally part of Kedah, the state—wedged against Thailand in the northwestern corner—was separated in 1842 when the Thais handed Perlis to Raja Syed Hussein whose successors have ruled there ever since.

Overleaf: *Viewed from Penang Hill, the peninsula's main range provides a backdrop to Southeast Asia's longest bridge.*
Opposite: *This Georgetown chef defty demonstrates the art of making* roti canai—*an Indian griddle-cake. Both photos by Jill Gocher.*

PENANG TOWN SIGHTS

A Stroll Through Old Georgetown

A labyrinth of streets, lanes, and alleyways which weave through a sea of red-tiled roofs makes Georgetown's old center a marvellous place to explore on foot. If the heat gets too much, or a tropical storm descends, a trishaw, locally known as a *becak*, is the perfect alternative. Many of the downtown streets date from the original town plan, and bear names of early administrators like Light and Farquhar, or survive as testimony to their original inhabitants like Lebuh Chulia, where the Chulias—Indian Muslims from the Malabar Coast—first settled.

Nowadays "street" is translated to the Malay *lebuh*, "road" to *jalan*, "lane" to *lorong*: Love Lane thus becomes Lorong Cinta. Some names have been changed by zealous town planners, such as Lebuh Pitt which recently became Jalan Masjid Kapitan Kling, after its famous mosque. Residents, however, often still use the old names.

A historic site may be the main reason to head down a certain street, but in Georgetown it is often what is glimpsed or experienced along the way which makes a walk in the old city most memorable: an old woman waving incense before an altar; a pavement palmist engrossed in his art; a trishaw piled high with smiling children; or the aroma of fresh coffee from a wayside stall.

Edifices from a more leisurely age

A good starting point is from the domed Clock Tower at the crossroads of Lebuh Light and Lebuh Pantai. A Chinese tycoon presented it to the city as a gift on Queen Victoria's Diamond Jubilee in 1897. Facing the seafront Esplanade, is Fort Cornwallis, built on the site where legend has it that Francis Light ordered his ships to fire cannonloads of silver coins into the thick jungle to inspire the natives to clear the land faster.

Apparently this ploy was used to keep the laborers busy while awaiting a shipment of axes from Melaka. The story doesn't mention whether they used *parang* machetes to hack at the jungle, or their bare hands. Only the stone walls remain and some fine cannon, including the 16th-century Seri Rambai (facing north) which is said to aid childless women if they place flowers in the barrel.

Around the Padang—the large playing fields where the colonials played cricket,

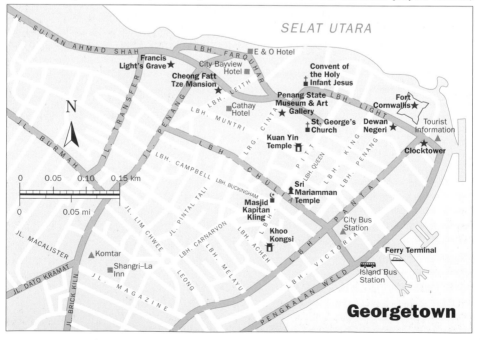

bowls and croquet—are many important buildings from the British era. To the west are some elegant, grey and white buildings built in the late Victorian style which formerly housed the municipal offices. On the southern side is the classical-styled Dewan Negeri (Penang State Assembly Building), and further up Lebuh Light is the old High Court (Mahkamah Tinggi). Relax on the seaward side of the Padang where hawkers sell *rojak* and cold drinks.

Continue along Lebuh Light to the Convent of the Holy Infant Jesus which occupies the site of Francis Light's original dwelling. Domestic science students still use part of what is believed to have been his kitchen. Venture past the convent's Georgian facade and into the interior where arched collonades, cloisters and couryards dating from 1852 lend a Spanish colonial touch. Old Eurasian nuns in beige habits pray at the art nouveau chapel with its honeycombed ceiling and carved pews, as sunlight streams in through the stained-glass windows.

West along Lebuh Farquhar is the celebrated **E & O Hotel** (Eastern and Oriental) built in 1884. Famous literary guests like Noel Coward and Somerset Maugham once dined in the still-functioning Grill Room and the Hollywood movie queen Rita Hayworth apparently sunbathed in her deckchair by the seafront. Originally owned by the Armenian Sarkies brothers, who also established Singapore's Raffles and Rangoon's Strand, the E & O still retains much of its old charm in the domed foyer, its spacious guest rooms, the dining room, and its unique harborside location. Past the E & O is an old walled cemetery where century-old frangipani trees with gnarled trunks litter their scented flowers over archaic tombs including that of Penang's founding father, Francis Light. The inscriptions on the headstones give a glimpse of the harshness of life for those early settlers.

Turn back along Jalan Sultan Ahmad Shah for the **Cheong Fatt Tze Mansion**, a rambling old home with faded stucco walls on the corner of Lebuh Leith. Hopefully, this 31-room residence built in 1870 will soon be restored for it is one of the last three—the other two are in Medan and Manilla—of its style surviving outside of China. It is still a private residence and visitors have to be content with a peek through the iron gates at its massive walls, wrought-iron verandahs and traditional Chinese tiled roof adorned with porcelain motifs. Inside, out of sight, are elaborate carved doorways, tiled courtyards and a spiral staircase.

Opposite the mansion is St.Xavier's Institution, an old Catholic School, and further along Lebuh Leith, in dazzling white, is the Cathay Hotel. Its plaster reliefs are paint-

Below: One of the oldest churches in the East, St.George's Anglican Church, built in 1817.

JILL GOCHER

ed lime-green and China blue, and the vast tiled lobby and spacious rooms are reminders of a more leisurely age. Turn left into Lebuh Mentri, where the old shophouses still retain their art nouveau tiles and carved woodwork, then take a left into Lorong Cinta with more decorated shophouses, corner coffee shops and Chinese clanhouses, back to Lebuh Farquhar. On the corner is the Gothic-style Cathedral of the Assumption with its twin spires, and down the street, the **Penang State Museum and Art Gallery** is crammed with fascinating memorabilia from Penang's past, including historical paintings dating from the early 1800s and exhibits on the Chinese triad wars in 1867.

Historic houses of worship

On the corner of Lebuh Pitt, shaded by massive angsana trees which shower the grounds with a "golden rain" of blooms every April, is St.George's Church built in 1817. A historical air pervades Southeast Asia's oldest Anglican church constructed in superb Georgian style.

The matching pavilion in the grounds is a monument dedicated to Francis Light. From here, walk down Lebuh Pitt to the smoke-enshrouded Kuan Yin Temple which honors the Goddess of Mercy, the favorite deity of Malaysian-Chinese. Pigeons swoop about the courtyard where beggars wait for alms from businessmen who come to pay homage to another popular deity—the God of Prosperity.

Renovated and redecorated since its inception in 1800, the temple still retains its original tiled roof elaborately decorated with symbolic porcelain figures. Opposite, wander down Lebuh China, the original "Chinese Street," and turn into Lebuh King which has some impressive old Chinese clan houses. At No 32, the 19th-century Tua Peh Kong, legendary scenes are carved into the granite wall panels and the roof ridges are adorned with tiled motifs.

Further south, Lebuh King becomes a "Little India" and in the early morning the pavements are taken over by tea and *roti* sellers. On the corner of King and Chulia, what looks like a small mosque is in fact a white-domed shrine to the Nagore Durgha, a saintly Muslim from southern India. Indians in checkered sarongs relax on the cool marble floor and tucked in around the perimeter are a cupboard-sized *mamat* stall crammed with cigarettes and other sundry items, and a tiny store where a hatter makes velvet fez-like caps known as *songkok*. On neighboring Lebuh Penang, Indian money-lenders known as *Chettiar* still dress in their toga-like *dhoti* and sit on wooden floors to conduct their business. In adjacent textile shops, parrot-colored saris drape from the ceilings and brassware gleams in the sunshine.

On Lebuh Queen, the elaborate archway of the Sri Mariamman Temple is invariably occupied by hundreds of pigeons which

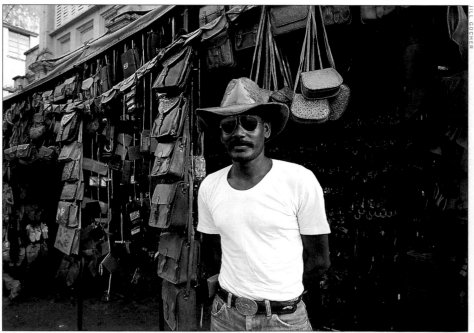

perch on the limbs, heads, and tridents of the dozens of Hindu deities. At the entrance arch, known as a *gopuram*, sari-clad devotees twist flowers into garlands for the gods. Within the temple, built in 1833, are shrines to the major deities and to the Nava Grahas—the nine planets of Indian astrology.

Return to Lebuh Pitt for its dominant attraction, the Kapitan Kling Mosque, built in 1916 to replace the original 1801 building constructed by the East India Company's Muslim troops. The Klings (a term now considered

derogatory) were the Indian Muslim traders from the Coromandel Coast and many of the mosque's patrons today are descendants of these early adventurous businessmen. In a tiny, covered lane beside the mosque some of these same Indians dish up perhaps Penang's tastiest *nasi kandar*—rice and curries—with a distinctive South Indian flavor.

Into the world of the clans

Walk further down Lebuh Pitt, past the shops selling lacquered tiffin-carriers, costumes for lion dances, and temple paraphernalia, to the corner of Lebuh Armenia, where Lebuh Pitt becomes Lebuh Cannon. The street's name derived from the clan wars of 1867 when the Tua Peh clan rioted and the British fired cannons to disrupt them. The Tua Peh clanhouse is still situated near this junction. Follow Lebuh Cannon to tiny, cobblestoned Lorong Cannon on the left. Pass under the archway, past the 19th-century Chinese town houses which line both sides of this narrow passage into Cannon Square.

This large courtyard, paved with granite, is the site of "The Dragon Mountain Hall," better known as the **Khoo Kongsi**, Malaysia's—and possibly Southeast Asia's—most elaborate clanhouse. Entry is free, but a pass to enter the Kongsi must be obtained from the signposted offices on the right. Every available surface of the building, both exterior and interior, is either gilded,

carved, enamelled, tiled, or painted. Reputed to weigh a massive 25.4 tonnes (25 tons), the roof is adorned with dragons and flowers made of porcelain tiles. An image of the Khoo clan's patron saint, a renowned 3rd-century Ch'in general, takes center stage in the main hall. In the left room resides the God of Prosperity, and to the right are carved and gilded ancestral tablets of the Khoo clan—Chinese bearing the Khoo name—dating back to 1840.

The forerunner of this clanhouse was even more elaborate, but on the eve of its completion in 1898 it burnt to the ground. "An act from above," was the unanimous verdict, as Penangites considered the ornate clanhouse too fantastic for the use of mere mortals and the gods responded accordingly. Across the courtyard, unnoticed by most visitors, is the stage for the *wayang*—Chinese operas staged for the gods. The theatre features beautifully-carved wooden doors and massive, circular roof beams.

Bustling street bazaars

Backtrack through Lorong Cannon, turn left, and at the end of the street facing Lebuh Acheh is the Masjid Melayu, the Malay Mosque founded in 1808 by a rich Muslim from Acheh in Sumatra. The distinctive minaret is in Egyptian style while the tiled roofs are traditional Javanese design. Follow this street up to Lebuh Carnarvon where craftsmen still turn out huge Chinese coffins made from tree trunks. Other shops specialize in paper Mercedes and replicas of domestic appliances which are burnt at Chinese funerals for the dead to use in their afterlife.

Opposite: Bargain hard with the fast-talking salesmen at the leatherware stalls off Jalan Penang. Above, left: Trishaws trundle past Masjid Kapitan Kling in Georgetown. Above, right: Garish pink buns are a favorite offering at the Festival of the Nine Emperor Gods.

Lebuh Carnarvon—especially around the old colonial market at the corner of Lebuh Campbell—is at its best in the early morning when the entire street becomes a market. Trishaws mass at the entrance awaiting housewives laden with their day's shopping. Stalls are not in any order, it is more like organized chaos. A butcher hacks up pork beside a mango seller, whose sales patter is drowned out by a neighboring stall which advertises "Buddha Cassettes Sold Here." Piles of fresh greens are stacked beside brooms and brushes. The rasp of a sugarcane crusher making juice, competes with the sizzle of bean shoots fried with noodles, and the haggling of old women as they sort out sea slugs and barter over salted eggs.

Follow Lebuh Campbell, past the goldsmiths with their shops full of gleaming wares, presided over by mostachioed Sikh guards with rifles; past Jalan Pintal Tali, better known as Rope Walk, to Jalan Kuala Kangsar—yet another bustling morning market. Here, chickens await their fate, and hogs' heads hang from butchers' hooks. Nonyas——Straits Chinese women in their distinctive batik sarongs and lacy *kebaya* blouses——throng the cake stalls which sell *nonya kuih*, pastel-colored delicacies made of rice flour and coconut cream. Bunches of Chinese sausages, like red candles, hang in the doorways of dry-goods shops where the pavements are filled with baskets of dried fish. A

cloth merchant surrounded by bolts of cotton, flings out a couple of meters of pink fabric for a customer's appraisal and across the way, housewives dip their arms, elbow-deep into buckets to test the firmness of last night's squid catch.

More market action centers around Jalan Penang; at the covered emporium of stalls known as Chowrasta Bazaar; at Picadilly Bazaar which specializes in cloth; and the pavement leather stalls at the beginning of Lebuh Chulia. Turn left on Jalan Penang for the hard-to-miss, 65-storey, KOMTAR building which dominates this end of Georgetown. Inside there are air-conditioned fast-food joints, department stores and clothing boutiques, but somehow it doesn't quite fit in with the rest of the city—and for smart shopping save your money for Kuala Lumpur's malls.

Georgetown has countless more attractions; there are dozens of lanes like Lorong Toh Aka off Lebuh Carnarvon with 19th-century, pastel-colored townhouses which still display their traditional calligraphic signboards; there are the antique shops on Lebuh Bishop; the Victorian-style commercial buildings and shipping companies along Lebuh Pantai; and the old Chinese clan piers at Pengkalan Weld—just to name a few.

Thai temples and tropical gardens

Further afield, on the outskirts of the city reached by either a pleasant walk or a short taxi ride, is the area known as Pulau Tikus. Follow Lebuh Farquhar west into Jalan Sultan Ahmad Shah (Northam Road), which is shaded by giant raintrees. Opulent, domed and turretted mansions—former residences of Straits Chinese tycoons—line both sides of this avenue which used to be nicknamed "Millionaires Row."

At the roundabout, turn left for the seafront Pesiaran Gurney (Gurney Drive), a very popular evening eating spot famous for its roadside stalls selling *laksa*—a fish and noodle soup garnished with basil—and its Chinese hawker centers and seafood restaurants. Go straight across the roundabout into Jalan Kelawai, and continue until Lorong Burma. Here, the renowned Thai temple, Wat Chayamangkalaram, houses a 32-meter (105ft) Reclining Buddha. A notice warns visitors against "photo-takin,", wearing hat or shoes, and to "beware of shoe thieves." Statues of fabulous serpentine creatures coil along the entrance path guarded by mythical Thai "birdmen."

The building which houses the Buddha is

of little artistic merit, but behind, unnoticed by most devotees, is an aesthetic stupa, adorned with reliefs of Thai temple dancers which was built in 1900. Directly across the lane, is the lesser-known Burmese Temple where white stone elephants guard the gateway. Inside, where an aura of serenity pervades, are filigree metal archways, a Burmese-style stupa.

Running parallel to Lorong Burma is Lorong Bangkok, a charming lane flanked on both sides by a complete ensemble of pre-war terrace houses in the same architectural style, undisturbed by any other development. Each two-storey house is painted in matching creams and yellows, and features Chinese tiled roofs, stained-glass doors and windows, and arched and columned verandahs. Wander up to Jalan Burma and into the Pulau Tikus township—heart of the *baba* and *nonya* (Straits Chinese), Eurasian and Thai communities—where there is an interesting morning market and many excellent food stalls and restaurants featuring *nonya* and Thai cuisine.

From Pulau Tikus town it is about 2 km (1.25 mi) to Penang Botanic Gardens. Follow Jalan Burma to Jalan Gottlieb, turn left passing the Penang Chinese Girls' School on the right and through an avenue of stately Cuban Royal Palms which have smooth grey trunks like Roman columns. Turn right at Jalan Kebun Bunga, where the road is lined with huge, century-old *angsana* trees. On the right

is the **Nattukkottai Chettiar Temple**, Penang's largest Hindu temple, and a center for the annual Thaipusam festival when penitents pierce their flesh with sacred skewers and shoulder decorated structures known as *kavadi*. Over the entrance arch are colorful plaster statues of deities flanking a peacock.

Multiplying monkeys

Along the road to the gardens, groups of monkeys gather. They used to be a major attraction at the gardens and a source of much revenue for the peanut sellers. However they bred so profusely that gang wars broke out when they became aggressive, and so now feeding is not permitted inside the gardens, hence their very dominant presence just outside the gates.

Paths lead alongside the stream and up to a waterfall—the gardens are also called Waterfall Gardens—and a trail starts from here to Penang Hill. There are some fascinating tropical trees here, including the cannonball tree, with its enormous spherical fruit; the brilliant, pink-flowered Thai *bungor* tree; and the *penaga*, or ironwood tree, which caused Penang's early colonial land-clearers such anguish.

Opposite: *Junior members of a Chinese street opera group dress up in outsized satin robes.*
Below: *Mythical winged dragons guard a globe at the Burmese Temple in Lorong Burma.*

PENANG ISLAND

Around the Pearl of the Orient

In the afternoon we drove outside the city, through groves of coconut-palms and gardens wonderfully green, to swim in a blue bay and sip drinks on the verandah of a comfortable club.

Patrick Balfour
Grand Tour—Diary of an Eastward Journey

Although not quite as idyllic as this 60-year-old description, Penang's coast still offers plenty of opportunities to indulge in similar sensory and aesthetic pleasures, as well as others as varied as a funicular railway ride to a cool hill retreat, a temple guarded by sacred vipers, classical Malay villages, and a farm of 3,000 butterflies.

The 70km (43mi) journey around the island is an easy day trip by car or motorcycle which can be hired at very competitive prices opposite the hotels at Batu Ferringhi. Buses also make the trip, but there are many

changes and it is a slow business. Bicycles are also fine for the north coast, but the winding hilly country through the western part of the island makes for tougher going. Penang Hill is worth a separate day trip, and has several pleasant walks.

The northern beaches

Heading out of Georgetown, follow Jalan Sultan Ahmad Shah which turns into Jalan Kelawei and then at the next roundabout turn into Jalan Tanjung Tokong. Along here, squeezed into the suburban sprawl, are some Chinese market gardens where neat rows of greens are tended by weathered old men in conical hats. When the road again joins the coast there are some small Malay roadside stalls that serve *laksa* and other Penang Malay specialities, as well as a good view back around the bay to Georgetown.

Further west, Tanjung Tokong and Tanjung Bunga were once bucolic fishing villages, but are now part of Georgetown's satellite suburbs. From here, the beaches begin, as do the luxury holiday resort complexes carved into the hillsides which loom above the serpentine road that has changed little in 20 years—although the surroundings and the volume of traffic have certainly kept pace with the times.

Shades of the past still linger at a miniature bay where an old two-storey retreat remains of what were once many seaside vil-

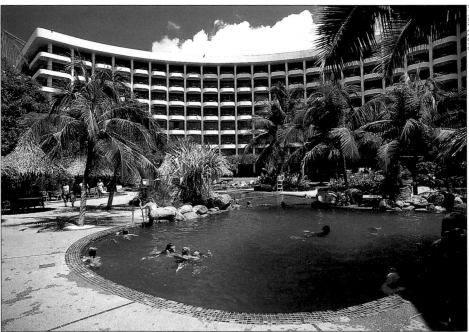

R. IAN LLOYD

las—now replaced by hotels and condominiums. The beaches improve the further west one travels, but the bay overlooked by the Ferringhi Beach Hotel is clean and good for swimming. Around the next point, 14km (8.7mi) from Georgetown is Batu Ferringhi—Malaysia's best-known beach. Its shoreline is dominated by luxury hotels and restaurants, souvenir shops, car-hire booths and moneychangers lining the road in front of the resorts.

Pockets of Malay kampungs, and a couple

of small guesthouses—remnants of the 1960s when Batu Ferringhi was a laid-back hippy hangout with thatched huts—still survive around the back of the shops and along the western end of the beach. Despite its brash veneer, and the fact that there are lots of better beaches in Malaysia, Batu Ferringhi has a certain magnetic appeal.

Elderly tourists on package tours—highly visible in their newly-acquired batiks and suntans—flock in from Europe and Australia. Children also adore the beach for the water is warm and inviting and there is always plenty of action going on such as para-sailing and windsurfing. From the beach you can see an outcrop of rock called Lovers Isle, with the mountains of Kedah shrouded in the distance by blueish mist, both lend an air of the exotic to the scene, especially as night draws near.

Restaurant prices are considerably higher here than in Georgetown, but many of the hotels serve superb food and on weekends they are often booked up by discerning Penangites themselves. It's a good idea to avoid the northern beaches at weekends for the bays and beaches become crammed with picnickers and holidaymakers. But, come Monday, the beaches are quite deserted, particularly Lone Crag Beach, a shaded bay 3km (1.9mi) north of Batu Ferringhi.

To the end of the world

Teluk Bahang, the most westerly town on

the north coast, was until recently a quiet fishing village completely devoid of high-rise hotels. However, even now with the inevitable addition of yet another monolithic resort, the local inhabitants still rely more on fishing than tourism for their living, and the village has lost little of its calm allure.

At the far end of the beach a wooden jetty heads out to sea where a flotilla of fishing boats is moored. There's plenty of maritime activity here, particularly at dusk when fishermen in small wooden sampans shuttle between ship and shore ferrying ice, bait and fish. The eastern end of the beach, away from the village, is good for swimming and sunbathing. Sunsets along this coast are particularly memorable—fishing boats silhouetted in a firey sea.

Next to the jetty, a trail leads from the aptly-named "End of the World Restoran" into the Pantai Acheh State Park, and along the roadless coast all the way to the lighthouse at Muka Head, a two hour trek. Another trail branches off to the southwest and heads through coastal forest—good for birdwatching and monkey-spotting—to end up at lonely Keracut Beach where there are toilet facilities and basic shelters.

The uncrowded west

Heading south from Teluk Bahang, watch out for the Batik Factory on the left where visitors can see batik cloth being produced. A little further on, 1km (0.6mi) from Teluk Bahang, is the **Penang Butterfly Farm**. Around 3,000 butterflies, including 50 Malaysian species, live out their fortnightly

*Opposite: Coconut palms shade the pool at one of Batu Ferringhi's luxury beachside hotels. **Above:** Catamarans and beach-boys are permanent fixtures along Penang's northern beaches. **Overleaf:** At the Penang Butterfly Farm this tropical butterfly makes a meal of flower nectar.*

lifespan here, flitting amongst luxuriant ferns and sipping nectar from tropical blooms.

In the large, netted enclosure there's a man-made waterfall, ponds full of vermillion carp, and butterflies everywhere. A notice on a glassed-in display of butterfly pupae tell visitors to "look out for those which may emerge at any moment." Admission is $1.60 and there is a huge, adjoining souvenir shop, blissfully air-conditioned to entice visitors to linger longer; some fascinating displays of scorpions, and such oddities as the world's largest moth and heaviest beetle.

At the Rimba Rekreasi (Recreational Forest), just past the Butterfly Farm, trails wind through the rainforest and a Forestry Museum contains exhibits on Malaysian

JEAN-LEO DUGAST

forests and the logging industry. From here, the road climbs up through old rubber estates and into higher country where durian trees tower overhead.

In the fruiting season, farmers work hard at clearing the undergrowth, preparing for the ripe durian to drop. These orchards are zealously guarded, for Malaysians have an obsessive passion for their most expensive and malodorous fruit.

Titi Kerawang to Teluk Bahang

Streams come tumbling down from the highlands, and just off the road at Titi Kerawang, is a waterfall and a natural swimming pool—deliciously cool after the tepid sea.

From the crest of the road there's a panoramic view across the lonely west coast; coconut plantations fringed by mangroves reach all the way down south to Pulau Betung, a tiny offshore islet.

The route winds down through nutmeg and clove orchards, past the turnoff to Pantai Acheh—a fishing village renowned for its pungent shrimp paste, past Sungai Pinang—a traditional rural Chinese village, and into a scenic region of Malay kampungs. Wooden homes on stilts, with frilly curtains flapping in the long glassless windows, are shaded by coconut palms and fruit trees and surrounded by neatly-swept, sandy yards and flowerpots full of pink bougainvilleas.

At Balik Pulau, Penang's "Durian Capital," 32km (20mi) from Georgetown, there's a main street of pastel-colored shophouses, and the town has a rural air unlike the rest of the island. Leaving here, the road forks at Genting. The right-hand route ends up at **Pulau Betung** where boats can be hired to explore the deserted beach of Pasir Panjang.

From Genting, the main road climbs up again through another range of hills, through more orchards and bamboo thickets, and then down to Teluk Kumbar, a fishing village on the south coast. A picturesque road turns off from here and follows the coast past wooded bays to Gertak Sanggul.

Although the beaches are muddy at low tide, there are marvellous sandy spots to escape the crowds, picnic, and watch the fishing boats come and go. Boats returning from the offshore fishing grounds come roaring into the bay creating curved walls of spray. After they anchor, the fishermen row into shore to collect their wives who help sort the fish and provide welcome drinks and snacks. At Teluk Bahang, beside a long jetty and rows of fishing boats, a tiny seaside restaurant serves up inspired *mee udang*—fried noodles with giant tiger prawns.

Holy venomous vipers

Continue to Bayan Lepas, the last of the traditional Malay villages before the start of the industrial complexes and surburban sprawl. Just before town a road leads through Kampung Seronok, with more Malay houses, and then to Batu Maung on the coast. Here, a shrine commemorates a hollowed-out impression on a rock believed by some Chinese to be the footprint of the great Admiral Cheng Ho who came ashore during his famous 15th-century voyages.

Once surrounded by rice paddies, the

Penang Island
(Pulau Pinang)

SELAT UTARA

Golden Sands Beach Resort
Ferringhi Beach
Rasa Sayang
Penang Mutiara Beach Resort
Lone Pine
Batu Ferringhi
Penang Parkroyal
Holiday Inn
Tanjung Bunga

Muka Head

Teluk Bahang

Tanjung Tokong

Pantai Acheh State Park

Batik Factory

Butterfly Farm

Forestry Museum

Penang Botanic Gardens
Gurney Drive Foodstalls
Pulau Tikus
Bangkok Lane
Wat Chayamangkalaram

Bukit Bendera (Penang Hill)
Bellevue Hotel

GEORGE-TOWN

Funicular Railway

Titi Kerawang Waterfall

Air Hitam
Kek Lok Si Temple
JL. AIR HITAM
State Mosque

Sungai Pinang

Jelutong

S. Pinang

S. Air Terjun

S. Kelian

JL. AIR HITAM

JL. PAYA TERUBONG

S. Air Hitam

S. Jelutung

JL. MASJID NEGERI

JL. PERAK

JL. KELAWEI

Gelugur

S. Tokok

S. Relau

Balik Pulau

Penang Bridge

Bukit Jambul Golf Course
S. Nibung

Equatorial Hotel

P. Genting

Relau

S. Ara

PULAU JERJAK

P. BETUNG

Snake Temple

P. Betung

Titi Serong

Bayan Lepas

SELAT SELATAN

Gertak Sanggul

Teluk Kumbar

Kg. Seronok

Bayan Lepas International Airport

Batu Maung

SELAT MELAKA

N

0   1   2   3 Km

0   1 mi

Snake Temple now sits beside the highway in the midst of factories and housing developments. Climb the entrance stairs, past the curio and drink sellers. Once inside, not much has changed in decades.

The old lady with the jade hairpin still sells joss-sticks at the counter. Incense-shrouded, with beams blackened from soot, the temple looks similar to many Chinese shrines, but with a difference, for here lazily draped around the altar are dozens of poisonous yellow and green-striped pit vipers, including some baby specimens which look like overgrown earthworms.

A wrought-iron stand behind the main altar, is what a temple assistant calls "the maternity ward"—where the pregnant snakes prefer to hang out. The vipers' drowsiness is apparently caused by the incense smoke which renders them relatively harmless, but at night they move freely around the temple and eat eggs which are left out for them.

Soon after its foundation in 1850 for the worshippers of the Taoist deity Chor Soo Kong, **The Temple of the Azure Cloud**—its correct title—was visited by these vipers who have made it their home ever since. Worshippers see the snakes as holy representations of the the deity and it is said that the population increases significantly in July, Choor Soo Kong's birthday month.

An interesting notice in the main hall, by order of the board, warns that "Mediums are forbidden to fall into a trance in the Snake Temple or its precincts to avoid causing inconvenience to worshippers or visitors." Marked with daubs of red paint on their heads, specially-milked, non-poisonous vipers are draped around daring visitors' necks for souvenir snaps by the resident photographer.

A giant among temples

Following the main highway north, take the coastal loop to Georgetown to view Asia's longest and the world's third-longest bridge. The Penang Bridge, built at exhorbitant cost, spans the 13.5km-wide (8mi) straits which separate the island from the mainland.

Further north at the modern State Mosque (Masjid Negeri), turn up Jalan Air Hitam which leads to both the funicular railway up Penang Hill, and **Kek Lok Si Temple**, Malaysia's largest Buddhist Temple crowned by the lofty "10,000 Buddhas Precious Pagoda."

Around the back of Air Hitam market a covered walkway lined with souvenir stalls selling plastic Bhuddas, t-shirts and a variety of other gaudy items aimed mainly at Malaysian tourists, climbs up to the temple complex where there are ponds full of sacred tortoises—their backs painted with red calligraphy—and halls crammed with Buddha statues.

At gilded altars, devotees shake bamboo containers full of "I Ching" fortune sticks, and Buddhist nuns with shaven heads hand out the pre-printed prediction cards. For an impressive panorama of the surrounding countryside, climb to the top of the 30-meter-high (98ft) pagoda through its seven tiers, in Chinese Thai and Burmese fashion. Inspired by a visiting Buddhist abbot's apparition—he envisaged the surrounding hills as a crane with outstretched wings, the symbol of immortality—local Buddhists chose the sight for a temple. Construction started in 1890 and took 20 years to complete.

Behind the Kek Lok Si Temple, a road winds 3km (1.8mi) to Air Hitam Dam which is a popular picnic and jogging spot with its reservoir perched at a cool 233m (764ft) above sea level.

Tea on a hilltop

Penang Hill's official name is Bukit Bendera (Flag Hill), but no one ever calls it that. Follow the signs to the railway station from the roundabout just before Air Hitam. By bus from Georgetown take a green (Lim Seng Seng Bus Co) bus to Air Hitam and then change to the shuttle bus which runs to the

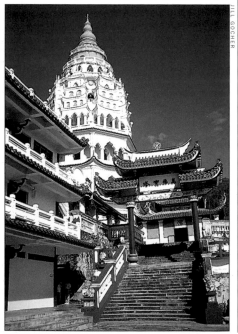

JILL GOCHER

railway terminus. Queues can be long and frustrating during public and school holidays but at most other times, especially early morning, there are few crowds. Services start at 6.30am and run until 9.15pm, and later until 11.15pm on Wednesday and Saturday nights.

Railway construction began in 1899 but the maiden journey was a fiasco due to an engineering fault. The train finally got into action in 1923 and has been ferrying passenger up the steep gradient through bamboo thickets and rainforest ever since. The half-hour journey passes a Chinese temple dedicated to the Jade Emperor, clumps of pitcher plants which can't survive in the lowlands, and English style bungalows to the top station at 731m (2,400ft).

At the summit, the air is noticeably cooler and can drop to 18 degrees centigrade. From the terrace of the Belleuve Hote—where early morning visitors can enjoy an English breakfast complete with silver tea service—there is a sweeping vista of Georgetown and toy-sized boats weaving through a glittering sea.

Strawberry and Tiger Hills

In the early decades of this century, Herman Hesse, the celebrated German novelist, apparently hiked up to this very spot for a drink at the Crag Hotel—the forerunner of the Bellevue. Energetic walkers still make the 8km (5mi) walk (3 hours) which begins at the

Moongate in the Botanic Gardens.

Penang's founder, Francis Light, was responsible for forging the original trail to the top and even though he was only in the colony for a few years he managed to build the first bungalow—setting a trend which is still followed today by moneyed Penangites—and even grew strawberries from cuttings he had imported from his Suffolk home.

At the aptly-named Strawberry Hill there is a Tea Garden, and a small Hindu temple and a mosque. A map posted at the hotel shows the layout of the many trails which wind around the hills. The popular, and easy 3km (1.9mi) stroll to Tiger Hill passes mock-Tudor stone cottages where swallows nest in the eaves, Indian gardeners trim hedgerows, and sunbirds dart about among the flowering shrubs.

Smaller trails along stone paths wind about the forested hillsides and all you can hear from the city of half a million inhabitants at your feet is a barely audible hum. From Penang Hill, Georgetown seems like another world away.

Opposite: The climb to the top of the "10,000 Buddhas Precious Pagoda" is the ultimate goal for pilgrims to the Kek Lok Si Temple.
Below: Joss-sticks, and sacred papers for burning are among the offerings for sale at the Snake Temple near Bayan Lepas.

R. MOH'D NOH SALLEH

LEMBAH BUJANG

The Valley of Hidden Temples

A 7th-century Sanskrit drama describes it as Katha, the Tamils knew it as Katahara, and a Chinese missionary who visited in 671AD called it Chieh-Cha, but they were all talking of the same place—Kedah. Scholars believe that this legendary kingdom was in the Bujang Valley where archaeological sites containing dozens of Buddhist and Hindu temple remains prove the existence of settlements from the 5th century. The valley is on the southwest side of Gunung Jerai, a 1,300m (4,265ft) mountain which was an important navigational aid for early sailors.

These are not spectacular ruins, being mainly sandstone and brick temple platforms, but they are fascinating nonetheless for they are among the only tangible remnants of the Malay Peninsula's pre-Islamic past. Archaeological activities began 150 years ago when James Low, a colonial civil servant, dis-covered the "relics of a Hindoo Colony, with ruins of temples," but it wasn't until the 1930s that an authoritative exploration was made by Quaritch-Wales and his wife who excavated and studied 20 of the 30 known sites.

Early theories speculated that these were Indian colonies, but archaeologists now believe that a prehistoric Malay settlement at Sungai Muda developed into a landfall for ships from India, and that by the 7th century it had evolved into an entrepôt. Buddhist inscriptions and images indicate Indian contacts from the 5th century, and the abundance of Chinese ceramics and Middle-Eastern glassware from the 8th century shows that the port was by then international-ly renowned.

This Buddhist phase operated well into the 9th century, but towards the end of the century the area around Pengkalan Bujang came into prominence and with it the emergence of Hindu temples. This era lasted until the coming of Islam in the 14th century.

Without a trained guide it is difficult to locate the temples scattered through planta-tions and rice paddies, but two of the best-known—Candi Bukit Batu Pahat and Candi Pengkalan Bujang—have been reconstructed near the excellent, Muzium Arkeologi Lembah Bujang (Archaeological Museum) which displays finds from the digs including sculptures, bronzes, ceramics, and models and photographs of each reconstruction.

TO ALOR SETAR

North Through the Rice Bowl

A blur of green rice fields glimpsed through the windows of an express bus is all most travelers ever see of southern Kedah while they rush through to Pulau Langkawi. But those who take time to explore this quiet agricultural region will discover timeless villages, superb scenery, historical sites and lots of curious looks from the friendly Kedah people.

If you can afford it, hire a car, for along the 93km (58mi) route from Butterworth to Alor Setar, the best scenery and sites are off the main road. Leaving Butterworth, follow the main road north past the suburbs and the airforce base. The rice fields start just before the Kedah border, where the Merdeka Bridge spans the Sungai Muda. A sea of paddy fields stretches to the horizon with wooden houses, surrounded by coconut palms and fruit trees, perched on islands of higher ground. Over half of the nation's home-grown rice comes from Kedah.

During the planting season women dressed in batik and conical hats made of woven palm fronds wade through the flooded fields planting out rice seedlings. Although many of the ancient customs have died out some survive. In order to ensure a plentiful crop, old midwives are still called upon to plant the first seedlings. In the old days, many magic spells were used, no strangers could enter the chosen seed bed, and when the crop was ripe for harvest the village magician would select suitable rice stalks for the "rice baby" which was given a symbolical birth. It is rare in these days of automation to witness these rituals, but they are still performed in remote hamlets.

Legendary trading ports

Turn off at Tikam Batu, for Kota Kuala Muda, a small town 8km (5mi) along the road, where an old brick gateway plastered with faded election posters is all that remains of the fort of Kuala Muda, built in the 18th century when this riverside port attracted spice and tin merchants from Europe, China, India and the Middle East. It's hard to imagine that this sleepy hollow was once a cosmopolitan trading center.

North of town is Pantai Merdeka, a popular beach overlooking the estuary of the Sungai Merbok. Along the way are dozens of traditional Malay houses, some still with thatched *atap* roofs and woven bamboo walls. The beach is not great for swimming, but there are good views across the estuary with the solitary peak of Gunung Jerai looming in the background.

Back on the main road north is Sungai Petani, the region's main commercial town, surrounded by rubber estates which are now giving way to plywood factories and industrial estates. In the main street is an unusual Moorish-style Hong Kong and Shanghai Bank. There are lots of restaurants and food stalls, for this is the junction town for the East West Highway. North of town, turn off at Bedong for the **Lembah Bujang Archaeological Park and Museum**. This road is also an alternative route to Alor Setar, following the scenic coastal rice-farming district, and a more pleasant journey than the

Opposite: Sandstone plinths from Hindu-Buddhist temples front a photographic display of archaeological digs at Lembah Bujang's Muzium Arkeologi. Below: Outside Kota Kuala Muda, a farmer rotary-hoes his rice paddy.

R. MOH'D NOH SALLEH

main road which is often crammed with diesel-belching lorries.

To the home of the Fanged King

At Merbok, turn off for Lembah Bujang, a further 2km (1.2mi) beyond. Outside of town take the Yan road which winds around the base of cloud-wreathed Gunung Jerai. Across the Melaka Straits are deserted offshore islands and along the coastal road are picturesque rice-growing kampungs. At Yan, drive to the beachfront, where even though it's too muddy for swimming, there's sea breezes and food stalls serve homemade Kedah-style *laksa*—fish and noodle soup, and deliciously cool *leng ci kang*—an icy drink made with barley, jelly and preserved ginger.

At 1,200m (3,937ft) the massive limestone outcrop of Gunung Jerai, the legendary home of Raja Bersion "The Fanged King," dominates the region. Access to the summit where there are overnight chalets, a restaurant and a Forestry Museum is from Guar Chempedak on the highway, or from the coastal route, turn off at Yan Kecil.

Private cars or government-run jeeps make the winding 13-km (8mi) climb to the top of the peak where views extend across the patchwork of rice paddies, over the Melaka Straits to Penang. Jungle paths wind through forests of rhododendrons and giant ferns—home to mousedeer, long-tailed macaque, slow loris and giant squirrels.

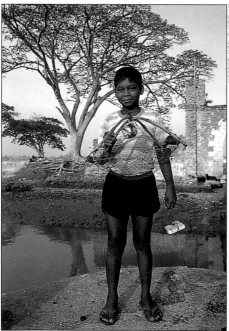

North of Yan at Sungai Limau, is the colorful Sultan Abdul Halim Mosque built early this century with cream and red scalloped archways. Further on at Kangkong, boys and chickens play in mounds of paddy husks and beside each home is a small replica of the house, where the family rice is stored.

The coastal route ends at a T-junction where the right fork goes to Alor Setar (9km/5.6mi) and the left to Kuala Kedah, Kedah's principal port, and the southern gateway to Pulau Langkawi. Rows of fishing trawlers with bright red cabins line both sides of this bustling river and smaller boats crisscross to the far bank where the Kota Kuala Kedah, the remains of an old fort, is located.

Upstream, a new bridge spans the water, but the easiest approach to the fort is to take a 20 cent boat ride from the jetty on the seaward side of the ferry terminal. The river heaves when a big Langkawi ferry takes off, and continually churns with the traffic of fishing boats, but surprisingly, amidst all this action, dolphins are still sighted playing in these estuarine waters.

Small terracotta bricks make up the walls of the fort which features an imposing gateway with a keystone archway dating from 1771. This brick fort replaced earlier wooden fortifications which were the scene of a battle with the Portuguese in the 17th century. Legend has it that this is where Sultan Abdullah met Francis Light when he ceded the island of Penang to him. However, when the Thais attacked in 1821, the British failed to honor their promises of assistance and the fort was conquered.

These days, goats scramble over the walls, courting couples sit on the old cannon, and teenagers race to the top of the lighthouse. Come sundown, everyone leaves and heads for the numerous seafood restaurants perched on stilts beside the river. Here, over a plate of chilli crabs or baked grouper, diners can enjoy the added spectacle of a fiery Melaka Straits sunset.

East West Highway

The spectacular East West Highway which traverses the central mountain ranges linking the northern West Coast to Kelantan on the East coast is approached by either turning off at Kuala Kangsar in Perak which is 108km (67mi) from Grik where the highway proper begins, or by the popular northern route which starts at Sungai Petani in Kedah, 35km (21mi) north of Butterworth. This road connects to Grik through the towns of Baling and

Keroh in the far east of Kedah. The East West Highway runs 124km (77mi) from Grik in Perak to Jeli in Kelantan, and the road continues from there to Kota Bharu.

Elephants may be the world's biggest land mammals, but in the dense rainforest their size doesn't make them any easier to see. However, on the East West Highway it is quite usual to sight their dung on the road just near Malaysia's only "Elephant Crossing" sign west of Pulau Banding. If you are incredibly lucky you may even catch a glimpse of these shy creatures.

After 11 years in the making, at a cost of $M400 million, when the East West Highway opened in 1982 it was under a night-time curfew for there were still rogue bands of communist terrorists—leftovers from the Emergency of the 50s and 60s—roaming this rugged border region between Thailand and Malaysia. Since early 1990, however, when the last of the remaining communists surrendered, the highway has been open 24 hours a day, although army posts still remain as the operation of finding all the booby traps still goes on.

In a roundabout way, this has worked to the benefit of the wildlife for the forests have been off limits to loggers for decades and much of the rainforest is still in its virgin state. Many elephants who have seen their former territories become plantations have now been happily relocated into the forests around Tasek Temengur, a man-made lake formed when the Perak River was dammed.

From Grik, the highway cleaves the mountain tops then descends to Temengur Lake and across a bridge to the island of Pulau Banding. Commanding a view of the lake and the surrounding mountains is a comfortable resthouse, perfect for a quiet night's stopover and the base for fishing excursions and boat trips to the lake's interior for possible elephant sightings.

East of the lake, the highway ascends to the top of the 1,031-meter high (3,382ft) watershed, where the air is fresh and bracing and the views across Perak to the south and up to Thailand in the north are magnificent. Descending on the eastern side of the ranges, the highway crosses into Kelantan state.

At Batu 14, just over a metal suspension bridge, are the Sungai Pergau waterfalls, where the boulder-strewn river hurtles down to the lowlands. Further downstream, the river widens and flows past a solitary limestone massif, Gunung Reng, which is pitted with caves said to have been the settlements of prehistoric Stone Age tribes. From Jeli, where the highway ends, it is another 113km (70mi) to Kota Bharu, the capital of Kelantan.

Opposite: *A fish trapper outside the walls of Kota Kuala Kedah, an 18th-century fort.*
Below: *Viewed from the East West Highway, Gunung Reng towers above the Pergau River.*

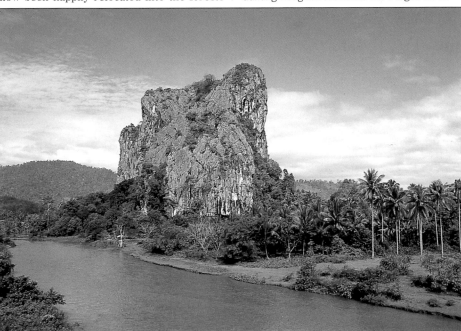

ALOR SETAR

Kedah's Courtly Capital

In Malaysia, where there are no great seasonal changes, the greenery which surrounds the towns looks similar throughout the year. But Alor Setar is an exception. The vast sea of rice fields which surrounds Kedah's capital in the northwest of the state changes dramatically with the seasons of cultivation.

When the paddy is growing, the landscape is bathed in a wash of brilliant green. Later, it takes on a golden hue when the grain is ripe. After the harvest, the fields are a bare virginal brown, and finally when the alluvial plains are again flooded for the next planting, Alor Setar is surrounded by reflections of clouds mirrored in the irrigated fields.

Alor Star (the "e" is often dropped), the commercial hub of the far northwest, may be experiencing a building boom in the wake of a fast-moving economy, but the town still retains much of its rich cultural heritage,

some splendid examples of royal architecture, and unpolluted skies which are the envy of the industrialized southern cities. Traditions and culture date back to the 4th century when the legendary kingdom of Langkasuka, held sway over much of today's northern Malaysia and southern Thailand.

The royal orchestra

Most of Alor Setar's historical sites are in the center of downtown. The obvious start for a tour of this courtly capital, is a curious three-tiered tower called the Balai Nobat, which houses the *nobat*. These sacred instruments of the royal orchestra comprise three drums, a gong and a flute, were presented to the Sultan of Kedah by Melaka's Sultan Mahmud Shah in the 15th century. Nowadays the orchestra only plays for royal inaugurations, weddings and funerals. Travelers wishing to view the *nobat* must make prior arrangements with the State Government Office opposite the Balai Nobat.

Close by, is the Balai Besar (The Large Audience Hall) a stately, open-sided building decorated with wood carvings, art nouveau wrought-iron, and upturned roof finials reminiscent of Thai architecture—remnants of the days when Kedah was under Siamese suzerainty. The 18th-century Balai Besar was demolished in 1904 to make way for the present structure which was built to stage the elaborate ceremonies for the marriages of

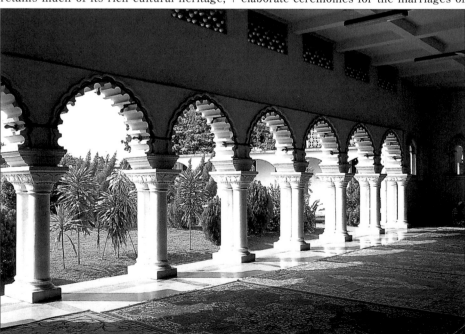
R. MOHD NOH SALLEH

Sultan Abdul Hamid's five eldest children, which ran for an unprecedented 60 days.

Beside the Balai Besar, a triple-arched gateway leads into the walled compound of the Istana Kota Setar, the former royal palace and now the Muzium Di Raja (**Royal Museum**) built in 1763. The palace was renovated after the Bugis attacked in 1771, and again following the Thai occupation from 1821 to 1842.

When the new palace was built at Anak Bukit, just outside of Alor Setar, the Istana

Kota Setar was taken over by voluntary organizations, but was restored to its original form in 1983 when Sultan Abdul Halim opened the Royal Museum to commemorate his 25-year reign of Kedah.

A royal dais, a bridal chamber, and videos of recent royal weddings can be viewed in the Front Hall; while the Middle Hall displays regal costumes, the family tree, and stamp collections, photographs and historical documents. However, the most fascinating collection is in the Astaka Hall at the back, where Sultan Abdul Halim's African hunting trophies, including a black rhinocerous' head and a set of elephants' tusks, adorn the walls. Other interesting exhibits include historical photographs of royalty in traditional dress, a royal *buayi* (swinging cradle), finely-tooled spears, and elephant's foot stools—a bizarre Victorian fashion.

A superb Moorish mosque

Ever since the 12th century, when the ruler of Kedah, Maharaja Derba Raja II, embraced Islam and took the title of Sultan Muzaffar Shah, the state has been a bastion of the faith. It is fitting that the most prominent building in Alor Setar—discounting a couple of new box-like highrises—is the majestic **Masjid Zahir**, a Moorish-style mosque, built in 1912. Located on Jalan Pekan Melayu, opposite the Balai Besar, this white and beige mosque features arched collonades, onion-shaped

domes, and intricate plaster reliefs including medallions with Arabic inscriptions.

Opposite Masjid Zahir, at the southern end of the town's historical hub, is the neo-classical, Balai Seni Negeri, the State Art Gallery. Arched verandahs, decorated gables and columns with floral capitals adorn this elegant former courthouse constructed in the best colonial fashion in 1912. Works by Kedah-based artists, photographers, and craftsmen are displayed at the gallery, open every day from 10am to 6pm, but closed from noon to 2.30pm on Fridays.

Out of town

Follow the Lebuhraya Darulaman, the main trunk road, north of town for 2km (1.2mi) to the Muzium Negeri (State Museum), a Thai-style building built in 1936. Among the displays are a variety of artifacts from the archaeological digs at Lembah Bujang and a collection of early Chinese ceramics. Opening hours are from 10am to 6pm, closing between noon and 2pm on Fridays.

Outside Alor Setar, to the east, is the Royal Mausoleum at Langgar. Follow Jalan Langgar through town, under the expressway and out through the ricefields, and just after the "25km Kuala Nerang" milestone, about 9.6km (6mi) from Alor Setar, turn off for Makam Di Raja on the left. The narrow road winds past wooden kampung houses into the large walled compound, the final resting place of Kedah's royal family for generations and also the burial site of Malaysia's popular first prime minister, and Kedah prince—Tunku Abdul Rahman.

***Opposite:** Prayer rugs cover the marble floors of the elegant Masjid Zahir, a landmark in downtown Alor Setar. **Above, left:** The facade of the early-20th century Masjid Zahir. **Above, right:** Thai influences are apparent in the architecture of the Balai Besar, "The Large Audience Hall".*

PERLIS

Touring the Smallest State

Perlis, Malaysia's smallest state, covering 795km² (307mi²) in the extreme northwest of the peninsula, shares more than two-thirds of its border with Thailand which has always exerted a powerful influence over the region. Although ruled by Malay chieftains subject to the Sultan of Kedah, the Thais raided Perlis for centuries.

Following an attack in 1821, the region came under Thai rule for 21 years, but when Kedah was handed back to the sultan, Perlis was given to Syed Hussain, the son of a former chief, who became the Raja of Perlis, although he still paid tribute to Bangkok.

In 1909, the Thais relinquished their Malay vassal states to Britain and an English Resident was installed at Arau, the royal capital. During the Japanese occupation during World War II, the Thais were handed back Perlis as a reward for becoming allies of Japan, but this brief annexation ended when the Japanese surrendered.

Perlis has no outstanding historical sites or glorious beaches, but is very picturesque and still looks much like the view a 1930s travel-writer glimpsed from his train window. "Marsh and jungle, rice-fields, rubber trees, undulating forest and distant hills were an endless panorama of delicious green..."

Driving north from Alor Setar there are two routes to Kangar, the nation's smallest regional capital. Travelers en route to Kuala Perlis for ferries to Pulau Langkawi can take the coastal road or the alternative route which heads north to Jitra, then to Kodiang, the border town 40km (25mi) from Alor Setar. Ricefields flank both sides of the road, and finger-shaped limestone massifs rear up from the plains. The distant blue hills denote the border between Malaysia and Thailand.

Arau, is the royal town and home to the Raja of Perlis, one of the world's longest-serving monarchs who ascended the throne in 1945. The red-roofed, Istana De Raja (Royal Palace) is a mixture of colonial and Moorish architectural styles. Opposite, crowned by golden domes is the Royal Mosque which can accomodate 7,000 worshippers. From Arau it is 14km (9mi) to Kangar, the quiet capital, where it is rare to meet another traveler. Just before the town, on the right, is Kangar's major attraction, the **Masjid Syed Alwi**, an attractive art deco style mosque built in the

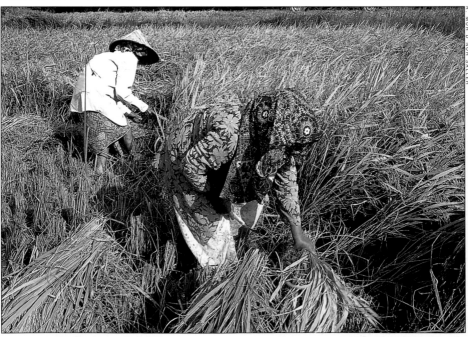

R. MOH'D NOH SALLEH

early 1930s. Black, onion-shaped domes crown the flat roof and the central dome has stained-glass windows in the shape of crescent moons.

Downtown Kangar is a mixture of old wooden and new cement shophouses. Food stalls abound around the busy bus and taxi station. On the outskirts, are an elegant 1930s State Secretariat and clocktower, and a lone high-rise office block. Take Jalan Tun Abdul Razak and turn off into Jalan Pengkalam Assam which has recently been renamed

after Dato' Wan Ahmad, a former royal secretary, and the late owner of Perlis' prettiest traditional Malay house. This whimsical, pastel-colored house built in the 1920s features tiled and hipped roofs, roof ridges of Chinese tiles, intricate wood carvings, decorated gables, otained glass panels, and doors painted with flower-pot murals.

Follow the Alor Setar road and turn off for the port of Kuala Perlis, the state's second-largest town and the gateway to Pulau Langkawi. This is a real working-class fishing town and at low tide is hardly attractive—surrounded by acres of mudflats and a pervading aroma of dried fish.

There seems little point in lingering and most people only stay long enough to board the first ferry to the islands. But when the tide comes in and the sun sets behind Pulau Langkawi, the open-air seafood restaurants which cover the wharf front open for business, and the place comes alive.

From Kangar, take the north road which terminates at Padang Besar, the border town 34km (21mi) north. Turn right, just out of town for Sungai Batu Pahat, 10km (6mi) from Kangar, a popular picnic and swimming spot which also has a golf course and a Snake Farm where a large collection of venomous snakes are kept for serum research. It is open to the public from Sunday to Wednesday 10am to 4pm and on Thursday from 10am to noon. Further along the main northern road,

turn right, past villages of traditional wooden houses, to Tasik Melati, a small lake popular with local picnickers.

Back on the main road, detour to Bukit Keteri for a closer look at the curious, limestone "sugar-loaf" hills. Follow the left-hand road to Chuping which turns off just before the cement factory at Bukit Keteri. High up, in the limestone cliffs on the right, notice the ladders hanging from cave entrances which are used by daring guano collectors who scale the cliffsides and enter the caves to search for bat excreta which is used for fertiliser. Further on at Chuping, lime-green sugarcane fields stretch to the horizon.

When driving around these northern districts be on the lookout for turban-clad motorcyclists with pet monkeys riding tandem. These are *beruk*, the pig tailed monkeys that clamber up palms to collect young coconuts. Further north, turn left for Kaki Bukit and nearby Gua Kelam "The Dark Cave," a 370-m (1,213ft) long limestone cave. A wooden walkway built over a subterranean stream winds through the floodlit cave and leads out to the Wan Tangga Valley. An Englishman in the 1930s enlarged the cave once used for transporting tin ore from a mine near the entrance.

At the end of the northern main road is the railhead of Padang Besar, a typical dusty border town of duty-free shops, restaurants, open-air markets, smugglers and border police. Malaysians flock across the border to Pekan Siam, a ramshackle bargain-hunters' market town on the Thai side of the border. Buses and taxis run from here to Hat Yai, the commercial and notorious nightlife center of Southern Thailand.

*Opposite: Women harvest rice using small crescent-shaped knifes which do not offend the rice spirits. **Above, left:** Limestone hills are characteristic of the Chuping area. **Above, right:** Datuk Wan Ahmad's home in Kangar is the most elaborate traditional home in Perlis.*

PULAU LANGKAWI

Archipelago of Legendary Islands

In the far northwest where the Indian Ocean funnels into the Melaka Straits, are a group of 104 idyllic isles, where only five years ago visitors could bicycle about on old crushed-marble roads, and it was a novelty to meet a car. Apart from one luxury hotel that was in danger of becoming a white elephant, accommodation was merely thatched huts on the beach.

But then it all changed, and Pulau Langkawi was discovered. An aggressive tourist promotion campaign and duty-free status may have been the main reason the islands rapidly appeared on the international scene, but many locals believe that it was something altogether more spiritual: that the seven-generation curse of Mahsuri had finally ended.

The curse

According to legend, in the late-18th century, when the beautiful Mahsuri lay dying, after being speared to death for a false accusation of adultery, she cursed Pulau Langkawi, saying that it would not prosper for seven generations. And indeed, the island, although blessed with great natural beauty, and formerly renowned for its abundant spices, did seem to suffer. The Thais and the Achehnese from Sumatra repeatedly invaded, the pepper crops failed, and historians even ponder why the strategically-sited islands were passed over by the British when they chose Penang for their base.

Now the seven generations have finally come to pass, and whether for psychological, spiritual, or economic reasons, the islanders' future now seems assured as hotel chains compete for the best real estate, and visitors arrive by the boat load. However, Pulau Langkawi still retains much of its former quietude and rural charm. Even in the peak Christmas season the beaches are still uncrowded compared with Penang's north coast, and dozens of totally-deserted islands are a short boat ride away.

The predominantly Malay population of around 28,000 lives on the main island of Pulau Langkawi, where forest-covered marble and limestone mountains dominate the interior and far northwest. The best beaches and most of the accommodation is on the west coast, with other picturesque beaches in the far northeast. The rice-growing villages of the interior, away from the tourist centers, are

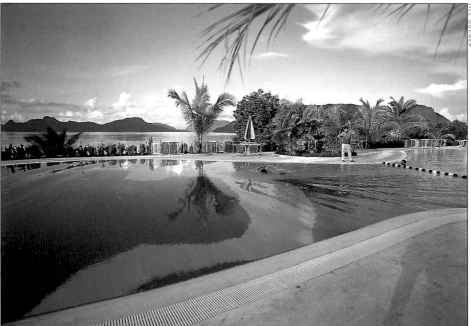

JILL GOCHER

still traditional. Kuah, the main port town is set in a bay overlooking a horizon of islands. Home to 3,000, it has most of the restaurants and shops.

Arriving

To get to Pulau Langkawi, travelers can fly or go by sea from Penang, but the most popular route is to take the high-speed ferry from either Kuala Kedah (1hr) or Kuala Perlis (40min) on the mainland. Once on board, the locals settle down to watch wrestling videos or re-runs of old Charlie Chaplin movies as the muddy mangrove coast is left behind.

The ferry charges through pale-green seas, and then enters the labyrinthine passages of the Langkawi islands—once the haunt of pirates, and still notorious for smugglers ferrying contraband from Thailand. Rocky islets with tiny, crescent-moon beaches pass by, then the first luxury hotel is sighted. The boat then swings around into Bass Harbour, where, framed by coconut palms beneath a mountainous backdrop, the island capital of Kuah sprawls along the foreshore, its onion-domed mosque reflected in the quiet glassy waters.

Taxis and minibuses ply from the bustling jetty into town and the duty-free shops where most domestic visitors head for. International travelers, however, usually head straight to the west coast beaches of Pantai Tengah and Pantai Cenang (22km/14mi), further north-west to Pantai Kok, or to Tanjung Rhu (23km/14.3mi) on the northern coast.

Bicycles are a slow, but relaxing way to enjoy and get around the island, and motorcycles and cars are also easy to rent. An excellent network of well-signposted, sealed roads extends throughout the 524km2 (202mi2) main island, and it's possible to bicycle around in one day.

Pungent odors and a beauty's grave

From the jetty, parklands fringe the harborside where sailboats lie at anchor, past the yellow-domed mosque to Kuah, named after the Malay word for "gravy" as the town featured in a legend known as "The Broken Cooking Pot." The once sleepy main street lined with wooden Chinese shophouses, has now extended into new blocks and word has it that the old shophouses are soon to be demolished.

Kuah has the cheapest and best variety of food on the island, there are numerous hawker stalls, an excellent food center—great for local seafood—next to the bridge, Chinese restaurants and an ever-increasing variety of seafood and western-style eateries scattered

Opposite: A panoramic view of a horizon full of islands greets swimmers at this resort hotel near Kuah. Below: Early morning reflections in a glassy sea at Pantai Chenang, Pulau Langkawi's favorite resort beach.

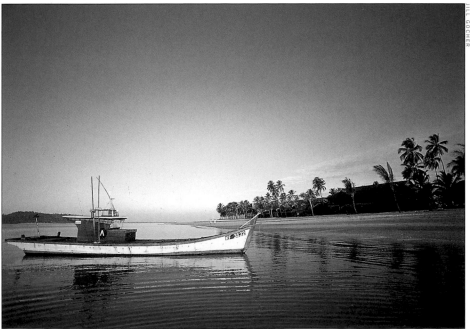

around the duty-free shops.

Heading west from Kuah, the town quickly reverts to rural kampungs, and at the Langkawi Golf Club the left turning heads to Empangan Malut—a Chinese-run village renowned for its dried fish business, pungent odors and lack of tourists. The next road on the right goes to Makam Mahusri, the tomb of Langkawi's heroine. Along this road, traces can still be seen of the original crushed-marble road built in 1962 and only recently upgraded. There are not too many places in the world where the marble is so abundant that it has been used for roadbuilding.

Turn off for Mahsuri's Grave, at Kampung Mawai in Ulu Melaka, which has been recently restored using the same white marble. Although the site has been somewhat commercialized the restoration is aesthetically done. There is a well, apparently used by Mahsuri, and at the adjacent, traditional Kedah-style house, demonstrations of paddy-pounding and weaving are staged.

White sands and longboat tours

Back on the main road continue along for Pantai Cenang, a long stretch of white sands, flanked by coconut palms and lodgings ranging from simple A-frame huts to five-star luxury hotels. Commanding a prime position at the head of the beach, and also top of the price range is the **Pelangi Beach Resort**, which is constructed in traditional Malay style using jungle hardwoods. The beach is best for swimming at high tide, and the flat firm sand makes for excellent jogging. Many of the chalets have sea views and it's very pleasant to stretch out with the sea breeze rustling the palms, watch the rainbow-coloured windsurfers slicing through the jade green waters and gaze out at the offshore islands, and the dragon-back mountains that provide a dramatic backdrop.

Wooden longboats, with shade-canopies to protect passengers from the fearsome midday sun visit a number of outlying islands. Popular three-hour tours generally stop at Pulau Singa Besar, where there's good beaches and a rather sad wildlife sanctuary. They then continue to Pulau Dayang Bunting, "The Isle of the Pregnant Maiden," where legend has it a woman who was childless for 19 years conceived after drinking the waters of the deliciously cool freshwater lake now named Tasek Dayang Bunting, "The Lake of the Pregnant Maiden." After World War II, when a Japanese soldier was apparently taken by a white crocodile here, no one dared enter the lake, but it is now a popular swimming spot, and infertile women still visit.

Boatmen will also point out the nearby 91-meter high (291 ft) Gua Langsir, "Cave of the Banshee," a bat-filled haunted cave, but few will venture near. Not because they fear the ghosts but because they want to avoid damaging their boats on the shallow, rocky shore.

Opposite Pantai Cenang is Pulau Bras Basah, where there are overnight chalets and serene, uncrowded beaches. Nearby are numerous tiny islands, excellent for day trips to play at Robinson Crusoe. South from Pantai Cenang there are more resorts at Pantai Tengah. The larger ones offer boat trips for snorkeling near the outer islands, but the best diving—and the only decent scuba-diving in the Melaka Straits—is at the **Pulau Payar Marine Park**, a three-hour boat journey to the south of Langkawi. Here, there are still sizeable "live" coral reefs and the waters are clear with good visibility.

Rice riddle

Continue along the coastal road past the airport, and take a right for Padang Matsirat, a small inland town, renowned for its "Field of Burnt Rice." The site is a nondescript, fenced-off square of ground, where after heavy rain, burnt rice grains appear on the surface.

According to legend, villagers burnt their rice rather than leave it to the Thais who invaded Langkawi only months after Mahsuri's execution. Among those killed was the chieftain who had ordered her death. Proof, say believers, of the effectiveness of Mahsuri's curse.

Back on the coastal road is Kuala Teriang, a small village where a wooden footbridge crosses a stream to the fishermen's settlement on the point. There's an untouristy atmosphere here. But for how long? A new resort—albeit low key—has just been completed in the next cove.

From Kuala Teriang the road follows the coast to picturesque Pantai Kok where the waters are clear and the sand a talcum-white. Small chalets cluster in the arc of the bay, and further around at Burau Bay is another luxury resort. Turn off just before here to Telaga Tujuh, "The Seven Wells." The walk through the rainforest is very pleasant, and the waterfalls are good if it's not the dry season when the 91-meter rock face all but dries up.

Northern beaches

From Pantai Kok take the main highway north and turn off to Teluk Datai where the road winds along the deserted western end of the north coast to a new golf course set amongst towering rainforest and a deafening insect chorus. The beaches along here are rocky, but there are good views across to Thailand's islands.

Return to the main road and continue northwest, past the over-rated Pasir Hitam,

"The Beach of Black Sand," and turn right at Padang Lalang for Tanjung Rhu. This road runs along the coast, with pretty views of offshore islands. Then a mangrove-fringed river enters from the right and follows the road to Tanjung Rhu, so named because of the *rhu,* or casuarina trees that shade the beach.

It's a quiet place, despite the presence of two resorts, and some food and souvenir stalls. Rising from the waters, just offshore, are a collection of curious limestone outcrops, and in the distance are the mauve silhouettes of distant Thai islands. Children love this beach because of the shallow lagoon and the vast sand flats at low tide.

Back at Padang Lalang take the main road back to Kuah which passes Telaga Air Hangat, a hot springs on the right, then rural villages and rubber plantations. Watch out for the striated marble cliffs to the left, 6km (4mi) from Kuah, where they sell and display everything from marble bathrooms to chess sets and a miniature marble version of the Kuah Mosque.

An alternative route from Kuah heads up through the center of the island past Ulu Melaka and roads lead off to a Forest Recreation Park at the foot of Gunung Raya, and another newly-finished road leads to the mountain's summit at 881 meters (2,890ft).

Opposite; *Children love the clear tepid waters of Pulau Langkawi.*

PART V

Introducing the East Coast

Golden beaches shaded by coconut palms which bend with the prevailing tradewinds stretch into the distance. Offshore, wooded isles shimmer in the South China Sea and rainbow-colored fishing boats ply the estuaries where villages perch on stilts.

This idyllic cameo regularly occurs along the east coast which comprises the states of Kelantan, Terengganu, and Pahang. There are no cosmopolitan cities, nor traffic jams. The beaches are deserted and unpolluted, traditional customs, arts and crafts still thrive, and the population is almost entirely Malay, in stark contrast to the ethnic diversity of the west coast.

The east coast maintained its original identity partly due to geographical factors: the mountainous interior deterred early road builders, and the annual monsoon closed river ports for up to six months a year. Although minerals were discovered, they were not present in the same quantities found in the west. The eastern mines also experienced transportation problems due to the vast distances involved. Consequently the east was spared the massive influx of tin mining and plantation workers.

The colonial British were keen to transplant the Union Jack to the east, but there were political problems. Both Kelantan and Terengganu were loosely under the suzerainty of the Thais, and although Malay sultans remained in control, they still had to make yearly tributes to the Thai court. In 1909 Kelantan and Terengganu were transferred from Thai to British rule against the wishes of the northern sultans, who preferred Bangkok's loose, more distant control to the pervasive influence of the western powers. However geographical isolation ensured that interference by the new overlords was kept to a minimum.

The sea has always been the lifeblood for east coasters and remains so today. Cowrie shells, used as pre-coin currency, were exported from the Malay coast 4,000 years ago, and early history records that tortoise-shell, corals and *trepang* (sea slugs), as well as inland products like camphor, incense, gold, and jungle exotica like bezoars—monkey gallstones used as talismans—were being traded for cloth, copper, ironwares, musical instruments, beads and pottery from at least the 5th century.

Arabs, Chinese, Indians, and traders from the vast Malay archipelago frequented the eastern sea lanes, and traded in ports like the legendary Langkasuka, and Marco Polo's Lokak—which some scholars suggest was in Kelantan. Construction of the inland railway from Gemas in Johor, to Tumpat in Kelantan during the 1930s, and the building of a road from Kuala Lipis to Kuantan in Pahang, effectively ended the east's isolation, but the vast coastline was still without roads until comparatively recently. In 1982, the East West Highway was completed, finally linking the northern coasts of the peninsula and reducing the road distance from Penang to Kota Bharu by over 600km (373mi).

Apart from Terengganu's recently-discovered oil and gas wealth, economically the east coast still lags behind the progressive west coast. But this works to the traveler's advantage as much of the east's traditions have been maintained. Kelantanese men still wear their original headgear, kite-flying and top-spinning are still popular, wood-carvers, gold and silversmiths, silk-weavers, and batik-painters still flourish, and in countless fishing villages life still follows the rhythms of the sea and the annual monsoon. Travelling the east coast is as much a journey through time as through space.

Overleaf: A Kelantanese with his kite, known as a wau bulan, or moon kite. Photo by R. Ian Lloyd. Opposite: Fisherman still wear turbans at Kampung Dasar Sabakon Kelantan's north coast. Photo by Radin Moh'd Noh Salleh

CRAFTS

Ancient Arts Perpetuated in the East

In the heyday of royal patronage when hundreds of palace ceremonies were practiced, Peninsular Malaysia had a great variety of arts and crafts. Their production was part of the daily routine of the *kampung* people. Preparations for the elaborate court ceremonies involved the whole community which worked within the palace grounds, and the mobilization of village experts brought about the creation of teams of highly-skilled and specialized craftsmen. Some of these traditional folk arts are still practiced today and flourish around Kota Bharu—the undisputed center of Malay arts and crafts.

Crafting a royal trousseau

In Kelantan, the silver and gold jewellery-making owed much to the patronage of the Sultan and his court. As these skills were always in regular demand, gold and silver-smiths normally lived on the perimeter of a royal palace. Most of their needs were supplied by their patrons and thus they were able to spend their time crafting painstakingly delicate and beautiful objects.

Long before a royal wedding there would be a period of intense activity when craftsmen produced ornaments and objects for the marriage ceremonies. Most were made of silver and included items such as trays, bowls, plates and ladles for the dining table, and kettles—often elaborately embellished—to hold the water for cleansing hands after eating.

The custom of betel chewing called for a whole array of utensils including containers for lime, tobacco, cloves, receptacles for *sireh* leaves, pounders and special cutters for the betel nuts, which were all contained in rectangular caskets. Formerly, betel chewing was such an integral part of Malay life that no expense was spared in fashioning the containers, and many of them fully reflect the splendor of those bygone days.

Every piece was the result of a painstaking process of hammering, etching and carving, and each bears the stamp of the ingenuity and skill of the craftsman. Goldsmiths fashioned pendants, chains, rings, anklets, armlets, and a particularly attractive elliptical-shaped cummerbund buckle called a *pending*, which was worn with ceremonial dress. Motifs were mostly drawn from the plant world, and the patterns of flowers, leaves and intertwining stems have much in common with the best Kelantanese wood carving. Repoussé and filigree were the main decorative techniques employed.

Equally important at every ceremonial function was the royal wardrobe. Traditional costumes were made from a silk cloth known as *kain songket* which is renowned for the diversity of its designs and considered to be the pinnacle of the Malay weavers' art. It is characterized by intricate patterns worked in gold and silver threads, and is of exceptionally fine quality.

The background is silk, woven traditionally on a simple four-posted frame loom with treadle operated heddles for the pattern threads. Hand-thrown bamboo shuttles produce a "floating weft" of gold or silver threads which creates patterns of lozenges, chevrons, and repeated floral motifs according to a prescribed blueprint.

Kain songket is usually produced in standard sarong lengths and is still popular as a dress for special occasions such as weddings and palace functions; it also regularly appears in the fashion houses of Paris.

The art of batik

Batik is by far the most popular textile made in Kelantan. Earlier batik was produced by wood-block printing, but now the stamps are made with thin zinc strips bent into the desired patterns and soldered together to form a printing block with a handle.

The cloth is spread on moistened strips of banana tree stems which provide a cool surface underneath so that the wax used to mark the pattern will not run when applied. Traditionally, beeswax was used but nowadays micro wax and paraffin combined with resin achieves the same result. Only one side of the cloth is printed. For the first stage the printer dips his stamp into a pan of wax, flicks away the excess, and then applies the stamp to the material.

The cloth is then immersed in the dye bath where the parts untouched by wax take in the dye. The area which has been dyed is then covered with another application of wax, with the uncovered parts absorbing the next color. It is almost impossible to avoid cracking the wax in the course of handling, and veining inevitably appears, even in the best of batik. The wax is completely removed by boiling in water, and the cloth is then washed to remove excess dye, dried in the sun, and pressed ready for the market.

In Kelantan, as well as most of Malaysia,

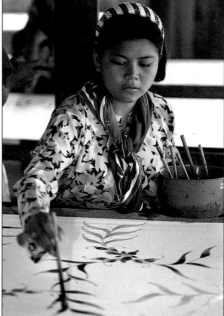

batik is also produced by simply hand-painting the design onto the cloth with a *canting* or wax pen. Floral or geometric designs are applied to Chinese silk or rayon which are sold as sarong lengths or made into colorful ready-to-wear clothing.

Woodcarvers used motifs similar to those found in metalwork and textile design. For centuries the Malay woodcarver enjoyed royal patronage: in the past all palaces were made of wood and were decorated with intricately carved panels, windows, doors, arches, and pillars. Being a country rich in timber resources it was not difficult for craftsmen to find suitable materials.

Much of the woodcarvers' traditional knowledge and skills have been handed down through the generations, and their work can be seen in old palaces and houses in Kota Bharu, and in Terengganu. Beautiful carvings also adorn musical instruments, as well as objects like the *rehal*—a wooden Koran stand—betel boxes, cake moulds, coconut shredders, food and tool boxes, walking sticks, kris hilts, and even the prows of fishing vessels.

—*Mohd. Kassim Hj. Ali*

Opposite: *Curving leaf and floral designs are typical themes for Kelantanese wood-carvers.*
Above: *Batik hand painted witht the* canting *wax pen is a speciality of the cottage-craft workshops near Pantai Cinta Berahi.*

TRADITIONAL PASTIMES

Shadow Plays, Giant Drums, Tops and Kites

The traditional pastimes once practiced throughout the peninsula during the natural breaks in the agricultural calendar and other festivals have all but died out along the west coast, but the east still embraces the ancient arts and in Kelantan their popularity is actually on the increase.

Wayang Kulit—**shadow puppet drama**

Historians believe that the shadow play is as old as civilization itself. Among the theories regarding its origin, one school believes that it came from China while another attributes its home to India because in every Southeast Asian country the repertoire includes stories from the great Indian epics—the *Ramayana* and *Mahabharata*. Others are convinced that it originated in Java because of the ancient terminology used in the dialogue.

Most historians agree, however, that the

shadow play was initially an animistic ritual, and traces of customary observances can still be witnessed in modern performances. The shadow play in Kelantan is particularly eclectic, combining Siamese, Javanese, Indian and Chinese influences. But the most conspicuous elements are of Javanese and Siamese origins. No one can say for sure when the shadow play was first introduced into Kelantan but it had gained a strong foothold by the start of the 19th century.

Performances were staged when offerings were made to the spirit of the rice-paddy, before and after a harvest, weddings, childbirth, circumcision, and during the Sultan's birthday and national holidays. It is still performed on a special wooden stage with an *atap* roof, usually located well away from dwellings to avoid accidentally "inviting" the spirits into homes when they are summoned by the puppeteer during the opening and closing ceremonies.

Behind the white screen onto which the shadows are projected are two banana stems into which the puppets are stuck. The good-natured characters are positioned on the right, while the forceful ones remain on the left. A lamp, suspended between the puppeteer and the screen, causes shadows to fall on the screen. The narration is accompanied by a small orchestra consisting mainly of percussion instruments.

The puppeteer, or *dalang*, has the enormous task of being director and manipulator of the puppets, actor, singer, narrator, and above all the musical conductor, all rolled into one. He also commands the power to contact the spirits whose blessing is sought before and after each performance. In the eyes of the audience he is both powerful and highly respected.

Wayan Kulit begin around 8pm and end at midnight. The number of puppets used for a performance ranges between 50 and 70 depending on the story being told. They are made from cowhide or goatskin and are hand-painted, although the colors never appear on screen. After the ritual and opening ceremony has been performed, there is a 30-minute prologue using the "tree of life" and a few characters from the main story to introduce the play to the audience. Then the main drama unfolds. At the end of each performance the puppeteer chants an incantation into the smoking incense to thank the spirits.

Into the air

Kite-flying, which dates back to the 16th cen-

R. IAN LLOYD

tury, is also very popular. The kites, or *wau*, as they are known, come in a variety of shapes and sizes, the most popular being the moon kite, so named because its crescent-shaped tail. Most kites measure about 2.1m (7ft) from tip to tail and 1.8m (6ft) across the wings. The frame is made by tying thin strips of bamboo together. The wings are covered with three layers of paper; a plain background, the bold decoration and finally intricate cut-out-designs depicting flowers, leaves or small animals. Each kite also has a bow which makes a humming sound during flight. Kite flying competitions are held between the best groups from each state and participants are judged not only on how the kite flies, but also on the shape, color and ornamentation, as well as the grace with which the kite can be manoeuvred and the music it makes in flight.

In most parts of the world, top-spinning is considered a children's pastime, but in Malaysia it is an adult affair. In Kelantan, contests are held between pairs of men to time how long each competitor's top, known as a *gasing*, can spin. Two large tops of equal size and weight are matched against each other. After the initial throw, each is skillfully transferred to a small stand where it may spin for an hour or more before falling. Another game, using smaller tops, is played between teams of men who attempt to knock their opponents tops out of a circular area until only one is left.

Top makers are very selective in choosing the correct type of wood. It must come from a certain species, and should be cut from the base of the tree, where the grain is most compact. After curing for three weeks, it is shaped on a homemade lathe. An iron or lead rim is then added, a steel spike inserted at the base, and a beautifully handcrafted ornamental silver cap is fitted on top. The finished article, shaped like a discus, measures 71cm (28in) in circumference and weighs between 5.4 to 7.2kg (12-16lb). Because of its size, children are discouraged from participating until they are sixteen.

The beating of *rebana besar*—the big harvest drum which measures 60cm (2ft) in height and 1m (3ft) in diameter is another popular activity. The skin is made of cowhide secured by a stout rattan hoop. Wooden wedges resembling the spokes of a wheel are beaten into the frame to give the skin to the required tension. The drums are usually played in pairs but on special occasions as many as six are used. The drum is placed on its side and struck using the palm of the hand. The sound is so penetrating that it can be heard a mile away.

Opposite: A Kelantanese villager makes ready to throw his top. **Above:** *Hidden behind the screen, the* Tok Dalang, *narrates the story and plays out the roles of his shadow-puppets.*

MAK YONG

Dance Drama in Honor of Mother Earth

The strains of the *rebab* coupled with the voice of the main performer reach a crescendo. The *Mak Yong*'s hands and entire body sway while the chorus girls sing in harmony. The audience is lulled by the refined dance steps and soothing songs into a fantasy land of drama and intrigue, and the musicians play a haunting tempo that seemed to reach to the inner depths of the onlookers' consciousness.

Mak Yong, as this performance is known, is a Malay dance drama which was acted out exclusively for the rajas and major chiefs until the turn of the century. For more than 300 years it was the favorite palace entertainment of the kingdom of Pattani in today's southern Thailand, and was then introduced to the rulers of Kelantan where it became equally prestigious and popular. Mak Yong reached the highest standard of refinement and artistic excellence in the courts of Pattani and

Kelantan. When royal patronage ceased, Mak Yong left the confines of the palace and became a popular folk entertainment among rural Malaysians, and performances still draw crowds today.

It is believed that Mak Yong originated as a ritual in honor of the spirit of Mother Earth, *Ma Hiang* or *Yong* (the term *Yong* means divinity), whose role was to watch over the rice crops. Thus, the main cast of Mak Yong is made up of women, consisting of four leading actresses who play the parts of the king (*Pakyong*), the hero, a young prince (*Pakyong Muda*), the queen (*Mak Yong*), and the heroine, a princess (*Puteri Mak Yong*).

The main characters wear elaborate traditional Malay costumes with headdresses, all sewn from *songket*—an exclusive silk-brocade fabric. Male actors only play supporting roles: comedians and court jesters known as *peran*, ogres, giants, jinns and others. There are also younger women in the cast who play chambermaids, known as *dayang*. A Mak Yong troupe also needs a male shaman, or *bomoh*, who plays a crucial role in ensuring the success of any performance.

Mak Yong are accompanied by musicians who play on an ensemble of *rebab,* a spiked fiddle, two *gendang* double-headed drums, and a pair of gongs known as *tetawak* which are hung facing one another. The *rebab* is a typical Malay chordophone that has three strings of metal wire played with a bow. The body is hollow, wide at the top, and tapered towards the bottom. The *gendang* and *tetawak*, are used in most forms of Malay traditional music. Mak Yong's music consists mainly of solo singing, accompanied by the *rebab*. The songs are divided into themes such as love, sadness, travel and lullabyes.

The Mak Yong's repertoire of stories focuses mainly on palace intrigues and romances between princes and princesses. Among the most popular stories are *Anak Raja Gondang* (The Gondang Prince), *Dewa Indera* (The Royal Demi-god), *Dewa Muda* (The Young Demi-god), and *Dewa Pechil* (Pechil the Demi-god). The Mak Yong stories, music and songs were traditionally handed down the generations as part of the Malay oral tradition.

Epics in the open air

Performances take place on stage, or in a theatre called a *panggong*, built of *atap* and bamboo, which is open on all sides. In the past, due to the strong ritual connection with the earth spirits, the *panggong* was built on the ground so that during the Mak Yong performers would be sitting or moving about on the ground. Nowadays it is raised a few feet above ground to allow for maximum visibility for the large audiences which often attend.

A typical Mak Yong usually lasts between three and five evenings, but can go on for longer. The story is made up of three main parts: the *buka panggong*, the opening of the theatre ceremony; the *menghadap rebab*, salutation to the rebab; and the *pecah cerita*, the story proper. All performances begin with the placing of the musical instruments in their respective positions on stage. The *rebab* is set on the eastern side of the *panggung*, while other instruments are placed behind it, filling the back part of the stage for the *buka panggong*. This ritual is typical of many Malay traditional dance dramas.

The *buka panggong* ceremony is only carried out on the first night and its main function is to ensure a safe and smooth performance. During this ritual, the shaman, actors, and musicians pay respect to the powers of the universe—earth, air, fire and water—in order to assure the elements of their friendly intentions. The ceremony begins with the preparation of the ritual paraphernalia and proceeds with the shaman, or *bomoh*, reading the ritual mantra to appease the spirits. He continues to conduct the *buka alat-alat muzik* ceremony to appease the spirits of the musical instruments, and salutation songs are

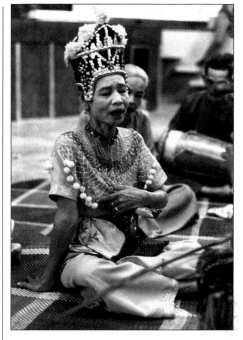

sung, accompanied by the ensemble.

The performance proper is preceded by a musical prelude known as *lagu-lagu permulaan*, the entry and introduction of actors and actresses, and the *menghadap rebab*. The musical overture may continue for half an hour and ends when the actresses have made their way on to the stage. In *menghadap rebab*, the leading actress (Mak Yong) sings a long aria, interrupted by short choral passages from other actresses.

As well as for entertainment, Mak Yong is also performed for spiritual purposes. These performances are mainly concerned with propitiating the spirits, and include *semah angin*, to balance the basic elements of a human body; *sembah guru*, a ceremony for the salutation of a teacher; *memanggil semangat*, the recalling of a lost soul; and the shaministic *main puteri*. The basic function of all these ritual performances is to bring about some kind of healing process where illness is believed to be caused by the loss of the soul or from spirit possession. These performances can either be held on stage or in the house of the patient who requires the service.

—Ku Zam Zam

Opposite: *A Mak Yong in the 1950s. The male figure merely plays a supporting comedy role while the main parts are played by women.*
Above: *The leading actress, or Mak Yong, sings a solo in this performance, circa 1960.*

BANGAU BOATS

Talismans from the Days of Sail

They are carved in strange and fantastic forms, designed to ward off the forceful demons of the sea and to protect the crews of the small fishing boats: they are the *bangau* and remain a curious legacy from the days when sail reigned supreme on the South China Sea.

Essentially a sail guard, or spar holder, attached to the prow of the boats, *bangau*, Malay for the cattle egret, were not merely utilitarian objects but artistically decorated talismans carved into a variety of shapes ranging from sea horses and dragons to characters from the shadow puppet plays.

Although some *bangau* were carved in the likeness of birds, few resembled their namesake which at first seems an odd choice as egrets are rarely seen at sea. But according to Mubin Sheppard, the only historian to undertake a detailed study of these decorations, the egret was probably chosen because of its well-known liking for fish. But there was formerly a deeper meaning behind the symbolism and decoration, for the *bangau* was where the *semangat*, or spirit, of the boat dwelt. Its presence helped the fishermen with their catch, kept fierce storms at bay and protected boatmen from sea demons which could cause freak winds, or throw a ship off course, never to be seen again.

From the 1950s onwards, as engines rapidly replacing sail the cumbersome spar-holders seemed fated to end up as mere historical ornaments on the museum shelf. But although the *bangau* fell out of favor on much of the east coast, it still survives in isolated fishing communities, particularly at Kampung Dasar Sabak, in the north of Kelantan, 10km (6mi) northeast of Kota Bharu, where a large fleet of 50 or more wooden boats, known as *perahu buatan barat* still proudly display these ancient figureheads.

Although now engine-driven, these boats retain the same basic design as their predecessors and the *bangau* is used to hold poles used for manoeuvering the boats to shore.

Myths of the oceans

The *perahu* boats are still painted and decorated in the elaborate Kelantanese style. Some *bangau* are carved to resemble mythological dragons, painted with realistic scales and glaring round eyes, which in Javanese

R MOH'D NOH SALLEH

tradition show a propensity for violence. Were these originally made to warn off the *naga umbang*, a huge marine dragon that tradition has it lurks in the depths of the sea?

Some rakish prows are shaped like the *garuda*, a demonic birdman which is a remnant from pre-Islamic Hindu times. According to legend, the *garuda* lives in the top of a huge coconut palm, representing heaven, which grows in the center of the ocean known as *pusat tasek*, and beneath its roots is a whirlpool which is the boiling pot of hell.

Alexander the Great, known to the Malays as Raja Iskandar, figures in a Kelantanese legend along with the *garuda* which wrecks the Raja's boat and flings him into the infernal whirlpool. But he survives and goes on to further exploits. This story is still faithfully told in the shadow puppet plays of Kelantan

A smaller version of the *bangau,* also a spar-holder, which shares the same horizontal beam, but on the opposite side of the boat, is known as an *ongkak*. On most east coast boats this is a mere 20cm (8in) peg, but on the decorative *dasar sabak* boats they too have become individual artists' fancies. The most popular representation is that of Raja Bota, a grotesque demon which appears as a villain in shadow puppet plays.

Dragons and long-knecked birds

On some of the more elaborate boats the entire front of the hull is painted with fire-breathing dragons, trident-wielding demons, and even the odd demure mermaid. All the boats are colored with rainbow stripes and beautifully maintained.

These days, engines have reduced the dangers of a fisherman's life, but it is still a hazardous business. The seamen are loathe to talk of the symbolism behind the *bangau,* for this is contrary to their Islamic teachings, but an old retired fisherman, mending nets on the beach, admitted that it "is better to keep the *bangau* newly-painted for one can

never be too sure of the fickle sea spirits."

Further down the east coast, the odd *bangau* is still to be found, and some of these actually resemble birds. At Penarik, in northern Terengganu, some *kolek*, crescent-shaped fishing boats with rakish sterns and prows, display *bangau* shaped like long-necked birds, but there the resemblance to the egret ends, for the heads are more like parrots. However, the small tuft of feathers carved on their heads could have been an attempt to imitate the bright orange feathers which the male egret sprouts during the mating season. But their origins remained obscure: the boat-builder was merely imitating a shape that his forefathers had copied before him.

The most elegant bangau of all, and the one that most resembles its ancient prototype, decorates a *kolek* boat at Beserah, just north of Kuantan. It depicts a snowy-white bird with a long neck and is very similar to the egret. It is possible the design originated from these more southern realms and then became more ornamented in Kelantan when it merged with other cultural symbolism.

Although most of today's east coast fishermen use stubby wooden diesel trawlers, there are still quite a few traditionalists who still put to sea each day in boats like the *perahu buatan barat*, the *kolek*, and the *sekochi*. And even though their matting sails have become obsolete, the *bangau* has defied modernity. These figureheads are still in pride of place on the bow—looking out in search of fish and protecting the fishermen from the wrath of the sea spirits, just as they have for centuries.

*Opposite: This Kelantanese fisherman renews the stripes on his traditional perahu buatan barat boat. **Above, left:** Fanciful designs adorn the prows of these boats at Kampung Dasar Sabak, Kelantan. **Above, right:** The bangau on the left is carved in the likeness of a shadow-puppet player. the smaller figure to its right is known as an ongkak.*

KELANTAN

Through the Land of Lightning

Kota Bharu, the capital of Kelantan, "the land of lightning," sprawls along the eastern bank of the flood-prone Kelantan River in the northern tip of the state. Hub of the fertile rice basin, and seat of the royal sultanate, the town is also the heartland of Malay arts, crafts and traditional pastimes.

The old royal center, north of Jalan Tengku Chik, is where most of the historical buildings are found. Between Jalan Hilir Kota and Jalan Hulu Kota, which translate as "the downstream and upstream roads of the fort," a high wooden wall, entered through elaborately-carved gates, leads to the **Istana Balai Besar**—the Royal Palace and Audience Hall—built in 1844. In the 1920s one of the few tourists to visit isolated Kelantan was invited here for Hari Raya breakfast with the sultan. He described the palace as "a wooden villa with windows of frosted glass." The building is still in its original state, but only the grounds are open to the public these days and photography is not permitted.

On the northern side of the square is Istana Jahar, another royal palace built by Sultan Mohamad II for his prime minister in 1887. Carved panels and wooden fretwork decorate this palace which has recently been renovated into the Royal Custom Museum. Follow the lane around the back of the museum to the Muzium di Raja, the Royal Museum, which is housed in the blue-and-white Istana Batu (The Brick Palace).

Opposite here is Kampung Kraftangan (Handicraft Village) built in traditional Kelantanese style. Open from 10.30am to 6pm, the complex displays the state's renowned crafts and exhibitions are held on subjects such as Islamic architecture, ceramics, batik-painting, textiles and silk-weaving. Programs are available from the tourist information office on Jalan Sultan Ibrahim beside the Muzium Negeri (State Museum).

Return to the square, past Istana Jahar, and facing Jalan Sultanah Zainab is the Masjid Negeri (State Mosque), a rambling 80-year-old mosque which comes alive on Friday, the Muslim prayer day, when thousands of worshippers pack the halls, and the streets outside are buzzing with hawkers selling religious books, chanting beads, headgear and traditional medicines. To the left of the mosque is the Islamic Museum, another

R. MOH'D NOH SALLEH

attractive old wooden building with a Pattani-style tiled roof, and next door is Kelantan's oldest brick building, formerly a bank, which has been converted into a War Museum.

A marvellous market

Walk back to Jalan Tengku Chick, past the three-storey Bazaar Buluh Kubu where shops specialise in Kelantanese batiks and songket, to the **Pasar Besar** (Central Market), the undisputed hub of town, and the peninsula's most colorful market. Munshi Abdullah, a scribe to Sir Stamford Raffles, Singapore's founding father, traveled through Kelantan 150 years ago and remarked on the diligence of Kelantanese women. These days they are still considered just as hardworking, and throughout the state they are seen cooking sweet corn by the roadside, tilling the rice and tobacco fields, bartering fish on the beaches, weaving silk, and painting batik. But, nowhere is the female presence as pervading as in the Pasar Besar where women traders totally dominate.

Dressed in batik, with their heads delicately veiled and adorned with gold jewelery, the feminine merchants chew on betel nut and haggle over prices while sitting amidst piles of colorful fruit and vegetables. The entire scene is bathed in a filtered yellow light which streams through the translucent roof. Pink lotus shoots, feathery fern tips, prickly durians, scarlet chillies and a bewildering variety of other produce contributes to the sights and aromas of Kota Bharu's greatest attraction. Upstairs are food stalls specializing in Kelantanese-style rice and curries, *nasi dagang*—rice and tuna, *nasi kerapu*—rice with herbs; and there are countless more stalls dealing in spices, dry goods, local biscuits and cakes.

Although nothing beats watching a real village performance of the shadow puppet play *wayang kulit*, or catching a festival where traditional contests in *gasing* (top-spinning), *silat* (self-defense), and kite-flying are performed, travelers can see these enacted each week at the Gelanggang Seni, the cultural center. In a small lane off Jalan Mahmud, not far from the Hotel Perdana, the center is open from February to October, but closed during the fasting month and the annual monsoon. Performances of top-spinning, *silat*, kite-flying, and *rebana* (giant-drums) are held on Monday, Wednesday and Saturday afternoons, and traditional dances and *wayang kulit* are held at 9pm on Saturdays and Wednesdays respectively. Kelantan hosts an international kite festival every May, the rebana drum festival in July, a top-spinning festival every September, and many traditional pastimes can also be seen at the annual *puja umur*—the sultan of Kelantan's birthday on March 30th and 31st.

The beach of passionate love

Malay silversmiths, obsolete in most other states, still thrive in Kota Bharu, and they can be found hammering away at their repoussé work and creating fine filigree at shops along the southern end of Jalan Sultanah Zainab. Most of Kota Bharu's other arts and crafts are produced along the road to Pantai Cinta Berahi, the famous beach of passionate love.

Songket weaving is centered in workshops around Kampung Penambang, 3km (2mi) from town, where women weave silk threads into handsome brocades—once the prerogative of royalty. Bolts of the shimmering cloth are on display, but they are not for everyday wear. Most of the buyers are Malays purchasing lengths for wedding costumes, or royal and official functions. Even a simple 2m (6.5ft) sarong length can cost hundreds of dollars.

Opposite: As the shadows lengthen, food stalls take over the carpark opposite Kota Bharu's Central Market. **Below:** *A wistful Kelantanese girl dressed in her lacy best for the Sultan's birthday celebrations.*

R. MOH'D NOH SALLEH

From Kampung Badang, 8km (5mi) from Kota Bharu, to the beachfront at 10km (6mi), are dozens of workshops where girls paint tropical flowers on hand-painted batiks and youths stamp cloth with traditional Kelantanese patterns. At other cottage factories, kite-makers paste delicate designs onto their *wau bulan*—moon kites—which can have a wingspan of 2m (6.5ft). Most of the craft shops are a short distance from the nearby beach of passionate love and it is pleasant to stroll from the beachside chalets around the palm-shaded lanes where there is always some work in progress.

The tradewinds always seem to blow along Pantai Cinta Berahi. The South China Sea pounds the shore and clouds the air with a fine mist. The long golden sands are excellent for walks but avoid the weekends when Kelantan's favourite beach is packed with local sightseers.

East along the coast is Pantai Dasar Sabak, famous for its painted fishing boats and the World War II site where the Japanese first came ashore to conquer the Malay Peninsula in 1941. To get there, take Jalan Pengkalan Chepa to the airport then on to Pantai Dasar Sabak where a bunker marks the historical wartime spot. At the beachside *kampung*, 1km (0.6mi) further east, fishermen still take to sea in beautifully-decorated *perahus*. In the absence of a harbor the boats are hauled up the beach by their chanting crews.

Wats, **rice and tobacco**

Kota Bharu is a good base for exploring the fertile Kelantan Basin, bordered by Tumpat in the north, Pasir Puteh in the southeast and Tanah Merah in the southwest. To get to Tumpat, the old railhead town 15km (9mi) from Kota Bharu, take the bridge across the Sungai Kelantan to Wakaf Bharu, then head north through rice paddies which become tobacco fields in the dry season.

Outside of town is one of the region's many Thai *wat* temples for this border area is home to Kelantan's Thai Buddhist minority. A large, gold-tiled Buddha stands beside the temple approached via a gateway decorated with elephants. Time-warped Tumpat hasn't changed much in decades; the old wooden railway station dominates the town and original shophouses line the main road. On Jalan Dato is the elegant District Office built in the town's heyday in the 1930s.

Cross the railway line, and just out of town where a lagoon flanks the road, boat-builders on the opposite shore can be seen crafting large ocean-going fishing boats from jungle hardwoods. Further along is Pantai Seri Tujuh, a popular beach and boating lagoon and venue of the international kite festival. Mid-morning, along the beach, fishermen cast a huge net offshore, then teams of men haul both ends up the beach until the fish are trapped into a flapping, silvery semi-circle, and then ladled into a waiting *perahu*. A few kilometers past Pantai Seri Tujuh is Pengkalan Kubur and the Thai border.

Southwest from here at Cabang Empat, turn right for Wat Phothivihan where swallows nest in the earlobes of Malaysia's largest Reclining Buddha housed in an ugly building which looks like a football-stand. Nearby, older and more aesthetic temples house Buddhist shrines. Follow this road to Repek where in the harvest season mechanical harvesters chomp their way through a golden sea of rice, and wooden threshing stalls dot the landscape.

At Repek, turn west for Kelantan's oldest and prettiest Thai temple—Wat Uttamaram. Monks in saffron-colored robes wander about the quiet, shaded grounds where cows graze, and wind chimes and temple bells tinkle in the breeze. This elaborately-decorated *wat* has fanciful flame-like, upturned roof ridges, an orange and green, multi-tiered roof, and fabulous dragons entwine the verandah columns. Continue along this rural road and turn left alongside the river to Rantau Panjang, a border town popular with Malaysian bargain hunters. On the Thai side is Golok, a seedy town renowned for its unabashed nightlife. Return from Rantau Panjang through Pasir Mas, an old riverine town and home to (it is generally contended) Malaysia's prettiest women. Kelantan's history abounds with tales of beautiful women

including the legendary warrior queen Cik Siti Wan Kembang who ruled during the 14th century and whose pet deer is immortalized on the state's official crest.

On Highway 8, 10km (6mi) south of Kota Bharu is Masjid Kampung Laut, possibly Malaysia's oldest mosque which was removed here from its former floodprone site beside the Kelantan River. Built around 300 years ago by Javanese missionaries after a lucky escape from pirates.

Another fascinating region is the little-visited eastern beaches around Perupok, Bachok and Kampung Melawi. Along the road from Kota Bharu, women can be seen tilling tobacco fields and rice-paddies, and hawkers shoulder poles strung with conical food-covers woven from pandanus leaves. On the coast, the beaches stretch in an unbroken line from one horizon to the other. Bachok's Pantai Irama has a beachside park and a rest-house, but the beaches are usually deserted, except for the odd fisherman. South at Kampung Melawi, a very traditional village way off the tourist trail, crescent-shaped fishing boats known as *kolek* still put to sea and the shoreline is strewn with shells. The palm-fringed beach extends from here all the way to Besut on the Terengganu border.

Below: At Pantai Sri Tujuh, near Tumpat in Kelantan's far-north, fishermen still haul their nets in by hand.

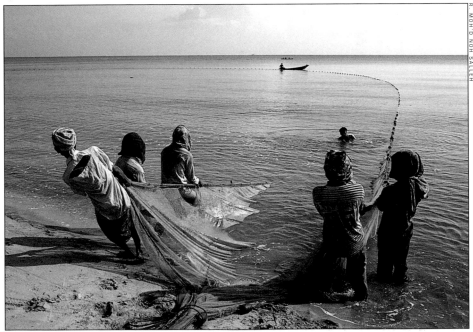

PULAU PERHENTIAN

Palm-Fringed Islands of the North Coast

I plunged into the clear turquoise sea. A large rainbow cod, startled at the intrusion, sought refuge under a pink tabletop of coral. Unperturbed, a giant clam sat alone on the sandy seafloor, its striped lips ready to crush its unsuspecting prey. Psychedelic parrot fish nibbled away at a coral branch, and orange-and-white-striped clownfish hid from predators amongst the lilac-colored tentacles of reef anemones.

Out of breath I resurfaced, alone in the sea, the jungle chorus from behind the beach sounding deafening after the silence of the underwater world. After the dive I ran up the deserted beach, drew a freshwater bath from the well, and sat down under the coconut palms to admire the view from Pulau Perhentian Besar: Malaysia's most quintessential tropical island.

At the northernmost tip of Terengganu, the Perhentian island group, are 21km (13mi) off the coast of Kuala Besut, a fishing town not far from the Kelantan border. Wooden fishing trawlers converted into passenger boats make the two-hour crossing across the South China Sea to the jetty on Pulau Perhentian Besar (literally big Perhentian) where there are chalets, a resort, talcum-white beaches and no villages.

Across the narrow strait which separates the two islands is Pulau Perhentian Kecil the "small" island, home to a fishing community, and has a couple of provision shops, coffee shops, and the islands' only mosque. The island is renowned for its clever musical villagers who are adept at *berdikir barat*, a rythmic rap-like repartee between two teams of singers who make up lyrics as they go along, accompanied by hypnotic drum beats.

Perhentian Besar is a perfect destination for travelers seeking solitude, and a chance to do as little as possible. The waters are clear and clean, the beaches dazzling white, the interior rainforest is still virginal, and there are several interesting small coral reefs close enough to shore that even the most inexperienced snorkelers can enjoy the tropical underwater world. Even when the island is booked solid at holiday weekends Perhentian Besar still seems half-deserted.

Modern travelers may have only been coming to Pulau Perhentian for less than a decade, but for centuries mariners have been

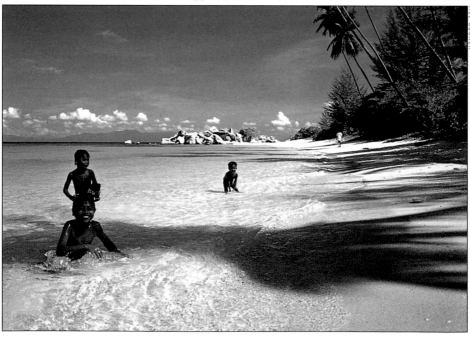

using the islands (literally translated-"the stopping-place islands") as a refuge from bad weather and a port to stock up on fresh water. Mentioned on Chinese sailing charts from the 15th century, Pulau Perhentian was a port of call on the prosperous maritime trade route, known as the second silk road, which flourished between China, Southeast Asia, India and the Middle East.

Kuala Besut, the jump-off port, is 68km (42mi) south of Kota Bharu. Goats recline on wooden verandahs, and sun themselves in the middle of the road in this sleepy fishing town. Sometimes a street market enlivens the waterfront road, and people from outlying villages crowd the stalls which are stocked with cheap Thai clothes, dried squid, woven pandanus mats and fruits and vegetables. There is always action at the dock: Kuala Besut is the home port of one of Malaysia's largest deep-sea fishing fleet, and dozens of smaller local trawlers.

Island boats run more frequently in the mornings, and on weekends, which in Terengganu and Kelantan fall on Thursday and Friday, but if you are stuck in the town overnight there are good beaches to the north and south, and a peaceful resort overlooks the beachfront, a few kilometers south of Kuala Besut on the way to Kampung Raja. For travelers arriving by car there are many private car parks in town where vehicles can be left overnight for a small fee.

Ferries leave from the wooden town jetty, and as all travelers are only in town to go to the islands it is virtually impossible to miss the boat as the boatmen and townspeople direct everyone to the next departing boat. They rarely leave on time—casting off only when they are full. The journey out is usually through glassy seas where flying fish skip across the surface and dolphins are occasionally spotted.

During monsoon season, from November through March, seas can get very rough and few boats make the crossing. Even if you get out in fine weather the seas can quickly mount and sometimes it is difficult to find a boat for the return journey. The water is also murky during this season, visibility is poor, and many east coast resorts close down. Boats, when you can get them, land at either the jetty near the resthouse or at the new dock close to the low-key resort.

Trails wind along the coast linking both jetties, and a track continues around the beaches to the north to the popular backpackers' beach which faces Pulau Perhentian

Kecil across the strait. The accommodation here is cheap and basic wooden huts with rock-bottom amenities, but the views, the water, and the beach more than make up for it. For travelers who like to relax in more comfort there is a small, resort south of the jetties on an equally pretty beach.

Canoes and snorkeling equipment can be rented from the chalets and the resort. The reefs in front of the beach are shallow at low tide and the corals and marine life can be easily observed. Take care though, when the tides are running, particularly in the channel between the islands, as the current can become very strong. All Terengganu's offshore islands are protected under Marine Park status.

Thick rainforest grows right to the beaches and well-marked trails wind across the island to deserted beaches on the windward side. Starting from the last chalet to the south of the new jetty, a trail winds uphill and descends to a long bay. Midway along this beach another trail heads inland to the resort and at the end of the bay another track leads across the island. This enjoyable trek which offers a break from the beach takes around two hours.

Opposite: *Children make the most of the crystal-clear waters at Pulau Perhentian Besar.*
Above: *A perfect day for beachcombing along Perhentian Besar's main beach*

TERENGGANU

An Ancient Port and Endless Sand

Beautiful fishing boats, a stone palace and flag pole atop Bukit Puteri, religious schools, a bustling Chinatown, and a predominance of fishermen, were all remarked upon by Munshi Abdullah, a Malay writer who visited Kuala Terengganu in 1836. These days, the state capital has boomed with Terengganu's new oil wealth, but beneath this veneer much of Abdullah's 19th-century observations are still relevant.

Situated beside the estuary of the river which the state is named after, Kuala Terengganu, 168km (104mi) south of Kota Bharu, is probably the oldest port on the east coast. Some scholars believe that it was one of two ports marked on Ptolemy's second-century map of the Malay Peninsula—the earliest-known cartographic record of the region—which was apparently drawn from information supplied by Indian sailors.

Later, Chinese and Arab annals record that Kuala Terengganu was a major trading port, and Javanese records from the 1360s show that it was part of the vassal states of the Majapahit Empire. But the most famous historical evidence is the Terengganu Stone, inscribed with the oldest-known Malay text in the Arabic script which was discovered 24km (15mi) upriver at Kuala Berang. This stone fragment records Islamic rules proclaimed by Raja Mandulika in the mid-14th century and proves that Terengganu converted to Islam at least 25 years before Melaka. Ever since Sayid Hussin, an Arab tin-prospector, found the historical stone in 1897 it has been kept in the National Museum in Kuala Lumpur, but there are plans to bring the Terengganu Stone back to its home state.

Kuala Terengganu

Kuala Terengganu sprawls along the riverbank and around a promotory to the South China Sea. The oldest, and most colorful part of town is centered around the waterfront and extends back to Jalan Masjid, while the modern "petro-dollar" part of town is along Jalan Sultan Ismail. Start a morning tour at the bustling **Central Market**, pass through the entrance flanked by women vendors who sit haggling amongst piles of bananas and durians, then weave your way inside through the rows of stalls which sell everything from sausage-like *keropok likur*, a shrimp delicacy, to traditional blue-and-white Terengganu batiks and locally-produced brasswares.

Chinatown starts at the market corner and lines both sides of Jalan Bandar. Its old shophouses which have housed generations of family businesses, are built in the distinctive southern Chinese style with curved roof ridges, arched windows, carved signboards, and decorative tiles. The small frontages are deceiving for these townhouses are cavernous family dwellings, often with warehouses attached, that stretch 30m (98ft) from the road and extend out onto stilts above the river. Old shops here sell local brasswares, nautical equipment and conical trishaw drivers' hats made of palm leaves.

East of the market, next to the post office, a staircase ascends 200m (656ft) to the summit of Bukit Puteri (Princess Hill) where fortifications have stood for centuries. From the old fort, which played an important role in the early 19th-century Civil War, there are panoramic views across the estuary to the fishing village of Seberang Takir.

A large brass bell, called a *genta*, made by a 19th-century craftsman from neighboring Kampung Tanjung is still housed beside the fort and was used in the past for warning the population of fires, and of men running amok. It was also rung during Ramadan to signify the breaking of the fast. Also on the summit is a lighthouse, a flagpole, and some fine old cannon including the legendary Meriam Beranak, "the cannon that bears children," with its offspring—a tiny cannon—beside it.

At the base of Bukit Putri is the royal compound, once enclosed by a high stone wall, which houses the apricot-and-white Istana Maziah, built in French provincial style in 1894. This former royal palace is still used for official functions. Behind the palace on Jalan Kota, are remnants of the old stone wall, and an entrance leads to some 19th-century wooden houses that are still home to Terengganu royalty, although the sultan now resides in a new palace on Jalan Sultan Mahmud, south of town. On the corner of Jalan Kota and Jalan Masjid is the Masjid Abidin which was originally built of wood in 1793 but has been substantially renovated. Inside are some beautiful wood carvings.

The boat-builders' island

Across the river from Kuala Terengganu is Pulau Duyung, a 50-cent ferry ride from either the jetty east of the market or from the riverside end of Jalan Sultan Ismail. On the riverine island, traditional carpenters still

Opposite: Trishaws are still a popular mode of transport along Jalan Bandar, a waterfront street lined with old Chinese shophouses.
Below: "Chick" blinds of split bamboo, painted with advertisements, shade the pavements and the shoppers from the fierce sun in the heart of Kuala Terengganu's Chinatown.

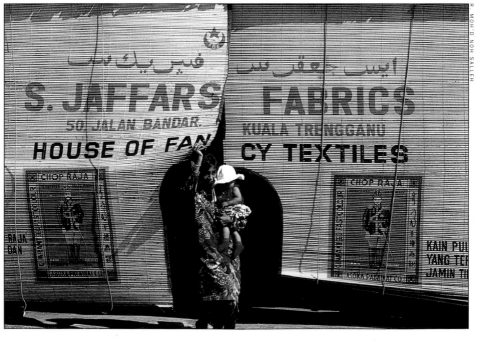

carry on the art of building wooden boats, using the prized red cengal wood from Terengganu's interior rainforests. The *pinas*, Terengganu schooners 18 to 21m (60-70ft) long, which once sailed to Bangkok and Saigon, haven't been built for decades but the craftsmen still use the same boat-building techniques to make ocean-going trawlers and wooden yachts for an international clientele.

Pulau Duyung is now connected by the new bridge to town, but it is much more pleasant to make the trip by water and view Kuala Terengganu across the river. Apart from the boat-builders, the island has interesting old *kampung* with traditional wooden houses, and on neighboring Pulau Duyung Kecil, connected by a path, is the ruins of a 19th-century mansion once owned by Tok Duyung, a famed Islamic religious teacher.

In the northeast of town in Kampung Tanjung and Kampung Ladang watch out for signs advertising Tembaga dan Batik workshops, usually in the ground floor of kampung houses, where traditional Terengganu-style batiks and brasswares are still made.

Other attractions further afield include the State Museum on the top of Bukit Kecil; Pantai Batu Buruk, a favorite tree-lined beach 1.5km (0.9mi) from town; Suterasemai, a silk-weaving center, 5km (3mi) south at Chendering; Masjid Hiliran, a historical 19th-century wooden mosque on Jalan Hiliran; and further out from there, along Jalan Kuala Hiliran then Jalan Losong Ferry is the Komplex Budaya, 3km (1.9mi) upriver at Kampung Losong, where some 19th-century wooden palaces have been resited beside the river.

From Kuala Besut in the far north, to Cukai, 261km (162mi) south, the Terengganu coast is practically one long beach. Fringed by coconut palms and casuarinas, these cream-colored sands are occasionally broken by estuaries. The only flaw in this otherwise impeccable coastline is the 40km (25mi) stretch between Kertih and Chukai, close to the Pahang border, where Terengganu's vast petroleum and gas complexes cast an Orwellian shadow over the surroundings.

The lonely north coast

North of Kuala Terengganu, the main road to Kota Bharu heads inland, but there is a quiet coastal road which begins just north of the recently completed Jambatan Sultan Mahmud, Malaysia's second-longest bridge, and follows the beaches 42km (26mi) to Kampung Penarik.

The good beaches start at Batu Rakit,

14km (8.6mi) from the roundabout north of the bridge and continue till Merang—not to be confused with Marang, the more popular fishing town south of Kuala Terengganu.

Follow the seaside road to Pantai Merang, a bay north of a small rocky headland where boats often shelter from the mid-year southwest winds. On a hill overlooking the beach is a resthouse and at the base are A-frame chalets. Food vendors set up beside the beach at weekends when the people from the surrounding kampung come here for picnics, and there's some basic, but traditional homestays operating just out of town for travelers who want a real kampung experience far from the other tourist haunts.

Offshore, to the northeast is Pulau Bidung Laut, which has recently been handed back to Malaysia after a decade as a United Nations shelter for thousands of Vietnamese boat people. Further north, the hazy-blue island in the distance is the divers' paradise of **Pulau Redang**, Terengganu's largest archipelago, 50km (31mi) from Kuala Terengganu, and the location of a billion-dollar resort development. Enviromental groups are keeping close tabs on the project as the reefs around these islands are Peninsular Malaysia's most pristine.

Boats run from Kuala Terengganu to Pulau Redang infrequently, boat charters are expensive, and the best way to visit is with an organized dive group or tours which include arrangements for camping and food. These

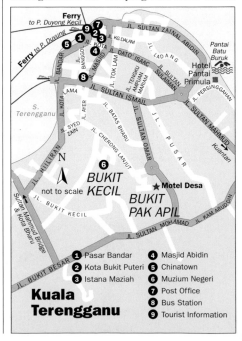

groups often depart from Pantai Merang which reduces the boat trip to around three hours. If you've got plenty of time you can always put up in a kampung house and take pot luck at scoring a boat back to the mainland.

Just north of Kampung Merang, turn off for Pantai Bari, another idyllic beach which is always deserted. From here the road runs along the coast to Kampung Penarik, with delightful beaches all the way, however don't make the mistake of thinking you can plunge in minus swimwear or topless: even if you think the beach is deserted someone's bound to show up, and conservative Terengganu is not the place to offend the locals.

Marang and Pulau Kapas

Heading south from Kuala Terengganu, follow Jalan Sultan Mahmud which turns into Route 3, the main East Coast Highway. At Rhusila, 10km (6mi) south, the heartland of the Parti Islam fundamentalists, some women wear *purdah* veils, and the men dress in turbans and the long Arabic *jubah*. Their seafront shops specializing in cheap basketwares and dried fish flank the highway and there is also a government-run Kraftangan shop with an excellent array of Terengganu fabrics and crafts.

Marang, 5km (3mi) further south, is the quintessential fishing town, with the prettiest harbor in Malaysia. Bird-like *kolek* boats, painted in pastel hues, and squat wooden

fishing boats anchor in the bay and come and go past the sand spit to the sea. Along the shoreline, racks of squid and salted fish dry in the sun, boats being repaired lie on the shore like beached whales, and in the distance behind the beach, Pulau Kapas, an offshore island, seems to hover in a midday mirage above the shimmering sea.

Most of the chalets and guesthouses are just south of town, across the bridge, at Kampung Rhu Muda, where there are good swimming beaches and cottage-craft workshops specializing in wood-carving and hand-painted batik.

Recently, some budget-priced chalets were built north of town facing a lagoon which runs along the back of a picturesque beachside kampung, where houses stand high on stilts to protect against the wrath of the monsoon seas which often sweep over the village. A wooden footbridge spans the lagoon to the fishing village, and it's a short walk from here to the beach. Old wooden shophouses line the tiny main street of Marang, which is alongside the waterfront to the left of the highway.

Some of these have now become back-

Below: *Dressed in traditional outfits with silk brocade headgear and short sarongs known as samping, Terengganu boys are as resplendant as the girls at an annual festival in Kuala Terengganu.*

packers' lodgings, like the Hotel California where Malay beach boys lounge on the verandah and strum their guitars. Others are small offices which cater for trips to Pulau Kapas, a short half-hour boat ride from Marang jetty. As the island is only 6km (3.7mi) offshore it is ideal for travelers who don't have the time to spend on a lengthy boat trip to some of the more remote islands. The beaches are clean and powdery white, the water is clear and excellent for swimming, but for good snorkeling and diving it's better to organize a trip to neighboring Pulau Rajah. The chalets are grouped together on the main beach which gets quite crowded, but there are more deserted bays around the southern headland.

Much of inland Terengganu is either monotonous oil-palm plantations or inaccesible mountainous rainforest, but 20km (12mi) outside of Kuala Berang, located 25km (15.5mi) southwest from Marang, is Empangan Kenyir, reputedly the largest dam and man-made lake in Southeast Asia. The enormous dam wall supports a vast network of sunken valleys—the flooded headwaters of the Sungai Terengganu. A road spans the top of the wall with spectacular views across the vast lake to the forested mountains beyond.

On the lakeshore are boats for hire, and tour companies organize overnight stays on houseboats and longer fishing trips. The lake has many famous freshwater species and the angling is excellent. There are also a number of waterfalls which can only be viewed by boat. Just before Kuala Berang, another road turns off to the left to Air Terjun Sekayu, a seven-tiered waterfall and forest recreation park, 18km (11mi) from the turnoff. The park is well maintained and there are trails up through the rainforest to the head of the falls. It is very popular with the locals, who much prefer to hang out at freshwater waterfalls than by the sea, but through the week it's quite peaceful. There is a mini-zoo with some white gibbons, and a resthouse and chalets for overnight stays.

The giant leatherback turtles

Heading south from Marang along the East Coast Highway, the road hugs the coast 41km (25mi) to Rantau Abang, a 19km (12mi) stretch of beach where the giant leatherback turtles come ashore every year to lay their eggs. Measuring 1.5m (5ft) long and weighing over 350kg (772lb), the largest of all sea turtles return to nest between the months of June and September, although August is the peak season. Numbers have declined rapidly in recent years and the government has introduced heavy fines for egg-collecting, and is making a major effort to ensure that the turtles keep returning.

It may look a bit bizarre to see fisheries officers zooming along the beach in dune buggies and locating turtles with walkie-talkies, but their presence, and constant patrolling in the nesting season, coupled with media exposure of the turtles' declining numbers has definitely changed peoples attitudes. Not so long ago onlookers climbed on the turtles' backs, sat waiting with transistor radios blaring and took flashlight photos. Now all of these activities are banned. Fisheries department officers collect the eggs after they are laid and place them in compounds until they hatch, then they are watched as they return to the sea. Parts of the beach are now out of bounds to the public and other sections are accessible if you buy a ticket.

This all may sound too organized, but the sight of these massive turtles lumbering up the beach by moonlight to lay their eggs, perhaps having swum from the Atlantic to return here, is an awe-inspiring experience and well worth being woken up in the middle of the night for. Don't expect to see them on your first night. You have to be lucky as even in the nesting season it is pot luck whether or not they will beach.

Why they return to Rantau Abang every year is yet another one of nature's mysteries. Some villagers believe that they are lured in by a large black stone which looks like a turtle, but experts think that the steep incline of Rantau Abang beach, which can be dangerous for swimming, is perfect for turtle-landing, although this theory is not foolproof for there are other sites along the coast which also offer a sharp dropoff.

A **Turtle Information Center**, run by the Fisheries Department is open during the season and has film shows and displays. There is ample chalet accommodation, from budget A-frames to the more traditional Malay-style chalets, and most have a restaurant. Alternatively there is a small complex of simple restaurants serving local fare just south of the Information Center.

Tanjung Jara, 10km (6mi) past Rantau Abang, is a private resort, but the award-winning architecture—based on the original designs of Terengganu's old wooden palaces—is worth stopping off to see even if you don't stay over. The entire complex is made of wood, stained in the traditional manner and decorated with wood carvings. Set around a

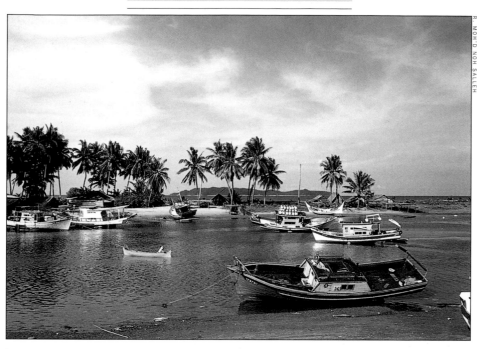

lagoon and along the beachfront, the resort blends in beautifully with the surroundings and is a great place to unwind in luxury. This resort is also kept informed of turtle-landings and visitors make the short trip north in a mini-van.

Dungun, just south of Tanjung Jara, was once a thriving port with an upstream ore mine, however, these days it's just another sleepy fishing port where salted-fish dry on racks in the sun, diesel-powered trawlers throb in and out through the estuary and housewives cycle to the riverside market. Kampung Seberang Pintasan, on the northern promontory, just down the road from Tanjung Jara, is the best place to watch the sun go down when the fishing boats are silhouetted in a river of molten gold.

Wooden boats crowd the riverbank at photogenic Paka, 20km (12.4mi) south of Dungun, a traditional east coast village which has changed little over the decades, unlike the next port south, Kerteh, which has been transformed by the state's vast offshore petroleum and gas deposits. Waste gas flames belch into the sky, and miles of serpentine pipelines dominate the road south past the huge gas-processing plant and refinery complex owned by Petronas, the national oil company. A safe distance from here, well-planned oil-workers' suburbs set in tree-lined streets border the highway to Kemasik where the scenery again reverts to Terengganu-style fishing villages. Pantai Kemasik, just south of town, is a long, white-sand beach with a distinctive offshore rock formation which is popular with oilworkers' families on the weekends. The highway south follows the coast past Kijal, a sleepy seaside village which is well-known for its delicious *kuini*, a type of mango. When it's not fruit season, the enterprising women hawkers sell *lemang* rice cooked in bamboo, with *rendang* a spicy, dry beef dish.

Chukai and adjacent Kemaman, 18km (11mi) south of Kijal, is the last port on the Terengganu coast before the highway crosses into Pahang state. Tourists rarely stopover here as they are usually en route to the beach resorts, but the town has a bustling market place alongside the riverfront, banks, and good local restaurants. At the nearby seaside village of Kuala Kemaman where old wooden houses stand high on stilts above the sand, every vacant block is covered with shrimp crackers drying on mats in the sun. There are no tourists here, and everyone still ekes out a living from the sea. In the mid-afternoon heat—siesta time—the only sounds are the soft lapping of waves and the tradewinds rustling the palms along the long beach which runs all the way south to Pahang.

Above: *At Marang, fishing boats moor in the lagoon, and in the distance is the popular resort island of Pulau Kapas.*

KUANTAN & PAHANG

A Vast Region Ruled by the Ocean

A long coastline of golden beaches, mountainous offshore islands, cool hill resorts, tranquil fishing villages, lotus-covered lakes, and rainforests with West Malaysia's highest mountain and longest river, all contribute to make Pahang, Peninsular Malaysia's largest state covering 35,965km² (13,886mi²), a highly popular tourist destination.

Because of the region's size many of these attractions are nearer and much more accessible from the west coast than the east. For this reason the Cameron Highlands are included in the Perak chapter, Fraser's Hill in Kuala Lumpur, and Taman Negara (the national park) and the Kenong Rimba Forest Park near Kuala Lipis in the Rainforests chapter.

Legendary kingdoms

Pahang is the Khmer word for "tin" and as the tin mines upstream from Kuantan at Sungai Lembing had been worked since prehistoric times some historians think that this is where the state's name derived from. Other interesting associations with the ancient Khmer from today's Kampuchea is that the indigenous Orang Asli, the Jakun, speak a Mon-Khmer dialect and there are legends suggesting that an ancient Khmer city lies buried in the silt under the waters of Tasek Cini. But archaeologists have yet to study the region seriously.

Settled since the Stone Age, Pahang was well known to early Chinese mariners who came for the sandalwood and elephant's tusks as Pong-fong, and later to Arabs and Europeans as the gold-rich kingdom of Pam, also known as Pan, Phaan, Paham, and Pahangh. But the state emerged as a separate entity only in the 15th century when it was captured by a son of the sultan of Melaka who started the Pahang dynasty at Pekan which is still the royal seat beside the Pahang River.

A riverside capital

Kuantan, situated about midway down the east coast, only took over from inland Kuala Lipis as the state capital in 1955, and although the town was mentioned as far back as the 12th-century when it was known as Tan-ma-ling, probably after the nearby promontory of Tanjung Tembeling, nothing tangible remains from antiquity and there are few historical buildings. The further south one travels on

R. MOH'D NOH SALLEH

the east coast the more homogenized the society becomes, and Kuantan also lacks the wealth of cultural traditions found in Kota Bharu and Kuala Terengganu. However, the town is pleasant enough and is a good base to explore the neighboring beaches, fishing villages and other nearby attractions.

As the closest east coast center to Kuala Lumpur (259km/161mi), this fast-growing town ringed by surburban developments is the commercial and industrial hub of Pahang. There are some old black-and-white colonial administration buildings fronting the Padang opposite Jalan Mahkota, and on the northern side facing Jalan Masjid is the fantastic, new State Mosque with its huge arched entrance reminiscent of Mughal-India, which features intricate mosaic-tile work, and four soaring minarets.

Jalan Mahkota and parallel Jalan Besar have some interesting old Chinese shophouses and in this grid is where most of the banks, offices, downtown hotels and restaurants are located. The shaded walkway which extends along the riverbank is pleasant in the evening and there are lots of foodstalls overlooking the river.

Beaches and fishing villages

Teluk Chempadak, a sandy bay enclosed by rocky headlands 4km (2.5mi) from Kuantan along Jalan Teluk Sisek is the town's major attraction. At the north end of the bay there's a paved promenade with handicraft shops, seafood restaurants, and cheap eating stalls. Trails wind through the rainforest which grows right to the water's edge around to another shaded bay.

In the early morning the jungle is alive with birds and it is easy to spot monkeys swinging through the trees. To the south of the promenade are two international-class hotels, and a range of alternative accommodation. There are plenty of better beaches on the east coast, but Teluk Chempadak is lively, great for watching the local action, good for swimming, sunbaking, jogging, jungle-walks, and eating seafood, and if you are an early riser the apricot dawn over the South China Sea is a treat.

Beserah, 10km (6mi) north of Kuantan along Jalan Beserah (the main highway north), is one of the east coast's most fascinating fishing villages. Take the turnoff to the beach where the foreshore is covered with wooden racks raised high on stilts where salted fish dry in the sun. Dawn is the best time to arrive, for the sea is like glass and some-

times even dolphins and dugong can be seen at this hour. Men shoulder the heavy rattan baskets of fish down to the drying racks and then a group of sarong-clad girls and women, both Chinese and Malay, squat on the decks and begin covering the split bamboo floor with the silvery, salted fish.

When the tide comes in, the sands underneath the stilted racks are covered with water and boys leap about in the shallows spearing fish. Across the tidal lagoon, before the sand dunes slope down to the beach, woven mats are spread out and covered with *ikan bilis*, the dried, anchovy-type fish that are a basic ingredient in Malay cuisine. Under tin roofs near here are sheds where the *ikan bilis* are cooked in vats of salt water before drying. The entire village runs on the salted-fish business and the day's action all centers around the afternoon catch. When the boats return depends on the season, but the locals usually know—give or take an hour—and it is a sight worth waiting for.

Offshore, the tubby trawlers unload the catch into beamy open boats which ride the waves into the shallows, and there, amidst the

Opposite: At Beserah, a fishing village north of Kuantan, women spread salted fish to dry on split-bamboo platforms raised on stilts off the ground. Below: This Pahang fisherman spends his mornings at sea and his afternoons mending nets under the coconut palms.

R. MOH'D NOH SALLEH

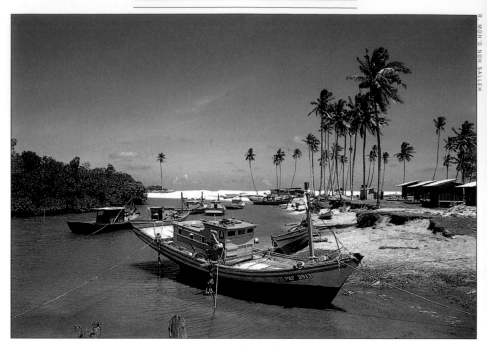

R. MOH'D NOH SALLEH

foaming surf, the fishermen transfer the baskets of fish onto a waiting cart pulled by water buffalo. When the cart is full, the driver shouts and urges the buffalo out of the water and the carts thunder up the white sands to the *ikan bilis* sheds. Perhaps, in years gone by, other fishing villages also used buffalo to transport the fish from boat to shore, but this is the only east coast *kampung* which still uses this method.

Recently some good, low-cost lodgings have sprung up in the beachside village where traditional wooden houses are shaded by coconut palms, and travelers can now make a stopover in this interesting *kampung*. South of the town, just over the bridge is a batik workshop, and close to the beach on this side, women make homemade *keropok*, dried prawn crackers.

Just north of Beserah, at Kampung Sungai Karang, the inland road goes to Pusat Cenderamata (1.8km/1mi), a craft center which has shellcrafts and jewelery made from local gemstones. About 5km (3mi) north at Balok, the long beach has fine white sands and is great for swimming. An international windsurfing contest is held here every December/January when the annual monsoon kicks up a good surf on the otherwise placid waters. There are resorts and some excellent seafood restaurants along the coast to Pantai Batu Hitam, where the beach is shaded by whispering casuarina trees.

North of here, the highway makes a detour around the Kuantan port, and then heads up the coast past the picturesque estuary at Sungai Ular. Here, wooden fishing boats with gaily-painted yellow cabins, and rainbow-colored sampans moor beside the river, and coconut palms tower above the seaside village. Fishermen sit in the shade mending their nets, and the womenfolk gather at the water's edge to buy fish fresh from the boats. For good snorkeling, local boatmen will ferry you out to tiny Pulau Ular, a nearby island which derived its name "snake island" from a legend which tells that it was formed by a giant sea serpent. This quiet village has some very basic huts, but is totally unaffected by the tourism which thrives both to the south and north.

Laid-back Cherating

Cherating, 47km (29mi) north of Kuantan, looks like a typical Pahang village on the highway, but turn off to Kampung Cherating and every *kampung* house seems to have turned into a mini-resort. This is the backpackers' favorite hang-out on the east coast mainland, and despite the proliferation of chalets and restaurants, the seaside village still retains most of its *kampung* charm for there are no high-rises or ugly cement buildings. The beach stretches for miles to the south, and is great for swimming and windsurfing. Even in the peak season there's an uncrowded feel to the place.

If you're not interested in the beach there are plenty of other cultural activities including trying your hand at batik-painting. The Souvenir Center near the highway has good courses, and this is also a good place to learn the art of weaving *mengkuang*—pandanus leaves—which locals weave into mats and baskets. Travelers can also get to participate in Malaysian sports like *sepak-takraw*, a game similar to volley-ball where a rattan ball is kept aloft without using your hands. Resort owners also run river trips up the Sungai Cherating to out-of-the-way traditional *kampungs* and they also organize trips to other places of interest.

Around the headland north of Kampung Cherating is Asia's first Club Med with 4km (2.5mi) of private beaches and five-star luxuries amidst self-imposed isolation. About 5km (3mi) north is Pantai Chendor, where green turtles—known as *penyu agar*, a smaller turtle than the giant leatherbacks—come ashore to lay their eggs from May to September. Just north of here is the border between Pahang and Terengganu.

Inland from Kuantan

For an interesting excursion to a Buddhist cave temple, a waterfall and an old mining town, take Jalan Bukit Ubi from downtown Kuantan and continue west, past the Lencongan Kuantan (Kuantan By-Pass) to the turnoff to Sungai Pandan waterfall about 18km from town. Follow the signs another 12km to the forest park with its spectacular falls which cascade down a tiered rockface. These falls are also approachable from the main Kuala Lumpur highway to Kuantan. Turn north just before the Kuantan airport.

Back on the Sungai Lembing road, just past the turnoff to the falls is the small village of Panching. At the Police Station take the right-hand fork for 4km (2.5mi) through palm-oil plantations to the solitary limestone hill which contains Gua Charas (Charas Cave). Fifty years ago a visiting monk from Thailand came here to meditate and the caves have been visited by Buddhists ever since.

At the base of the hill is a small temple, and a steep 50m (164ft) staircase ascends the cliff-face to a cave containing a reclining Buddha sculpted from the natural limestone. It is best to visit early morning when the otherwise gloomy cavern is illuminated by sun-rays from an opening in the cave ceiling. Leading off from here, and higher up, are more caves, but torches are needed for exploration.

At the end of the road, 34km (21mi) from Kuantan, is Sungai Lembing, an old mining town which went to sleep when Malaysia's only major underground tin mine closed down. There is little to do here, but the old town is interesting to wander around; nothing new has happened here in decades, since the bottom fell out of the world tin market.

The unpainted, old wooden shophouses, the magnificent, century-old raintrees draped with ferns, and the ruins of grand colonial mansions overlooking town are all memories of a grander past. Tours of the old mine can sometimes be organized in advance through the Tourist Information Centre at the LKNP Building near the Kuantan post office.

Just before Sungai Lembing, the right-hand road which crosses the river leads to Gunung Tapis, an isolated and mountainous rainforest region which is accessible only with a four-wheel-drive vehicle. The scenery is magnificent, and there are some beautiful waterfalls, but there are no facilities and potntial visitors must bring all their own food and camping equipment.

Opposite: *Fishing trawlers, painted in the characteristic Pahang colors (each state has its own color combination) crowd the estuary at Sungai Ular, an untouched fishing village.*
Below: *Walking trails lead through the lush rainforest to the tops of these falls at Sungai Pandan, west of Kuantan.*

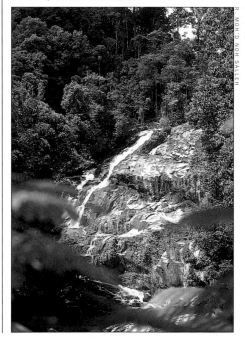

R. MOH'D NOH SALLEH

PEKAN

Polo and the Pahang Sultanate

Chickens scratch around the old wooden houses, and children cycle along the bucolic road. It looks like any other *kampung*, but then the quietude is shattered by an insistent throbbing. The children dismount, and peer through the high fence bars as a helicopter lands, and their sultan disembarks in front of his gold-domed palace. There is still a feudal air to Pekan, the royal capital of Pahang.

Located 44km (27mi) south of Kuantan, on the southern bank of the Sungai Pahang, West Malaysia's longest river, Pekan was described by 15th-century court annals as having "rivers running fresh to the sea, plentiful gold and jungles stocked with elephants." Conquered by Mansur Shah, the son of the Sultan of Melaka in 1458, Pekan has been the home of Pahang's dynasties ever since. The present sultanate trace their lineage to Bendahara (Prime Minister) Wan Ahmad who took the title of Sultan in 1882 after a long civil war.

Pastel-colored, 19th-century shophouses along Pekan's main street face a riverbank shaded by ancient raintrees. Nearby, is the excellent **Sultan Abu Bakar Museum**, a 70-year-old brick mansion, once the British Resident's home and later the sultan's palace. Royal regalia, textiles, neolithic artifacts, and treasures from a recently-recovered Chinese junk are among the many collections on display.

Across the bridge is Masjid Abdullah, an art deco mosque built in 1929, and the multi-domed Abu Bakar Mosque built by Sultan Abu Bakar who ruled Pahang from 1932 to 1974. At the end of Jalan Istana Abu Bakar is the opulent royal palace, its marble entrance topped by huge replicas of arched elephant's tusks—the symbol of Pahang's royalty. The palace overlooks spacious polo grounds where international tournaments are held. Sultan Haji Ahmad Shah, Pahang's current sultan and his sons are all expert players and promising Pekan youths are sent to Argentina to learn the finer points of the "sport of kings."

Other interesting sights around Pekan include the old Istana Leban Tunggal, an original wooden palace, and the Silk Weaving Center at Pulau Keladi.

Below: Sultan Ahmad of Pahang (center), shaded by a yellow umbrella—a color reserved for royalty—is flanked by his personal staff outside his palace at Pekan in 1885

MUZIUM NEGARA

TASEK CHINI

Malaysia's Answer to Loch Ness

"It's head was a big as a tiger's and it had horns like a deer," exclaimed Pak Lasah, a centenarian of the Jakun people, while describing the legendary serpent-like creature he spied in Tasek Chini, a series of shallow lakes in central Pahang. Others, including a British engineer in the colonial days, also glimpsed the elusive *naga*, but like its Scottish kin, the "monster" of Lake Chini is still awaiting discovery.

Other legends about the lakes are equally intriguing. Stories persist that an ancient, walled Khmer city once existed here, but when threatened by attack, the inhabitants used a system of aquaducts to submerge the city, intending to drain it later. Aerial photographs showing unnatural straight lines indicate that a town may have existed near the lake, and linguists point to similarities in the language and culture of the Kampuchean Khmer and the local Jakun people, but tangible proof is lacking. The lakes have always been sacred to the local Malays as they are said to be the abode of Seri Pahang, a legendary white crocodile.

Tasek Chini can be reached by road from the town of Chini, off the Kuantan/Segamat Highway, but the more sedate way is by boat from Kampung Belimbing, a village on the northern bank of the Sungai Pahang, 83km (51.5mi) west of Kuantan. Once across the broad Pahang River, the boats wind their way 4km (2.5mi) along the winding Sungai Chini. Snaking lianas drape to the water's edge where the riverbanks are anchored by the buttress roots of giant trees. After the gloom of the jungle, the lakes dazzle with color. The waters are also home to many delicious freshwater fish, and from June to September, the lakes are covered with lotus flowers. Wreathed in cloud, 823-m (511ft) high Gunung Chini, said to be the breeding place of the legendary serpents, looms behind the lake.

The boats dock at a floating jetty beside a small resort hidden by rainforest—an ideal spot to stay overnight. Wooden longboats can be chartered for fishing, and to visit the nearby Orang Asli villages. Or you can cruise the lakes, hoping for a glimpse of the legendary serpent, or traces of the mysterious lost city.

Below: The enigmatic Tasek Chini, a system of lakes in the backlands of Pahang.

R. MOH'D NOH SALLEH

PART VI

Introducing the Rainforests

Smothering the central mountainous ridges, stretching the entire length of the Malay Peninsula, from the Thai border in the north to the southernmost state of Johor, are the great green heartlands: home to 14,500 species of plants and trees, 600 varieties of birds, over 200 different mammals as well as untold thousands of invertabrates and insects.

These fecund realms are among the most ancient of the world's rainforests, for when the last Ice Age brought havoc to the ecosystems of the Amazon and Central Africa, the Malayan jungles were scarcely touched and continued to thrive undisturbed.

"It is a world in which man seems an intruder," wrote Alfred Russel Wallace, the great biologist, when he viewed the virgin forests of the Malay Archipelago in the mid-19th century "Where the weird gloom and solemn silence combine to produce a sense of the vast, the primeval, almost the infinite."

In Wallace's day, man had made scarcely a dent on this green mantle which in many places stretched from the shores of the Melaka Straits to the the South China Sea. Not that it's potential was unknown, for the Orang Asli, the indigenous dwellers of the interior, had for millennia been trading aromatic woods, rattans and resins with the coastal Malays who, in turn, bartered with merchants from China, India, Arabia and the Malay archipelago.

Prized products included rhinceros horn which was made into cups and ground into powder for use as a fever cure—the main reason for the decline of the one-horned rhino which Marco Polo took to be the mythical unicorn. And gallstones from honey bears which were worn as talismans.

Although these resources were utilized, the rainforests themselves remained inviolate until the British colonials discovered rubber, when immense acreages of West Malaysia's lowland rainforests were cleared for the new cash crop. The central forests remained rela- tively untouched until the last few decades, when land schemes transformed many forests into oil palm plantations, and logging made inroads into previously virgin tracts.

Recently, however, in the wake of growing domestic concern over the state of the environment, and mounting international criticism of over-logging, Peninsular Malaysia had become increasingly more ecologically conscious. No more rainforests are to be felled for land schemes, and logging has been scaled down in an effort to conserve valued forest resources.

Despite decades of punishment the West Malaysian rainforests are still vast, covering around 60% of the peninsula. There are large areas of undisturbed jungle throughout the central ranges, and some of the forests along the East West Highway are still in a virgin state, although access is difficult.

Taman Negara, Malaysia's original National Park, is only accessible by river, but it is still one of the best places to really experience the rainforest, for here there are large tracts of lowland dipterocarp forest. These rainforests which occur up to 304m (1000ft) above sea level are home to elephants, tigers, tapir, rhinoceros, deer, bear and wild boar, and are the richest and most dense tropical forests, where often over 240 species of trees grow in a single hectare.

Slighly higher up is the less dense hill dipterocarp which gives way at around 800m (2,624ft) to mist-shrouded montane forests. As well as Taman Negara, other accessible rainforests include the Kenong Rimba Jungle Park outside Kuala Lipis in Pahang, and the newly-explored, but less accessible Endau-Rompin region between Pahang and Johor.

Overleaf: Many Orang Asli, like this Temiar hunter from Kuala Woh in Perak, still use blowpipes. **Opposite:** Each rainforest tree species has its own season, flowering and fruiting independently. Photos by R. Ian Lloyd

ORANG ASLI

Original Peoples of the Peninsula

Known collectively as the Orang Asli, or "original people"—a term introduced in the late 1950s—Peninsular Malaysia's aboriginal people consist of about 20 tribal populations, numbering more than 90,000.

Orang Asli languages fall into two major groups. First, there are those that are local dialects of Malay—a member of the Austronesian language family spread throughout island Southeast Asia and the Pacific. Second, there are "Aslian" languages, belonging to the Mon-Khmer division of the Austroasiatic family and therefore related to Vietnamese, Cambodian and many other languages in mainland Southeast Asia. These languages give a valuable clue to the question of the "origins" of the Orang Asli (*see Prehistory, page 24*).

The most popular classification divides the Orang Asli into three major sub-divisions; the Semang (or Negritos), the Senoi, and the

Aboriginal Malays (or Jakun). This system works neatly, however, only for about half of the Orang Asli groups.

The Semang live in the northern parts of the Peninsula and number around 2,000. Interestingly, this number has remained constant since the early 1800s, so they are not dying out, as has sometimes been claimed. They comprise a network of small populations who formerly lived mostly by nomadic hunting and gathering. Their physical appearance—darker skinned, more curly-haired and slightly shorter than other peninsular populations—has long been assumed to result from their biological kinship with other so-called Negrito peoples in the Philippines and Andaman Islands. But recent research suggests that they may be more related to their fellow Orang Asli, and that their appearance results from genetic change following millennia of close adaptation to living in the forest depths.

There are at least six named groups of Semang, differentiable by their linguistic, cultural and social features: the best known are the Kentaqs, Kensius, Jehais, Mendriqs and Bateks. While some still retain the option of turning to a nomadic lifestyle, most now live in relatively settled circumstances, not far from the roads or larger rivers leading to small towns like Baling, Grik, or Kuala Krai. They operate largely within the cash economy, through selling collected or farmed produce, and by earning wages as laborers.

The Senoi—which means "human being"—number around 40,000, and occupy the upland, middle portions of Perak, Kelantan, and northern Pahang. The two main groups, the Semais and Temiars, lived until recently by slash-and-burn cultivation, supplemented by fishing, trapping and the trading of forest products. Nowadays, they cultivate fruit and rubber for sale, and have also taken up paid employment and even entrepreneurship.

The Aboriginal Malays of Johor, Negeri Sembilan and southern Pahang, who number around 30,000, differ from the other Orang Asli in speaking dialects of Malay as their own language. They are mostly the descendents of the same people from among whom the Malays also emerged centuries ago. The two main groups are the Temuans of Selangor, Negeri Sembilan and Melaka, and the Orang Hulu of Pahang and Johor.

They live largely by swidden agriculture, but they also specialize in the collection of forest products for trade with the outside world. Even now, they are major suppliers of wood oil, resins and cane. In holding on to this distinctive economic niche, they developed a pattern in which the members of each village maintain closer relations with their non-Orang Asli partners than with people in other Aboriginal Malay villages. They also differ from the more widely-connected and egalitarian Semang and Senoi societies in preferring to marry close relatives and maintaining ranked sets of local headmanships.

The slopes of Gunung Benom in central Pahang are home to a great variety of Orang Asli groups who do not fit neatly into Semang-Senoi-Malay classification. Significantly, the name Benom is not Malay, but an old Mon-Khmer world for "mountain." The sedentary and relatively accessible Jah Hut are famous for the high quality of their wood carvings. The secretive Che' Wong live deeper in the forest and they forage, farm, and collect for trade. On the northern slopes of Gunung Benom live the Batek Nong, the most southerly Semang group in the Peninsula. The Lanohs of the middle Perak river valley, between Lenggong and Grik, have been regarded as Negritos, but their language is related to Temiar and they have been more sedentary than nomadic.

Further south, the Semelais, Semaq Beri, Temoq and Mah Meri have similar lifestyles to Aboriginal Malays, but they speak Southern Aslian languages. Their residence patterns range from the sedentary (Mah Meri) to nomadic, from coastal (Mah Meri and occasional Semaq Beri) to interior (the rest), and from dry land (Temoqs, many Semelais, most Semaq Beri) to lakeside (Semelais living on Tasik Bera). Livelihoods vary from fishing, farming, hunting, gathering and collecting for trade. The Mah Meri also produce fine wood carvings for the art market, in a different style those of the Jah Hut.

In Johor there are Aboriginal Malay populations whose history and way of life links them more with the sea than the land. The Orang Kanaq on the west coast near Benut also live on the Indonesian side of the Straits of Melaka. Although Muslims, they regard themselves as Orang Asli, perhaps because their distinctive language is not a Malay dialect. The Orang Kanaq, who originate from Riau, have puzzled observers by maintaining their tiny population of 30-40 people for several generations. The Orang Seletar, who live in the mangroves along the narrow strait separating Johor from Singapore, are the descendants of the Orang Laut, or "sea people," who played a crucial role in the early

Orang Asli Groups of Peninsular Malaysia
(Approximate distribution)

Languages included on the map: THAILAND, PERLIS, KEDAH, Kensiu, Kentaq, Jehai, PENANG, Lanoh, Temiar, KELANTAN, Menriq, TERENGGANU, PERAK, Batek, Semai, Semaq Beri, Jah Hut, Che Hut, PAHANG, Wong, SELANGOR, Temoq, Temuan, Semelar, Mah Meri, NEGERI SEMBILAN, MELAKA, Orang Hulu, JOHOR, Orang Kanag, Orang Kuala, Orang Seletar, SINGAPORE

Legend
Languages
- Northern Aslian
- Central Aslian
- Southern Aslian
- Malay Dialects

Boundaries
— International
— State
- - - Ethnic groups

history of the region. A few Orang Seletar families who continue to live in boats make a living by catching fish and crustacea along the shorelines.

Usually, visitors wishing to see Orang Asli need to get off the beaten track. However, the road from Tapah to Cameron Highlands passes through Semai country, and some villages are beside the road. Temiars can frequently be seen in Grik and Gua Musang, and the East West Highway passes through Jehai and Temiar country. Taman Negara is within the territory of the Bateks, several of whom work as guides and porters.

Tourists should note, however, that Malaysian law entitles the Department of Orang Asli Affairs (JOA) and local police to limit the access of outsiders to Orang Asli settlements. To avoid problems, seek advice beforehand. When visiting settlements, try to do so in small numbers to avoid swamping the people's resources and invading their privacy. Small gifts are appreciated, as are offers to buy any of their handicrafts. However, these can be expensive, especially Jah Hut and Mah Meri wood carvings and "real" used blowpipes from the Temiars and Semais.

—*Geoffrey Benjamin*

Opposite: Necklaces of trade beads and a bark headband are the favored body ornaments of this Temiar tribesman from the Perak foothills.

TAMAN NEGARA

Forests from the Dawn of Time

From high up in the misty mountains, the serpentine river winds its way down through the overhanging jungle. Vines and creepers loop from tree to tree like the rigging on ghostly galleons, and where the sunlight penetrates along the riverbanks, flowering lianas with clusters of orange blossoms splash color through the evergreen rainforest. Up in the tree tops where the great trunks suddenly burst into branches are huge hanging fern gardens and equatorial orchids that bloom, as the Malays say, "for the eyes of God alone."

Inside the giant bamboo stands are luminescent fungi that glow in the dark and on the ridges grow pitcher plants that devour insects. White-faced monkeys rattle the tree-tops and, frightened by the boat's engine, flee chattering into the depths of Taman Negara, Malaysia's largest and oldest National Park, which sprawls 4,343km^2 (1,677mi^2) through the backlands of Pahang, Kelantan and Terengganu states.

In Malay, Taman Negara, means simply "The National Park," and within its boundaries are found every type of inland forest habitat ranging from dense lowland rainforests to the "cloud" forests of the montane regions. Crowning the mountainous range which bisects the park from east to west is Peninsular Malaysia's highest peak, the remote Gunung Tahan, 2,187-m (7,175ft) high. It is a difficult, but rewarding climb for travelers willing to undertake the 9-day trek to the summit.

Established as a sanctuary since 1937, the park's interior rivers run pure and unpolluted and century-old trees still endure, safe from the chainsaw and the bulldozer. There are spectacular waterfalls, towering limestone massifs, and within this green heartland live the vast majority of the country's highly diverse wildlife.

Seeking out the shadow-dwellers

Species native to the park include the shy and elusive elephant; the tiger—who the Orang Asli say causes those who sight it to not eat for a week; the *seledang*—the wild cattle which early hunters feared more than the tiger; and monkeys, deer, otters, leopards, squirrels, bats, rats, shrews, and a fantastic spectrum of birds and insects.

But travelers have to be aware that the

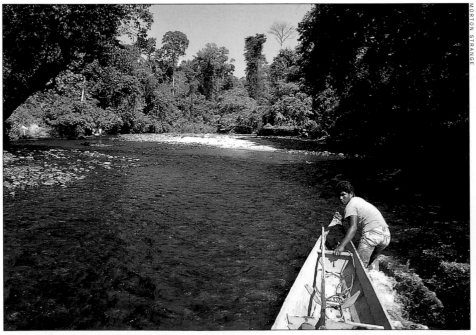

MORTON STRANGE

tropical rainforest is nothing like the African savannah and that most of the animals are nocturnal. Even experienced jungle bashers may spend a week in the dense jungle and see nothing more exciting than a mound of elephant dung, a flash of feathers and a legion of leeches. They may see you, but the shadow play in the gloom of the rainforest floor provides excellent camouflage and their superior sense of smell ensures that most of the larger creatures will always be well out of sight.

Wild pigs and deer often graze and root around the chalet areas, and birds can be easily sighted. Tapir, and *seladang* can sometimes be viewed at salt licks from the overnight hides. For travelers with patience, the ability to appreciate the rainforest and endure its discomforts, and a large measure of luck, Taman Negara can still provide an unforgettable reward—the sight of one of the rarer mammals.

The river approach

The only access to the park is by boat along the Sungai Tembeling which forms the southeastern boundary. The 59-km (37mi) boat journey from Kuala Tembeling, the closest road access to the park, is a unique experience. It take three to four hours along the river, and sometimes longer in the dry season when passengers have to disembark in particularly shallow sections.

Beyond the 35-km (22mi) marker, Taman Negara begins on the western riverbank while the eastern side is cultivated land and *kampungs* all the way to Kuala Tahan; the site of camp headquarters where the silt-colored Tembeling meets with the clear, tea-colored Sungai Tahan which originates in the untrammeled reaches of Gunung Tahan.

After the restful river journey, lulled by the hypnotic jungle chorus, Kuala Tahan, the administration and accommodation center, seems incredibly busy. Wooden longboats jostle for position at the wharf, coming and going with boatloads of tourists. At the reception, forms are filled out, fees paid, chalets, beds, boats, treks, guides and everything else is organized while throngs of visitors eat ice-cream sundaes at the restaurants. But only a few hundred meters inside the ever-present jungle, it is surprising how the crowds are quickly swallowed up by the sheer immensity of the park.

All trails start from Kuala Tahan, and they range from easy one-hour strolls around the area near the headquarters to gruelling 9-day treks up Gunung Tahan. Always start out as

early as possible, for this is when the birds and animals are active and it is also the most pleasant time to walk. Even though the rainforest is considerably cooler than the cleared land, the lowland regions are still hot and humid and even the fittest traveler may find walking a struggle in the middle part of the day. If you are not used to trekking in equatorial jungles the best way to begin is to start out on shorter trails and get acclimatized before attempting longer walks.

Trails and hides

The trail to Bumbun Tabing (*bumbun* means "hide") takes around 90 minutes (3 hour there and back) and is excellent as a starter. For much of its length it meanders along the eastern bank of the Sungai Tahan where deep pools like Lubuk Simpon (15 minutes from base) are great for a refreshing dip. Nearby grow spectacular *tualang* trees, the highest "dominants" in the rainforest. These grey-barked giants, which often reach 76m (250ft) high, stand head and shoulders above the canopy.

At the junction of the Bukit Teresek trail, hikers can either follow the Bumbun Tabing

Opposite: During the dry season boats have to be hauled upstream in some shallow section of the Sungai Tahan. Below: A baby monkey snuggles up to its mother on the forest floor in Taman Negara.

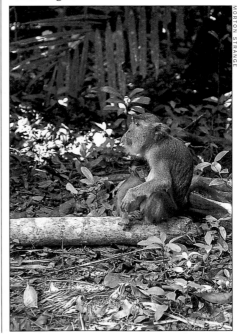

MORTON STRANGE

trail or take a detour along the prettier Rentis Neram (*rentis* means trail) which follows the riverbank overhung with ancient *neram* trees, a type of myrtle with smooth trunks and ribbons of bark.

Bumbun Cegar Anjing, an overnight hide, is reached by fording the river along the Rentis Neram. Deer often browse here on a grassy old airstrip and sighting of *seladang* are not uncommon. At Bumbun Tabing, a hide overlooking a natural salt lick at the end of the trail, wild pigs and barking deer are often sighted and the unique tapir with its long trunk and black and white markings is sometimes spotted here. Just before Bumbun Tabing the Rentis Tahan-Trenggan begins.

About 1km (0.6mi) along, the left branch leads to Gunung Tahan, and the right-hand track meanders through lowland rainforest, where monkeys and gibbons are often sighted, to Bumbun Kumbang, a 13-km (6hr) walk from headquarters. This overnight hide is good for viewing tapir, sambar and barking deer, and can be alternatively reached by a 45-min boat journey and a 45-min walk from the river.

To maximize chances of spotting animals at all hides it is best to be inside a few hours before nightfall. For night viewing, it is advised to rotate watches and to shine a torch onto the clearing every 15 mins. Animals are apparently not disturbed by torchlight and hang around long enough to be observed.

MORTON STRANGE

Bukit Teresek, a hill lookout at the end of a short but steep trail from Kuala Tahan is an excellent place to view the rainforest from above. Along the trail in the early morning, the "wak wak" cries of gibbons and the piercing squeals of giant squirrels can often be heard and are sometimes glimpsed swinging through the canopy.

From the highest lookout, panoramic views stretch across the roof of the lowland rainforest and on clear days extend to Gunung Tahan, the table-topped mountain to the left of center. Viewed from above, the canopy crowns vary from vermilion to copper tones, and through the entire spectrum of greens. Nowhere is there a grouping of the same colors for in the tropical rainforests each species only appears sporadically and each has it own seasonal rhythms.

Other walks from headquarters include the interesting Rentis Belau, which starts on the opposite bank of the Sungai Tahan, climbs a couple of spurs and then traverses magnificent lowland rainforest. A detour leads off to Gua Telinga, a limestone cave, about an hour's stroll from base, where a rope walk leads through the dark cavern—home to thousands of bats and the non-poisonous cave-racer snake which crushes the bats and then swallows them. Further on are the hides at Bumbun Belau and Bumbun where salt licks attract tapir, and sambar and barking deer.

Climbing the peninsula's highest peak

Gunung Tahan is of course the ultimate goal for the serious trekker, but preparations must be made well in advance as the entire trip takes around nine days and all supplies must be carried from headquarters. The 61km (38mi) trail traverses several river crossings, climbs up and down hills and mountains before the main peak is reached. The journey is both arduous and exhausting, but well worth the time, expense and effort if you are fit enough to enjoy it.

The first day to Sungai Melantai is a five-hour walk through reasonably easy terrain, but the second day to Kuala Puteh is a tough trek which covers 26 hills and takes a good eight hours. The third day's trek to the scenic campsite at Kuala Teku is spent fording the Tahan and in dry seasons six crossings are usual, whereas if the river is high the trail follows some high spurs to avoid danger.

The real climb starts on the fourth day and ascends to Wray's Camp—named after a co-leader of the 1905 botanical survey—at

1,100m (3,600ft). This region is montane oak forests where elephant tracks are common. From here, most climbers stay overnight at three higher camps in order to make the final push for the summit early in the morning. At this altitude, amongst the cloud forests, where trees seldom grow higher than six or seven meters (20ft), and orchids and pitcher plants thrive, the overnight temperature often plummets to four degrees Celsius.

From the highest Padang camp the trail climbs to the summit plateau, which rises from 1,400m (4,600ft) to 2,187m (7,174ft). In this peaty, rocky world stunted tea-trees only grow a meter high and mists can quickly swirl in and obscure the trail. After traversing a gully of bonsai trees, mosses, ferns and orchids, the path finally climbs to the summit where if the climber is lucky with the weather, spectacular birds'-eye views sweep across the world's oldest rainforests to the horizons.

Fishing and birdwatching

For travelers who are not keen on spending hours tramping through the rainforest, Taman Negara also offers some interesting boat trips and excellent fishing for these rivers are home to over 200 species of fish. The one-hour jaunt to the rapids and swimming holes at Lata Berkoh is a pleasant and relaxing excursion and there is a overnight fishing lodge 200m (656ft) downstream.

Anglers often catch the famed *sebarau*

carp here in quiet pools near sunken logs and *toman* (snake-heads) are found in still, deep pools. The Malayan *mahseer* (*kelah*), popular with sports fishermen, prefers pools along the swifter river sections, and the best sporting fish of all, the *kelesa*, which often leaps high into the air when hooked, inhabits deep water pools.

Other popular river trips include the exciting, rapid-studded stretch between Kuala Tahan and Kuala Trenggan and then up this latter river to Kuala Kenyam. This is a favorite venue for birdwatchers as the prolific wild fruit trees here attract a fantastic array of species. Further upstream, the river trip continues past banks draped with huge *neram* trees, and traverses undisturbed rainforest up to Kuala Perkai which also offers excellent fishing and has an overnight lodge.

Some visitors may complain that there are few animals left, for no one is assured of a sighting, which should always be considered a bonus rather than a certainty. It is true that most of the larger mammals live in the far-off untrammeled and most inaccessible regions, but the park was originally proposed as a place where wildlife could live undisturbed by man, and during its half a century of existence Taman Negara has most certainly lived up to that purpose.

Opposite: *The common palm civet is often seen from hides around Taman Negara.*

KENONG RIMBA

Deep in Elephant Country

It happened on a day pregnant with promise. We were about a mile into the jungle and the early morning mist still blanketed the canopy far above our heads. The previous night's rain dripped from giant leaves, an ultramarine butterfly colored the gloom and a sharp mosquito-like bite signalled my first leech encounter of the day. Then Ahmad, our guide, stopped abruptly, pointed to a large pile of hay-like dung in the middle of the muddy path, and calmly announced, *"tahi gajah"*—elephant droppings.

It was clear that this was no special event for Ahmad who was born and bred here, but I had often tramped along rainforest trails in the hope of spotting at least some small sign of these giant pachyderms. Finally, in the northwest region of Pahang state, at Kenong Rimba, which translates as "the primeval jungles of Kenong," I had seen and smelt tangi-

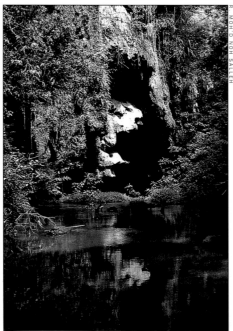

ble evidence that the Malayan elephant really does exist.

Further along we were rewarded with an even more conclusive proof: elephant footprints in the mud, three times the size of my palm print. But they were already a few days old and the rainy season had just finished; a signal for the elephants to move deeper into the forest.

Setting this region aside as a jungle reserve was the brainchild of Hassan Tuah, who now runs tours from his tiny office in Kuala Lipis, Pahang's old colonial capital. After a long battle with bureaucrats and timber tycoons he succeeded in seeing Kenong Rimba established as a state park. He is unerringly enthusiastic about the park: its virgin forests, its limestone caves, and its prolific wildlife. "Our northern borders meet Taman Negara," he explained, "and much of the larger wildlife lives in the undisturbed rear section of the park."

A town worth exploring

Kuala Lipis is the jump-off spot for Kenong Rimba, and is an interesting old town to spend time in while en route to the park. Located where the fast-flowing Sungai Lipis meets the Sungai Jelai (which laters turn into the Pahang, Peninsular Malaysia's longest river), Kuala Lipis was one of Pahang's earliest settlements, renowned as a trading center for gold and jungle products centuries before it became the colonial capital in 1898.

After Kuantan took over as the state capital in 1955, little happened in Kuala Lipis and the sleepy town still maintains many colonial buildings and a main street lined with picturesque old wooden shophouses. At the hilltop resthouse, formerly the British Resident's home, a museum houses Neolithic tools, pottery, brassware and fabrics. Other historic buildings include the Clifford School, built in 1913, and the Lipis District Offices constructed in 1919.

From Batu Sembilan to the forest

Next morning, in the pitch-dark long before dawn, we met Ahmad at the Kuala Lipis railway station, and take the local train to Batu Sembilan (Ninth Mile) where settlers, who hacked their farms from the jungle were smoking *kretek* (clove cigarettes) and drinking coffee, waiting for the mist to rise.

In a grey dawn, we walked to the jetty and boarded a longboat for the 20-minute run down the Jelai River and then into its tributary, the Kenong River which the park is named after. From the Kampung Dusun jetty, on the fringes of civilization, it is a half-hour walk to where we came across more evidence of the elusive giants.

The elephant caves

Limestone hills, pockmarked with caves and draped with vines, thrust upwards through the forest canopy. At Gua Batu Tangga, "the cave of rock steps," curious ledges line the rear of the cavern, and a little further on is Gua Batu Tangkup, where elephants shelter

during the torrential monsoon. The trail into the cave narrows between boulders which have been polished marble-smooth over the centuries by the mighty mammals squeezing past the entrance. Inside the cavern the earth has been beaten-down flat and there are more piles of elephant dung. Stalactites hang from the roof and it is easy to imagin those regal creatures sitting in this primeval shelter, dry as a bone, while the monsoonal rains pound the world outside.

Sweet potatoes, aloe and bat guano

As we pressed on through the forest the trees become higher and filtered sunlight flickered through the canopy high overhead. A strong aromatic scent filled the air. A tree was flowering on the roof of the jungle. Beside the track, the ground was dug up, for here, Ahmad explained is where the Batek, a sub-branch of the indigenous Negrito people, have been digging for sweet potatoes.

Further along the trail we met two couples, the men short and muscular, and the women with wooden combs stuck in their hair and their sarongs hiked up high to enable them to move freely through the jungle. They were out searching for *gaharu*, a fragrant aloe wood used to make joss-sticks, which constitutes a major source of their income. When they finally bounded off down the slippery track their barefoot tread was sure and certain, unlike ours as we stumbled

over tree roots in our so-called jungle footwear.

We stopped for lunch beside the virgin stream of the Sungei Kesong, under the limestone massif of Gunung Kesong. Fish darted about in the shallows of these clear waters far from the muddied streams polluted by loggers. Great mud slides on the banks indicated that we were not the only ones to have lingered here, for these marks were made by elephants crossing the shallow stream.

Upstream, we entered the aptly-titled Gua Hijau, or Green Cave, where the walls are stained bright green. Bat guano lay thick on the ground and inky black recesses lead into a labyrinthe of undiscovered passages.

Beyond the trail

Further afield there are other places worth seeing. A longer trek leads to the Seven Steps Waterfall in the far north of the park, or adventurous travelers can even climb the limestone ranges of the Kesong Valley to search for the elusive and rare desert goats, believed to be kept by dwarfs.

On the edge of the park, beside the river at Kampung Dusun, are a series of rapids where the village women wash clothes on a flat limestone shelf and a short trip downriver by dugout canoe leads to Gua Batu Tinggi, where the river flows through a cave.

Kenong Rimba harbors many a mystery, for these tropical rainforests contain plants which are still little known to scientists. Most importantly, however, it serves as a haven for wildlife amid a rapidly changing landscape.

Opposite: The caves of Gunung Kesong reflected in the waters of the river of the same name, at this shallow crossing favored by elephants. ***Above, left:*** *Figs sprout, not from the branches of this lowland rainforest tree, but from the base of its trunk.* ***Above, right:*** *Vines and ferns intertwine in the lush riverside foliage.*

ENDAU ROMPIN

Mysterious Denizens of the Forest

Home to Malaysia's largest population of the Sumatran rhinoceros, one of the world's rarest animals, Endau Rompin, a reserve covering an area of 93,000 hectares of tropical lowland forest, sits astride the boundaries of Johor and Pahang states. On the southeastern side of the peninsula, the park falls in a biogeographic area known as the Riouw Pocket with flora akin to that of western Borneo. However this phenomenon is not evident in Endau-Rompin's fauna which is representative of the mammals, birds, reptiles, amphibian and fishes found in the peninsula.

Hairy beasts and fairy tribes

The indigenous Orang Ulu who use these forests for hunting and gathering, live in Kampung Peta, just outside the park boundary on the Johor side, and at Kampung Mok, located on the Pahang side. The elders of Kampung Peta possess a rich heritage of legendary tales featuring hairy giants, fairies, spirits and dragons. For each strange rock formation there is a fairy tale to explain its shape. The uncannily quiet plateau at Padang Temambung, a shrubby grassland habitat covered with what appears as a criss-crossing of paths is a sacred place—the home of a Chinese fairy princess and the gateway to the Orang Ulu heaven. The landslips at Gunung Beremban have been attributed to the awakening of the earth dragon, which occured when a careless individual brought vinegar up to the peak and aroused the sleeping dragon with the pungent smell.

Endau-Rompin is also believed to be inhabited by the Malaysian version of Bigfoot, known as Serjarang Gigi, "widely-separated teeth". The beast is a hairy giant, well over 3m (10ft) tall with arms as big as a normal person's thigh.

When things go missing in camps or the village, the incidents are attributed to fairy tribes known as the Orang Bunian, and visitors are advised not to bathe naked in the streams in case their behavior offends the fairy women.

Much of the beauty of Endau Rompin—its numerous waterfalls, rapids, pools and clear forest streams—is due to the geology of the park. At the Upeh Guling Waterfall there are a series of holes caused by the erosive swirling action of stones and pebbles in the river current. A rock formation at Gunung Janing resembles a sailing ship, and at the source of the Sungai Endau is another formation which looks like a crouching man swallowing the river and letting the water pass through him which the Orang Ulu call The Old Man of Endau.

Considerable areas of the park consist of sedimentary successions overlying or capping more resistant volcanic or granite bedrocks. This provides the setting for the formation of plateaux and mesas and causes rapids and waterfalls at each interphase with a distinct drop in elevation along the rivers and streams which are full of deep pools.

Geology has also played a part in creating a mosaic of ecological habitats. Hikers who start from Kuala Jasin and then climb up Gunung Janing pass by riverine forest, lowland dipterocarp forest, up through hill dipterocarp and into a pure stand of fan palms. Further along is a patch of swamp forest with pitcher plants and monkey puzzle trees.

A rich array of fauna

The bird life in the riverine and lowland forests is rich with bulbuls, flycatchers, spider-hunters, sunbirds, drongos, magpie robins, flowerpeckers, orioles, pigeons, and the entire spectrum of the avian fauna of the peninsula. Encounters with tigers, deer, wild boar, gibbons, leaf monkeys, macaque, squirrels, tree-shrews, tapirs, civet cats, otters and even rhinoceros can also be had by the lucky few who have time to spend on extended trips into the forest.

Monitor lizards can often be seen basking in the sun by the old logging tracks or along riverbanks. Flying lizards and agamid lizards are often sighted playing among the branches of trees. Snakes are present but harder to see. Tortoises and terrapines can occasionally be sighted in the streams and in the forest. Crocodiles are reported in the main river but are rarely found in the park.

Frogs are abundant along the streams and rivers and their chorus and calls permeate the evening air. A popular riverside frog *rana blythi* from Sumatra appears in the Guinness Book of Records as one of the world's largest frogs. Here, the species can attain over a kilogramme in weight.

The rivers are good fishing grounds for the bony-tongued *arawana*, and the carp known locally as *sebarau*, both of which are good sport fish. Lurking in deep, river pools are the giant catfish and the fearsome giant snake-head which has been known to attack unsuspecting swimmers who venture into their territorial pools.

Looking for birds and animals in the forest is a challenging pastime for park visitors. Hikers can explore the forest, climb the often tough hill trails, and there are good rapids for white-water enthusiasts. Travelers can also visit Kampung Peta where the Orang Ulu produce mats woven from pandanus leaves, and other artifacts made from wood and rattan.

Hikers are advised to purchase leech socks, to at least deter these ever-present bloodsuckers. There is little to fear from snakes, but if a tiger is known to be around do not venture into the forest on your own, it is always much safer to go with a group. Ask and follow the advise of the rangers and inform them if you do decide to hike on your own. Hire a guide if you are uncertain of the way as it is better to be safe than sorry. By following these basic guidelines Endau Rompin will provide the travelers with an unforgettable nature experience.

—*Kiew Bong Heang*

Opposite: Early-morning mist still hovers above the rainforested hills of Endau-Rompin, an untouched and remote region, currently being set aside as a state park. **Below:** *Wallowing in a salt lick, this rare Sumatran rhinoceros is one of a group of some 20 individuals—the Peninsula's largest group—which lives in the Endau-Rompin region.*

WWF MALAYSIA

PART VII

Introducing Melaka

"Malacca fascinates me more and more daily. There is, among other things, a mediaevalism about it. The noise of the modern world reaches it only in the faintest echoes," wrote Isabella Bird, the intrepid Victorian traveler who visited Malacca, now Melaka, in 1879.

In the course of the last century, progress has of course caught up with the town, but remnants of its six centuries of history remain. Sailing *perahu* from Sumatra still dock at the riverside and their merchant sailors still barter charcoal for rice. The labyrinthine lanes of Chinatown still harbor age-old family businesses, and squeezed in between 18th-century shophouses are ancient temples, historic tombs, and elegant old mosques. At the centre of the old port town is the renowned Town Square with its terracotta red Dutch buildings, and the Portuguese ruins on St. Paul's Hill.

Interwoven in the early history of this ancient trading capital is the story of Negeri Sembilan—formerly a series of nine territories to the north of Melaka—which was first settled by the matriarchal Minangkabau people from Sumatra in the early decades of the 15th-century. Although not as well-known as Melaka, Negri Sembilan is a scenic state which still maintains a strong Minangkabau identity in its characteristic architecture which features "buffalo-horn" roofs, its spicy *nasi padang* cuisine, and its cultural tradition of Adat Perpateh, a unique matrilineal system.

Queen of the spice trade

It seems that the older a city is the more fanciful are the legends that surround its birth, and Melaka is no exception. Around the last decade of the 14th century, Parameswara, a fugitive Sumatran prince, sailed up the Melaka Straits in search of a new kingdom and put ashore at an obscure fishing village where, according to legend, his royal hunting dogs were intimidated by a miniscule mousedeer. This auspicious sign (apparently Kandy in Sri Lanka was founded after a similar occurrence) convinced Parameswara that this was to be the site of his capital and he called it Melaka after the tree that he was resting under.

There were other less whimsical reasons for the choice, for the port was sheltered and conveniently situated at the crossroads of the monsoons to enable merchants from Arabia and India to sail down on the southwest trades, and the traders from China and the Spice Islands to arrive with the northeast monsoon. With the young prince's royal pedigree and the port's favorable location Melaka soon became a bustling entrepot where spices, scented woods and jungle exotica were exchanged for Indian textiles, and porcelain, silks and metalware from China.

Melaka's rise to fame was meteoric and in less than a century the city became the paramount trading port of the vast Malay world. Dominant among the traders were the Muslim Indians, wealthy and respected merchants whose religion commanded considerable prestige in the region. Upon Parameswara's conversion to Islam, when he became the first sultan of Melaka, the port was thrust into the international class, for at this time Egypt controlled the Spice route to Renaissance Europe and allowed only Muslim shipping.

On the hill overlooking the harbor, the sultans and their court enjoyed a life of medieval opulence, residing in gilded palaces, borne aloft on silk-caparisoned elephants, seated on golden thrones and waited on by hundreds of slaves. Sultan Mansur

Overleaf: A Straits Chinese wedding group wear satin robes from China, but the bride's headdress is copied from Malay traditions. Photo circa 1900. **Opposite:** *Malay children pose on the original terracotta paving and lean against the solid wooden doors of Melaka's Stadthuys. Photo by Radin Moh'd Noh Salleh*

Shah's reign, from 1459 to 1477, considered as the Golden Age of Malay power and culture, was enlived by legendary happenings, intrigues, scandals, and the exploits of Hang Tuah, Hang Jebat and Hang Kasturi—the three musketeers of the Melakan Sultanate.

The Portuguese conquest

In the words of a Portuguese historian, by the end of the 15th century, Melaka was "the richest sea port with the greatest abundance of shipping that can be found in the whole world." Tales of the "wondrous Golden Chersonese" and the "city where the winds meet" were heard and heeded by the Portuguese who were lusting to overtake Arab domination of the spice trade.

After an abortive first attack on the city in 1509, the Portuguese were forced to retreat, but they returned in full force two years later under the command of Alfonso de Albuquerque, the Governor of Portuguese India (Goa). Their timing was perfect for there were palace squabbles and the sultanate had lost the support of the Orang Laut, the sea tribes, which were vital for a naval battle. Although the Malays fought furiously, led by Sultan Mahmud on his war elephant, they were overcome and the monarch and his court fled south to Johor.

The Portuguese, eager to make their mark on their new conquest, immediately started construction of A Famosa, an impos-

ing stone fort that encircled the base of St. Paul's Hill, and constructed churches, administrative buildings and churches using some of the stones from the sacked Malay palace and mosques. The fort dominated Melaka for centuries until the British destroyed it in 1806, and the Porta de Santiago is today the only surviving gate.

Trade initially flourished, but then slackened when the wealthy Muslim traders defected to the Islamic ports in Sumatra. Joao de Barros, a Portuguese traveler who visited Melaka in 1540 prophetically remarked that "the Portuguese arms and boundary marks placed in Africa and Asia (...) are material things and time may destroy them; but it will not destroy the religion customs and language which the Portuguese have left in those lands." His prediction still rings true: the Portuguese Eurasians of Melaka are still zealous Catholics, still speak Cristao, an archaic form of Portuguese, and maintain many ancient cultural traditions although the links with their mother country were broken over 350 years ago.

The Dutch burghers take over

Troubles, however, besieged the Portuguese Empire, the tiny homeland did not have the manpower or money necessary to ensure the survival of their far-flung dependencies, and corruption and greed undermined the crown's treasury. Throughout the Portuguese

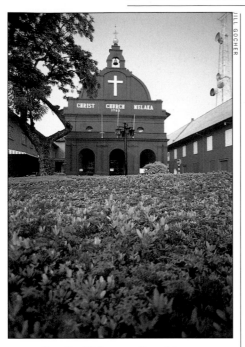

occupation the Malays continued to wage war against Melaka from their new southern base in Johor.

When Dutch traders first contacted Johor at the start of the 17th century they were welcomed as possible allies against both Portugal and Aceh who had wrecked Johor's trade and repeatedly destroyed its capitals. After entering into treaties with Johor, which still controlled the Orang Laut as its personal navy, the Dutch gained control of the Melaka Straits, captured Portuguese vessels and were so sure of their succession as Melaka's overlords they even measured the ramparts of the A Famosa fortress by moonlight.

With the help of Johor it took the Dutch six months to win Melaka. In 1641, with most of the town decimated, the burgers of the Dutch East India Company took command. Unlike the Portuguese, they were only interested in commerce, not crusades, and Islamic traders returned to Melaka and many mosques, some of which still survive, were built. The Hollanders proceeded to rebuild Melaka in the image of a Dutch trading town. A Famosa was repaired and the date 1670, together with the United East India Company's coat of arms was engraved on the Porta de Santiago, and can still be seen today.

The rebellious Minangkabau

To the north, however, the fiercely independent Minangkabau settlers of today's Negri Sembilan were not about to pay Dutch taxes and they rebelled under their charismatic leader Raja Ibrahim. Denounced by the Dutch as a presumptuous imposter, he claimed to be able to poison the wind, bewitch firearms and render himself invisible. Raja Ibrahim was the first to call on all fellow Muslims, regardless of race, to fight the infidel Dutch, but he failed to enlist the support of the Bugis who were settling neighboring Selangor, and who had always been suspicious of the Minangkabau.

In the 18th century, the Minangkabau of Negri Sembilan, who were no longer being protected by Johor and were at the mercy of the Selangor Bugis, turned to their Sumatran homelands and imported Raja Melewar, a prince from their traditional royal house, who could unite and defend them. He was proclaimed as the Yang di-Pertuan Besar of Negeri Sembilan in 1773 and his heirs have ruled the state from their royal capital, Sri Menanti, until the present.

Melaka passed out of Dutch hands in 1824 when under the terms of the Treaty of London, all the lands west of the Melaka Straits fell to the Dutch including the English territory of Bencoolen in Sumatra, and everything to the east including Melaka came under British rule.

Later, during the mid-19th century, Sungai Ujong, the largest of the nine territories of today's Negeri Semblian, was the center of a tin rush and continual disputes arose over who controlled the Linggi River, the major channel for the tin trade. This in turn disrupted the tin trade with the Straits Settlements of Melaka, Singapore and Penang, which were under English control, and the colonials, worried about declining profits, intervened and placed a British Resident in Negri Sembilan in 1874.

The warring territories gradually accepted the British status quo—they had little choice—and finally a treaty was signed between the Yang de Pertuan Besar Mohammad, the four major chiefs (known as Undang), and the British in 1895. When Malaya gained independence from the British, Mohammad's son Abdul Rahman became the first Yang di Pertuan Agong, the paramount ruler of independent Malaya.

Opposite: Porta de Santiago is the only surviving gateway of the great fort of A Famosa which once encompassed all of St. Paul's Hill.
Above: Christ Church, built by the Dutch in the mid-18th century, faces Melaka's Town Square

BABAS & NONYAS

The Merging of Two Cultures

Along Melaka's seafront drive, the gentle tradewinds stir the sultry air and waft into palatial old homes which overlook the Melaka Straits. On one breezy verandah, a foursome of elderly women sit around a table playing *cherki*, a little-known card game similar to dominoes.

Their pastime is unusual—for mahjong is the popular game for women of their age—but their clothes are also odd, for instead of wearing the ubiquitous Chinese pantsuits they are dressed in the Malay fashion of batik sarongs and embroidered *kebaya* blouses, their hair swept back in chignons and secured with golden hairpins. And something else is different too, for their chatter is not any Chinese dialect, but Malay, the tongue of their adopted homeland.

These women comprise a veritable "who's who" of Melaka's most prominent families. They are members of the unique ethnic minority known as the Straits-born Chinese or *peranakan*, which means "born here" in Malay. Many families can trace their family tree back centuries, to the days when their adventurous ancestors sailed from China in junks laden with brocades and pearls to barter and trade at Melaka. Some of these merchants married local Malay women, and some families even claim royal descent.

Of noble beginnings

According to a 15th-century court history, when the Ming Emperor sent his daughter Princess Hang Li Poh to marry Sultan Mansur Shah "500 youths of noble birth" accompanied her. They settled at the foot of the hill known since then as Bukit Cina, "Chinese Hill," and took up local brides. From these early alliances the distinctive Malayanized culture of the Straits Chinese evolved which is totally different from that of later Chinese immigrants who came to Malaya during the British colonial days.

From the beginning, the *nonyas*, as the

women are called, and the *babas*, their menfolk, were wily and clever at trade. Many became exceedingly wealthy and developed an opulent lifestyle—a combination of the Chinese talent for making money and the Malay love of enjoyment. In the 17th century, Dutch monopolies forced many *babas* to the British ports of Penang and Singapore, but Melaka has always remained their cultural heartland.

A life of leisure

Pampered by servants, the *nonyas* spent their leisure time visiting, gossiping, and chewing betel-nut: a Malay habit. Their abiding passion was beadwork which they picked up from the Minangkabau women and most of their trousseau, including wedding slippers, pillow ends, belts and bed decorations were intricately beaded, all for their most spectacular event—the *nonya* wedding.

The traditional wedding ceremony, rarely seen these days, ran for 12 consecutive nights and was a glorious mixture of Chinese and Malay tradition. The elaborately embroidered gowns were imported from China, but the bride's golden headdress, glittering with diamonds, was Malay.

A love for spicy and piquant food also sets the *peranakan* apart from other Chinese as their cuisine uses Malay ingredients like coconuts, *belacan* (dried shrimp paste), chillies and abundant spices. Delicate cakes and pastries were laboriously prepared and today's nonya are still adept at cooking these traditional *kueh* (cakes). Following the Malay style, the *peranakan* eat with their fingers. Chopsticks—handed down through generations—were never actually used for eating, but merely for ceremonial purposes at the family's ancestral altar.

The Golden Age

Melaka's Heeren Street, now called Jalan Tun Tan Cheng Lock after a famous *baba* millionaire/politician, has long been their ancestral center, and is lined with Chinese-style town houses some of which date from 18th-century Dutch times. These cavernous homes, often 46m (150ft) long, incorporate Chinese, Malay, Portuguese, Dutch and English influences—a mosaic of Melaka's multi-cultural past.

Even their porcelain was different, for the wealthy *nonyas* ordered custom-made sets direct from China. Just over a decade ago no one wanted the bright enamelled wares decorated with peony flowers and phoenix birds—the *peranakans'* favorite symbols—but today, Nonyaware, as it is known, is highly prized by ceramics collectors. Their unique silverware, known as Straits Chinese Silver, is also sought after by antique dealers, and by *nonyas* whose families were forced to give up their heirlooms during the Great Depression of the 1930s.

Many *babas* had run rubber plantations during their "Golden Age" under British rule, but when rubber fell in value to five cents a pound—compared to 1912 when the same weight had raised five dollars—businesses were ruined overnight. Some *babas* found the sudden change too much to endure, for many of that generation were hedonists who had never worked a day in their lives preferring to live off the family fortunes. Opium smoking, gambling, womanizing and expensive cars had already eroded many a *peranakan* fortune. Some *babas*, however, were successful and prominent in their own right, and today their descendents are still wealthy.

Just over a decade ago, the *babas* and *nonyas* were in danger of dying out, but fortunately their culture has experienced a revival. Although many customs are no longer practised, Malaysians and Singaporeans of Straits-born descent have become more conscious of their heritage. *Nonya* food continues to be popular, there's been a spate of nostalgic books, and the new generations are paying top prices for Nonyware porcelain and Straits Chinese silver.

Opposite: *Symbolic animals and flowers carved in teak decorate this gilded screen at William Chan's ancestral home in Melaka's Jalan Tun Tan Cheng Lock.* **Above:** *Wearing traditional sarong and* kebaya, *Mrs. Chua (center) and her* nonya *friends while away the hours playing a traditional card game called* cherki.

MELAKA TOWN

A Stroll Through History

Situated on the west coast of the peninsula, beside the straits named after it, Melaka—the nation's oldest town—is unique in that it has directly experienced all of the major phases of Malaysia's history; from the establishment of the Malay Sultanate in 1396, through the Portuguese, Dutch, and English colonial eras, followed by the Japanese occupation and finally independence in 1957.

Located 147km (91mi) south of Kuala Lumpur, and 245km (152mi) north of Singapore, bustling, modern Melaka, capital of the state of the same name, now sprawls into the surrounding rice paddies and onto land reclaimed from the straits. But at its heart Melaka still retains much of the ancient aura of "the queen of the spice trade."

Walking is by far the best way to get about town—with trishaws as a good alternative. The old downtown layout is still much the same as it was centuries ago with the merchants' hub (Chinatown) on the northwest bank of the Melaka River, and the government and administrative area on the southeast side.

The best place to start a stroll is at the famous **Town Square**, sometimes known as the Red Square because of its distinctive terracotta-red buildings, or the Dutch Square, because most of the historical buildings around its edge date from the Dutch colonial era in the 17th to 18th centuries.

The **Stadthuys**, built in 1650, and recently restored to its former glory, is the square's most dominant structure. The former governor's residence, it is one of the oldest buildings in the East. The massive masonry walls, which now house a historical museum, were constructed on the foundations of the old Portuguese fort.

Early etchings show that the building was originally whitewashed—it wasn't always red—and during the Victorian era, the English used it to house visiting guests. A 19th-century traveler reported that "there must be more than forty rooms in this old place, besides great arched corridors, and all manner of queer staircases and corners."

To the left of the Stadthuys is the Christ Church, painted a brilliant post-box red, built in 1753 with bricks imported from Holland. Inside, the original hand-carved pews still serve for the multi-cultural Anglican congre-

R. MOH'D NOH SALLEH

gation who come on Sunday to listen to any of three sermons in Mandarin, English and Tamil. Seventeen wooden beams, 15m (49ft) long, each hewn from a single rainforest tree, span the nave. Church records date back to 1641 and set in the floor are 16th-century Portuguese tombstones which predate the Dutch conquest.

Beside Christ Church, stands an attractive red building with an arched verandah, built in Dutch style in 1931. This was the town post office until recently, when it was converted into the Youth Museum.

In the center of the square, carved from English marble, is the Queen Victoria Fountain, which was constructed in 1904 to celebrate the monarch's 60-year-long reign. Beside the fountain is the Tan Beng Swee clocktower constructed by a rich Straits Chinese family in 1886.

Opposite, is the **tourist information office**, and to the right a bridge spans the Melaka River. It was built in the late 19th-century to replace an earlier one constructed in the 17th-century, which in turn had replaced the original Melaka Bridge which was slightly upriver from here. Historical accounts describe the first bridge as being built of stone, strong enough to support the sultan's elephants, and wide enough to house the town's main bazaar. In 1511 the Portuguese successfully conquered Melaka by storming the bridge from the shelter of a junk which

they had floated upriver on a spring tide.

From the Town Square, follow Jalan Kota, passing some more old Dutch houses on the left, until you reach Melaka's most enduring symbol, the old stone gateway of **Porta de Santiago**. This is all that survives of the original walls of the great Portuguese fortress of A Famosa which once encompassed all of St. Paul's Hill.

Contained within its massive, laterite walls were a castle, two palaces, government buildings, five churches and two hospitals some of which were built from the stones of the previous Melakan Sultanate's buildings. Above the archway of Porta de Santiago is the date 1670, and the coat of arms of the VOC (Dutch East India Company) which were added by the Dutch when they were repairing the fort after taking over from the Portuguese.

In 1807, A Famosa fort was blown up by the British who feared that when Melaka returned to Dutch rule after the Napoleonic wars that it would pose a trade threat to their recentl—established port of Penang. Munshi Abdullah, in his *Hikayat Abdullah* tells of "pieces of the Fort as large as elephants, and

Opposite: Calendars featuring Tamil screen idols and Hindu deities, chunks of rock sugar, altar offerings and sundry goods crowd onto the "five-foot-way" of this Indian store in Melaka's Jalan Bunga Raya.

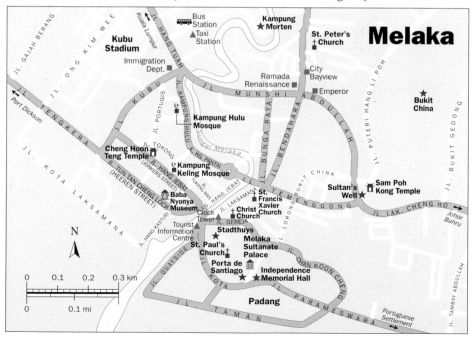

even some as large as houses, were blown into the air and cascaded into the sea." Sir Stamford Raffles, the founder of Singapore, stepped in and saved the last remaining gateway, Porta de Santiago. But it was too late, for in the words of Munshi Abdullah "the Fort was the pride of Malacca and after its destruction the place lost its glory..."

From the stairs behind the gateway, a path climbs to the summit of the hill crowned by the ruins of Sao Paulo (St.Paul's Church) which gave the hill its name. Built by the Portuguese in 1521, the Protestant Dutch later destroyed the roof and used the building as a fort. Leaning against the church walls are massive granite tombstones, dating from Dutch times, carved with poignant inscriptions—testimony to the Hollanders' short, difficult lives in the tropics.

A miraculous occurance

The empty crypt was once used as a temporary burial site for St. Francis Xavier who had often visited the city he called "the Babylon of the East", in reference to its debauched inhabitants. The saint was attributed with miraculous powers, and many of these tales are still believed by Melaka's Portuguese Eurasians. Apparently, after the body had been sent to Goa from Melaka, the Pope requested the saint's arm to be sent to Rome. According to the tale, when the limb was severed, blood flowed from the wound even

though St.Francis Xavier had been dead for 62 years. By the church tower, the statue of the saint is also armless for the same limb was broken off, not long after its erection, by a falling branch. Proof, say superstitious Melakans, of the saint's unearthly powers.

Opposite Porta de Santiago, is the **Independence Memorial Hall**, with displays and videos chronicling the nation's fight for freedom. Crowned with onion domes this colonial building was once the Malacca Club, where planters came to drink and play cards. The novelist Somerset Maugham stayed here and was told the true murder story of a wife and her lover who conspired to kill her husband which inspired him to write his short story *Footprints in the Jungle*. The club features prominently in his tale, as does Melaka which he calls Tanah Merah.

Carry on around Jalan Kota for the **Melaka Sultanate Palace**, a multi-gabled, wooden reconstruction of the famed 15th-century palace of Sultan Mansur Shah. It houses a cultural museum with dioramas depicting court life in the Malay kingdom's "Golden Age" and historical and cultural displays. The palace features beautiful wood carvings, and was built at immense cost, but it still isn't as splendid as the original which according to the Sejarah Melayu, had gilded beams, and a roof of copper and zinc shingles.

Past the palace, on the next corner is an interesting old Dutch cemetery with tombstones dating from the 17th century. Follow Jalan Mahkamah along the side of the cemetery into Jalan Gereja, then take the lane to Jalan Laksamana to view the twin-spired Saint Francis Xavier Church which was built in Gothic style in 1849.

Continue up this street to the busy crossroads which lead into Jalan Bunga Raya and Jalan Bendahara, the two main shopping streets. On this the corner are some interesting Indian shops selling spices, incense and colorful Hindu calendars and posters.

Cross the bridge over the Melaka River, into the labyrinthine lanes of old Chinatown. Directly after the bridge, turn left into Lorong Hang Jebat, a narrow thoroughfare flanked with pastel-colored, antique shophouses. Turn right into the Jalan Kampung Kuli, past the silversmiths' shops to Makam Hang Jebat, where a white-walled archway leads to the ancient tomb of Hang Jebat, one of the famous warriors of the 14th-century Melakan Sultanate.

Backtrack to Lorong Hang Jebat, then turn right into Jalan Tukang Besi

(Blacksmiths' Street) where smiths still pound away at metal heated over charcoal forges, and where tinsmiths beat out objects ranging from the religious to the mundane, from lanterns and altars to watering cans and bathtubs. At the next block this road becomes Jalan Tukang Emas (Goldsmiths' Street) and although the jewelers themselves have now moved elsewhere, family businesses still continue their age-old trades. To the left is the Sri Poyyatha Vinayagar Moorthi Temple, one of Malaysia's oldest Indian temples, built in 1781.

On the next corner, dominated by a pagoda-style minaret, is the Masjid Kampung Keling. Built in 1748, the mosque features a three-tiered, pyramid-shaped roof, and a majestic Victorian chandelier hangs from the ceiling of the white-tiled prayer hall. Melaka's Indian Muslim community, formerly known as Keling, who originated from the Coromandel coast, still frequent this mosque built by their trading ancestors in Dutch times.

This same road now becomes Jalan Tokong, where colorful shops sell religious paraphenalia, and craftsmen make fake videos and Mercedes out of paper to be burnt at Chinese funerals. On the left, an elaborate archway leads to the main courtyard of the Cheng Hoon Teng, the oldest Chinese temple in Malaysia founded in 1646 by a Chinese refugee fleeing the Manchus. Translated as the Abode of Green Merciful Clouds, the temple is primarily dedicated to Kwan Yin, the goddess of mercy, whose bronze image imported from India in the 19th century bears more than a passing resemblance to Queen Victoria.

Devotees light bunches of joss sticks and toss I-Ching fortune sticks in front of the main altar, and before the lesser ones of Kwan Ti, the god of wealth (the patron saint of tradesmen) and Machoe Poh, the queen of heaven (guardian of fishermen and travelers). Behind the main building are halls devoted to Confucious and other deities, and one houses carved ancestral tablets. The temple's massive tiled roof is elaborately decorated with porcelain figures from Chinese mythology, and there are beautiful carvings and giltwork in the halls.

Take the next turn right into Jalan Portugis, then right into Jalan Masjid for Kampung Hulu Mosque built in 1728 which features the pagoda-style minaret and pyramid roof which are a hallmark of Melaka's 18th-century mosques. Follow Jalan Kampung Hulu, turn left into Jalan Kubu—a

curving street lined with pastel-colored Chinese shophouses—and continue along here to Jalan Hang Jebat, also known by its former name of Jonkers Street. This is one of Melaka's most famous thoroughfares and has been a center for merchants since the town's beginning. The first historical sight on the left is the mausoleum of Hang Kasturi, one of the renowned warriors attached to the 15th-century court of Sultan Mansur Shah. He attained notoriety by having an affair with one of the sultan's concubines, and as a result was killed by the legendary Hang Tuah. Opposite, is the Hui Kuan, the Hokkien merchants' guild, which has beautiful stone carvings beside the entrance.

Antiques street

Further along are the antique shops which Jonkers Street is renowned for. Melaka's Indian Muslims still dominate the antique trade, carrying on in the tradition of the late T.J. Kutty, whose descendants still run his original 1930s business. Gone are the days when old wares could be bought for a song, but Melaka is still Malaysia's best venue for buying antiques. Straits Chinese Silver is best

Opposite: Shop columns painted in Chinese calligraphy are a common sight in Melaka's old Chinatown. **Below:** The proprietress of Fatimah's, an antique shop on Jonkers Street, with rows of charcoal-burning irons.

R. IAN LLOYD

at Tian Wah on neighboring Jalan Hang Kasturi. Klasik, an antique shop on the right, specializes in Nonyaware porcelain, reproduction blackwood chairs inlaid with mother-of-pearl, and red-and-gold Chinese furniture. Fatimah's, on the left, is good for old Dutch sideboards, gas lamps, blue-and-white ceramics and charcoal-burning irons. Wah Aik, a traditional cobbler, on the left, makes handmade shoes, including miniature replicas of those for Chinese bound feet.

After lunch, a well-known pork satay seller sets up beside the coffee shop on the corner of Jalan Hang Lekir, and down the bridge end at No.2 a tiny shop serves the most fragrant chicken rice in Melaka. One old *baba* townhouse on the right, has been converted into a restaurant, and although the prices are inflated, the interior decor is original, there are some beautiful gilded wood-carvings, and diners can lunch on marble-topped tables.

Just before the Melaka River bridge turn right into Jalan Tun Tan Cheng Lock, formerly Heeren Street, which means gentlemen's street in Dutch. However, before exploring this architecturally-renowned street make a detour down to the riverbank. Downstream, elegant Sumatran *perahus* still dock, and the far bank is lined with wooden barges that transport goods to the ships anchored offshore.

From the Heeren Street jetty, or from behind the tourist information center on the opposite bank, visitors can board boats for a 45-minute cruise of the Melaka River. The boats travel downstream past the *perahus* and the barges to the estuary, and then head upriver along the old canal flanked by hundred-year-old townhouses and warehouses to Kampung Morten, a picturesque Malay *kampung* where wooden boardwalks link the houses. A miniature lighthouse characterizes the beautiful old home of the late Haji Hashid which is now a private museum.

Heeren Street is where the rich *babas* built their townhouses, some of which date from

the 17th-century, although the most elaborate were built during the 19th and early-20th century. Once, only those lucky enough to know a *peranakan* family ever managed to visit one of these Melakan ancestral homes, but since William Chan opened his family residence, **The Baba Nonya Heritage** at No. 50, visitors can now enjoy an in depth tour of one of Melaka's most elaborate homes and get a unique insight into the *peranakan* lifestyle.

Built in what is known as Chinese Palladian style—a fusion of High Victorian,

R. IAN LLOYD

Chinese and tropical architecture—the 27-meter-long house (88ft) was built in 1896. A huge panelled screen, intricately carved and gilded in unusual two-tone gold leaf, separates the main hall from the *tiah gelap*, the room where unmarried maidens could peer out at male guests. Archways carved with dragons, phoenix birds, and flowers decorate the formal rooms where portraits of ancestors peer from their gilded frames at opulent marble tables, blackwood furniture inlaid with marble and mother of pearl, and priceless antiques. A magnificent teakwood staircase winds upstairs to the flamboyantly-decorated bedrooms and downstairs is an original 19th-century kitchen.

Further down Jalan Tun Tan Cheng Lock, set back from the road on the left, is the Chee Mansion crowned by a tower on the roof that for many years was the highest structure in Chinatown, and was also used as a navigational aid for sailors on the Melaka Straits. An eccentric blend of Dutch, Portuguese, Chinese and English styles, the house was built by a Eurasian architect in 1919 for the wealthy Chee family whose fortunes were made from rubber and banking, and whose descendants still live in the house today.

Walk back to the bridge, then follow Jalan Laksamana, past the Indian shops selling Javanese batiks and prayer rugs, and the bookshops selling English-language books. At the next intersection turn right into Jalan

Temenggong. Two blocks along here, past some excellent coffee shops which specialize in Indian *roti canai* and *murtabah*, is the Melaka Sikh Temple which has a prayer hall with an arched verandah and a decorative front entrance.

Continue to busy Jalan Munshi Abdullah and the hill directly in front is Bukit Cina, the huge Chinese graveyard hill, reputed to contain at least 12,500 tombs, some dating back to the 15th century. To the left, at the base of the hill beside Jalan Puteri Hang Lih Po, is the Chinese temple of Sam Po Kong. Set around a white-washed courtyard, the temple is dedicated to Cheng Ho, the famous Muslim Admiral of the Chinese Fleet who sailed to Melaka in the 15th century.

Adjacent to the temple is the Perigi Raja, the well of the Princess Hang Lih Po, who returned to Melaka with the famous admiral in 1459 to become one of the wives of Sultan Mansur Shah. Apparently, she and her 500 handmaidens lived near here at the base of Bukit Cina which is the largest and oldest Chinese graveyard outside of China.

Starting from just along Jalan Puteri Hang Lih Po, a good jogging trail winds up and around the hill for about 3km (1.9mi) and passes some ancient graves dating from the Ming Dynasty (14th to 17th century), and some huge horseshoe-shaped tombs of the Kapitan Cina who were the heads of the Chinese community during colonial times.

Two 15th-century Malay Chieftains are buried on Bukit Tempurong Plain, and some old *keramat*—sacred Muslim graves—are found on the northeast foot of the hill. From the top of the hill, the panorama sweeps from the green paddy fields beyond the town, past the hilltop St.John's Fort, out across the straits to Pulau Besar and other offshore isles, and then back to the patchwork of red-tiled roofs of old Chinatown and the highrises of Melaka's new commercial district.

Return to Jalan Munshi Abdullah, and turn right into Jalan Bendahara. Two blocks up on the right, with a distinctive Iberian facade, is St. Peter's Church, which was built in 1710. Malaysia's oldest-functioning Catholic church is the traditional place of worship for Melaka's Portuguese-Eurasians, who trace their roots back to the 16th-century Portuguese conquest. The first Augustinian fathers arrived in 1587 and their traditions are still upheld, especially at Easter when the mass culminates in a candlelit procession when a statue of Christ is borne aloft around

Opposite, left: Gilded "ancestor" tablets at the Cheng Hoon Teng Temple, Malaysia's oldest Chinese temple.Opposite, right: Wooden clogs known as terompah, *because of the sound they make when walking on hard surfaces, are a common sight in Chinatown's sundry shops. **Below:** Melaka's Portuguese Eurasians gather at St. Peter's for an Easter procession.*

R. IAN LLOYD

AROUND MELAKA

Warrior Tombs and other Straits Sights

On the outskirts of Melaka town and around the compact state are many historical sights, and some of Malaysia's oldest and most picturesque kampungs, with traditional wooden houses with their distinctive high-pitched roofs and tiled staircases.

Some attractions, like the Portuguese Settlement, St.John's Fort, Tranquerah Mosque, and the new State Mosque, are a short trishaw ride from downtown. While the sights further afield are accessible by both taxi and bus, it is best to rent a car for a day to explore the scenic countryside.

North along the straits

Heading west from the Melaka River bridge, follow Jalan Tun Tan Cheng Lock which becomes Jalan Tengkera, and continue along the seafront of the Melaka Straits to Masjid Tranquerah. This beautiful mosque built in 1728 features the distinctive Melaka-style, pagoda-shaped minaret and a Javanese-style tiered roof. In the grounds is the grave of Sultan Hussein Shah of Johor who ceded Singapore to Raffles in 1819.

After the mosque, this road becomes Jalan Klebang, where many rich *baba* families built mansions during the turn-of-the-century rubber boom. Set in spacious seaside lawns, some of these stuccoed residences with their shuttered windows and arched foyers, are still in pristine condition; others are dilapitated haunted houses, and a few have been revamped into restaurants and hotels.

At **Klebang Besar**, about 8km (5mi) from town, the Malay foodstalls perched on the sandy beachfront are a great place to watch the sunset and dine on satay and baked fish. Turn left at the Tanjung Kling Mosque with its unusual octagonal minaret, and just down this road on the right is the presumed tomb of Hang Tuah, the greatest warrior of the 15th-century Melakan Sultanate. Many historians dispute the State Government's claims that this is the legendary grave, but there is no doubt of its antiquity and many superstitious Chinese come here to get divine inspiration for lucky lottery numbers.

From the grave, follow the road around to **Pantai Kundor**, a traditional Malay fishing village overlooking a sandy beach. Further north, after Masjid Tanah, turn left for the best swimming on the coast at Tanjung

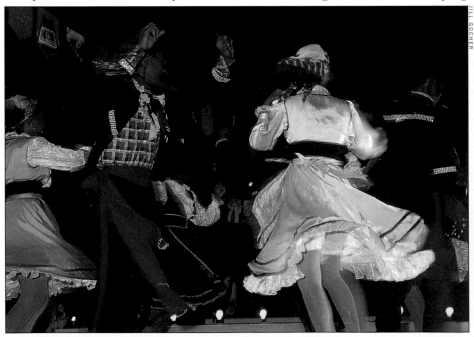
JILL GOCHER

Bidara—a long sandy beach where the calm waters are studded with granite boulders.

Heading southeast from Melaka town, follow Jalan Parameswara, turn left into Jalan Bukit Senjuang, and then take the sharp right turn up the hill to the 18th-century St.John's Fort, 3km (1.9mi) from town. From the white-walled Dutch fort there are panoramic views of the surrounding countryside. According to legend, an underground tunnel runs from here to Porta de Santiago at the foot of St. Paul's Hill. Apparently the entrance was bricked over centuries ago and its location remains a mystery to this day.

European heritage preserved

Return to Jalan Parameswara and turn off at Jalan d'Albuquerque for the **Portuguese Settlement**, home of the Eurasian descendants of the Portuguese who conquered Melaka in the 16th century. It looks similar to any Malay village, but the streets bear names like Texeira and Sequiera, and some of the population look decidedly Iberian. Cristao, an ancient Portuguese tongue, is still spoken here, and some old cultural dances and traditions are still carried on.

At the Portuguese Square visitors can watch cultural performances on Saturday nights, and the surrounding restaurants serve up spicy Portuguese-style cuisine. At Easter and Christmas, families celebrate in "open house" style and visitors are welcome to join in. During the Feast of St. Peter's on the 29th June, fishermen decorate their boats which are blessed for the coming year.

Traditional kampungs flank the road south to Muar. At Umbai, 13km (8mi) from Melaka, turn right to the jetty at Pengkalan Pernu, where boats ply across the straits to **Pulau Besar**, "the big island," which has clean sandy beaches, good for swimming, and a luxury resort.

Further south, at Serkam, turn right to Makam Tun Teja, the mausoleum of the heroine Tun Teja, the beloved consort of Sultan Mahmud Shah, who died here in 1510 while fleeing the Portuguese invasion. The white-washed mausoleum is surrounded by rice paddies where women still use traditional curved knives to harvest the rice.

A formidable dwelling

Just past Merlimau, 23km (14mi) from Melaka, turn right to the **Penghulu's House**, the prettiest traditional house in Malaysia. This beautifully-ornamented home was built by Malay carpenters in 1894, and

features a colorful staircase of art nouveau tiles, fine wood carvings, a central courtyard, a decorated pillar known as a *tiang seri*, and an original interior. The descendants of the Penghulu—the chieftain of Merlimau—still live in the house and visitors are welcome, as are donations which help with the upkeep.

Modern tourist attractions

For sights north of Melaka, follow the signs for Kuala Lumpur. At Pringgit, view the fantastic **State Mosque**, built in traditional Melakan style but in extremely grand porportion. Continue to Ayer Keroh, 10km (6mi) from town, where Melaka's newest attractions are all located within a short distance of each other. **Mini Malaysia** has full-size replicas of all the 13 states' different traditional houses. Nearby is the Melaka Zoo; the Hutan Rekreasi, a forest recreation park with shaded jogging trails; a golf course and two resort-style hotels. Other attractions include a crocodile farm, a snake farm, a butterfly farm and a Chinese theme village.

Opposite: Skirts swirl at the Portuguese Square every Saturday night when the local residents hold a cultural show featuring Portuguese dances. ***Above:*** *A descendant of the famous* penghulu, *or chieftain, who built this renowned home at Merlimau, rests on the art nouveau tiled steps which lead to the* serambi *or verandah.*

NEGERI SEMBILAN

Wooden Palaces and Living Stones

Settled since the 16th century by Minangkabau settlers from the Sumatran highlands, the mountainous state of Negeri Sembilan located south of Selangor, north of Melaka, and east of Pahang, is often overlooked by travelers en route to either Melaka or Kuala Lumpur, especially since the construction of the North South expressway which bypasses all the state's major towns.

Seremban, the state capital, 64km (40mi) south of Kuala Lumpur, grew up around the same time as the latter, but always suffered by comparison. Just over a century ago it was a mainly Chinese town which served the local tin-mining industry, and was only accessible by boat up the tortuous, winding, Sungai Linggi river, an 18-hour journey from the coast. Towards the end of the century, however, it was linked by rail and road and consequently became the colonial capital. A num-

ber of important government buildings were constructed, some of which still survive today. The newer industrial areas, built in the last decade, have sprouted in satellite towns away from downtown, and as a result, the heart of old Seremban still retains much of its old charm.

The English always practised the "divide and rule" policy of keeping the Asian and European sections of town separate, and the layout of Seremban town still basically follows the old pattern. In the commercial end of town—the original Chinatown—in the grid of streets between Jalan Tuanku Munawar and Jalan Yam Tuan, many turn-of-the-century shophouses built in the Southern Chinese style still survive, jammed between newer concrete additions that sadly lack the architectural details of their predecessors.

All the government buildings—both old and new—are on the higher ground to the east of Chinatown. Beside the Gothic-inspired, Catholic Church (Gereja Katolik) on Jalan Yam Tuan, walk east to Jalan Dato' Abdul Kadir and to the concrete bunker-like State Secretariat on the corner of Jalan Bukit. In direct contrast is the adjoining State Legislature Building, also built in contemporary style but featuring elegant Minangkabau roofs with their sweeping curves and upturned eaves. Across the road is its predecessor built in 1912, a marvellous neo-classical building withcolumns and archways which is now the State Library.

Follow Jalan Dato Hamzah, which overlooks the attractive Lake Gardens, or Taman Tasek. Shaded parklands, popular with picnickers and joggers surround around a man-made lake. At the park's pavilion, music and cultural shows are staged on the weekends. Opposite the Lake Gardens are more colonial buildings, built in the same style as the State Library, which now house the District Land Office. Further down the road is the Masjid Negeri, or State Mosque, which has an unusual scalloped roof supported on nine pillars, which represent the original nine territories of Negeri Sembilan.

Minangkabau palaces

Rather inconveniently sited, but worth a visit nonetheless is the **State Museum** (Muzium Negeri) and Cultural Park (Taman Seni Budaya) located 2km (1.2mi) west of town along the link road to the North South Expressway. The Cultural Handicraft Center, built after the fashion of a wooden Minangkabau palace, displays handicrafts and historical artifacts, but the most interesting part of the complex are the Istana Ampang Tinggi and the Rumah Minangkabau, two original Minangkabau style houses.

Built in 1861, the former is now the State Museum. The superior, rainforest hardwood is stained with *damar minyak* which repels termites, and the roof is of thatched *atap*. The house was originally an upriver royal residence and was moved to downtown Seremban in 1953 where it served as the museum. It was recently relocated to the Cultural Park.

Of the same style, but of more elegant proportions, the **Rumah Minangkabau** is a beautiful example of 19th-century Malay craftmanship and could well have been the palace which Victorian author Isabella Bird visited in 1879 at nearby Mambau. She "thoroughly liked his house (...) There was a rich, dim light in the room, which was cool and wainscoted entirely with dark red wood."

The extremely low doors built into chiefs' houses are believed to have been designed that way so that the respectful visitor always has to bow when entering. Beautiful wood carvings of verses from the Koran adorn the interior panels, and the entrance stairs are also carved. The two-tiered roof with its curved ridge, characteristic of Minangkabau houses, is made from hand-cut wooden shingles. The Rumah Minangkabau was dismantled from its original site at Mambau in 1924

and shipped to England where it was part of the Malaya display at the Royal Wembley Exhibition. Later it was relocated at its present site.

Sri Menanti, the royal capital, 33km (20mi) east of Seremban, is reached by following Jalan Zaaba through town and then turning off on the road to Kuala Pilah. This route follows Malay kampungs and then winds up through the scenic Bukit Putus pass, site of an 1875 skirmish when the local Malays rebelled against the British and stockaded the pass. However, a force comprising the Royal Artillery and the Ghurkas eventually drove out the defenders.

Just over the crest of the hill is Hutan Rekreasi Ulu Bendol, a picturesque forest park where the Bendol River cascades over smooth granite boulders, and trails weave through the rainforest. From here the road winds down to the vale of Terachi. Shaded by fruit trees, and adorned with trailing bougainvilleas, traditional Minangkabau houses decorate this attractive kampung. Opposite the police station, is an unusual 70-year-old coconut palm with a corkscrew trunk

Opposite: The colonial grandeur of Seremban's imposing State Library. Below: Minangkabau memorabilia like this antique gong, are on display at the Istana Ampang Tinggi, the 100-year-old wooden palace in the grounds of Seremban's cultural center.

which apparently bears extra-sweet fruit.

At Terachi, turn right for Sri Menanti and follow the road through picturesque kampung to the seat of the Negeri Sembilan royal family whose Sumatran ancestors first settled here four centuries ago. The opulent Istana Besar built in the 1930s, with an azure-colored tiled roof, is the home of the current Yang di-Pertuan Besar.

The nearby **Istana Lama**, the old palace, and the general appearance of Sri Menanti's sleepy town has changed little since it was described by Cuthbert Woodville Harrison in his *Illustrated Guide to the Federated Malay State* (1923). "The palace itself is built entirely of dark red wood in Malay style, the two ends raking skywards to flamboyant gables. Set against the background of dark green hills with a broad lawn in front it is the fitting culmination of the Sri Menanti valley and its dozens of little Malay houses, any one of which might serve as model for the Astana itself." The Istana Lama is beautifully decorated with wood carvings and apparently the 99 supporting pillars represent the 99 warriors of the different clans. There are plans to turn the old palace, built in 1902, into a museum.

East then south

Kuala Pilah, further east, the largest town in the region, is a good place to taste typical Minangkabau cuisine. Specialities include beef *rendang*, a dry, coriander-flavored curry, and chicken and vegetables cooked in coconut cream with firey *cili padi* (bird's eye chillies).

North of downtown on Jalan Bahau is an interesting old archway with a roof of Chinese design which was built by the local Chinese in 1905, in honor of Martin Lister, Kuala Pilah's first British Resident. Directly opposite is the old Sim Tong Temple which has an elaborately-decorated roof ridge, featuring dragons and other Chinese symbolism, and inside are some priceless wood carvings

imported from China at the turn of the century.

Port Dickson, Negeri Sembilan's well-known beach region, is 29km (18mi) southwest of Seremban. Take Jalan Rasah out of town, past Rasah and Mambau to Lukut, where a 1km (0.6mi) detour around the back of town leads to Kota Lukut, a hilltop fort. Overlooking the Lukut River, it was built in 1847 by Raja Juma'at. Substantial stone walls made with laterite (a soft red stone which turns hard when exposed to the elements) still remain, and moats and the foundations of

buildings inside the fort complex can still be seen, remnants of those fighting days when the Bugis from Selangor and the local Minangkabau vied for control of the lucrative tin trade.

Port Dickson itself, 8km (5mi) south of Lukut, is a large port town with oil refineries which offers little of interest to visitors. Take the town bypass to the southern beaches which are extremely popular with both locals and citysiders from Kuala Lumpur who flock here every weekend and public holidays. Although not in the same class as east coast beaches, the 18km (11mi) stretch of sandy coastline offers a diversion from the inland and is good for windsurfing and canoeing.

Athough many local people swim here, the southern Melaka Straits are quite polluted and the hotel swimming pools are probably a safer bet. Along the popular beach fronts at Pantai Bagan Pinang and Teluk Kemang are hotels, resorts, and plenty of restaurants and foodstalls well-known for their inexpensive seafood.

At the southern end of the beach stretch, 16km (10mi) from Port Dickson, turn off for **Blue Lagoon**, a resort bay, and Tanjung Tuan (Cape Rachado) where an old colonial lighthouse overlooks a rainforested promontory with expansive views across the Straits of Melaka. On extra clear days, the swampy Sumatran coast can apparently be spied across the water. Visitors here are beseiged by cheeky monkeys, who raid picnic baskets and crawl over cars. The promontory is also a popular stopover for migratory birds and during September/October and March/April there are large concentrations of hawks and eagles. Further south at Pasir Panjang there are camping and picnic grounds set in a forest recreation park which overlooks the Straits of Melaka.

A tomb and stones which grow

At **Pengkalan Kempas**, further west on the road to Linggi is the 15th-century tomb of Sheikh Ahmad Majnun Shah, a holy man who rebelled against Melaka's Sultan Mansur Shah. An inscribed pillar by the grave gives two contradictory descriptions of the Sheikh; the inscription in Jawi says he was a saintly religious man, while the other in Sumatran Kawi script claims he was a traitor. Legend has it that the circular hole, 11.5cm (4.5in) in diameter, below the inscriptions, was used to test oaths, and that it would apparently tighten around a victim's arm if he was lying.

Of much greater antiquity than the tomb, and even more mysterious, are the three adjacent carved megaliths which date to around the 2nd century, and stand about 2m (6.5ft) high. They are called "the spoon", "the sword" and the "the rudder" because of their respective shapes and the latter has curlicue floral carvings. No in-depth archaeological study has been undertaken on the stones

which obviously date from the pre-Islamic era. The Sheikh's grave was obviously sited here because it was already considered a sacred place.

Megalithic stones, known locally as *batu hidup*, "living stones," are found in many sites around Negeri Sembilan and in northeast Melaka. Some villages believe that these stones grow—hence the name—while others maintain that they were merely gravestones. Though not as celebrated as the Pengkalan Kempas collection, other such stones are found at Tampin near the Melaka border.

Negeri Sembilan's other attractions on the main highway south, include the **hot springs** at Pedas, 20km (15mi) from Seremban on the main highway south, and the picturesque Minangkabau houses at the next towns of Rembau and Kota.

For travelers with their own transport there is delightful drive north along the Kuala Lumpur road to Setul, then turn off for Ulu Beranang and Broga, a picturesque kampung region with some old wooden mosques and scenic villages against a backdrop of the mighty hills of the main range.

Above, left: *Curved roof ridges and long shuttered windows are features of rural Minangkabau houses like this one at Terachi.*
Above, right: *These mysterious carved megaliths are found beside an ancient grave at Pengkalan Kempas.*

PART VIII

Introducing Johor

Johor, the most southerly state on the peninsula, is also one of the most developed, with vast oil-palm plantations and a fast-growing industrial sector. Nevertheless there are still picturesque kampungs from Muar to Pontian on the Melaka Straits, some beautiful forest reserves, offshore islands, historic ruins as well as the bustling capital of Johor Bahru with its royal palace brimming with antiques.

Chinese traders in the 9th century spoke of a legendary kingdom known as Lo Yueh "a place where traders passing back and forth meet." Historians speculate that it was located in Johor but there is no tangible evidence. Johor's history really begins when Sultan Mahmud Syah of Melaka fled from the Portuguese in 1511 and set up his court on Bintan Island in the Riau-Lingga archipelago.

Following his death, his son, Sultan Alauddin Riayat Syah, moved his royal base to Pekan Tua, close to today's Kota Tinggi, and established the kingdom of Johor which quickly became the dominant Malay power on the peninsula. The courtly traditions of Melaka were faithfully adhered to and the Johor royal court set the standards by which all other peninsular kingdoms were judged.

During the 16th century Johor suffered numerous raids by the Portuguese and the Acehnese from Sumatra, and when the Dutch first appeared in the early 17th century, Johor saw them as an ally. Consequently when the Dutch attacked Melaka the armies of Johor provided assistance. After the successful conquest, the Dutch governor of Batavia acknowledged that "without their help we would never have become master of that strong place."

Johor was still a power to be reckoned with in the late-17th century due mainly to the skills of the powerful Laksamana, who commanded the allegiance of the Orang Laut, or Sea People. But times were changing. After Sultan Ibrahim's suspiciously early death, the Laksamana family were driven out and the Orang Laut reverted to piracy, which threatened Johor's trade. In 1699, believing that Johor's decline was due to the weak rule and atrocities of the sadistic Sultan Mahmud, the nobles of the court had him murdered. This act changed the course of Malay history for according to tradition, only God could punish a ruler, especially those of "white blood" descended from the Melaka line. Sultan Mahmud had no heirs, and in the words of a Thai chronicle, "his lineage disappeared and was never heard of again."

The enormous scale of *derhaka*, or treason, within the palace worked to the advantage of the powerful Bugis. After fleeing civil wars in Sulawesi and setting up bases in Selangor they began infiltrating the Johor court, then being run by the unpopular Bendahara family that had conspired to kill Sultan Mahmud. They were so successful that Bugis underkings effectively ruled Johor for most of the 18th century.

In 1819, the factionalized court worked to Stamford Raffles' advantage, when, by playing one group off against the other, he acquired the island of Singapore. By the end of the 19th century, the Temenggung line finally ousted the Bendahara family and established the dynasty which still runs Johor today. Most notable was "the father of modern Johor" Temenggung Abu Bakar who later took the title of Sultan. He wisely introduced a constitution prohibiting his state from aligning with European powers, but his son Ibrahim ruled at the zenith of British power and was finally persuaded of their right to rule. Ironically Sultan Ibrahim remained in power long enough to see the situation reversed in 1957 when Malaya achieved independence.

Overleaf: *Crystal furniture and priceless antiques on display at the Istana Besar, the royal palace in Johor Bahru.* **Opposite:** *Malay girls wearing the traditional long blouse, known as* baju kurung Johor. *Photos by R. Ian Lloyd*

JOHOR BAHRU

Where Mainland Asia Ends

Just across the narrow straits which mark the border of Singapore and Malaysia, Johor Bahru has always suffered in comparison to its fast-paced and sophisticated neighbor in the south. Formerly used an entry and exit point, today Malaysia's most southerly capital is experiencing a boom. Attracted by the stable political situation and low wages, investors are pouring into the state and Singaporeans flock here on the weekends to take advantage of their stronger dollar, cheap markets, low-priced seafood, and the thriving, underground nightlife.

Despite, Johor Bahru's new image, the town still has a relaxed ambiance which is distinctly refreshing for visitors eager to escape the sterility and organization of Singapore. Local wags say that their more repressed southern neighbors come here to let loose—as soon as they cross the border,

smokers head for restaurants where they can puff away uninhibited, food freaks can enjoy the proliferation of cheap outdoor eating, and gum-chewers can chomp legally.

Once known as Tanjung Puteri, Johor Bahru means "New Johor," and was the creation of Sultan Abu Bakar, who moved his capital here in 1866. This southern gateway still bears his stamp: many of the town's historic buildings were built during Abu Bakar's reign. Most of Johor Bahru's 750,000 inhabitants live in sprawling outer suburbs but the town's commercial hub is in the grid of streets north of the causeway where quaint old shophouses are rapidly giving way to high-rises.

Most parts Johor Bahru worth visiting are along the road facing the straits. Address confusion can easily happen along here: the road changes names four times along its length. Although the town's sights are somewhat spread out it is a pleasant stroll from one to the other as a shaded promenade runs the entire length of the seashore road which begins as Jalan Ibrahim at the causeway which links the two nations.

Officially declared open in 1924, the causeway has always been a vital link to Singapore carrying road and rail traffic, gas and water. A section was blown up by the British during World War II in an attempt to stop the Japanese invading, but it proved a futile excercise. Less than a month later the

Japanese repaired it and took possession of Singapore Island.

At the general post office, take a detour up the steep road on the right to the imposing, Sultan Ibrahim Building, which houses the state government offices. Known as "the fort", because of its massive, 65m (213ft) granite tower, it is a dominant feature of Johor Bahru's skyline. Built in the early 1940s, the offices are a mixture of Saracenic and art deco styles, and display fine stone-carvings and mosaic work. Further along Jalan Ibrahim, past the 19th-century courthouse, is the Istana Besar with a brilliant blue roof of glazed tiles.

The Royal Palace was built by Sultan Abu Bakar in 1866 and was recently renovated as the Muzium Di Raja (**Royal Museum**) housing the incredible antique and heirloom collection of the royal family of Johor which was mainly collected by the anglophile Sultan Abu Bakar and his son Ibrahim on their many European jaunts. Despite the fact that Abu Bakar was regarded as being a very "British" Malay—he played cricket and would quote Tennyson—he was a shrewd ruler, who although on intimate terms with the British royal family, staunchly resisted English intervention in Johor.

The opulent palace is still much the same as described by a grandchild of Queen Victoria: "The interior is lined with white marble,and arranged in a sort of Moorish fashion (...) everything combines to give an air of magnificence, and comfort." The Royal Museum is filled with priceless antiques and exceptional features include the crystal furniture in the Reception Room, the golden thrones in the Throne Room and the Hunting Room adorned with stuffed trophies of Johor's once prolific wildlife. Istana Besar is surrounded by beautifully-landscaped lawns and gardens which are open to the public. There's a children's playground, an orchid garden, and and a Japanese tea-house, presented to Sultan Ibrahim by the crown prince of Japan in 1939.

Further west, on a hill overlooking the seafront, is the Sultan Abu Bakar Mosque, built in 1900 at a cost of $400,000. Four octagonal minarets with fan-shaped stained-glass windows surmount the prayer hall of Johor's largest mosque. Around the circular driveway, hawkers lay out colorful prayer rugs from Turkey to tempt the devout, and tourists looking for souvenirs. Opposite, on Jalan Gertak Merah is the Johor Zoo, which is popular with children. Below the mosque is the

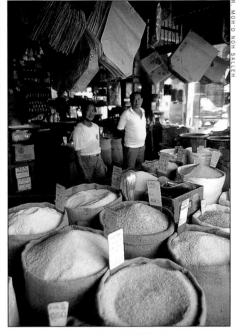

Islamic Center, built in Middle-Eastern style, and nearby is Tepian Tebrau, an open-air food center, renowned for its cheap seafood.

Past the hospital, turn right for MAWAR, a complex with a government-run Kraftangan (handicrafts) shop where craftsmen give demonstrations, it also has a restaurant and tea terrace. Opposite, is the JARO workshop, a rehabilitation center well-known for its leather bookbinding, basketware, and other crafts made by the handicapped.

Further around the seafront, overlooking the straits from its commanding hilltop situation is the Istana Bukit Serene, the home of the Sultan of Johor. Other places of note around town include the Arulmigu Rajamariamman Devassthanam Temple, Johor state's largest Hindu temple, which has a tiered entrance arch bedecked with statues of gods and goddesses. The temple is right in the heart of downtown, opposite the new Kota Raya Plaza hotel and shopping complex on Jalan Ungku Puan. Behind town on Jalan Mahmoodiah is the Royal Mausoleum in a beautifully-maintained Muslim graveyard shaded by fragrant frangipani trees.

Opposite: Crammed with Singaporeans returning from a weekend in Malaysia, the Causeway, which links Johor Bahru with the island republic also carries vital supplies of gas and water. Above: Different types of rice on sale at a Johor Bahru dry-goods store.

SOUTH OF MUAR

Through West Johor's Scenic Village

Stretching from the old port town of Muar in the northwest corner of Johor state, to the tip of mainland Asia at Tanjung Piai, the 200-km (124mi) coastal road traverses some of the prettiest rural villages in Malaysia. Muar, also called Bandar Maharani, sprawls along the banks of the Muar River. Sumatran *perahus* still dock at the town jetty and boatmen can often be seen hoisting their mighty canvas sails at the rivermouth.

Muar is mentioned in the 16th-century *Malay Annals*, as the founder of Melaka had considered the port for his capital, but later opted for Melaka as its prominent hill made for better defence. Muar is considered as the heartland of Johor culture, and the dialect is considered the purest Malay on the peninsula. Both men and women wear the distinctive, collarless Johor-style *baju* shirt and the region is famous for its *ghazal* music which

originated from Arabia.

Downtown Muar, dominated by 19th-century shophouses, is very much a Chinese town at its heart. Coffee shops still have marble-topped tables and bentwood chairs, and there are many interesting dry-goods shops and old-style businesses. South of the commercial center, overlooking the river, is Bangunan Sultan Abu Bakar, an elegant, neo-classical government building which dates from the turn of the century, when its royal namesake revitalized Muar's architecture. Nearby, the courthouse, police station, customs house and high school all date from this same era. South, along the riverbank parklands shaded by ancient raintrees, is the stylish Masjid Jamek built by Sultan Ibrahim. From here, a walkway leads to Tanjung, the riverside park which has picnic tables and food stalls selling local specialities.

Magical Mount Ophir

North of Muar, take a detour to the legendary Gunung Ledang, called Mount Ophir by the British. In the 15th century, Melaka's Sultan Mansur Shah wished to marry the beautiful Princess of Gunung Ledang. Her dowry list of trays of mosquito's hearts and a vat of tears didn't perturb him, but he withdrew his marital offer when she requested a cup of his son's blood.

The waterfalls of the 1,276m (4,186ft), the cloud-wreathed mountain make it a favorite

R IAN LLOYD

venue for weekend climbers and picnickers. It is also where local *bomoh* shamen are reputed to go for their esoteric training and to commune with the same fairy princess that had bewitched Sultan Mansur. To get to the mountain take the road from Muar to Tangkak and 11km (7mi) north of here, on the road to Segamat, turn off at Sagil for the waterfall and the start of the summit trail.

South of Muar, the road to Batu Pahat, 50km (31mi) south, winds through some delightful kampung regions, famous for their

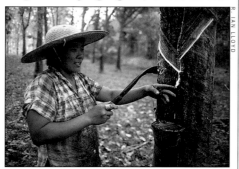

tropical fruits such as *duku*, rambutan, and durian, and during the fruiting season the roadsides are flanked by fruit stalls. Traditional Muar-style wooden houses, with long shuttered windows and covered porticos, painted in pastel shades and surrounded by palms and fruit trees, line the sides of the road. At Parit Pecah, 18km (11mi) south of Muar, there is a unique Bugis house with a high pitched roof of wooden shingles. This 100-year-old house is the only surviving one of its kind in Malaysia. The region, south of here to Batu Pahat, is famous for its numerous *bomoh*, and patients come from all over the country and Singapore to seek cures from these traditional medicine men.

Batu Pahat, surrounded by characterless suburbs crammed with electronics and textile factories, looks a thoroughly uninteresting town. But it's well-known for its cheap and excellent Chinese and Malay food, and the old downtown area is worth a visit. Sailing boats from Sumatra still dock along the riverfront, and the market area has many old shophouses decorated with plaster curlicues and circular columns displaying Chinese calligraphy, where blacksmiths, tin-smiths and basket-makers still work

Seafood at Asia's tip

Travelers enroute to Johor Bahru, can either turn here for Ayer Hitam and take the main highway south, or they can opt for the longer,

but more interesting Route 5 along the coast. Leaving Batu Pahat, this road winds through hilly country, past vegetable farms and market gardens down to the flat coastal plain criss-crossed by canals. Along this scenic road, villagers shell coconuts and dry cocoa on mats, and the tidal canals are filled with wooden fishing boats.

At Benut, 50km (31mi) south of Batu Pahat, there is an early 20th-century mosque, and 24km (15mi) further on at Pontian there is a tree-lined seafront drive with good food-stalls and a view of the wooded offshore isle of Pulau Pisang.

It is 59km (37mi) from Pontian to Johor Bahru, but the coastal road continues to Kukup, a renowned seafood haunt, 19km (12mi) south. The entire town is perched on stilts above the mangroves and the buildings are connected by boardwalks. Chilli crabs, baked fish, garlic prawns, and a variety of other culinary pleasures are served at any of a dozen seafood restaurants. Tour boats depart from the jetty for the floating fish farms and to Pulau Kukup, a nearby mangrove island.

To get to Tanjung Piai, the tip of mainland Asia, follow the road to Serkat, turn right at the mosque and then follow the signs to the end of the road. Two wooden jetties lead to a couple of small restaurants set high above the straits. Across the pearly waters is a horizon full of Singapore-bound shipping and in the distance are the jagged outlines of the island republic's towering downtown skyline. The menu board at Restoran Atan says it all: "Southernmost of Asia is at Our Feet."

Opposite: Heading back to the depot through an avenue of rubber tress, a tapper shoulders buckets of latex collected from this estate near Batu Pahat. *Above, left:* Trees must be tapped in the cool early morning when the latex flows best. *Above, right:* Floral decorations adorn the minaret of the Benut Mosque.

EAST JOHOR

Ancient Forts and Beach Resorts

The importance of rivers as the major transport arteries of the past can be seen by the number of peninsular states that were named after their principal rivers, Johor being one of them. The Sungai Johor, which begins in the hills west of Kota Tinggi, is not the state's biggest river but it has figured in Johor's history since the very beginning. Along its banks the early sultanate built capitals and forts, and some of the region's most historic events took place here.

Gruesome beginnings

Kota Tinggi, the gateway to East Johor, 40km (25mi) north of Johor Bahru was probably the location of Pekan Tua, the royal capital established by the Melakan sultanate after they were ousted by the Portuguese. A jumble of wooden and concrete shophouses, the town is typical of rural Johor.

In the surrounding kampungs, there are a number of famous graves including the mausoleum of Sultan Mahmud, the last "white blood" sultan of the Melaka line, who was murdered by his nobles in 1699.

According to Malay history, a nobleman, Megat Sri Rama delivered the fatal blow. He would seem to have had good reason: his pregnant wife had been disembowelled on the sultan's orders. But because this was an act of *derhaka*, or treason, he suffered for years from a wound made by the dying sultan's sword, and legend has it that his descendants never set foot in Kota Tinggi for fear of Sultan Mahmud's revengeful ghost.

Located at Kampung Makam, just north of town, this yellow-canopied tomb is still a pilgrimage site for many Malays. The regicide was a momentous event in Malay history: not only because only God can punish a sultan, but because he had no heir, and his ancient lineage died with him.

Back along the road are more historical tombs including that of Bendahara Tun Habib, whose descendants founded the current royal families of Johor, Terengganu and Pahang states.

A crowd-pulling cascade

Kota Tinggi's biggest attraction is the **Lombong Waterfall** (Air Terjun Lombong) which is located 14km (9mi) northwest. During the rainy season the 37-m (121 ft) high falls are thunderous and the surrounding rainforest is covered with misty spray. The swimming pools at the base are cool and refreshing and there's a restaurant and overnight chalets scattered amongst the rainforest. Throughout the week it is very peaceful, but on weekends it becomes inundated with local tourists.

North of Kota Tinggi, turn off to Desaru, a popular beach resort 54km (35mi) to the east along a highway through huge oil-palm plantations. About halfway along, turn off to Teluk Sengat, then follow the signs 8km (5mi) to Johor Lama, for the ruins of Kota Batu, or Stone Fort, that the Portuguese wrested from the Malays in 1587.

The national museum cleared away the undergrowth in 1960, and a rectangular area with earth ramparts and some original blocks of stone are still visible. Much of the fort, which commands a superb position overlooking the broad Johor river, is still covered in thick bamboo.

Built by Sultan Alauddin Riyat Shah in 1540, the fort was defended by 8,000 Malay

R. MOH'D NOH SALLEH

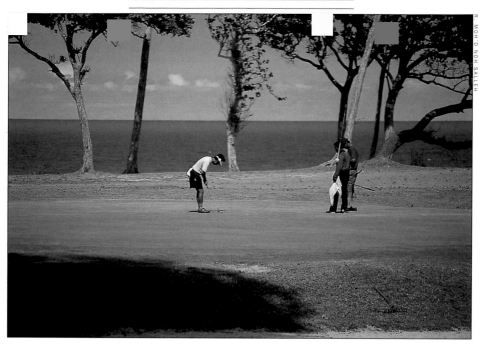

and Orang Laut (Sea Tribe) warriors who resisted the first Portuguese attacks. But, when the enemy gathered reinforcements and renewed their onslaught two weeks later, Johor Lama was overtaken.

Portuguese historians claim the conquistadores made off with a fortune in gold, hastily buried by the departing Malays, and spoils included 2,000 sailing boats and 2,500 guns and muskets. Boats often make the trip to the fort's jetty from the opposite bank of the Johor river at Kong Kong, 35km (22mi) east of Johor Bahru.

From the fort, continue past the durian trees, and the little wooden houses to sleepy Kampung Johor Lama on the riverside. Beneath a forest of coconut palms there's a mosque with a wooden minaret, some colorfully-painted houses, and a long jetty where fishermen spread their nets to dry and boys splash about in inflated inner tubes. Many of the inhabitants here are descendants of the Orang Laut, the original navy of the early Johor sultans.

Desaru, Johor's most popular beach resort, is 11km (7mi) east of the turnoff on Route 92. The golden-sand beach is flanked by trees, which give rise to its name "place of casuarinas." The clear, blue waters are excellent for swimming and windsurfing, and are by far the best beaches within a two hour drive from Singapore. There are a couple of big resort hotels, and an exclusive golf course which faces the South China Sea and has the rainforest behind.

The deep southeast

Continue south 28km (17mi) for the fishing villages at the southeastern tip of Johor. At the end of the road take the left fork for Teluk Ramunia, past the shipyards, to Sungai Musuh, where there are picturesque waterways crammed with wooden fishing boats. From the palm-fringed coastline are views of the busy shipping lanes to the metropolis of Singapore, and the violet hills on Pulau Bintan in Indonesia beyond.

Some enterprising villagers have built chalets, and although the beach is not as good as Desaru, the kampung atmosphere makes for a pleasant stay. Back along the coast is Sungai Rengit, a fishing village renowned for its seafood, and at Tanjung Pengelih there is an overgrown British observation post built during World War II. Across the straits, the geometric horizon of Singapore's housing blocks looks very near, but it is a world away from the calm of Johor's sleepy southeast.

Opposite: Freighters en route to Singapore harbor hover on the horizon while villagers search for shellfish in the shallows of the Johor Straits off Pengarang. **Above:** Golfers enjoy the breezes from the South China Sea at Desaru's waterfront golf course.

SOUTHERN ISLANDS

Jewels in the South China Sea

Swallows circle overhead and the trade winds murmur through the casuarinas along the seafront walkway at Mersing. Joggers hurry past, families stroll by, and couples relax in the cool of the evening and gaze out to a horizon studded with the silhouettes of more than 64 offshore islands. Some are mere rocks thrusting up from the seabed, others are isolated "Robinson Crusoe" hideways, and many more are well-known resort isles including the renowned Pulau Tioman.

Mersing, a bustling port town 124km (77mi) north of Johor Bahru, and 186km (115mi) south of Kuantan, is the gateway to all these islands. Passenger boats depart from the town's jetty, and many resorts have offices in town (*see Practicalities, page 266*).

Although Pulau Tioman is in Pahang, boats still depart from Mersing. Wooden trawlers, known as "slow boats" which have

been converted to passenger ferries make the four to five hour journey, but there's also less-frequent faster boats which cut the journey to around two hours. There are also an island airport with flights from Kuala Lumpur and Singapore—the landing is tricky and spectacular—but the best way to appreciate the island (if you have the time) is to take the sea approach.

Spectacular Pulau Tioman

Manoeuvering their way through the fishing trawlers and the traffic of the Mersing River, the island-bound boats negotiate the shallow harbor and enter the sparkling waters of the South China Sea. Lulled by the heat and the diesel throb, passengers drowse as the wooden boat slices through the glassy sea. Faint islands appear like rocks in a Japanese garden, and flying fish scoot across the water.

Hours pass and the once-distant, mountainous massif of Pulau Tioman, the largest island along the east coast, now comes into focus. Dominating its skyline are the horn-like granite peaks of Batu Sirau and Nenek Si-Mukut, which rear 914m (3,000ft) above a wilderness of virgin rainforest. The forest creeps down to a coast ringed with bays of white-coral sand, and lapped by turquoise waters. No other island off the peninsula can match Tioman for sheer geographic splendor.

Located 32km (20mi) off Pahang's coast, the 113km^2 (44mi^2) island, has only become a

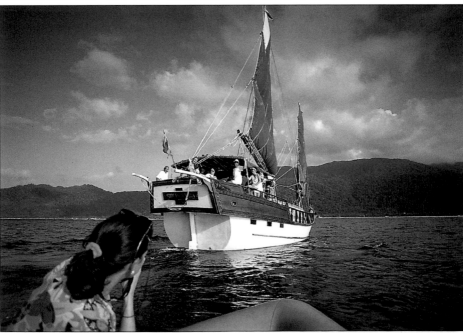

JILL GOCHER

popular traveler's destination in the last decade, but it was known to the ancient mariners of the spice trade for at least a millenium before. The pinnacle peaks provided an unmistakable landmark, and the island offered sheltered ports all year round. Early Chinese sailors knew the island as Zhumashan, "the mountain of *rami*" because of the abundance of the nettle-like *rami* plants which they used to make rope.

Pottery finds which have been unearthed at Juara on the east coast, and Teluk Nipah in the southwest indicate that the island was an important port of call from the 11th to the 19th century. When motors replaced sails the island was no longer visited by traders and slumbered in obscurity until it was rediscovered by adventurous travelers in the 1960s.

Until recently, the bulk of Pulau Tioman's 1,500 inhabitants were dependent on fishing for a livelihood but this has been fast replaced by tourism as the island's major money earner. During the peak holiday periods the beaches and resorts become quite crowded, and visitors outnumber locals, but during the annual monsoon the island reverts to its former quietude.

Except for isolated Juara, a village on the remote east coast, and Mukut, a fishing community on the south coast, most of the population lives along the protected northwest shores around the large village of Tekek where most of the resorts, and the island's main jetty is located. Tekek also has a mosque, a school, a couple of shops and lots of little restaurants, chalets, huts, and a delightful sandy beach.

The island's only road, 3km (1.9mi) long, runs from the airport just north of Tekek to the Tioman Island Resort, the island's only luxury hotel, situated on a long, sandy beach. The swimming is excellent here and there is good snorkeling around the reefs which encircle Pulau Rengis, the small rocky islet just off the coast from the resort. A group of Hollywood movie makers set up camp near here over 30 years ago to shoot beach scenes for the Cinemascope musical "South Pacific." The location of their camp is now occupied by the resort's golf course.

The backpackers' mecca

A concrete path only wide enough for motorbikes runs north past chalets and patches of rainforest to the headland at Tanjung Musuh. Here, it reverts to a trail over a rocky promontory and down to Kampung Ayer Batang, the favorite travelers' beach and the location of some of the best and original "thatched-hut" resorts like Nazeri's and ABC. Now dozens of other establishments have sprung up along the bay with these two pioneer resorts at either end.

Beaches north and south

The southern end of Ayer Batang beach is creamy-white sands and is excellent for swimming. Anchoring fishing boats have killed a lot of the coral, but there are still some soft corals, anenomes, colorful fish, and evening snorkelers often spot hawksbill turtles. Rainforest creeps to the back of the resorts, and *biawak*, iguana-like lizards up to 1.5m (5ft) long, can often be seen. The orange-billed mynah bird, known as the *tiong*, which some locals believe gave Tioman its name, is often heard mimicking other birds. Lesser flying foxes, *keluang kecil* (actually a type of bat) are only found on the offshore islands and make their home in the coconut palms along the foreshore. At dusk they noisily set out to forage in the jungle.

The beach at the northern end is rocky and not as good for swimming as the south end. A trail heads from the far end of the beach and climbs the headland to Penuba Bay where there are some chalets and a pretty beach. The trail continues past Monkey

Opposite: A revamped junk serves as a cruise ship in the waters off Pulau Tioman.

Johor's Islands

Bay, which has steep dropoffs good for scuba diving, although it is much easier accessed by boat. It is possible to walk all the way to Salang, a beautiful bay in the far northwest which is popular with dive groups, but the trail is rather unkept. If you don't like trekking go by boat.

The trail to Juara

Most of the 19-km (12mi) long by 12-km (7.4mi) wide island is still covered by virgin rainforest, and is home to an uncommonly-large mousedeer population. Sometimes these elusive creatures, which stand only 22cm (9in) at the shoulder, can be seen along the cross-island trail which connects Tekek to Juara on the east coast.

Take the turnoff to the mosque, and follow the footpath which climbs through thick rainforest to the top of the watershed. The waterfall here is good for a refreshing dip. The path then descends through jungle and through a rubber plantation and coconut palms to Juara.

Around 40 families live in this isolated community which now survives more on tourism than on rubber tapping or fishing. There are chalets and a couple of small restaurants. The seas are crystal clear and the beach is long and sandy. Deep-sea fishing trawlers and squid boats often shelter in the bay which has been used by sailors for centuries. Evidence of the port's antiquity came to light in 1976 when villagers digging the ground to make a football field, chanced upon ancient Chinese ceramics dating from the 12th century. More porcelains were discovered at Teluk Nipah, in the southwest, and ceramics from both sites are now on display at the Sultan Abu Bakar Museum in Pekan.

The southeastern settlements of Kampung Genting, Teluk Nipah and Mukut are still quite traditional. Boat services are sporadic, so these places are only feasible if you have time on your hands. A round-the-island boat service goes to the waterfall which is a short walk from Kampung Asah, just east of Mukut. It's a pleasant spot to cool off amidst the rainforest, but the real charm in the south is the spectacular scenery and the untouristy atmosphere. Freshwater streams cascade down from the granite peaks which soar over the village, and the beaches to the west of Mukut are deserted even in the holiday season.

Good diving

A novice snorkeler can still find plenty of interest on Tioman's beach reefs, but the best diving is at Pulau Tulai, about 5km (8mi) off the coast from Salang, in the far northwest. The island is often nicknamed coral island, and chalet owners run boats there. The best corals are found off the rocky coast where snorkeling is best done from a boat. There are boulder-sized brain corals, gardens of staghorn coral, and in the deeper waters are candelabra-shaped sea whips. Marine life is plentiful and striped angelfish, butterfly fish and the darting clownfish contribute to the rainbow-colored underwater world.

The second-best known island off Mersing is Pulau Rawa. Located 16km offshore, this quintessential tropical island with its dazzling white beach and turquoise waters is home to the region's pioneer resort run by a member of the Johor royal family. Apart from the sun and the sea, there is little to do here, as the island is small, but as it is only a 45-minute boatride, Rawa is a popular weekend jaunt and is ideal for travelers who want a short island hop.

Big pig and general's hat

Pulau Hujung, further south, is a small forested isle with beautiful beaches, also popular with day trippers. There are some private retreats here, but there is no overnight accommodation. Close by is Pulau Tengah, which is just starting to be developed and has a small resort. This island looks bare compared to the others in this group as it was used as a temporary camp for Vietnamese boat people during the early 1980s and most of the jungle was cut down. A rusting metal ship grounded on the sandy shores provides a grim reminder of their hurried flight.

Pulau Babi Besar, "big pig island," is the largest of the small archipelago comprising Pulau Hujung ("the end") and Pulau Tengah ("the middle"). Only five years ago this hilly isle supported a small fishing village and tourists were rare, but now low-key resorts dominate the western shores where all the best beaches are found. During the week the island is still very peaceful. Cow trails lead through the copra plantations, past wooden kampung houses, and weave in and out of pretty bays with white sand and clear blue waters.

Known to the ancient Chinese mariners as "general's hat island" the conical silhouette of Pulau Tinggi, literally the "lofty island," looms to the south. Some locals say that it was used as the long-distance shot of Bali Hai in the movie *South Pacific*, which was partially filmed on Pulau Tioman.

The solitary, granite peak, over 609m (2,000ft) high, rears above the dense rainforest. The lower reaches are swathed by coconut plantations which descend to the pristine, white beaches. A new resort has recently been opened here, but the villagers still rely principally on copra and fishing for

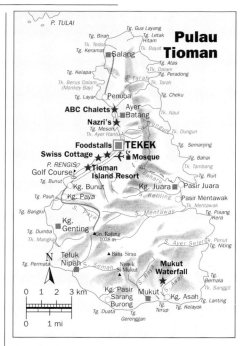

their livelihood.

In contrast to mountainous Tinggi, Pulau Sibu the next island to the south (two hours from Mersing) has only small hills and much of the island is easy to walk around. The first resort only opened five years ago, but now there are a range of places to stay. This island still retains a pleasant kampung atmosphere. Solar electricity was introduced to Pulau Sibu as a government-assisted pilot scheme and the solar panels which stand outside each kampung house provide power without the thumping of generators.

Two untouched islands

Remote Pulau Aur, and Pulau Pemanggil, are at least six hours by boat from Mersing and are the most untouched of all the islands in the Johor archipelago. Far from the muddy effects of mainland rivers, the waters are crystal clear with abundant marine life and prolific corals.

Facilities are only available on Pulau Aur where rooms are basic kampung-style and the boat service is highly irregular, but for travelers wanting to really get away from it all, these two islands are untouched and marvellously uncrowded.

Opposite: This panorama from the promontory at Tanjung Mesoh, shows Pulau Tioman's mountainous interior, still covered in virgin rainforest, and its long, palm-shaded beaches.

PART IX

Introducing Singapore

Nations are usually products of their history. While marveling at the sky-scraping, chrome-and-glass facade of Singapore, the visitor might be forgiven for thinking that this tropical island republic must surely be the exception to that rule.

The trick for understanding Singapore is to look beyond and beneath that facade. Do not be deceived by the glitzy Westernized, sophistication of the cosmopolitan Singaporeans, for just below the surface they are unequivocally Asian.

Singapore's history has been determined as much by its geography as anything else: situated at a crucial crossroads for trade, shipping, and now communications, between the related twin cultures of Malaysia and Indonesia, and within reach of the former Khmer, Thai and Indian empires too.

In 1819, when Stamford Raffles of the East India Company arrived to sign treaties with the local Malay ruler, the Temenggong or Viceroy for the Sultan of Riau-Johor, his party found fragmentary remains of the 14th-century palace of the ancient kings of Temasek, as Singapore was once called, on the hill now called Fort Canning.

Standing at the mouth of the Singapore River was a huge boulder, mysteriously inscribed with a script that has never satisfactorily been deciphered, and in the first act of "urban renewal" vandalism in Singapore, this was blown to pieces by a British engineer in 1843, to make way for new construction.

A Singaporean playwright, Robert Yeo, recently wrote a play which centered on a dialogue between Raffles and Singapore's former Prime Minister Lee Kuan Yew, seeing them as kindred souls. It is true that Lee, the country's first elected prime minister of an independent Singaporean government in 1959, and regarded as the patriarch of the nation, occupies a place in Singapore's history as monumental as that of Raffles, that of the founder of modern Singapore. But signifi-cantly, there is a statue of Raffles in the city centre, not of Lee, and old colonial street names have never been changed. Lee's Singapore has always striven to balance the mystique of the Oriental god-king with the rationality of the corporate technocrat.

Raffles—the founding father

In the 1820s, Raffles laid down the communally-based design of the city center—a design which persists even today. His blueprint survives in the Central Business District (essentially, the colonial British area) clustered around the commercial artery formed by the Singapore River, in Chinatown, south of the river, and Kampung Glam centered around Arab Street, the stronghold of Malays and other Muslims from the region.

Perhaps most importantly of all, it was Raffles who determined that Singapore would be a free port and would welcome all comers, provided they contributed to its economic development. These founding principles remain unchanged today.

Raffle's open-door policy stimulated the immigration of wealthy and entrepreneurial Chinese merchants from Malaya, Indian workers from the sub-continent, and a flood of poor but industrious southern Chinese escaping the turmoil of their homeland during the 19th and 20th centuries. Hence, Singapore's three million population today roughly comprises 78% Chinese, 14% Malays, 7% Indians, and 1% "others" including Eurasians.

Back in the prosperous, and somewhat smug, colonial 1920s and '30s, Eurasians and Chinese were still not quite the thing at the Singapore Cricket Club, and even British soldiers below officer's rank were routinely

Overleaf: The Manhattan-like skyline of Singapore's central business district.
Opposite: Dressed in Chinese brocades, a Singaporean girl carries on her ancestors' cultural traditions.

refused entry to that oasis of gentility, the Raffles Hotel.

World War II changed everything. Singaporeans passing the Padang shortly after the British surrender to the invading Japanese on February 15, 1942, were treated to the hitherto unimaginable spectacle of ragged Europeans lined up like cattle, preparing for internment in Changi Jail.

But on September 12, 1945, the Padang was again witness to historic events: on the steps of City Hall, Admiral Lord Louis Mountbatten received the Japanese surrender for the British.

The Japanese surrender notwithstanding, the mystique of colonial power had been shattered for ever by the British defeat. By 1959, Singapore had won internal self-government under its first fully-elected government, dominated by the People's Action Party (PAP), under the leadership of feisty Cambridge-educated lawyer, Lee Kuan Yew, Singapore's however was a singularly bloodless battle for independence, achieved largely through the political process.

Lee Kuan Yew rebuilds the nation

Lee and his colleagues proceeded to tackle Singapore's many ills: a burgeoning population ill-matched with growing unemployment, inadequate education and housing facilities, and a virtually empty treasury. Convinced that the PAP was a communist party, foreign investors at first shied away from the new Republic. As if this were not enough, the PAP had to deal with internal political rifts between its largely communist left and the moderate-socialist right—on which side Lee himself stood. These tensions were reflected in widespread social unrest during the early 1960s, focusing around the proposal to merge with Malaysia, which was supported by Lee Kuan Yew.

Merger did in fact come in 1963, but only after a huge security sweep rounded up and detained indefinitely trade unionists, students and other agitators. Detention without trial remains an option on the government's books today. Lee is credited with being possibly the only Third World leader to have ridden the communist tiger to power without being devoured by it.

The Malaysia experience did not work, culminating in the trauma of Singapore's virtual expulsion to full independence in 1966. A much-toughened government set about the taming of the trade union movement, as well as extensive industrialization and massive rehousing programmes, all of which were to prove highly successful strategies in terms of economic development.

Above all, a Raffles-style milestone decision was made to invite and encourage foreign capital and expertise, and to teach Western science, technology and languages in school. Herein lies the key to Singapore's

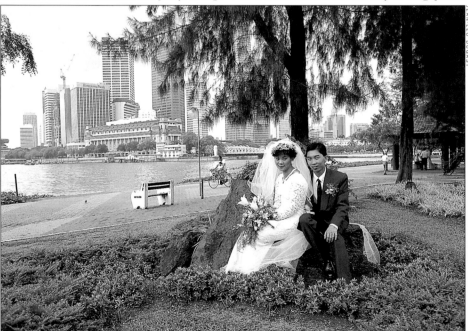

now unique character, in many ways quite alien to that of her Southeast Asian neighbors.

While it is true that the PAP put in place networks and structures, including measures to control the press, which fortified its power throughout society and made opposition extremely difficult, it was perhaps Lee's charisma and ability to keep the national "rice-bowl" full that kept him and his party in power for so long. The PAP still runs Singapore today.

Lee remained in charge until November 1990, when he handed over to the current Prime Minister Goh Chok Tong. However, Lee still sits in Cabinet, as does his son Brigadier-General Lee Hsien Loong, as Deputy Prime Minister.

Where East meets West

Singapore is a city that forces you into constant double-takes. Nothing is what it seems. The Asian gent in the western suit with computer Basic at his fingertips is conveniently reversible into a Confucian sage lecturing you on the virtues of "filial piety," and the vices of the decadent West.

The Indian restauranteur still wears his traditional white *lungi* (wraparound skirt), hangs Hindu images in his shop, and eats with his fingers off a banana leaf, but uses a closed-circuit TV to check on empty tables upstairs.

The gorgeous young air hostess may seem a Suzie-Wong lookalike, but actually she is most likely extremely chaste and living with her mother. This is not so much a schizophrenic nation as a multi-phrenic one. Asian television newsreaders speak old-style "BBC English," but local Chinese are returning from universities overseas with American accents, while baseball-capped kids tote "ghetto-blasters" along Orchard Road. On the streets, the dominance of the English language combined with Asian mother-tongues has produced a genuine Creole, jestingly referred to as "Singlish."

The dignified forms and gentlemanly foreplay of British justice are still here, yet the laws and their application seem at times somewhat severe: death for drug trafficking, a US$200 fine for littering, and so on. Underlying it all though is the ancient Chinese concern for the good of the collective, the community, rather than that of the individual. This is also a brash "money-faced" and food-obsessed place given to reminding itself that it is the best and the first. Local banks strive to build the tallest skyscrapers in the region, super-efficient Changi Airport is

indisputably one of the world's best, and the port is the world's busiest, to name but a few superlatives already achieved.

The biggest worries facing Singapore today are the problems of success. The Republic is already the third-richest nation in Asia, after Japan and Brunei, holding about US$29 billion in foreign reserves. Nobody wants, or needs, to be a servant in Singapore any more. Singaporeans import their maids from the Philippines, Sri Lanka and Indonesia.

Typically, having virtually won the race, Singapore is not resting on its laurels. Under the new, more velvet-gloved, regime of Goh Chock Tong, the concerns for gracious living, leisure and recreation, personal freedoms, literature and the arts, history, environmental and heritage conservation, all of which come naturally to affluent societies, have at last been given more room to breathe than in the past.

Singaporeans are urbane, well-traveled and well used to hosting the five million tourists visiting their country each year. They will receive you warmly, providing only that you do not step on their toes by criticizing them or their country.

—*Ilsa Sharp*

Opposite: *The gardens overlooking Singapore's harbor: a favorite backdrop for wedding photographs.* **Below:** *Chinatown's streets becomes a bazaar during the Chinese New Year celebrations in January/February.*

PEOPLE

Island of Cultural Contrasts

When visitors touch down at Singapore's ultra-modern Changi airport, their first impressions are fashioned by the high-tech buildings, and the orderliness of the beautifully-manicured gardens. These impressions are soon followed by the realization that this small island bustles with people of various races. How surprised they would be to learn that just 170 years ago, the land they are standing on was both hilly and swampy, devoid of any permanent buildings, and inhabited by a few hundred *orang laut,* or sea people, who made this tropical isle their home.

Today, Singapore and its surrounding islands has over three million inhabitants, but the number swells annually as some 5.4 million visitors pass through the island for business and leisure. Together, they contribute to making Singapore one of the most densely-populated countries in the world with a total

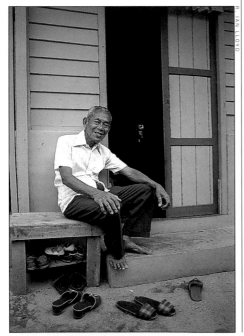

of over 5,200 people per square kilometre. Why was there such a phenomenal increase in population when most countries have increased their numbers no more than ten fold?

The early history of Singapore tells of its dominance by various sultans who at times settled in the nearby Riau islands or in neighboring Johor. Singapore, with its low lying hills and swampy shores was not a particularly attractive place to live, although a few enterprising Chinese had established small plantations of gambier and pepper. The seafaring *orang laut* who roamed the region, created shore settlements and came and went as the whim took them.

However, in 1819 when Stamford Raffles established a trading post on Singapore, records show that there were 30 Chinese, although this information was gleaned more by hearsay than an official count. It was not until 1860 that a census of population was made and by that time the handful of inhabitants had swelled to a grand total of 80,792.

A mecca for Asian migrants

This radical change in demographics occurred as under British rule Singapore prospered rapidly as a port and attracted waves of migrants from nearby territories and from mainland China. Malays from the peninsula were not slow to recognise the opportunities and moved southward with the wave of Chinese migration. Just three years after Raffles first landed, Malays comprised some 60% of the 10,683 inhabitants of Singapore but with the influx of Chinese from the mainland the proportions were soon to change.

By mid-century, migration was a well-organized affair that included women as well as men. By the 1860s the Chinese became the majority and that ratio has continued till today: they now comprise 78% of the 3,315,500 citizens and residents.

Arriving with Raffles in 1819 were 120 Indian soldiers and several Indian clerical assistants. Scope for work was wide and others soon followed from Malayan Penang, India and Ceylon. When Singapore became a penal station in 1823, the British transported a few hundred convicts who were put to work constructing buildings, and indentured laborers were shipped from southern India to work for the government. Entrepreneurs, too, moved from Bengal, Gujurat and Punjab, and so the mix of Indians from the sub continent was established. Other major groups attracted to the burgeoning isle included the neighboring Javanese, Bugis, Balinese and peoples from Sumatra.

By the end of the century, Singapore had become a thriving entrepot and a well established settlement, and its success continued to attract migrants. Because many of the settlers came to the island without families, it was inevitable that some intermarriage would occur. Single Chinese married Malay women and a new group of people, *peranakans*, was created. Individually referred to as either *nonya* for women, or *baba* for men, the *peranakans* have their own style of dress, customs, and a delicious hybrid cuisine. Westerners married Asians and the offspring of these unions became the Eurasians who now number over 200,000.

A cosmopolitan society

Attracted by its cosmopolitan atmosphere and the opportunities for work, more and more foreigners have come on a strictly controlled, temporary basis to Singapore. The Asian faces one sees on the streets today may belong to the Japanese, Thai, Filipino or Korean communities, all of which live and work in the republic for a finite period of time. In addition, expatriate English, Australian, American, French, German and New Zealanders form small but strong communities here.

Thus the basis for the remarkable mix of people that make up the rich fabric of Singaporean society was established, each bringing to the island their own culture and customs, religion and mythology.

The Hokkien, Cantonese and Teochew ancestors of today's Singaporean Chinese came from southern China bringing their Buddhist, Taoist and Confucian beliefs. Although over 70% of Chinese follow these faiths, a large number are Christian.

Much has been done to integrate the different races to form a homogenous Singaporean identity, and the policies that have fashioned this have largely succeeded. Young people are proud to be Singaporean, irrespective of race, and now intermix freely. The days when the Chinese, the Malays and the Indians each lived in different districts are largely gone, as the same racial ratios that contribute to the total population are followed in allocations in housing estates and educational institutes. One interesting outcome of this melange of backgrounds is the emergence of a local English dialect, Singlish, which is peppered with Malay and Chinese words.

Because the dynamics that have created Singapore are still at work today, the country and its people, continue to change. Singapore does not stagnate, nor will its people.

—*Fiona Nichols*

Opposite: *This Malay leaves his shoes outside the door, a habit of all Asian Singaporeans.*
Above: *Indian women wear red sarees to signify their married status.*

FESTIVALS

Preservation of Age-Old Traditions

Although Singaporeans commemorate at least 20 festivals, only 10 of these are official holidays as one of the sacrifices in the strive for economic success was a reduction in the number of public holidays. But this has not affected the survival of many time-honored festivals and the nation's cultural diversity presents a fascinating showcase with celebrations happening every month.

As many festivals follow lunar calendars the dates change from year to year, so it is best to check at tourist information offices for dates and venues.

Starting from the beginning of the Roman calendar, New Year's Day, January 1, is celebrated at midnight with fireworks displays over the Esplanade. Thaiponggal, on January 14, is a South Indian thanksgiving celebration when devotees offer rice, vegetables, sugar cane and spices to their deities. In the tem-

ples, particularly the Perumal Temple on Serangoon Road, they sing and chant prayers to the accompaniment of bells, clarinets, drums and conch shells.

Thaipusam, held during January or February, is the most colorful and dramatic Hindu festival. Held in honor of the deity Lord Subramaniam, it is a time of penance and rejoicing. On festival day, male devotees enter into a trance-like state, pierce their bodies with skewers and the hooks of the *kavadi*—a metal wheel decorated with peacock feathers—and then walk in procession from Serangoon Road's Perumal Temple to the Chettiar Temple on Tank Road.

Chinese New Year, also known as the Lunar New Year, held during January or February, is celebrated for 15 days until the final day known as Chap Goh Mei.

On Chinese New Year's Eve, Chinatown's streets are packed with hawkers and throngs of customers. During the holiday, the Chinese visit relatives and friends, don new clothes and shoes, and present money packets, or *ang pau*, to younger relatives. Traditional dishes are eaten, and lion and dragon dances are performed. The celebrations end with a Chingay Parade of colorful floats, stilt-walkers, dancers and acrobats along Orchard Road.

Hari Raya Puasa, the major Muslim festival which marks the end of the fasting month, or Ramadan, occurs in April or March. The

Malay areas of Geylang Serai, Bussorah Street and Arab Street are packed with food stalls selling special delicacies, and the shops are crammed with fabrics, carpets and clothing. Muslims celebrate with prayers, then after the traditional feast they don new clothes and visit relatives and friends.

Later in April, the Chinese celebrate Qing Ming when they visit graveyards, and offer food and burn joss sticks to honor their deceased ancestors. Good Friday, on April 17, is a public holiday when Christians attend special church services.

In May, Vesak Day commemorates Buddha's birth, enlightenment and death. At Buddhist temples, saffron-robed monks chant prayers and distribute food to the poor. Pigeons are set free and devotees bring donations to the temple.

In June, the Dragon Boat Festival is celebrated in honor of the poet Qu Yuan who committed suicide by drowning. Dragon-boat teams from all over the world converge here for the annual race. Also in this month, Muslims celebrate Hari Raya Haji which commemorates the Haj or pilgrimage to Mecca. Muslims gather for prayers, and sheep and bullocks are ritually slaughtered and the meat distributed to the poor.

During July or August, is the Festival of the Hungry Ghosts, the seventh month of the lunar calendar, when Chinese believe that the restless souls of the dead roam the earth. To appease these unhappy spirits bonfires of joss paper are burnt and grand street operas, known as *wayang*, are held.

Every August 9, National Day, Singapore's independence is celebrated with a grand parade and fireworks. Later, in August or September, the Mooncake Festival is held when the Chinese exchange mooncakes: sweet pastries stuffed with red bean or lotus-seed paste. This festival is also known as the Lantern Festival, and colorful lanterns are lit during the celebrations.

The Birthday of the Monkey God, is celebrated in September at the Monkey God Temple on Eng Hoon Street when a sedan chair, believed to be possessed by the deity, is carried in procession, flanked by mediums who slash their bodies with blades. Another Chinese celebration, the Festival of the Nine Emperor Gods, is held over nine days during September to October, when it is believed the gods visit the earth to grant good fortune.

Kusu, an offshore island, is the venue for a month-long pilgrimage observed by both Malays and Chinese which has its roots in two legends. In one, the island was once a turtle which was rescued by a Malay and a Chinese fisherman. The other, concerns a diety Tua Pekong, who saved the lives of an epidemic-stricken crew.

From October through November, three Hindu festivals are celebrated. The first, Navarathiri, which means "nine nights", takes place at Tank Road's Chettiar Temple and devotees celebrate with traditional dances and a procession. The next, Thimithi, or Fire Walking Festival, is enacted at the Sri Mariamman Temple on South Bridge Road, when devotees, protected by prayers and faith, walk bare-footed across a four-meter pit of red-hot coals. The third, also a public holiday, is Deepavali, the Festival of Lights, when Hindus celebrate the victory of good over evil, houses are gaily lit, and devotees throng the temples.

The year ends with Christmas, when Orchard Road becomes a sea of lights, and Singaporeans celebrate with a shopping and partying spree which continues through to New Year's Eve.

—*Yeow Mei Sin*

Opposite: *A Chinese opera group known as "A Pair of Flying Swallows" performs in a Singapore street theater.*
Below: *His chest pierced by dozens of metal skewers A Thaipusam penitent prepares to make his pilgrimage.*

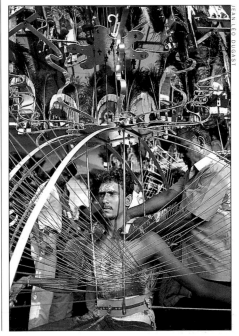

SPIRIT MEDIUMS

Mediators Between God and Men

Midnight, on a narrow lane, people gather around a circle on the pavement, its circumference delineated by a white cord. Facing each other across the circle are a silent adolescent boy holding a black, triangular flag marked with eight trigrams of protection, and a white satin-clad medium wearing the tall, squared-off hat of Twa Ya Peh, the opium god.

Lit by candles, the circle is piled high with offerings: stacks of gold leafed rice paper charms; oranges, pears and limes; bowls of water and rice; five brown eggs painted with human features; a tiny wooden coffin with a needle-sharp spike fitted lengthwise through it.

The excorcist

Singapore's Chinese spirit mediums are intermediaries between gods and men, vehicles for the gods to act on earth. Sia Chai has been a medium for over 30 years. Recently a

couple sought his advice as their son was possessed by a female ghost. He wouldn't eat, wouldn't speak, couldn't sleep. An exorcism was suggested to force the ghost out from the boy and return it to the spirit realm.

Assistants bustled about making preparations. One explained, "We begin with a chant to the Five Generals. We ask them to tell the opium god that we need his help. Only then will he come and enter the medium." Twa Yeh Peh prefers offerings of Guinness Stout and cigarettes. Some gods are vegetarian, some abstain from intoxicants. The opium god indulges.

While the assistants chant a deep, slow dirge, the medium enters trance. Slowly at first, he sways then he swings like a see-saw. The medium's dance is controlled fury. A trace of blood drips from his tongue, cut to inscribe characters on charm papers.

Trapping the ghost

Tenderly, he washes the boy's face with a blue cloth soaked in holy water. Drawing back, in a series of tai-chi-like moves, he proceeds to wrest the demon from the boy, pulling it forward with his outstretched hand, drawing it toward his own body. He crumples to the ground in a huddled heap with a gutteral animal snarl, a primeval, spine-tingling shriek. The boy sits motionless, perched on a stool, the crowd stunned into stillness for a frozen moment. The medium has impaled the unseen ghost onto the needle and shoved it into the tiny wooden coffin.

It is over. The medium wakes from trance and the boy and his family walk off to catch a taxi. Later, the temple assistants were asked about the boy. "Back to normal," they replied.

Gods for every occasion

Spirit mediums, known in Hokkien as *tang-ki's*, or "divining youth," are an intrinsic part of popular Chinese religion which encompasses Taoism, Shenism (*shen* means "deity"), ancestral veneration and Buddhism, with a sprinkling of Christian and Hindu elements. Popular Taoist gods represent nearly every facet of physical and psychological life: city god, kitchen god, god of walls, baby god, seven-year-old god, god of war and of poetry Beloved rulers and warriors were deified upon death, over generations, as history became myth and myth a history of the divine.

Rebels, renegades and criminals whose struggle against false, cruel authority touched the hearts of the people might also achieve godhood. Like the "Hanged Man" of the Tarot, these were men who sacrificed themselves to bring about spiritual transformation in the world. The opium god is a "hanged god". So is Jesus.

In an elaborate iconographical system, each god, spirit or demon is identified by color, clothing, weapons and position in the multi-leveled hierarchies of heaven and hell. Gods and spirits can manifest in our world and exert an active influence for good or ill on the events of our lives.

It's not hard to find a medium. Some are associated with Buddhist and Taoist temples. Some operate from small roadside shrines, easily recognizable by the black triangular flags out front bearing the *pa kua*, the eight trigrams of the I Ching. On the front sidewalk shrine, the tiger stalks around an incense-filled urn. Yang counterpart to the Yin dragon, the tiger keeps the *kuei* (malicious spirits) from entering the temple. The open front door reveals an elaborate, tiered altar, crowded with hand-carved wooden images of the gods, bright with paint and gold leaf.

Trance and mortification

The Chinese lunar calendar marks full and new moon birthdays of the gods and other significant days when mediums perform in streets and temple courtyards. Some flail barbed-wire balls about their backs and shoulders, other wield blades as big as meat cleavers. Hot iron balls are kicked from medium to medium in a demonic soccer match. Although mortification is the most dramatic part of a spirit medium's activity, it's probably the least significant part.

Many mediums never practice any form of mortification at all. Most female mediums do not. Its purpose is to make visible the medium's state of trance, to give tangible proof that he is indeed inhabited by a deity. How else could he be master over fire, oblivious to physical pain? How could he insert hooks through flesh, pierce flesh without bleeding?

People have their own reasons for visiting a medium. They believe in the gods. They hear, through word of mouth, that the medium can heal illness or predict the future. Perhaps they have exhausted all other possible remedies for their problem before they decide to take it to the gods. Most usually try Western medicine before consulting a medium for a remedy, but if it doesn't work or is inappropriate, they may consult a medium.

The chosen ones

These vehicles for the gods may be plumbers, electricians, hawkers, housewives or mothers, but what sets these people apart from the ordinary is that they are chosen as vessels for the gods. While in trance, they are entered by one or more of the great pantheon of Taoist gods.

The god, acting through the medium, can advise, administer medicine, change *kuay oon* (bad luck) into good, subdue demons and deal with the whole range of problems that we mortals generate with such wild abandon on this karmic wheel of life.

—Barbara Anello

Opposite: *Brandishing a sword this youthful medium performs at a temple in Owen Road.*
Above, left: *The medium, dressed in green robes, gives advice while under trance.*
Below: *This medium performs a symbolic dance beside a bonfire of sacred papers.*

ARCHITECTURE

Pockets of Old Amid the Brand New

In the 1960s, before the demolisher's hammer put paid to much of Singapore's traditional architecture, the urban areas were dominated by highly-decorative, terrace-style shophouses and townhouses. This distinctive style known variously as Singapore Eclectic, Straits Chinese Baroque, or Palladian Chinese, combined rococo plasterwork, Malay wood carvings, European wall tiles, Chinese roof tiles, and Portuguese-style shutters.

Visitors may easily imagine that Singapore's architecture now consists only of high-rise apartments and shopping complexes, but surprisingly, there are still quite a few pockets of traditional streetscapes. These surviving architectural legacies are reminders of the not too distant past when Singapore was one of Asia's most exotic ports of call.

Stamford Raffles, Singapore's founder, started the trend back in the 1820s by decree-ing that shophouses must be constructed of masonry with tiled roofs—to guard against fire. His other public requirement which made such a lasting impression on the streetscape was the "five-foot-way", known in Malay as *kaki lima*, a continuous covered passage formed by the second floor overhanging the first, which afforded protection from the merciless equatorial sun and the torrential afternoon downpours.

Many early traders were wealthy Straits Chinese who had made their fortunes in the Straits Settlements of the Malay Peninsula. When they moved their businesses to Singapore, they imported the eclectic urban architecture that already existed in Melaka and Penang which utilized Chinese, Malay, Portuguese, Dutch and English influences. Elements shared by shophouses in all the Straits Settlements are five-foot ways, facades decorated with bas-relief plasterwork, jalousies—literally from the French for "jealousy"—slatted window shutters to provide ventilation and privacy, Chinese tiled-roofs, and ornate eaves, balustrades, pilasters and other baroque embellishments, and delightful combinations of pastel colorings.

Townhouses were built in the same fashion, but the ground-floor shopfront was taken over by the formal sitting room entered by the *pintu pagar*, literally "fence door," a heavily-carved half door which provided privacy when the *pintu besar*, or main door, was open.

Directly in front of the door was the family ancestral altar, usually a carved and gilded affair presided over by stern-faced ancestor portraits. Most houses have small frontages, but are surprisingly large inside.

Geomancy and symbolism

Chinese architectural traditions have always been involved with *feng sui*, or geomancy, and these townhouses were no exception. South was the preferred direction to face as this was the most harmonious situation. All houses

had at least one inner courtyard, known as air-wells, which apart from giving light and ventilation, also facilitated the collection of rain water which brings good luck. Fish-shaped drainpipes, symbolizing "plenty", would channel the water towards the front of the house, believed to mean "wealth wisely spent," rather than to the back of the house where it would be "wasted wealth."

Symbolism was rampant in all decorative features as well as the coloring. Bats denote happiness, deer symbolize high status and wealth, cranes are for longevity and pheasants mean joy. Phoenix birds symbolizing "marital bliss" and peony blossoms for "eternal springtime" were the favorite symbols of the Straits Chinese. Colors were also very important, and both the Malays and the Straits Chinese loved pink—a sign of good fortune, and green—which symbolizes spring and peace.

If it hadn't been for tourism, most of these streets of remaining shophouses, and their residential equivalents, would have been history years ago. Singapore's town-planners only stopped their wholesale demolitions when they realized that travelers were bypassing their city for the more traditional towns of Melaka and Penang. When the first restored shophouses, known as Peranakan Place, opened on Orchard Road they were an overnight tourist success, and now many older buildings have preservation orders on them.

Colorful and attractive, the newly-restored shophouses of Tanjung Pagar, south of Chinatown, now house trendy boutiques, and are fashionable business addresses, but they are a trifle too sterile. However, there are still many traditional terrace houses and shops which still house their original inhabitants, and retain the character of old Singapore.

Emerald Hill Road, pronounced a preservation area in 1981, has 112 terrace houses built from 1902 to 1930. Despite being designed by 13 different architects the streetscape is an aesthetic blend of richly detailed townhouses. To get there, walk up the side road through Peranakan Place on Orchard Road.

Chinatown, particularly in the old grid around Pagoda, and Terenganu Streets, has many fine examples of two and three-storey shophouses with five-foot ways in an architectural style similar to the old Portuguese colonies of Macao and Melaka.

Along Desker Road, off Serangoon Road, are turn-of-the-century shophouses painted in delicate greens and blues, featuring fretwork eaves, decorative jalousies, and large arched windows bordered by neoclassical pilasters.

Some of the most ornate Singapore baroque shophouses still survive in the old Malay area of Geylang Road east of the city, and in the neighboring *lorongs* (lanes). The facades are covered with decorative tiles and an over-abundance of plaster bas-reliefs featuring Grecian urns, Chinese mythological characters and fruit and flowers. Also on the east coast are the picturesque terrace houses of Joo Chiat Road, dating from the 1920's which feature Doric columns and beautiful windows.

Opposite: Swing doors, known as pintu pagar, *give privacy to townhouses when the main door is open.* **Above, left:** *Fanlights, and slatted jalousies are features of Singapore's baroque-style shophouses.* **Above, right:** *Roses add an English touch to this tiled facade in Chinatown.*

FOOD

Feasts in Asia's Capital of Cuisine

As a tiny and unusually cosmopolitan island, Singapore has an extraordinary variety of food ranging from simple Asian peasant fare to the courtly cuisine of imperial China, and the exotic flavors of east-meets-west haute cuisine. If Singapore is not the culinary capital of Asia, then it certainly ought to be.

To understand the nation, one has to understand the Singaporean's passion for food—something akin to a national pastime. The average citizen eats between four and seven times a day—little but often. A typical day might start with a savoury rice porridge, noodles or a filling Indian *roti canai* and the day unfurls around the appetite. Soups for lunch. Take-away fried rice or tropical fruits for a small snack. Maybe a dessert of sickly sweet cakes or ice shavings topped with coconut milk. A curry, or seafood extravaganza could well be an evening meal and there is

always a late night nibble before heading home.

Singaporeans think nothing of driving across the island to sample their favourite dish at a popular cafe. More often than not they eat at local hawker centres, selecting an inexpensive meal from one of the stalls and sitting at communal round tables. Because of the cosmopolitan ethnic mix, there is a veritable pot pourri of cuisines and what is called Singaporean food is the result of a felicitious blend of Indian, Malay and Chinese styles. The Chinese brought the wok, with rice and noodles (which Marco Polo borrowed and called "spaghetti"); Indians brought spices and thick sauces; and the Malays incorporated seafood and vegetables to form a style of cuisine that is hot and spicy, eaten in small quantities with rice.

Being an island nation, seafood is particularly important here: and this usually means the hot and fiery variety. Whilst these dishes can be eaten in a sophisticated city hotel, they are much more fun and easier to enjoy in a hands-on meal under the stars, down by the sea.

Along Singapore's east coast, there is a huge food centre whose range of expertise extends much further than chilli and pepper crab, drunken prawns, deep-fried squid, Thai-style fish and steamed shrimp. At Ponggol, overlooking the straits that separate Singapore from Malaysia, are rowdy and unsophisticated restaurants perched on the shoreline, hanging over the water from whence the fish recently came. Here, there are no nouvelle cuisine decorations and minimalist portions. The food is wholesome and fresh (it is still alive in a tank when you arrive at the restaurant and if you have the heart, you can select your own fish, crabs and prawns), and social etiquette encourages eating with the right hand.

Then there is satay, a dish favored originally by the island's Muslim neighbors. These fine kebabs of beef, chicken or nowadays pork, skewered, marinated and then

cooked over a charcoal fire, are one of Singapore's finest delicacies. Dipped in a rich peanut sauce, and consumed with cubes of fragrant steamed rice, they appeal to even the most jaded of palates.

And what the Chinese didn't bring to Singaporean cuisine, the Indians added Originally it was the southern Indians who came, bringing their spicy tropical preferences, coconut and vegetarian curries served on banana leaves; then northern Indians and Punjabis arrived with recipies for their rich traditional cuisine that relied on baking and dry cooking. Fish head curry is a tremendous favorite in Singapore and one finds that Sundays, the day when most locals eat out with family and friends, are inevitably popular days for this dish. The cheeks are the best part, and the eyes a delicacy!

Serangoon Road, the part of town known as little India, is the place for traditional, South Indian banana-leaf curries—some of the best value menus in town. Custom dictates you eat with your right hand, but restauranteurs will happily bring spoons and forks for the less adept diners.

While there are plenty of Chinese and Indian restaurants around Singapore there are far fewer Malay restaurants yet the cuisine has immense merits. Much Malay food includes the usual Asian ingredients—chillis, ginger, tumeric, garlic and coconut—but features more stewed dishes than Chinese.

Indonesian dishes offer many similarities to Malay. *Nasi campur*—rice with a selection of meats, fish and vegetables—is common to both countries but the Indonesians tend to go easier on the chilli and heavier on the coconut flavor. The most popular style of cuisine is the very spicy, Padang (Sumatra) style. It is Indonesia's answer to *nasi campur*, and you pay according to the number of portions consumed. Large chilli-sauted prawns, rich beef *rendang* stew, spicy vegetables, eggs with chilli sauce, mouth-watering chicken curries and spiced or fried fish, all characterize *nasi padang*.

Smart Chinese dining is plentiful in Singapore. The decision lies with which style of cuisine. Cantonese, Shanghainese, Pekinese, Hainanese, Hunanese, Taiwanese, Teochew, or Sichuan—these are just for starters. There are also herbal restaurants where meals are quasi-medicinal with dishes cooked in healing herbs. Alternatively, Singaporeans in the know will head for restaurants where restorative health is promised from such culinary items as bear's paw, sea slugs, bull's penis and, in the pre-SPCA days, live monkey's brains and snake soup. Not for the faint hearted!

Singapore's dining options, however, extend far beyond the boundaries of Southeast Asia. Korean, Japanese, Vietnamese and Thai restaurants abound. Fine French, Italian, Swiss, Russian, German, Spanish, Lebanese and even Mexican restaurants can be found in the republic but the best tip is to do as the locals do: eat Singaporean. *Selamat makan.*: enjoy your meal.

—*Fiona Nichols*

Opposite: *Chinese chicken rice, Malay satay sticks and an Indian curry.* **Above, left:** *Banana leaves serve as plates for curry and rice in this outdoor restaurant in Little India.* **Above, right:** *Noodles, eaten with spoon and chopstick, are a favorite snack at any time of the day.*

COLONIAL SIGHTS

A Tour of the Colonial Past

When Stamford Raffles stepped ashore in 1819 to plant the East India Company's flag—in effect, the British flag—he was presented with an imperial planner's dream, a virtually blank sheet of paper on which to design a do-it-yourself colonial city. There were scarcely any bothersome local buildings which had to be drawn around, or demolished, except for the Malay Temenggong or Viceroy's small village at the mouth of the Singapore River, which Raffles promptly moved to a less central location.

The impact of the empire

"Colonials" get a bad press nowadays. Yet men like Raffles were imbued with high and serious purpose. Of course, commerce and dominion motivated him and his ilk, yet there was far more to Raffles than mere money-grubbing. Steeped in Malay history, culture

and language, Raffles was familiar with the romantic mythology shrouding Singapore's early history. It was his extensive background reading that brought him to the tiny island in the first place. To underline his own, and Britain's, place in local history, he cannily chose to build his own bungalow, Singapore's first Government House, on "Bukit Larangan," or "Forbidden Hill," as Fort Canning was then called. Sacred and taboo to the Malays for centuries, the hill had been the preserve of their kings. Raffles no doubt hoped that British rule would acquire for itself some of the semi-magical kudos attached to this hill if he built his residence there.

Like all the finest British colonials, Raffles burned with missionary zeal to bring the light of civilization, education and justice, and to some extent, Christianity, to his native charges.

A surprising number of the men gathered around Raffles were Scots—St. Andrew's Cathedral was named after their patron saint. These were the men who shaped the city, particularly in that colonial heartland radiating from the Padang, the seafront cricket ground still at the city center today. But none more than George Drumgold Coleman, Superintendent of Public Works, who worked in Singapore from 1822-1844. Coleman Street, next to the City Hall, is named after him. He set much of the architectural tone of early Singapore, with his taste for classical Palladian style. Skilfully, he adapted this style to the tropics with features like wide verandahs for shade and rain-shelter, and louvred windows to filter the intense sunlight.

Initially, however, central Singapore was the creation of Raffles' own fertile brain. In typical British style, his town plan was premised on concepts of class, caste, creed and race. He allocated separate spaces to merchants, craftsmen, and cultivators, and to the Europeans, Chinese, Malays, Bugis (from Indonesia), Arabs and Chuliahs (South Indian Muslims).

Raffles' mark on the city is still visible today. For his own kind, Raffles reserved the Padang area. In those days, the sea ran at the very edge of the cricket ground. Reclamation first extended the land in 1890, and again in the 1980s. Besides cricket matches, many major events of national importance took place on the Padang—the rounding up of British civilians under Japanese occupation, the subsequent surrender of the Japanese, and the later political rallies for independence.

For the early British settlers, the Padang was a social magnet, and just before dinner, the pallid European wives and daughters, perspiring in crinolines, bonnets and gloves, would come here for their daily social ritual, the "Turn", when they would take their horse-drawn carriages along the Esplanade waterfront, salute and greet one another, stroll on the greens, and eye potential husbands exercising their mounts.

It is not easy for young Singaporeans today to admit or even to perceive it, but the tentacles of the British Empire still reach deep into their psyches—in their language, their legal system, in their sports, and in the way they run their social clubs. And not least, in the surviving grand old buildings that still encircle the Padang.

A Padang perambulation

Start your walk standing on Cavenagh Bridge. Ahead is the tower of the Victoria Memorial Hall in Empress Place, and behind, is Fullerton Building, housing the GPO, just as it did when it was first built in 1928. On the same site was Fort Fullerton, constructed in 1830 to defend the city. Beside the Fullerton Building, is Battery Road, named after the heavy gun battery arming Fort Fullerton. It leads into Raffles Place, first named Commercial Square when it was created by Raffles in 1823 by levelling a hill and filling in a swamp. This was the meeting place for the merchants of his day, and it is still a center of big business today—the Stock Exchange is housed here.

When Raffles arrived, this section of the Singapore River was littered with skulls, the macabre remains of the victims of early pirate raiders. Cavenagh Bridge itself was assembled in 1869, from steel parts manufactured in Scotland—before that, one had to cross the river by ferry. By 1910, traffic across the bridge had swollen, with rickshaws and bullock-carts trundling alongside electric tramcars and the first motor cars. Hence the construction of the new Anderson Bridge right next door, reducing Cavenagh Bridge to a mere footbridge. You can still see the sign there announcing that ox-carts, horses and vehicles exceeding 3-cwts (hundredweight) are prohibited from crossing.

Cross the bridge into Empress Place, named after Queen Victoria of England, to view the Dalhousie Obelisk of 1850 to your left by the river, and the magnificently restored Empress Place Building, once known as the Government Buildings and originally built as the Court House in 1864. This grand old neoclassical building is now a

Opposite: A turbaned Sikh welcomes guests at Raffles Hotel, watering-hole for the rich and famous for over a hundred years. Below: On the banks of the Singapore River, against a backdrop of old and new architectural styles, the statue of Stamford Raffles surveys the city that he founded.

R IAN LLOYD

museum housing major exhibitions of art-treasures, as well as restaurants and shops.

Ahead of you are the Victoria Memorial Hall and Theatre, complete with chiming clock tower. The theater, on the left side, dates from 1862 and was originally the Town Hall. The memorial hall, the right-hand half, is now the concert-hall home of the Singapore Symphony Orchestra, it was built in 1905 as a tribute to Queen Victoria.

The 2.4-m (8ft) tall statue of Sir Stamford Raffles stands proudly outside the Victoria buildings. First erected in 1887, it bears a plaque praising Raffles, "to whose foresight and genius, Singapore owes its existence and prosperity."

Walking towards the back of the Victoria buildings, towards Parliament Lane, you come to Parliament House on your left, the oldest surviving government building in Singapore, on the site of the original Temenggong's camp in 1819. The core of the building is the house built for British merchant John Argyle Maxwell in 1827 by architect Coleman, fitted with a small lookout tower. Parliament now sits in an extended version of his home, which he first rented to government in 1841.

Behind the fence just past Parliament is a tall bronze Elephant Statue, a gift to Singapore from King Chulalongkorn (or Rama V) of Siam, now Thailand, in 1871. As you stand with the elephant on your left, you look straight ahead down High Street, Singapore's very first road, hacked out of the jungle by Raffles' officers in 1819.

Turning right up St. Andrew's Road, the domed Supreme Court on your left dates from 1939. Note the elegant murals above the grand entrance, by Italian artist Cavaliere Rudolfo Nolli. On the right, the Singapore Cricket Club building comprises a core dating from 1884, with additions in 1910 and 1921. It offers all sports—not just cricket—and is a favorite watering hole for local Indian lawyers, and Chinese and expatriate businessmen.

Next to the Supreme Court on the left is City Hall, once known as the Municipal Offices, completed in 1929. City Hall got its name only in 1952 when Britain first conferred the title of "city" on Singapore.

At the other end of the Padang is another 19th-century sports club building, the Singapore Recreation Club. This was where the all-white and largely British members of the Cricket Club allowed the "coloreds," the Eurasians, to have their own sports club. To this day, there is a strong Eurasian flavor to the "SRC" as it is locally known.

Turn left from City Hall and walk up Coleman Street. On your right is the early English-style St. Andrew's Cathedral, completed in 1862 and built largely by Indian convicts. It is coated with a unique plaster made of shell lime, egg white, sugar and coconut water, hand polished with rock crystal. Cross North Bridge Road and walk up Coleman Street to Hill Street. On your right, is probably Coleman's most exquisite creation, the Armenian Church, Singapore's first Christian church, built in 1835 for the small but prosperous Armenian community. To your left, is the fancifully turreted, red-brick Central Fire Station, built at the turn of the century. Further up Canning Rise is the Masonic Hall, headquarters for the Freemasons, dated 1879.

A sacred hill

Walk up Canning Rise, past the Anglo-Chinese Primary School on your left (on this site since 1886), and climb the next staircase up the hillside parkland to your left which leads to Fort Canning, the once forbidden hill of the kings. On the hill, you can view the historic headstones of the colonial Christian Cemetery dating from 1823, including that of architect Coleman, besides the Malay shrine and grave of Iskandar Shah, the last king of Temasek, 14th-century Singapore. Note also the elegant Gothic Gateway designed in 1844 by Captain Charles Faber. Also on the hill are British army buildings from the 1930s, now a cultural center, and the original underground bunker used by the British General Percival during War War II to direct the unsuccessful defence of Singapore against the Japanese.

Retracing your steps down Canning Rise, take the staircase through the carpark of the distinctive red-brick National Library, built in the 1950s. You can walk through the library grounds onto Stamford Road. Next to the library is the elegant, silver-domed National Museum and Art Gallery complex, dating from 1887, and well worth a stopover.

Cross Stamford Road, then turn left into Queen Street for the Cathedral of the Good Shepherd designed by Denis McSwiney, a pupil of Coleman, in the 1840s. Ahead, on Bras Basah Road, is the silvery dome of St. Joseph's Institution school of 1852, now awaiting restoration and refurbishment, possibly as an art center. At Bras Basah Road, turn right. This road was named after the Malay for "wet rice"—traders used to bring the rice up the Stamford Canal on boats and dry it on the canal banks. The canal has been filled in only in recent times. Continue past Victoria Street, and past the tranquil, but rather derelict-looking Convent of the Holy Infant Jesus. There are controversial plans to adapt the Convent as a cultural-cum-entertainment center.

Passing Raffles City on your right you encounter Raffles Hotel on your left. Time for

a tea-break in the Tiffin Room or in one of the hotel's shady courtyards, there to dream of the days when the sea lapped the hotel's front steps, and the jazz-bands played for the naughty tea-dances of the 1920s.

Walk around the Beach Road side of Raffles City, cross the Padang and Connaught Drive road to the seafront Queen Elizabeth Walk, formerly the Esplanade. Assuming you can resist the temptations of the Satay Club food stalls, observe close by an elaborately sculpted fountain, complete with triumphant cherubs. The Tan Kim Seng Fountain of 1882 was a rather foolish use of Mr Tan's philanthropic donation of $13,000 towards the improvement of Singapore's water supply.

Along Queen Elizabeth Walk is the Cenotaph monument to honor the dead from both World Wars, and at the end of the seafront walk is the Lim Bo Seng Memorial in honor of a Chinese resistance hero who was tortured to death by the Japanese in 1944. From here you can look across the mouth of the Singapore River to the (sometimes water-spouting) 8-m (26ft) tall statue of the Singapore Merlion, crafted by a local sculptor in 1972—a national symbol created by the Singapore Tourist Promotion Board.

—Ilsa Sharp

Above: *This sculpted family sits outside the recently-restored National Museum and Art Gallery built during the colonial era.*

CHINATOWN

A Step Back in Time to Old Singapore

Chinatown is located in the grid of streets running south from the Singapore River where the early immigrants first came ashore off their cramped and miserable junks after the tortuous journey from China.

Despite ongoing modernization, the area still retains a noisy and colorful ambience of its own. Chinese Singaporeans still shop here for joss paper, lanterns, oil lamps, altar plaques, sweet meats, fresh fish and cheap vegetables. Chinatown's fortune tellers, temple mediums and medicine men still do a roaring trade, and calligraphers, letter-writers and fortune-tellers can be found along the covered pavements known as "five-foot ways".

Chinatown is easily accessible from both Raffles Place and Outram Park MRT stations. From the latter, walk up Eu Tong Sen Street to People's Park Complex and Pearl's Hill Centre which is a favourite with locals for

electronic goods. Opposite, on Smith Street, are wooden-clog makers and further down at Ann Siang Hill there is an old mask-maker. In nearby Sago Lane are the death houses where elaborate coffins are carved out of whole tree trunks.

Hindu and Chinese temples

North along South Bridge Road is the Sri Mariamman Temple with a staggering amount of Hindu religious figures all fighting to catch the eye on the tower over the entrance. This is Singapore's oldest Hindu temple and is an important site for Hindu festivals, such as Thaipusam, Thimithi and Deepavali. Around the Sri Mariamman temple are the streets of old shophouses which give Chinatown its rustic character.

Take a walk down Pagoda Street, Temple Street and Trengganu Street and you'll see a side of Singapore fast disappearing. The fortune-teller, cobbler, vegetable seller and letter-writer go about their daily business even though their clientele seems to be dwindling.

A good place in which to immerse oneself into the Chinese culture of days gone by is the Chinaman Scholar Gallery at 14B, Terengannu Street. Go up the stairs to the second floor and you might think you just walked through a time warp. Collector and antique dealer Vincent Tan has recreated the ambience of a Chinese scholar's home from the '30s. Visitors are offered tea as he patiently explains the paraphenalia and old photographs.

Walk down Cross Street and into Telok Ayer Street for the Fuk Tak Ch'i Temple which honors Buddhism, Confucianism and Taoism, summarily known as the Shenism. First completed in 1820 and then rebuilt in 1825, it is one of the oldest Chinese temples in Singapore. Further south is the Nagore Durgha Shrine where Palladian doors and Doric columns blend harmoniously with Moorish architecture to give this mosque its distinctive design.

Close by is the Thiam Hock Keng Temple, or Temple of Heavenly Happiness. Among Hokkien Chinese, this is the premier place of worship, and is a splendid example of Chinese rococo architecture. Hokkien immigrants, disembarking off their junks, made this temple their first destination on Singapore soil where they would light joss sticks to give thanks to the gods for their safe passage.

In 1821, a joss house was built, and today's temple was built on the same site in 1840. To the left of the Thiam Hock Keng Temple are the minarets of the Abrar Mosque. The Tamils used to call this the Koochoo Pally, which means "small mosque", because its original structure was but a mere thatched hut built in 1827. In 1850, the hut was replaced by the present building.

Preserving the past

In the southern part of Chinatown is the Tanjong Pagar Conservation area—"yuppie Chinatown"—where old shophouses have been revamped into pastel brilliance. Craig Road, Tanjong Pagar Road and Duxton Road all hold a good number of pubs and restaurants done up to the nines. The rows of shops sell handicrafts, artworks, souvenirs and even furniture. Restaurants serve anything from Thai, Chinese, and French to Italian food. The Pewter Museum on Duxton Road houses 800 exhibits tracing the history of pewterware and demonstrations by craftsmen.

The picturesque Jinrikisha Station at the corner of Tanjong Pagar Road and Neil Road can be rather misleading for it now houses a seafood restaurant. Jinrikishas—hand-pulled rickshaws—were a popular mode of transport before the World War II, but were then replaced by the bicycle trishaw.

Further afield, is the Seiwan Arts Centre on Eu Tong Sen Street, formerly the Thong Chai Medical Institution, with its displays of Chinese arts and crafts. Constructed in 1892, this beautiful Chinese building has an open courtyard, and ornate pillars and beams. The Wak Hai Cheng Bio Temple, sandwiched by modern, commercial buildings on Philip Street was built in the 1850s. Its focal point is its roof, which is decorated with miniature sculptures depicting life in ancient China.

In the center of the commercial district east of Chinatown, between Robinson Road and Shenton Way, is the Telok Ayer Festival Market, a classical wrought-iron building which was Singapore's first municipal fish market. Since it's recent restoration it now houses a food center.

Chinatown used to have dozens of coffeshops, and you can still find some, although it is getting harder to be able to sit down on a bentwood chair and sip a cup of potent local coffee placed on a marble table top. These days much of the food is to be found in hawker centres where numerous stalls sell an amazing variety, from fried noodles to pig's intestines. The Kreta Ayer Complex, opposite People's Park Complex, has a hawker centre on the second floor where specialities include *yong tau fu*, beancurd, chicken rice, or wan ton noodles.

—*Shane Callahan*

Below: *Streetside calligraphers are busiest at Chinese New Year when homes and businesses are decorated with good luck and long-life messages.*

LITTLE INDIA

Serangoon Road and Arab Street

Indian immigrants first settled around the region of Serangoon Road during early 19th-century British times when they were brought in to construct some of Singapore's most famous landmarks like the Istana—now the President's home, the City Hall and Saint Andrew's Cathedral. Today, this road, and its little side-lanes are still dominated by the Indian community.

There are spice grinders, fortune tellers, goldsmiths, flower-garland vendors, vegetable sellers, tailors, and Indian music-tape vendors. You can pick up hand-crafted bangles or anklets, leather sandals, saris, cooking pots of all shapes and sizes and ornate brass and gold jewellery.

To get to Little India take an MRT train to Dhoby Ghaut, then wander past the Cathay Cinema and up Selegie Road to Serangoon Road. You know you're there once you see

crowded Zhujiao Centre, just past Bukit Timah Road, where people from all over the island come for good deals in groceries and food. It's a great place to see how the customers haggle and also to taste what true local cuisine has to offer.

"Banana-leaf" restaurants

Food is a major preoccupation here. On every street corner hawkers set up shop. Look at the prata seller as he skilfully flips his sheet of dough over and over. The result is bound to be a treat. In most of the Indian restaurants, banana leaves serve as plates. Usually there is no cutlery for one is expected to eat using the fingers of the right hand (the left is considered unclean). Rice is scooped onto your leaf until you call out to stop and various spicy accompaniments of meat, fish or vegetable dishes can be chosen. The ever-popular Komala Vilas' on Serangoon Road is strictly vegetarian, and as well as "banana-leaf" curries they serve delicious Dhosai, a lighter form of fried bread, served with coconut chutney and curry.

Signs of religion are everywhere. Not just in the area's abundant temples, but also in restaurants and shops which all have prominently-displayed portraits of Shiva the destroyer, Hanuman the monkey god, Ganesh the elephant god and Krishna as a baby. Vendors in their tiny corners can also be found selling religious garlands made from jasmine and orchids.

Serangoon Road's Indian temples are colorful, adorned with statues of deities, and bustling with worshippers. The Sri Srinivasa Perumal Temple has broad red and white stripes while the nearby Sri Sivan Temple is gaily decorated with brightly-colored figures. The Sri Rama Temple also has a splendid entrance guarded by giant Hindu gods.

The most noticeable temple on Serangoon Road must be the Sri Veeramakaliamman Temple with its splendid entrance. Around late October, when Deepavali, the Festival of Lights, is celebrated, Serangoon Road is aglow with oil lamps, temples are adorned with floral decorations, and devotees carry the shrines of their deities in procession.

Two blocks north on Race Course Lane stands the Mahatma Gandhi Memorial Hall which had its foundation stone laid by Jawarharlal Nehru, the late Indian prime minister. A solid grey structure stands at the corner of Serangoon Road and Towner Road. The main place of worship for the 18,000 or so Sikhs in Singapore, the Central Sikh

Gurdwara, is also a gathering place for activities with its clinic and library. A prayer hall with a 13-meter-wide dome has enshrined in it the Ganth Sahib, or holy book.

The Chinese have also made their mark in Little India. On Race Course Road is the Leong San See or Dragon Mountain Temple. Dedicated to Kuan Yin, the Chinese goddess of mercy, the temple has an impressive altar, decorated with birds, flowers and a phoenix. Nearby, the Buddhist Temple of 1,000 Lights houses a 15-meter seated Buddha. The temple is so named because the Buddha is framed by a string of lights.

Unlike much of Singapore, slick shopping malls are not so plentiful here. Old-style shophouses still dominate the streets where the pervading aroma is of exotic spices; and where the women are draped in elegant sarees, and the men are dressed in the distinctive white *dhoti*. Textiles, in every imaginable hue crowd the shops, and Indian pop-music blasts from the shopfronts.

A good place for electronics, perfumes, and traditional Indian costumes is Serangoon Plaza. On Buffalo Road, a tiny alley leads into a courtyard housing a hawker centre and a series of renovated shophouses—a recently-completed government conservation project. Most of the local residents, however, shy away from the modern-look eatery preferring their old tried-and-tested coffee shops and restaurants.

Arab Street

Turn down Dunlop Street for Abdul Gafoor Mosque, built in 1910, and noted for its framed family tree which traces the line of Muslim prophets. East of here, is another interesting ethnic enclave centered around Arab Street which is famous for traditional Muslim businesses dealing in textiles. rattan goods, perfumes, leatherwares, spices, prayer mats, and Indonesian batik.

The area's most prominent landmark is the golden-domed Sultan Mosque on North Bridge Road, named after Sultan Hussein of Singapore, which was constructed in 1924 to replace an earlier mosque which had been funded by Raffles. The little lanes around Arab Street are also worth walking through, especially Jalan Bussorah, which has some interesting old houses.

Famous Bugis Street of yore is now an MRT station, but its successor, a recreated version, stands opposite on Cheng Yan Square. The gaudy transvestites have gone, and along with them, Bugis Street's raunchy atmosphere. The new version is a tamer attraction where you can still dine under the stars, and shop for copy watches and souvenirs.

—Shane Callahan

Below: *A Brahmin priest strikes a lookalike pose beside this Hindu deity at a Serangoon Road temple.*

MRT Stations

B1	Bukit Batok		N4	Newton
B2	Bukit Gombak		N5	Novena
B3	Choa Chu Kang		N6	Toa Payoh
C1	Raffles Place (2 Stns)		N7	Braddell
C2	City Hall (2 Stns)		N8	Bishan
E1	Bugis		N9	Ang Mo Kio
E2	Lavender		N10	Yio Chu Kang
E3	Kallang		N11	Khatib
E4	Aljunied		N12	Yishun
E5	Paya Lebar		W1	Tanjong Pagar
E6	Eunos		W2	Outram Park
E7	Kembangan		W3	Tiong Bahru
E8	Bedok		W4	Redhill
E9	Tanah Merah		W5	Queenstown
E10	Simei		W6	Commonwealth
E11	Tampines		W7	Bouna Vista
E12	Pasir Ris		W8	Clementi
M1	Marina Bay		W9	Jurong East
N1	Dhoby Ghaut		W10	Chinese Garden
N2	Somerset		W11	Lakeside
N3	Orchard		W12	Boon Lay

Singapore Island

MALAYSIA

SENOKO INDUSTRIAL ESTATE
Sembawang End Park
SEMBAWANG
Tg. Irau
P. SELETAR

SELAT JOHOR

YISHUN
Tg. Punggol
Tg. Tajam
Serangoon Harbour
Tg. Batu Kekek
KG. NOORDIN
KG. MALAM
Tg. Balal
P. UBIN
KG. MAMAM
KG. CHE JEVAH
Pulau Ubin Village
KG. MELAYU
Tg. Chek Jawa
Sungai
Seletar
Reservoir
JALAN KAYU
PUNGGOL
P. SERANGOON
P. KETAM
KG. JELUTONG
Tg. Jelutong
Changi Beach
Changi Village
Changi Golf Course

YIO CHU KANG
ANG MO KIO AVE 5
HOUGANG
PASIR RIS
Pasir Ris Beach
LOYANG
CHANGI

ANG MO KIO
ANG MO KIO AVE 3
TAMPINES EXPRESSWAY
E12
Changi Airport

Lower Pierce Reservoir
THOMSON
SERANGOON
TAMPINES ROAD
Changi Prison
BISHAN
BOUNDARY ROAD
The Crocodile Farm
TAMPINES & SIMEI
E11

PAYA LEBAR
Bedok Reservoir
E10

MacRitchie Reservoir Park
TOA PAYOH
JALAN TOA PAYOH
DEFU INDUSTRIAL ESTATE
KIM CHUAN
BEDOK
PAN ISLAND EXPRESSWAY
Tanah Merah Golf Course

PAYA LEBAR WAY
BEDOK NORTH
E8   E9
NEW UPPER CHANGI ROAD
XILIN AVENUE

N5
E5   E6   E7
KATONG
UPPER EAST COAST ROAD
EAST COAST PARKWAY

National Stadium
OLD KALLANG AIRPORT ESTATE
MARINE PARADE ROAD
East Coast Sailing Club & Lagoon

CITY
TANJONG RHU
Singapore Tennis Centre
UDMC Seafood Centre

Geylang
Big Splash
East Coast Park

Singapore Crocodilarium
Marine Parade Park

Benjamin Sheares Bridge
MARINA BAY
SELAT SINGAPURA

Railway Station
Mt. Faber
EXPRESSWAY
Keppel Harbour
World Trade Centre
P. BRANI
Tg. Pagar

0   1   2   3 km
0   1 mi

N

Sentosa Island

P. SENTOSA (SENTOSA ISLAND)
P. TEKUKOR
P. SERINGAT (P. RENGED)
TEMBAKUL (KUSU ISLAND)
P. SAKIJANG BENDERA (ST. JOHN'S ISLAND)
P. SAKIJANG PELEPAH (LAZARUS ISLAND)
SUBAR DARAT
P. SUBAR LAUT

Tg. Rimau
Fort Siloso
Rasa Sentosa Hotel
Siloso Beach
P. RENGGIS
Underwater World
Ruined City & Lost Civilisation
Nature Ramble
Butterfly Park & World Insectarium
Ferry Terminal & Fountain Gardens
Rasa Sentosa
Pasar Malam
Musical Fountain
Pioneers of S'pore & Surrender Chamber
Art Centre
Rare Stone Museum
Maritime Museum
Serapong Golf Course
Mt. Serapong
P. BRANI
Tg. Teregeh
SELAT SENGKIR

Central Lagoon
The Beaufort
ALLANBROOKE RD
Coralarium
Telok Durian
BURAN DARAT
Holiday Chalets
Golf Course
Tanjong Beach
Sentosa Golf Club
Tg. China

0   0.25   0.5   0.75 km
0   0.25 mi

N

AROUND THE ISLAND

Theme Parks and Offshore Islands

In order to attract tourists to linger longer, Singapore is rapidly developing new attractions, preserving historical ones and introducing new forms of activities. Amid the concrete symbols of progress are nature reserves, beaches, theme parks, offshore islands, and a host of recreation spots. The compact size of the island, a mere 573km² (221mi²), together with its excellent public transport system makes getting around an easy affair.

West of the city

A good place to start an island tour is at Mount Faber, off Telok Blangah Road. To get there take the MRT to Tanjong Pagar, then take a taxi. The scenic alternative is to ride up on the cable car from the Jardine Steps Station next to the World Trade Centre. From the summit there are panoramic views of Singapore and its offshore islands. Focus on the port area—you will see why Singapore is ranked as the world's busiest. Take a stroll, rest at the tea house, or take the cable car to Sentosa Island.

From Mount Faber, catch a taxi to Alkaff Mansion, in Telok Blangah Green. Formerly the 19th-century home of the wealthy Alkaff family, it has now been restored into a charming restaurant. The architecture is not purely colonial, but is blended with Asian and Arabic styles. Here, you can lunch or dine in the same rooms which were set for grand dinners and parties during the colonial heydays.

Further west at Pasir Panjang is Haw Par Villa, also known as **Tiger Balm Gardens**. Singapore's first theme park was built by the Aw brothers with the profits from their immensely popular Tiger Balm—a medicinal ointment. Open weekdays from 9am to 6pm, and until 9pm on weekends, the park charges $S16 for adults, and $S10 for children under 12. To get there take an SBS bus No 10 or 30. This Chinese mythological theme park presents multi-media shows, boat rides, and animated presentations which bring to life the statues of Chinese gods, goddesses, legends, beasts and demons.

Tang Dynasty Village, Singapore's latest theme park, is further west in Jurong, the huge industrial complex. Open weekdays from 10am to 7pm, and from 9am on weekends, admission is $S15 for adults and $S10 for children under 12. To get there take the MRT to Lakeside Station, then take bus No 154 or 240. In this largest Chinese historical and cultural theme park in Asia, architecture, street scenes and activities are recreated from Chang-An, China's Tang dynasty capital (618 to 907AD).

Nearby are the Chinese and Japanese Gardens, open from 9am to 7pm. Admission for adults is $S2.50, children under 12 pay $S1.20. The Chinese garden, which is Sung Dynasty influenced, is linked by a bridge to

the Japanese garden. On the Chinese side are courtyards, pagodas, fountains, bridges and a river on which visitors can paddle or row boats. At the **Penjing Garden** are bonzai plants from all over the world. The Japanese Garden features stone lanterns, shrubs, hillocks and a tea house.

Adjacent is the CN West Leisure Park, open Tuesday to Friday from noon to 6pm, and weekends from 9.30am to 6pm. Admission for adults is $S4, children under 12, $S2. To get there take the MRT to Chinese Garden Station, then take a taxi. Singapore's largest aquatic park features a 15-meter-long water slide, a wave pool, and a bumper-boat ride.

Further south, at Jurong Hill is the **Jurong Bird Park**, the largest birdpark in Asia and one of the world's best. Open daily from 9am to 6pm, the park charges $S6 for adults, and $S2.50 for children under 12. To get there take the MRT to Boon Lay Station, then take bus Nos 251, 253 or 255 from the interchange. Over 5,000 birds of 450 species are housed here and attractions include the penguin parade, the world's largest collection of Southeast Asian hornbills and a variety of bird shows. Opposite the birdpark is Jurong Crocodile Paradise, home to 2,500 crocodiles, where visitors can watch crocodile-wrestling shows daily at 11.45am and 3pm.

Singapore's oldest and most scenic parklands, The **Botanic Gardens**, on the corner

of Napier and Cluny Roads, are open daily from 6am to 11pm and till midnight on weekends. To get there take the MRT to Orchard Station, then hail a taxi, walk, or take a bus along Tanglin then Napier Road. Fifty-four hectares of tropical jungle, manicured lawns and beautifully landscaped gardens make the Botanic Gardens a favourite spot for picnics, strolls, workouts or simply a good rest. Over 2,000 plant species grow here, including Brazilian rubber trees, which were introduced to Singapore by Sir Henry Ridley. Once, monkeys roamed the grounds, but they have since been relocated. The orchid pavilion has some 12,000 orchid plants including Singapore's national flower, the Vanda Miss Joaquim.

Northwest of here, more or less in the center of the island, is the **Bukit Timah Nature Reserve** which covers a 163-m-high hill—Singapore's highest point. On its slopes is a nature reserve of tropical rain forest where monkeys, birds, butterflies, and snakes make their home. Hiking up Bukit Timah Hill is an exhilarating experience, aided by well marked tracks along its slopes. Beneath the canopy of trees, admire the wild orchids, ferns, mosses, vines and creepers that flourish in this 81-hectare reserve. From the summit, is a panoramic and unrivalled view of Singapore. To get there take a bus up Bukit Timah Road to Eward Circus, then walk up Hindhede Rd. (20 mins) to the reserve.

In the far north is **Mandai Orchid Gardens**. Ride the MRT to Yishun then take a bus No 171. The Mandai Orchid Gardens are next to the Zoological Gardens, so you

Opposite: A manta ray hovers over head at Underwater World at Sentosa Island.
Above, left: A sculpted nymph amongst the hothouse greenery of the Botanic Gardens.
Above, right: Waterside pagodas and an arched bridge are among the attraction of the Chinese Garden at Jurong.

should really try to combine the two in one trip. This is Singapore's largest orchid garden, and a huge variety of blooms now grow in this lush tropical garden which was formerly a swamp.

The **Singapore Zoo**, open daily from 8.30am to 6pm, charge $S7 for adults and $S3 for children under 12. To get there just stay on the bus from Mandai Orchid Garden. There is also a Zoo Express, a twice-daily shuttle which brings visitors from major hotels to the zoo. Coupons can be purchased at hotels (Adults $S29, children $S17). Singapore's zoo is rated one of the best in the world. Mapped on the open plan concept (as in the San Diego Zoo), it sprawls over 28 hectares and houses almost 1,700 animals belonging to 170 species.

If you do not want to walk it, then take the tram. There are various theme areas: Primate Kingdom for the apes, Antartica for the sealion and penguins, and Children's World, where visitors can touch the animals. The zoo's most famous personality is Ah Meng the orangutan, with whom visitors from all over the world have had breakfast (9am) and tea (4pm). Other notable personalities are the Bawean hog deer, the Komodo dragon and Sumatran tiger—which are all on the endangered list.

Due north from the city is the **Kong Meng San Temple,** a huge Chinese temple sited on Bright Hill Drive. To get there, ride the MRT to Braddell Station, then take a taxi. The temple complex includes a crematorium, where thousands of urns of ashes are stored. This temple is particularly busy during the Qing Ming festival, when the Chinese honor their dead. Throughout the complex are beautiful examples of Chinese architecture and sculpture. Occasionally, Chinese operas are staged here.

In the same direction, but closer to the city, is the Siong Lim Temple, on Jalan Toa Payoh. To get there, ride the MRT to Toa Payoh, then take a taxi or bus. Visible from the Pan Island Expressway, this temple is a majestic piece of architecture, complete with decorated gateways, courtyards, and beautifully-carved Buddha statues. Dating back to 1908, its construction was financed by wealthy Hokkien businessmen.

The East Coast

Massive land reclamation projects have reshaped Singapore's shoreline and many of the East Coast's attractions are on land that not so long ago was part of the Singapore Straits.

The **East Coast Park** runs alongside a 5-km long beach which features shaded beaches, cycling and walking paths, food centers and many recreational attractions. To get there it is easier to catch a taxi as access by public transport is difficult.

At the East Coast Sailing Club, windsurfers and lasers can be hired by the hour, and they also offer lessons. Canoes are rented at the Lagoon Food Center and bicycles can be hired from a booth near the Rendezvous Food Center next to the club.

At **Big Splash**, the aquatic amusements feature Southeast Asia's longest water slides. Simulated wave movements can be experienced in the Wave Pool. Otherwise, flow with the currents in the Flow Pool. Children will find safer amusements in the Children's Splash Pool, complete with miniature water slides.

The **Singapore Crocodilarium** at 730 East Coast Parkway, open daily from 9am to 5.30pm puts on wrestling shows, twice daily.

Further east, and north of Changi Airport, is the Changi Prison Chapel and Museum located at Changi Prison. Popular with with former prisoners-of-war, it is a memorial to the 85,000 prisoners held captive during the Japanese Occupation in World War II. The museum displays sketches, watercolors and photographs collected from that time. Notable are the collection of vivid photographs by George Aspinall. There are also rail spikes from the Thai-Burma railway

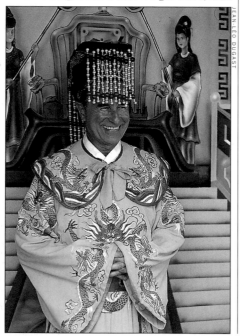

where many POWs died. The chapel is a replica of that constructed by the POWs. Open on weekdays from 8.30am to 12.30pm and 2pm to 4.45pm. Saturdays from 8.30 am to noon. Sunday services are held at 5.30pm. For further information telephone Singapore Sightseeing, 4736900. To get there take the MRT to Tampines, then take a taxi.

Offshore Islands

Off the coast of Singapore are around 58 smaller islands. About 24 of these are inhabited, some are in restricted zones and are inaccessible, while others range from deserted isles to popular tourist resorts.

Sentosa, formerly Pulau Belakang Mati, is an off-shore island totally dedicated to fun and recreation. Museums feature Singapore's history, rare stones, and maritime developments. There are nature trails and cycle paths through secondary forests, a pristine beach with powder-fine sand, roller skating rinks, a butterfly park, restaurants, a hawker centre and a luxury hotel.

At the popular **Underwater World** visitors can experience the feeling of being in the ocean depths without actually being there. When you walk through its moving perspex tunnel, you will be surrounded by 2,000 species of marine life. Ferry services to the island operate from the World Trade Centre from 7.30am to 11pm. Adults are charged $S8.50, children under 12, $S4.50, which includes the two-way ferry ride, entry fee, monorail rides and shuttle bus to the Coralarium. Visitors can also take the cable car from Mount Faber.

To get to the smaller southern islands of Kusu and St. John's, take the regular ferry services from the World Trade Centre. Return fares are $S6 for adults and $S3 for children under 12. Check schedules beforehand. From Kusu there's a 25-min boat ride with fantastic views of Singapore's skyline. The island has a couple of small beaches and the famed Tuah Peh Kong Temple which is crowded with pilgrims at the annual celebrations in October. Steps lead to the summit of the island where there are some sacred keramat—Muslim shrines. The shaded beaches at St. John's Island, 10-mins further by boat, are excellent for swimming and picnicking.

Further afield are the Sister's Islands, Pulau Hantu and Pulau Seking. To get there you can hire boats from Clifford Pier or Jardine Steps, which cost about $30 each, though prices can vary. Sister's and Pulau Hantu are popular with snorkelers and Pulau Seking has a quaint Malay village with houses on stilts.

—Yeow Mei Sin

Opposite: *Dressing up for the camera is a popular pursuit at Singapore's Chinese mythological theme parks.* **Below:** *Breakfast with Ah Meng, the celebrated orangutan.*

Travel Advisory

All prices are in US dollars unless otherwise stated. Information was gathered and accurate in November 1992. Prices and schedules change so check with a travel agent.

VISA FORMALITIES

All visitors must possess a passport valid for at least six months, or an internationally-recognized travel document endorsed for travel in Malaysia. Nationals of all British Commonwealth countries (except India) and the following countries are granted visa-free entry for 14 days, or one month if requested: Austria, Belgium, Brunei, Denmark, Finland, France, Germany, Iceland, Indonesia, Ireland, Italy, Japan, Liechtenstein, Luxembourg, Netherlands, Norway, Philippines, Singapore, South Korea, Sweden, Switzerland, Thailand, Tunisia, United States.

Extensions can be made easily at immigration offices for up to three months, but proof of onward journey (airline tickets) and whether you have sufficient funds is usually required. Employment is forbidden on a tourist visa. Citizens of Bulgaria, Czechoslovakia, Hungary, Poland, Rumania, Russia and Yugoslavia are allowed to enter Malaysia for up to seven days without a visa.

GETTING THERE

By air. Besides the national carrier **Malaysian Airlines** (MAS), 35 international airlines fly in and out of Kuala Lumpur's Subang International Airport and Penang. MAS fly from London, Amsterdam, Brussels, Paris, Frankfurt, Zurich, Istanbul, Amman, Jeddah, Dubai, Karachi, Delhi, Colombo, Madras, Bangkok, Medan, Jakarta, Denpasar, Manila, Hong Kong, Taipei, Seoul, Tokyo, Perth, Melbourne, Darwin, Adelaide, Sydney, Auckland, Honolulu, Los Angeles, Mexico City, Johannesburg. MAS also have shuttle flights from Singapore, and daily flights from Kuching (Sarawak) and Kota Kinabalu (Sabah).

A discounted fare on cheap airlines like Aeroflot via Moscow costs around $780 RT from London. Air Lanka, and Air India, via Colombo and Delhi or Bombay, are around the same price. MAS fly direct from London for $1320 RT. Discount fares from the US, via the West Coast, can cost as little as $900 RT. Book ahead in the Christmas period as this is a busy time with Malaysian overseas students arriving home for the holidays and with winter in the northern hemisphere this is the prime time for Malaysian resorts.

Make sure you've got return bookings on the cheaper airlines as these are often overbooked. Travelers can buy one way tickets from home and then purchase onward fares from the cheap travel offices in Penang where a variety of discounted fares can be purchased including multi-stop Pacific loops.

By sea. In the old days this was a feasible way to travel, but these days the few ships that do take passengers and stopover at Penang or Klang (Kuala Lumpur's port) are exhorbitant and irregular.

However, there's nothing like a sea voyage to relax you and gently ease you into the equatorial climate. Enquire at travel agents or shipping lines well in advance. It is again possible to come from Madras, India, by ship to Penang as this famous old service has recently recommenced with the revamped MV Vignesswara. Enquire with the Shipping Corporation of India, Madras. There is also a thrice weekly, express ferry service from Medan (Sumatra) to Penang, and from Dumai (Sumatra) to Melaka (*see Melaka Practicalities, p. 262*).

By rail. The train line runs all the way from Bangkok in the north, through Peninsular Malaysia, to Singapore in the south. KTM-Malayan Railways runs from Singapore to Butterworth, and from there travelers change to the Thai International Express to Bangkok. It is a marvellous journey, and a great way to see three countries at once.

Tickets can be bought at either end, or from Kuala Lumpur which is cheaper than Singapore. The International Express departs Bangkok at 3.15pm and arrives in Butterworth at 12.10pm the next day. Travelers can also enter the East Coast by rail as a line branches off from Haadyai (Southern Thailand) to Sungai Golok just over the border from Rantau Panjang, Kelantan.

By road. Peninsular Malaysia shares its land borders with Thailand and Singapore. Coming from the north, share taxis run from Haadyai, across the border at Bukit Kayu Hitam to either Alor Setar in Kedah or to Penang. Local buses also run from Haadyai to Sadao, then change buses for the border at Padang Besar in Perlis.

CUSTOMS

Visitors can bring in one liter of liquor, one carton of cigarettes, and personal possessions like cameras, watches, cassette-players, laptop computors, cosmetics and others. Narcotics, pornography (includes *Playboy*) and firearms are prohibited. Malaysia's drug laws are infamous and all too true, with death penalties for even trafficking in small amounts of marijuana.

The export of antiques must be accompanied with a licence from the Director General of Museums. There is no limit to the amount of currency which is allowed into or out of the country. If you have a dutiable item with you, the customs will assess its value and you will have to pay 50% of this amount as a deposit which is refundable when you leave the country.

GETTING AROUND

Malaysia is an extremely easy country to get around with minimum fuss and bother. There are various options such as air, train, bus and the excellent system of "share" taxis (see below). To really see the countryside at its best nothing beats hiring a car, particularly when traveling to more out of the way places. However, this can get costly over the long term. Trains are slow, but pleasant, and often follow more scenic routes than the roads. Express buses are faster than trains and quite comfortable, but are not advisable for the faint-hearted as the drivers often blatantly disregard road rules. Long-distance air-conditioned taxis are double the bus fare, but more enjoyable.

Hitch-hiking is still done (by International travelers) on Malaysian roads, but it is considered a pretty low-class thing to do, particularly considering how cheap the local transport is. It is highly unadvisable for women, even when traveling in pairs, to hitch hike, as there is a very real possibility of being picked up by men who imagine that women who get into stranger's cars are extremely loose.

By air

Malaysian Airlines (MAS) has reasonably-priced domestic flights from Kuala Lumpur to Johor Bahru for $37, Penang $42 and to Ipoh, Alor Setar, Pulau Langkawi, Kuantan, Kuala Terengganu, and Kota Bharu for similar prices. There are other services which connect some of these major towns, like Kuala Terengganu to Penang, Alor Setar to Kota Bharu, Johor Bahru to Kuantan for example. Air travel is the quick alternative, but offers little in the way of scenery, although the patterns of oil-palm plantations creeping into the rainforest, and the incredible greeness of the landscape is spectacular from above.

There is also a smaller service called Pelangi Air which operates a flight to Kerteh, the "oilies" town in Terengganu, and also flies from Kuala Lumpur to Pulau Tioman off the East Coast. This latter flight provides a hair-raising landing on the mountainous island, but marvellous sea and landscapes along the way. Flights are only booked-out during public and school holidays, when extra flights are put on to handle the crowds, but at all other times there should be no problems getting a seat. MAS also have special night flights and advance purchase fares which are cheaper than the regular flights.

Families, or couples without children can also get a 25% reduction on return fares within Malaysia. There are also discounts for "groups" of three or more, but you must pay at least a week in advance. For travelers arriving from Sarawak or Sabah, it is much cheaper to fly to Johor Bahru than to take flights to Singapore. For prices and times contact Malaysia Airlines,

Bangunan MAS, Jl. Sultan Ismail, 50250, Kuala Lumpur, tel. (03) 2610555, for 24-hour reservations, reconfirmations, and flight information tel. (03) 7463000.

By train

Kertetapi Tanah Malayu (KTM), Peninsular Malaysia's train system was built by the British during the colonial era and still retains many of its elegant old railway stations from that period, including the fantastic terminal at Kuala Lumpur. It is a comfortable, relaxing and extremely reasonably-priced way to view the country, and often the rail goes through countryside which is only otherwise observable by private cars as buses take the main routes which are the most uninteresting. Although buses are quicker, the main roads, especially the North/South route between Kuala Lumpur and Penang are often jammed with lorries which can make travel by bus quite nerve-racking.

There are two main rail lines; the West Coast line which runs from Bangkok through Butterworth and Kuala Lumpur to Singapore; and the East Coast line which branches off at Gemas in Johor and runs to Tumpat in Kelantan. There are two types of trains, the mail or regular services which are slow as they stop everywhere, or the express trains known as the Ekspres Rakyat and Ekspres Sinaran which only stop at major stations and are therefore the most popular for long-distance travel. The most expensive is 1st Class air-conditioned, then 2nd Class air-con, 3rd Class non-air-con. 1st Class is almost double the price of 2nd but is hardly worth it if you want to save money. Both these classes can be booked a month in advance and have in-house videos and sub-Arctic air-con. Third Class is basic, cheap and sometimes very hot, but is a great way to meet the locals.

A Railpass, available only to foreigners, can be purchased at the main railway stations. This gives unlimited travel in any class, for 30 days for around $70, or 10 days for $34, but it is often cheaper, especially if you want to travel 2nd or 3rd Class, to just buy the tickets when you need them. As an example, a 2nd Class air-conditioned fare from Kuala Lumpur to Butterworth costs only around $11, so if you want to make the Railpass economical it means a lot of time spent traveling in trains.

On **overnight trains**, sleeping berths are extra and must be booked and paid for when you buy your ticket. Children between the ages of four and 12 are charged half the adult fare, and children under four travel free of charge. There are buffet cars on all express trains where snacks and light meals can be purchased. Contact Kuala Lumpur Railway Station, tel. (03) 2747442 for details of times and fares.

An elaborately revamped Eastern and Orient Express which will cater for the well-heeled who like to travel in colonial splendor, is due to start running in September 1993 and there are even plans afoot to turn the splendid Moorish-style offices opposite Kuala Lumpur Railway Station into a expensive old-style hotel catering to those journeying on the "Raj"-type train. Call Venice Simplon Orient Express Ltd, London, UK (071) 928 6000 for information and reservations.

By road

Express, air-conditioned buses run between all of the peninsula's main towns. These are fast, they generally leave and arrive on time, and are reasonably comfortable with padded seats and cool air-conditioning although the seats are often placed a little too close for long Westerners' legs. They usually travel fast and the drivers have a penchant for overtaking on blind hills and generally disregarding road rules, although this is not as bad as in the past as the outrageous death toll on the highways has prompted the police to sometimes carry out undercover spot checks and as a result most drivers are now slightly less unnerving.

Probably the worst thing about the buses is where they stop for food breaks, usually in the drab outskirts of towns at "truckers stops" where the food is awful, compared to the marvellous cuisine that can be found the length and breath of the peninsula. However, they are still an extremely popular and convenient way to get around the countryside, especially to towns that are not serviced by the railway.

All **inter-state buses** (except for the East Coast and interior Pahang) run from the crowded Puduraya Bus Station in the center of Kuala Lumpur. Touts selling tickets for "pirate" (unlicensed) buses will accost you on the overpass to the bus station telling you how the bus you want is full and how they have cheaper fares, but ignore them as they are not offering discounts, and continue on to the bus company booths inside the terminal. The times and prices are listed on the front windows of the booths. Different companies run south and north, but just walk along until you find the destination you want, it's easy enough. If the next bus, say to Ipoh, is full, then there is usually another bus-company booth close by that also runs to the same destination. Prices are reasonable, for example, the route from Kuala Lumpur to Butterworth, costs $6 and takes around 8 hours.

All **East Coast buses** run from the new Hentian Putra, opposite The Mall (shopping complex) on Jalan Putra in the northern section of Kuala Lumpur. There is another station, Hentian Pekeliling, on the ring road, Jl. Tun Razak, not far from Hentian Putra, which services Kuala Lipis and other inland Pahang towns. Local buses run between all the minor towns in Malaysia and are slow, but reasonably comfortable and extremely cheap. The drivers are also not quite as maniacal, and although they are not air-con everyone keeps their win-

dows open and the wind keeps the buses from getting oven-like. The quickest and best way to travel though is by "share" taxis which ply the routes between all the peninsula's major towns. These are sometimes air-conditioned Mercedes with comfortable seats, and even cassette-players which invariably play Malay love songs or Chinese pop.

There are **long-distance taxi** stations, usually near the express bus stations at all the main towns. In Kuala Lumpur, the taxi terminal is upstairs from the Puduraya Bus Station. You must make it clear that you want to share the taxi, otherwise sharp-talking cabbies will try to talk you into chartering it which costs four times as much. When you approach popular taxi stations the drivers will all be calling out their destinations, like "Melaka" etc., and you just head for that taxi.

Sometimes you are the last passenger and they take off immediately, other times you have to wait until the taxi fills. This may be only ten minutes if it's in the morning, or maximum half an hour. However, if it's late afternoon and no-one wants to go there, the wait may extend to one hour, but don't worry as the taxi driver has to return, and sometimes if no-one else shows up he takes off half empty and then just looks for fares along the way. Prices are about double the bus fare, but are worth the extra as the drivers often take you straight to your hotel. (*See Practicalities for prices*).

Car rentals

Malaysia is one of the easiest countries in Asia to hire and drive your own car. Drivers need a valid International Licence or often a valid licence from your own country will do. Companies prefer to deal with people paying with credit cards, although you can pay by cash, but they usually ask for a hefty deposit. Rates start around $44 per day for the cheapest vehicles, although if you look in the Malay Mail (Kuala Lumpur's afternoon tabloid) you can sometimes find them for quite a bit less.

Driving is on the left-hand side of the road, and rules are much the same as in any other country. Wearing seatbelts is compulsory in the front seats. On highways and expressways the speed limit is 110kph and 80kph on trunk roads. In built-up areas and towns the speed limit is usually 50kph. Most Malaysian drivers, however, pay little heed to these speed limitations, and as there is little enforcement they usually get away with it. As well as suicidal drivers, motorists must be constantly aware in the kampung areas of bicycles and stray animals, especially at night. There is an excellent system of roads across the entire peninsula, but some stretches of the main west coast highway can get very crowded with lorries.

The North/South Expressway (Lebuhraya Utara Selatan) will be totally finished in late 1994 and the stretches already completed make long-distance driving a relaxed affair, although the road only goes through rural areas and by-passes all the towns. Although Malaysia have their own oil, petrol is not cheap at 45 cents a liter. Malaysian Motorhomes, 20 Jl. Pinang, Kuala Lumpur, tel: (03) 2418541, rent out their fully-equipped motor homes which sleep four, are air-conditioned and have built in bathrooms. This is a great way to see the country, particularly the inland and off-the-beaten track places.

PLANNING YOUR ITINERARY

Because of Peninsular Malaysia's extensive road and rail network it is an easy country to travel around, and it is quite feasible to circumnavigate the entire peninsular in a two-week stay. However, for travelers with less time, or for those who like to really appreciate a place it makes sense to limit your travels to a smaller area and opt to either visit the west coast or the east coast. The west is more multi-cultural, has most of the major towns and cities, and some of the peninsula's most famous destinations like Penang, Kuala Lumpur and Melaka. The east, on the other hand is laid-back, mainly Malay culture, and has beautiful beaches and tropical islands.

The interior regions like Taman Negara, the National Park, are a totally different experience, and travelers wishing to spend time here should allow for at least week to really make the most of their experience. If the hothouse atmosphere gets you down while on the West Coast you can always head into the hills to Cameron Highlands or the other hill stations to relax in the cooler weather and do some jungle trekking. Except for these hilly regions, the rest of the peninsula is hot and humid, and it is advisable to get an early start when sight-seeing.

For travelers interested in Malay culture, the east coast, and in particular the area around Kota Bharu, Kelantan, is the most traditional. Many people still produce arts and crafts, and the fishing boats, and many of the leisure activities like kite-flying and top-spinning are very traditional. For history buffs, Melaka with its many historical sites and original Chinatown, is the obvious destination, closely followed by Georgetown, Penang, which is great for exploring on foot. For beach lovers, the west coast's top spot is Pulau Langkawi, followed by the northern beaches of Penang, while the east coast is really one long beach excellent for swimming. The most pristine beaches are found on the offshore islands including Terengganu's Pulau Perhentian, Pulau Redang; Pahang's Pulau Tioman; and the offshore islands of East Johor.

ACCOMMODATIONS

In all the major cities and towns, travelers have a good choice of accomodation from luxury hotels in the major destinations to thatched-roof huts on the beach. All hotels above budget-standard charge 10% service charge and five% government tax on top of the bill, although this is sometimes included in the listed price. During the off season, which is the monsoon (Oct-Feb) on the east coast, and June to September in Penang and Pulau Langkawi, prices drop quite considerably. Except for peak periods like national and school holidays you can safely ask for "discount" prices. Hotels often have "promotional-rates" happening as well, so it's wise to enquire first as these can often save you up to 30% on the listed rate.

The **luxury lodgings** are world-class and the regular hotel chains like Hilton, Sheraton, Holiday Inn, provide the same service as their sister hotels elsewhere. Some of the luxury hotels that stand out, mainly because of their beautiful Malay-style wooden architecture, are the Pelangi Beach Resort at Pualu Langkawi and the Tanjung Jara Resort at Dungun (east coast). Not all the main towns have luxury hotels, but most have comfortable first-class to intermediate standard hotels. These are always fully air-conditioned, have hot-water in the private bathrooms, and provide TV, IDD phones, and often room service.

There are cheap and basic **old Chinese-run hotels** in every major and minor town on the peninsula. Some of these are clean and neat and a great bargain, and others are hot, noisy and dirty. (*See Practicalities for details*). Some of these hotels have air-conditioning and private bathrooms, but most have overhead fans and shared bathrooms. Some of these establishments double as brothels, especially in Ipoh, but this is only a problem if you are a single woman. Check out the room before you register.

In many of the beach destinations there are **chalets** (small huts usually containing twin beds) which vary from very cheap and basic to air-conditioned ones with attached bathrooms. The cheapest accomodation is usually "A" frame thatched-roof huts with a mattress. One sheet and a pillow with a pillow-slip is usually provided, but if you are roughing it, it's a good idea to have a couple of sarongs that you can use as a spare sheet, and use one of these as a towel as some of the cheaper places don't provide towels. Make sure you've always got some mosquito coils as this will ensure you always get a good night's sleep. Many of the more, outlying island resorts don't have electricity but they provide a kerosene lamp. In some of the older-style resorts there are no showers, but merely a *mandi*—a tub of water which you douse yourself with using a plaster dipper. Bring your own toilet paper with you as this is often not supplied.

Peninsular Malaysia's best bargain accomodation is a left-over from the colonial days, the *Rumah Rehat*, or **Resthouses**. These are usually in the outskirts of town, and are sometimes a little hard to get to if you don't have your own transport. Originally, resthouses were constructed to look after the needs of the colonial civil servants, planters, and merchants when they journeyed "out-station", and basically they serve the same purpose today.

Some resthouses, like Pekan (Pahang), The Gap (Fraser's Hill), still survive in their original colonial form. Others like Mersing (Johor), and Taiping and Kuala Kangsar in Perak have been rebuilt, but still offer the same services at very low prices. As resthouses are such a bargain they are often booked out by Malaysians, so it is a good idea to always phone ahead to make a booking.

Rooms are huge and can often sleep an entire family, they usually have private bathrooms, and often have their own verandahs. Some have air-conditioned rooms as well as ones with overhead fans. Practically all resthouses have restaurants attached and as the proprietors don't make much money on the rooms, they usually offer a good array of tasty food as this is what they make their profit from. In smaller towns, sometimes the Resthouse is "the" place to eat, and the food is usually excellent.

TOUR AND TRAVEL AGENCIES

Tours are only useful if you have limited time, or you are the type who can't be bothered finding out how to get somewhere on your own. The Malaysian Tourist Promotion Board (formerly TDC) run city, country, and night tours for reasonably prices from their information center (MATIC) in Jalan Ampang, Kuala Lumpur. Also the tourist information office in Kota Bharu, Kelantan, does interesting cultural and historical tours (see Practicalities, p.154). Look in the "Tours and Travel" section of the Malay Mail, Kuala Lumpur's afternoon tabloid, if you are interested in getting cheap local tours to Pulau Tioman, Cameron Highlands, Pulau Langkawi and other favorite destinations. These are usually quite reasonably-priced but you have hotel rooms on a twin-sharing basis.

These tours are very popular with Malaysians and it is a good way to meet the locals. International tourists are also catered for by the big travel companies in the cities and major towns. Reputable companies include Mayflower Acme Tours, Kuala Lumpur (03-6267011), Johor Bahru (07-241357), Kuantan (09-1866), Penang (04-628196), Pulau Langkawi (04-911330); Reliance SMAS Tours, Sungai Wang Plaza, Kuala Lumpur, (03-2488833). Ask at these tour agents for special tours like "Malaysian Gardens," which are often organised for groups.

WHAT TO BRING ALONG

You could travel to Malaysia and leave everything but your passport and money at home and get by very nicely. Light cotton clothing is worn all year round, and is cheap and easily available. The only problem with buying clothes here is that larger Western sizes are sometimes difficult to buy outside of Kuala Lumpur, so if you are on the large size it's better to at least bring along your own pants.

T-shirts and cotton shirts are cheap and readily available, and, in fact, many famous brands names are made in Malaysia and then sent overseas. For excellent "safari" type clothing, the "East India" boutiques in Metro Department stores in Kuala Lumpur stock a great array of cotton pants with lots of pockets, shirts, folding hats, and skirts and long shorts—all made of real cotton and excellent wear for travelling or trekking in the rainforest. Although hiking boots, and jogging shoes are available here it is best to bring your own as they will be nicely worn in. Reeboks and other brands are cheaper here than in Australia and Europe, but are no bargain for visitors from the USA.

Leave all your mini-skirts, backless dresses and sexy clothes at home. For even though many Chinese and Eurasians dress like this in the city, they don't get the stares that mat-salleh (westerners) do when dressed the same way. Even when dressed modestly you will still get plenty of looks, so unless you want a lot of unasked for attention it's best to dress in loose-fitting comfortable clothes. They are also much nicer to wear in the hot, humid climate. If you intend to go to the highlands areas like Cameron Highlands, bring along a light sweater, cardigan, or even a sweatshirt will suffice as the nights can get rather chilly.

If you wear glasses, bring your prescription along as spectacles are very cheap—even name brands—and there are opticians in every town in Malaysia. If you are on medications bring your prescriptions along and ask your doctor for generic names for your medicines as these are often sold under different names in Malaysia. Toiletries are readily available, both locally-made and imported and visitors shouldn't have any trouble buying their favorite brand of toothpaste or deodorant. For the best choice, stock up in Kuala Lumpur's big supermarkets before heading off on your travels.

If you are travelling on the cheap other sensible accessories include a small torch, water canteen, a day pack, pocket knife, and a money pouch. Rubber slip-ons, known as "slippers" in Malaysia, "thongs" in Australia and "flip-flops" in Britain, can be bought cheaply and are very useful for walking over hot beaches, and wearing when having a shower in shared bathrooms. Malaysians are not big on present giving, and a big smile to accompany your "terimah-kasih" (thank you) is all that is needed. If you feel like giving a small gift, coins from your own country or stamps are often appreciated.

LANGUAGE

The national language is Bahasa Malaysia, or Malay, which is spoken not only throughout

Malaysia but is the mother tongue of the vast Indonesian archipelago, southern Thailand, and the southern Philippines. For any traveler interested in spending time in this region, a basic knowledge of the language goes a long way to making travel more insightful, more economical and much easier. Even if you only know a few words, Malays will be delighted to hear you speak their language and will be much more responsive towards you.

Classical Malay attained its heyday during the 15th-century Melakan Sultanate, but this fine form of the language suffered duing the colonial British era when Malay took second place to English. However, after Independence, Bahasa Malaysia, which is based on Classical Malay, took over as the National Language.

Basic Malay is easy to learn although the formal language which is used in newspapers and books requires serious study and is much more complex. The language has taken on different words from the various cultural influences which have altered the Malay way of life. Arabic loan words are many, mostly arriving with Islam, and include the prayer times like *magrib*—the evening prayer or the Arabic word for "west".

Most Malay names like Mohammad, Mahmud, Azizah, Fatimah, etc., originate from Arabic as all Muslims, even those with nicknames, must have an Arabic name which God will use to call them on the Day of Judgment. Sanskrit arrived even earlier when Hinduism was introduced by Indian traders and loan words include titles like Raja, Megat, Indera, and words like *maya*—illusion, and *guru*—teacher. The Portuguese, after their conquest of Melaka introduced furniture and words like *meja*—table, and *almari*—wardrobe are still used today. Other minor influences include Hindustani, Persian, Chinese languages, Turkish, Thai and Tamil. English loan words are many and are usually easily recognisable like *polis*—police, *bas*—bus, *klinik*—clinic, *teksi*—taxi, and others.

Malay varies however, from region to region, and there are quite different variations spoken in Kelantan and Terengganu on the East Coast. Isolated communities also have their own distinctive dialect like on Pulau Tioman where the old remaining families still speak a version which only occurs on that island.

Apart from the national language, English is widely spoken in the cities, major towns and tourist destinations. It is the language of commerce and can be understood at all banks, post offices, and most large hotels. Even in small towns there is usually someone that can speak English, although don't expect to find English-speakers in isolated kampungs.

Chinese languages are widely spoken amongst the Chinese, some of whom still know very little Malay even after generations of living here. Hokkien and Cantonese are two of the more popular dialects. Tamil is spoken by the Indian minority who originated from South India, and Hindustani and northern Indian dialects are spoken by many Muslim traders who immigrated from these regions.

Spelling and pronunciation

Bahasa Malaysia is not a tonal language and is therefore less difficult to learn than Thai or many Chinese dialects. There are no articles, *kampung* means "the village", or "a village". Plurals are indicated by doubling the noun *layang-layang* means "swallows", *kupu-kupu* means "butterflies". Tense is usually indicated by adverbs, the most popular ones being *sudah* which means "already", and *belum* which means "not yet".

Malay is not a difficult language to pronounce but there are a few basic rules to remember. Bahasa Malaysia has made some changes to bring it in line with Bahasa Indonesia so that the growth of the language can be better coordinated. "Ch" is now spelt as "c", but is also pronounced as the latter; sy is "sh"; ng is as in "singer"; g is always hard as in "go". Vowels are as follows: a as in "father", never as in "pat"; e is very soft and hardly pronounced—negeri is spoken as "n-gri"; i as in "feel" or "machine"; o as in "hope"; u as in "tool".

Adjectives always follow the noun, as in *baju* (shirt) *merah* (red)—*baju merah*. For further instruction, and for popular phrases it is advisable to buy a small "teach yourself" book which you can read up on while waiting for buses. Even a smattering of Malay, including numbers, can be extremely useful, especially when bargaining. And if you know a few basic phrases like *berapa harga*, "how much," this will sometimes be enough to lower the price.

MONEY AND BANKING

All prices quoted in this book are in US dollars and at the time of writing, the rate was around $US2.50 to the Malaysian dollar known as the ringgit. At the beginning of the same year, however, the rate was $US2.69, so it is hard to ascertain what it will be like in a year from now. Government policy is to keep the ringgit low in value to make exports competitive, but the ringgit has been strengthening on its own due to the country's fantastic economic growth.

Notes come in $M1 (soon to be phased out), $M5, $M10, $M20, $M50, $M100, $M500, and $M1000. Coins are known as sen (cents) and those in use are 1, 2, 5, 10, 20, 50 *sen*, and a new $M1 coin.

Carry small notes when you travel in taxis, coins for local buses, and don't expect small shops to have change for large bills. All major credit cards are accepted at large hotels, restaurants, department stores, handicraft shops, airline ticketing agencies, and many other shops. They are also extremely useful when hiring cars. In the large towns and cities there are many licensed money changers and numerous banks which change money and travelers' cheques.

Banks have a small commission, but money-changers have no charges, although their rates are much the same. Department stores and major hotels also change money, but this should be done only as a last resort as their exchange rates assure that they make a hefty profit.

Banking hours differ from state to state. Melaka, Negeri Sembilan, Pahang, Perak, Penang, Selangor, and the Federal Territory (Kuala Lumpur) follow the standard Western working week with banks closed on Saturday afternoon and all day Sunday. Kedah, Perlis, Kelantan, Terengganu and Johor follow the Islamic week and banks are closed on Thursday afternoons and all day Friday. Banks open at 10am and close at 3pm through the week and on the half-day holiday they open at 9.30am and close at 11.30 am.

TAX, SERVICE AND TIPPING

As all major hotels and restaurants add a 10% service charge, tipping is not necessary and unlike some countries where the service will drop if you don't tip big, Malaysia doesn't follow that rule. Of course, like anywhere else, tips are appreciated, but don't feel obligated. In smaller restaurants, it is enough to leave the small change.

SHOPPING

From bustling night markets to air-conditioned shopping malls, Peninsular Malaysia is a great place to shop. The only places where bargaining is not the done thing is in department stores where "fixed-price" means what it says, and in government-run handicraft stores. Anywhere else—bargain. Don't expect to bring the price down too much, however, as this is not India, and prices first quoted are usually not too exhorbitant.

A good word to learn in Malay, even before the numbers, is *mahal*—"expensive"—as this is an essential part of bargaining. If you are not into bargaining, and even some Malaysians do this, ask for their "discount" price. This is usually at least 10 to 15% off their first quoted price. Always bargain when buying electrical goods, cameras, cassette-players and even when buying film in bulk. Don't expect to get much off the quoted prices of handicrafts, especially when you are at the source, like the batik workshops in Kelantan. They may drop the price by a few ringgit, but their mark-up is not much, and they are selling at half the price of what you would pay for a similar item in the city boutiques.

Remember to get international guarantee cards for cameras and other electrical goods. Kuala Lumpur is the best for buying these, and

for designer clothes (*see KL Practicalities, p. 234*). If a tout accosts you and offers you "copy watches," these are fake designer watches which sell from upwards of $12. Real brands, however, are reasonably priced. Kuala Lumpur's government-run handicrafts shops have a good variety, but prices are much lower at the source. Kota Bharu is the place to shop for *songket* (silk brocade), traditional silverwares, hand-painted silk batiks, traditional stamped batiks, wood-carving and interesting souvenirs like kites, and baskets.

Melaka and Penang are good for antiques, the latter is best for antique furniture, and porcelain. Penang is good for curios (*see Penang Practicalities, p.244*). The Mah Meri, from Pulau Carey (*see p. 69*) produce beautiful "spirit" carvings out of a reddish wood. Those interested in primitive art can go to their village and see them working. The Jah Hut, from Central Pahang also make wood carvings. Enquire at the tourist information centers in Kuala Lumpur.

ETIQUETTE

Malaysians are hospitable and friendly people, and readily forgive visitors all kinds of faux pas. However, it helps to know a few basic rules. Dress modestly, and women should always wear a bra, otherwise you get a lot of unwanted attention.

Before entering a house, mosque, and Indian and Buddhist temples take off your shoes at the door. If you are offered food it is impolite to refuse it; a sip or a nibble is sufficient not to offend. Never help yourself to food before you are invited to eat. When offered food you should accept with your right hand, as the left is considered unclean.

Politeness, humbleness, and patience are considered as great virtues, and it is considered quite low class to argue, show affection, or raise your voice in public. It shows respect when you visit a mosque to wear long trousers or a skirt, and cover your arms. Don't worry unnecessarily though about what is the correct behaviour, as Malaysians know that you are a foreigner. Just relax, be courteous, smile a lot and you will be totally accepted.

FESTIVALS

With such a multi-cultural population there is hardly a week in the annual calendar when a festival is not going on. Some national holidays and festivals occur on the same day every year, but most of the major holidays are based either on the Chinese, Muslim or Hindu calendars which are lunar, and the dates change each year.

The following monthly guide of major festivals is approximate except for specified dates, check with the tourist information centers for the latest dates of lunar festivals. In addition to these important events there are many smaller festivals, like the International Kite Festival in

Kelantan (July), Fraser's Hill International Bird Race (June), Kelantan International Drum Festival (July), Melaka's Festa San Pedro (June), and dozens more including sultans' birthdays.

January. Thaipusam. Hindu festival and procession when tranced penitents pierce themselves with metal hooks and spikes and shoulder elaborately-decorated yokes. Best at Kuala Lumpur's Batu Caves, and in Penang.

February. Chinese New Year. Celebrated for 15 days when Chinese visit relatives, decorate their homes and shops with red banners, and celebrate with lion dances and firecrackers.

February. Chap Goh Meh. End of Chinese New Year when temples are packed with worshippers and huge joss sticks are burnt.

April. Hari Raya Puasa. The start of the fasting month of Ramadan, known in Malay as puasa, when Muslims refrain from eating and drinking from sunrise to sunset. Special cakes are available during this time and the fast culimates with month-long Hari Raya when all Malays have open house and treat relatives and friends with special food and cakes.

May. Wesak Day. To celebrate Buddha's birth, enlightenment and nirvana, special prayers are given at all Buddhist temples.

June. Hari Raya Haji. To celebrate the annual haj or pilgrimage to Mecca special prayers are held at mosques, and sheep or cattle are sacrificed for the needy.

July. Maal Hijrah. The New Year of the Muslim calendar is celebrated with religious discussions and Koran recitals.

August 31st. Merdeka Day. Celebrated with parades, processions, and fireworks to commemorate independence from British rule.

September. Prophet Muhammad's Birthday. Special prayers and Koran recitals are held at mosques to celebrate this spiritual event.

September. Moon Cake Festival. Chinese festival to mark the victory of the peasants over their Mongolian worlords in ancient times. Special lotus-flavored moon cakes are eaten and colorful lanterns are displayed.

October. Deepavali. Hindu festival of lights to celebrate the triumph of good over evil. Indian families offer prayers and hold "open-house" when relatives and friends visit.

December. Christmas. Celebrated by Christans, and particularly joyous in Melaka where the Portuguese Eurasians pack the churches for midnight mass and hold "open-house" with special food treats.

TIME

Peninsular Malaysia is eight hours ahead of Greenwich Mean Time. Sunset is about 7pm and sunrise around 7am.

HEALTH

Although it is generally safe to drink Malaysian water from the tap, must locals boil their water to be extra safe. Hotels always provide boiled drinking water, and there is plentiful bottled mineral water on sale. Clinics (*klinik*) are available in all towns and are efficient with western-trained doctors who all speak English. There are government-run hospitals, and private specialist hospitals in all major towns.

ELECTRICITY

As Malaysia runs on 220 volts, 50 cycles, it is not possible to use American-made appliances without an adaptor. These are easily bought in electrical shops throughout the country.

AIRPORT TAX

International flight departures are taxed $M15, flights to Singapore and Brunei $M5, and domestic flights $M3.

EMBASSIES AND CONSULATES

All below numbers refer to offices in Kuala Lumpur, dialing code (03).

Australia 6 Jl. Yap Kwan Seng (2423122). Belgium 12 Lorong Yap Kwan Seng (2485733). Britain 185 Jl. Ampang (2482122). Brunei MBF Plaza, Jl. Ampang (4574149). Canada Plaza MBF (2612000). China 229 Jl. Ampang (2428495). Denmark 123 Jl. Ampang (2416088). France 192 Jl. Ampang (2484122). Germany 3 Jl. U Thant (2429666). India 142C Jl. Ampang (2617000). Indonesia 233 Jl. Tun Razak (9842011).

Italy 99 Jl. U Thant (4565122). Japan 11 Psn. Stonor (2427044). Netherlands 4 Jl. Mesra (2426844). New Zealand 193 Jl. Tun Razak (2486422). Norway Bangunan Ankasaraya, Jl. Ampang (2420144). Singapore 209 Jl. Tun Razak (2616277). Spain 200 Jl. Ampang (2484868). Sweden Bangunan Ankasaraya, Jl. Ampang (2485981). Switzerland 16 Psn. Madge (2480622). Thailand 206 Jl. Ampang (2488222). United States 376 Jl. Tun Razak (2489011).

INTERNATIONAL AIRLINES

All below numbers refer to offices in Kuala Lumpur, dialing code (03)

Aeroflot, Wisma Tong Ah (2610231). Air NZ, Wisma Golden City (2425577). Airlanka, Bang. Perangsang Segemal (2740211). Alitalia, Plaza See Hoy Chan 2380366). American Bang.Angkasaraya (2480644). British Plaza See Hoy Chan (2325797). Cathay Pacific, UBN Tower (2383377). China Bang. Amoda (2427344). JAL, Bang. Pernas International (2611722). KLM, President House (2427011). Lufthansa, Bang. Pernas International (261 4666). MAS, Bang. MAS Jl. Sultan Ismail (7463000). Qantas, UBN Tower Jl. P. Ramlee (2389133). Singapore, 2 Jl. Dang Wangi (2923122). Swissair, Bang. Angkasaraya (2426044). Thai, Bang. Kuwasa (2937100). United Bang. MAS, (2611433). UTA, Plaza See Hoy Chan (2326952).

Kuala Lumpur Practicalities

Includes Fraser's Hill, Genting Highlands, Shah Alam, Klang, Carey Island, Jugra and Kuala Selangor. Prices in US dollars. S=single; D=double; AC=air-conditioning. Telephone code for Kuala Lumpur is 03.

Most of Kuala Lumpur's best-known sights are within easy walking distance from each other in the heart of downtown, and the attractions on the fringes of the city can easily be visited by taxi. Plan your day so that you are walking in the early morning or late afternoon and spend the hot part of the day either relaxing in your hotel or shopping at one of the many air-conditioned shopping malls. The out-of-town trips are best done by car, but for those with plenty of time they are also accessible by public transport.

GETTING THERE

Kuala Lumpur is the main international gateway to Malaysia and the hub of the domestic air, train and bus services.

By Air

Subang International Airport, in neighboring Selangor state, 22km (13mi) from the city center, is served by the national flag carrier, Malaysia Airlines, and by 35 other international airlines. Terminal 1 handles all international flights, including Singapore, and Terminal 2 is for all domestic flights. **Taxis** from the airport operate on a coupon system and these can be bought at a booth beside the main entrance. Hand it to the driver at the end of the journey. A trip downtown should cost around $7. Bus No. 47 services the route from the Klang bus terminal at Jalan Sultan Mohamed (downtown). **Buses** run hourly and off peak the journey takes around 45 minutes, but the traffic jams on the Federal Highway access road are legendary: give yourself more time during the morning and evening rush hours.

By bus

Modern, air-conditoned, express buses to Kuala Lumpur run from Singapore's Lavender Street terminal, and from the Ban San terminal at the corner of Arab and Queen Streets. The eight hour journey costs $10, and most buses leave in the morning. Buy bus tickets in Singapore from Masmara, tel: 02-7326555, from the bus station or at 05-53 Far East Plaza, 14 Scotts Road, or from Kuala Lumpur-Singapore Express, tel: 02-2928254. Express buses also ply to Kuala Lumpur from all major West Malaysian towns. All long-distance buses depart and arrive from Puduraya Bus Station on Jalan

Pudu, except for East Coast buses which use the Putra Bus Station on Jalan Putra, and the Pekliling Bus Station on Jalan Tun Razak which serves West Pahang.

By train

Kuala Lumpur is connected by rail from Bangkok in the north to Singapore in the south. The Singapore train station is on Keppel Road, tel: 02-2225165, and five daily trains run to Kuala Lumpur. Expres Rakyat departs at 7.45am and arrives 2.30 pm, and Ekspres Sinaran departs 2.45pm and arrives at 9.25pm, 1st class AC $30, 2nd class AC $17, 2nd class non AC $15.5. The cheaper mail trains stop everywhere and are much slower. For travelers arriving from the north, tickets can be purchased in Bangkok for the entire trip to Kuala Lumpur, however, you must change trains in Butterworth.

GETTING AROUND

Walking. It is best to walk around the downtown area as the traffic is often horrendous, and even though taxi drivers know where jams occur they still get stuck, for KL has no alternative transport to the road.

Taxis. Still the best way to get around town if the distances are too great to walk or if the weather—always hot and humid—has taken its toll. All the major hotels and shopping complexes have taxi stands, or alternatively you can just hail them from the side of the road. Avoid taking taxis from outside the Puduraya Bus Station as this is a notorious place for rip-offs, instead walk about a block away and hail one. Taxis should always use their meters, and usually do, except when going on long trips like the airport when they will usually quote a fare. Fares are very reasonable by international standards.

Buses. Another alternative, but these are hot, cramped, and confusing for visitors who are only staying a few days. Minibus drivers are notorious for their outrageous driving techniques, and blatant disregard of traffic rules, so a ride in one is a unique KL experience, but not for the faint-hearted. Have spare change ready, most destinations cost 50 sen and are marked clearly on the front of the buses. To get to Petaling Jaya, Subang Airport, Shah Alam and Klang, take buses from the Klang Bus Station on Jalan Sultan Mohammed (just south of Central Market); to get to Batu Caves take a taxi, or a No.11 minibus from Jalan Pudu, or a Len Seng No. 69 or 70 from Jalan Ampang. For Zoo Negara (National Zoo) take a 177 Len Chee, or a 170 Len Seng bus along Jalan Ampang.

Car Hire. Most leading international car-hire firms have offices at Subang Airport and in Kuala Lumpur, including Avis, 40 Jalan Sultan Ismail, tel: 2423500; Budget, 163 Jalan Ampang, tel: 2611122; Hertz, 2nd floor, Kompleks Antarabangsa, tel: 2433344. Other local firms include Orix Car Rentals, 42-2 Jalan Sultan

Ismail, tel: 2423009; STT, 19 Jalan Dang Wangi (opposite Singapore Airlines), tel: 2981557; SMAS, Shangri-La Hotel, Jalan P. Ramlee, tel: 2307788. Expect to pay around $42 per day. Also check the classifieds in the Malay Mail (afternoon tabloid) for cheaper rent-a-cars.

INFORMATION AND TOURS

The best place for information is MATIC (Malaysia Tourist Information Complex), in a restored, historical villa at 109 Jalan Ampang, tel: 293664. They also put on traditional dance and dramas in their theatre. The former TDC is now called Tourism Malaysia, and is further out of town at Putra World Trade Centre (Beside the Pan Pacific Hotel and opposite The Mall), on Jalan Tun Ismail, tel: 2935188.

There is also an information center at Terminal 1, Subang International Airport, and the Kuala Lumpur Tourist Information Centre is at the corner of Jalan Parlimen and Jalan Raja (opposite the Padang), tel: 2936664. A number of travel and tour agents do KL and outside tours, but the best value is from MATIC. Their three-hour city tour leaves at 9.30am and 2.30pm includes Chinatown, Railway Station, colonial buildings, Muzium Negara, National Mosque, Istana Negara, Masjid Jamek. The country tour takes in "Embassy Row," a batik factory, Batu Caves, a Malay village, rubber-tapping, and Selangor Pewter: both tours cost $9 per person. A nightlife tour including dinner and a cultural show at Yasmin's, a Malay restaurant and a tour of Chinatown by night costs $22.

ACCOMMODATION

Kuala Lumpur has a great variety of accomodation—from the most luxurious to the sleaziest—and is reasonably priced by international standards. Most of the luxury hotels are in the "Golden Triangle" centered around Jalan Ampang, Jalan Sultan Ismail and Jalan Bukit Bintang, about 1.6km (1mi) east of downtown, while most of the cheaper accomodation is just north of downtown near Jalan Tunku Abdul Rahman.

Luxury ($125 and up)

Shangri-La Hotel, 11 Jalan Sultan Ismail, tel: 2322388, fax: 2301514. Consistent award-winner for its cuisine, and well-known for its tropical gardens which give the hotel a cool shady ambiance although it's deep in the commercial district. $148 S, $164 D, suites from $208.
Pan Pacific, Jalan Putra, tel: 4415555. North of town center away from the main hotel area, but next door to the Putra World Trade Centre. Beautifully decorated rooms and coffee shop well-known for its buffet and western snacks. $160 S, $176 D, sometimes offers 25% discounts.
Regent of Kuala Lumpur, 160 Jalan Bukit Bintang, tel: 2418000. Renowned for its service and it's opulent decor, the city's most luxurious and expensive hotel is located in the heart of the shopping and nightlife center.

$172 S, $190 D, suites $320-$2,400.
Kuala Lumpur Hilton, Jalan Sultan Ismail, tel: 2422222, fax: 2442157. Luxurious, comfortable rooms in the heart of the business district. Popular discotheque. S $144, D $156, ask for discounts (sometimes available) $124 D.

First Class ($75-$125)

Holiday Inn on the Park, Jalan Pinang, tel: 2481066. Located just behind the main hotel area, this quiet hotel used to have the best view in the city overlooking the racecourse, but sadly this is now to become yet another monolithic high-rise complex. Rates will probably drop when construction begins. $116 S, $132 D.
Concorde Hotel, 2 Jalan Sultan Ismail, tel: 2442200, fax: 2441628. Centrally located. Attracts young travelers mainly because of its adjacent Hard Rock Cafe and trendy boutiques. $104 S/D, and ask for discounts.
Hotel Istana, 73 Jalan Raja Chulan, tel: 241 9988. KL's newest luxury hotel with an opulent "palace-like" decor boasts a massive pillarless ballroom. Prices are reasonable as amenities are as good as the luxury class hotels. $104 S, $116 D.
Federal Hotel, 35 Jalan Bukit Bintang, tel: 2489166, older-style hotel with comfortable rooms situated in the heart of the shopping and nightclub district. $76 S, $84 D.

High Intermediate ($35-$75)

Hotel Malaya, Jalan Hang Lekir, tel: 2327722. Located in the heart of old Chinatown and within easy walking distance of all the major downtown sights, bus station and GPO. Restaurant serves Western and Chinese food. $64 S, $74 D.
The Lodge, 2 Jalan Tengah, off Jalan Sultan Ismail, tel: 2420122. The cheapest hotel in KL's most expensive junction, opposite The Hilton and Istana Hotels. Older, motel-style rooms with AC and hot showers, swimming pool, and excellent outdoor pavement restaurant. $60 S/D.
Hotel Pudu Raya, Puduraya Bus Station, tel: 2321000. A great place if you're traveling by bus or share taxi as KL's main stations (except for buses to the East Coast) are downstairs. All rooms AC with own bathroom. $39 S, $44 D.

Low Intermediate ($15-35)

Champagne Hotel, Jalan Bunus, off Jalan Masjid India, tel: 2986333. Great location in the fascinating "Little India" area. In the center of the cheap shopping district, surrounded by cheap Muslim Indian and Malay restaurants, and excellent-value lunch and night-time food centers. Rooms are comfortable and clean with own hot-water showers, AC, $23 S/D.
Chamtan Hotel, 62 Jalan Masjid India, tel: 2930144. Slightly more "up-market" than the Champagne Hotel around the corner. Good value, hot showers, AC $26 S/D.
Asia Hotel (formerly South-East Asia), 69 Jalan

Haji Hussein, off Jalan Tunku Abdul Rahman, tel: 2926077. Long-established mid-range hotel has good rooms with TV, hot showers AC, but is in the interesting, but fairly notorious Chow Kit market area. $42 S/D.

Kowloon Hotel, 142 Jalan Tunku Abdul Rahman, tel: 2926433, is in the middle of the cheap shopping district, great for bargain clothes, fabrics and shoes and close to all downtown sights. Rooms are all AC with hot showers and TV. $28 S, $32 D.

Budget (Under $15)

Coliseum Hotel, 100 Jalan Tunku Abdul Rahman, tel: 2926270. A historical landmark, this hotel is basic and pretty seedy, but the restaurant and bar, once frequented by Somerset Maugham and other notable novelists, is extremely popular and serves famous steaks. All rooms share baths, $9 S non AC, $12 D AC.

Tivoli Hotel, 134 Jalan Tunku Abdul Rahman, tel: 2924108, just up the road from the Coliseum, is cleaner, but as basic. All rooms with fans and shared bathrooms. $7 S, $8.50 D.

Colonial Hotel, 39 Jalan Sultan, tel: 2380336, is another basic, old-style hotel located in the heart of Chinatown. Fan and shared bathroom cost $7 S, $9 D, and $10 AC.

Travellers' Moon Lodge, 36 Jalan Silang (the street south of Jalan Tun Perak), tel: 2306601. Very friendly and centrally-located close to Chinatown and the bus station. Popular with backpackers. Dorm beds $3.50, S/D $9 with fan and shared bathroom. All prices include toast and jam and tea or coffee for breakfast.

Sunrise Travellers Lodge, 89B Jalan Pudu Lama, tel: 2308878. Popular with backpackers because of its closeness to the bus and taxi station at Puduraya. Prices are much the same as the Travellers' Moon, and include breakfast.

YWCA, 12 Jalan Hang Jebat, tel: 283225. Located just east of Chinatown. Clean, comfortable rooms only for women, couples and families. $6 S, $10 D (women), $14 D (couples), $20 family.

Meridien International Youth Hostel, 36 Jalan Hang Kasturi, tel: 2321428. In Chinatown and close to Central Market and all the major sights. Dorm beds (members) $2.60, (non-members) $3, rooms $8, all with common bath.

KL International Youth Hostel, 21 Jalan Kampung Attap, tel: 2306870. Close to Railway Station, clean and comfortable. Dorm beds in AC rooms are $5 for first night, and $3.20 after that.

DINING

Penang may be more well-known for its local cuisine, but KL has the most variety, for not only are the different regional cooking styles served up, but there is also a great range of international restaurants. Eating out is a passion with Malaysians, and most will frequent the outdoor food stalls which dish up a fantastic array of economically-priced meals. The majority of families buy *bungkus* (wrapped to take-away) meals at least once a week. Restaurants are also extremely popular, but are frequented more on special occasions. Malaysia has reasonably strict food and hygiene controls, particularly in KL, and it is perfectly safe to eat at outdoor eating stalls.

Hawker food

Popular food centers are the "Hilton" food stalls, behind the Hilton Hotel on Jalan Sultan Ismail, which are open for *nasi campur* (rice and curry lunch) where diners select what they like, buffet-fashion from a fantastic array of meat, vegetable, seafood and local Malay salad dishes known as *ulam*. Another good spot for this style of lunch is the outdoor food stalls in the center of Jalan Masjid India. At the northern end of this road, beside Semua House the hawkers open from dusk till dawn and sell great satay, *nasi lemak*—rice in coconut cream, and heaps of other Malay specialities. There are also food centers upstairs in Central Market; in the basement of Lot 10 on Jalan Bukit Bintang; the ground floor of Ampang Park on the corner of Jalan Tun Razak and Jalan Ampang; and on countless sidewalks and corners throughout the city and its suburbs.

Malay

Because of the proliferation of excellent Malay stall food there is not as many restaurants as you would expect featuring the local cuisine. Famous for its cultural shows and its excellent "home-style" but high-priced cooking is **Yazmin Restaurant,** in a revamped colonial bungalow at 6 Jalan Kia Peng, tel: 2415655. Cost for buffet and cultural show is around $18 each. Good for northern—**Penang and Kedah-style**—food is **Rasa Utara,** 34-35 Lower Ground Floor, Bukit Bintang Plaza, Jalan Bukit Bintang, tel: 2419245. Try the *roti jala*—a delicate lacy pancake—with beef *rendang,* a dry curry, and their local iced drinks including sugar cane juice and fresh coconut. Prices are reasonable, around $10 for two. For **seafood** in a pleasant lakeside setting head for the **Nelayan Floating Restaurant** at Taman Tasek Titiwangsa, 3km (1.9mi) north of downtown off Jalan Tun Razak. The path around the lake is a pleasant place for a jog if you feel like working up an appetite. Along Jalan Tuanku Abdul Rahman and Jalan Masjid India are a number of working-class, **economically-priced Malay** restaurants which open from very early breakfast to late at night.

Chinese

Petaling Street, in the center of Chinatown, closes to vehicular traffic at night and becomes a **night market** where you can dine amongst the lively din of hawkers' shouts and competing cassette shops. Jalan Bukit Bitang and the lanes that run off it are also Chinese areas that offer a great choice of stallfood. In Chinatown, try the *bah ku teh*, believed to have originated in Malaysia, a spicy pork soup always served with Chinese tea, and popular around mid-morning. *Yong tau foo*—deep-fried bean curd, fish balls and vegetables in a chilli sauce—another renowned snack is best opposite the Indian temple on Jalan Ulu Klang on the way to the zoo.

The Chinese, although economical with most other things, love to splurge on a meal, and will pay exhorbitant prices for the privilege of eating abalone, sharks' fins, or birds' nest soups. A favorite **up-market restaurant** is the **Golden Phoenix** at the Hotel Equatorial on Jalan Sultan Ismail, tel: 2617777 which specialises in exotic seafoods and venison dishes. The glitzy, kitsch architecture and decor of the **Eden Seafood Village** on the corner of Jalan Raja Chulan and Jalan Sultan Ismail, tel: 241 1093, is a bit like their food which is a mixture of Chinese, Western and Malay. Select your own live seafood from tanks.

Two good places for expensive **dim sum**—steamed and deep-fried tidbits—are the **Shang Palace** in the Shangri-La Hotel on Jalan Sultan Ismail, tel: 2322388, and the **Teochew** Restaurant, 272 Jalan Pudu, tel: 2416572. Other popular but pricey restaurants include the **Hai-Tien-Lo** in the Pan Pacific Hotel on Jalan Putra, tel: 2935555, which has one of KL's most impressive menus; the **Ming Palace** at the Ming Court Hotel on Jalan Ampang, tel: 2618888 which specializes in spicy **Szechuan cuisine**; and the **Hakka Restaurant** at 231 Jalan Bukit Bintang, tel: 9858492, which does home-style Hakka cuisine and live seafood.

Nonya

The Chinese/Malay cuisine of the Straits-born Chinese, *peranakan*, is not as prolific here as in Penang and Melaka, but the **Restoran Sri Saloma** beside the MATIC information complex on Jalan Ampang, tel: 2434817, is good and reasonably priced, as is the **Restoran Dondang Sayang**, Lower Ground Floor, The Weld, Jalan Raja Chulan, 262 3831 which does delicate *nonya* desserts.

Indian

The best place to find cheap and tasty **North Indian food** is around the Jalan Tuanku Abdul Rahman/Jalan Masjid India area, especially for economical *roti canai*—Indian pancake with lentil curry—breakfasts, and afternoon snacks of murtabah—pancakes stuffed with spicy meat or sardines. **Bilal Restaurant,** 33 Jalan Ampang, tel: 2380804, once the premier North Indian food spot in town has now been outclassed, but is still good value for chicken and mutton curries. *Naan*—oven-baked flat breads, and chicken tandoori have recently become hot favorites at many food stall centers. **The best,** although out of town, is at the hawker center opposite the shops close to KL International School in Ampang. Two good **Mughal-style** restaurants at Medan Tuanku, off Jalan Tuanku Abdul Rahman (one block north of Jalan Dang Wangi), are the **Omar Khayyam** at No.5, and Shiraz at No.1.

For **vegetarian food** there are a number of small restaurants in the downtown area of Leboh Ampang and Jalan Tun H.S.Lee just north of Jalan Tun Perak. These places are **very cheap** and do good *dosai*—thin crepes stuffed with potato curry and other South Indian specialities. **Curries** served on banana leaf are filling and economical around the Brickfields area, just south of the Railway Station. For upmarket vegetarian food served on traditional stainless-steel trays, try **Devi Annapoorna** Restaurant, at 94 Jalan Maarof, Bangsar, 3km (1.9mi) from the city center.

Western

Fast food is easy to get in KL. There are at least a dozen **McDonalds** in KL. **Kentucky Fried Chicken** are at Plaza Yow Chuan, Jalan Ampang, and along Jalan Tuanku Abdul Rahman. **Pizza Hut** are in the basement of The Weld, Jalan Raja Chulan, and the basement of Yow Chuan Plaza on Jalan Ampang. **Delifrance,** for pastries, rolls and coffee has a popular cafe in Lot 10, Jalan Bukit Bintang, and on the ground floor of The Mall on Jalan Putra.

The best American-style food in town is at the **Hard Rock Cafe** in the Hotel Concorde on Jalan Sultan Ismail. It's pricey, but the meals are huge, the coffee's great, and the music's loud. **The Lodge** outdoor restaurant on the corner of Jalan Raja Chulan and Jalan Sultan Ismail serves medium-priced and tasty steaks and grilled fish and is a good spot to people watch. **The Oasis** in City Square, Jalan Tun Razak, does cheap lasagne; and in the basement of Lot 10 on Jalan Bukit Bintang, **Cal's Diner**, a replica of an American diner complete with in-house movies and old jukeboxes does good hamburgers, coffee and desserts.

Japanese and other Asian

There are a number of expensive Japanese restaurants around KL including the **Keyaki** in the Pan Pacific Hotel on Jalan Putra; the **Chikuyo-tei** at Plaza See Hoy Chan, Jalan Raja Chulan; and the Genji in the Petaling Jaya Hilton. More moderately-priced and **excellent value** are the **Hoshigaoka Restaurants** at The Mall and at Lot 10 where a plate of sushi costs around $6, and there are a number of cheaper set meals. **Korean cuisine** is also popular—try the **Koryo-Won Restaurant** in Kompleks Antarabangsa, next to the KL Hilton. For the best **Thai food** head for Cili Padi in The Mall.

NIGHTLIFE

The favorite after-dark occupation for KL'ites is the *pasar malam* or night markets. Chow Kit area heading south into Jalan Tuanku Abdul Rahman is a maze of stalls and markets and down the back lanes it is still the sleaze center of town, haunt of *pondan* (transvestites), prostitutes, and drug addicts, although it's not as upfront as in Bangkok.

Cultural shows of traditional dance and drama are often staged at the MATIC tourist information complex in Jalan Ampang and sometimes at Central Market. Information offices have brochures which list what's happening each month. **Nightclubs** usually cater to Chinese businessmen unwinding after work, as do the karaoke bars in the Bukit Bintang area. If you want this unique experience check out the huge **Deluxe Nite-Club** upstairs in Ampang Park on Jalan Ampang. Pubs are not the English or Australian type, but are more like American bars. The bar at **Coliseum Hotel** on Jalan Tuanku Abdul Rahman is noisy and popular with Indian lawyers and the **Vatican** on Lebuh Pasar Besar is another favorite watering-hole.

Hard Rock Cafe in the Concorde Hotel play good recorded rock and sometimes have live bands. KL's nightspots come and go, and what's popular one month can well be closed the next. A popular venue is now around the back of the luxury hotel strip on Jalan Sultan Ismail, where some old colonial mansions have been revamped into nightclubs. **Betelnut**, on Jalan Pinang, the most popular, spins 60s and 70s music; and 10 Kia Peng has a wine bar, disco and art gallery. Other popular discos include the **Tin Mine** in KL Hilton, **Rumours** in Hotel Concorde, Club Oz in the Shangri-La, **Voodoo** on Jalan Ampang, and **Jimmy Dean's** in the annexe at Lot 10. Riverbank at Central Market and **All That Jazz**, 14 Jalan 19/36 in Petaling Jaya both have live jazz bands.

MUSEUMS AND ART GALLERIES

Muzium Negara (National Museum), Jalan Damansara, tel: 2380255. Open 9am to 6pm daily. One of Southeast Asia's most interesting museums with cultural dioramas and special theme exhibitions.
National Art Gallery, 1 Jalan Sultan Hishamuddin, tel: 2300157. Open 10am to 6pm daily, closed on Fridays from 12.15 to 2.45pm. Permanent exhibitions of local and foreign artists.
National Handicrafts Museum, 11 Jalan Conlay, tel: 2413117. Displays local traditional handicrafts and has crafts demonstrations.
P.Ramlee Memorial, 22 Jalan Dedap, Setapak. tel: 4231131. Former house and now museum dedicated to P.Ramlee, Malaysia's late, great film-maker/song-writer/actor and singer. Has videos of his movies and memorabilia from the 50s and 60s—great for film buffs.
Maybank Numismatic Museum, 1st floor, Menara Maybank. tel: 2308833. Open 10am to 6pm. Notes and coins of early Malaya to the present.
Forest Research Institute Malaysia (FRIM) Museum, Kepong, tel: 6342633. Open 8am to

4.15pm daily except Friday lunch and Saturday afternoons. Old colonial forestry museum set amongst beautiful forested grounds. Good for short jungle walks.
Gedung Raja Abdullah—Tin Museum, Jalan Raja Abdullah, Klang. tel: 3327383. Open 10am to 6 pm, closed on Fridays. This historical warehouse has displays on Selangor's early history and the growth of the tin industry.
Orang Asli Museum, km 24 Jalan Pahang, Gombak. tel: 6892122. Open 9am to 5.30pm, closed on Fridays. Excellent displays of handicrafts and culture of Peninsular Malaysia's aboriginal peoples.

SHOPPING

Kuala Lumpur has recently become an attractive shopping destination rivalling Singapore because of the ringgit's more favorable rates. The cheapest shopping—for clothing, shoes, cassettes, and fabrics is at the Chow Kit market area, Petaling Street night market, most *pasar malams*, and along Jalan Tuanku Abdul Rahman. Globe Silk, Mun Loong, are both small department stores on the latter street which are popular with local bargain hunters although it's sometimes difficult to get western sizes.

Bukit Bintang Plaza and adjoining Sungai Wang on Jalan Bukit Bintang are extremely popular for buying clothing, shoes, cameras, and electrical goods. Their Metro department store, also in the basement at City Square on Jalan Tun Razak, has good brand-name clothing like Esprit and East India Co (good for safari-type traveling gear) at reasonable prices and in Western sizes. Across a lane from these adjacent plazas is Imbi Plaza which caters almost exclusively to computer shops where both hardware and software are on sale. Lot 10, KL's latest trendy shopping venue, across the street, has many up-market designer boutiques, the Japanese department store Isetan, sportswear shops, and cheap cassettes and CDs.

Handicrafts are cheapest on the east coast, but good quality, albiet more expensive traditional arts and crafts are at Kraftangan, on Jalan Raja Chulan Bintang; and at Infokraf opposite the Padang on Jalan Sultan Hishamuddin. Central Market has a large range of good souvenir T-shirts, batik clothes, cheap but well done local watercolors, and cheap curios. Batik cloth and clothing is also good at Batik Malaysia Berhad on Jalan Tun Perak. Royal Selangor Pewter, the world-famous pewter manufacturer has outlets all over the city and its factory at 4 Jalan Usahawan 6 at Sentul, 3km (1.9mi) northeast of downtown is well worth a visit to see pewter being made.

BANKING AND MONEY

The major banks are all located in the dowtown central business district and open from 10am to 6pm Monday to Friday, and from 9am to 12.30pm on Saturdays. Money changers have slightly better rates and are prolific around Jalan Masjid India and Jalan Tuanku Abdul Rahman area, and at all major shopping complexes. Department stores change currency as do all large hotels but their rates are not as good.

AROUND THE NORTHEAST

To get to **Batu Caves**, the limestone massif renowned for its temple cave 13km (8mi) northeast, catch a taxi, for a No. 11 minibus from Jalan Pudu or Nos.69/70 Len Seng bus from Jalan Ampang. For **Templer Park** and **Kanching Forest Reserve** take either bus Nos 66, 72, 78 or 83 from Puduraya.

Fraser's Hill (Bukit Fraser)

To get to this colonial hill station, 101km (63mi) north of KL, charter a taxi from Puduraya ($25), or a cheaper method is to get a share taxi to Kuala Kubu Bharu ($2.50) then catch the 8am or noon buses to Fraser's Hill, a 2-hour bus journey. Or you can charter a taxi from Kuala Kubu Bharu to the hill station for $12. Motorists should not e that the 6km/4mi road from the Gap to Fraser's Hill, is one-way during the day. Traffic goes up at 7am until 7.45 and then every second hour until 7.40pm; down traffic is on alternate hours from 8am.

Accommodation and dining

The top place to stay is the attractive but over-priced, **Smokehouse Hotel**, which caters to a small but wealthy clientele. Located 1.5km from the village, rooms cost around $150.The most popular upmarket hotel is the **Merlin Resort** in the center of the village overlooking the golf course, tel: 09-382300. Comfortable rooms with good view cost $83 S/D on weekends and $67 on weekdays; prices include American breakfast. **Fraser's Pine Resort**, a complex of holiday apartments, tel: 09-382122, on Jalan Quarry, 1.5km (0.9mi) from the village center, overlooks jungle-clad hills. It has tennis and squash courts, a sauna, and kitchens and lounges in all apartments although only the expensive ones provide cooking facilities. One bedroom suites $96, 3-bedroom suites $156.

The best deal are the old stone bungalows run by the **Fraser's Hill Development Corp.**, which can be booked at the information center beside the clocktower, tel: 09-382201. Most are charming old houses with pretty flower gardens and great views. Some have housekeepers that provide good Malay-style meals. Rooms with attached bathroom cost around $18 S/D. The very central, but characterless **Puncak Inn**, above the shops, charges around $24. Probably the best deal of all is **The Gap Resthouse**, a marvellous colonial-style building with elegant old rooms, marvellous views, and a reasonable-priced dining room, but it's 6km from Fraser's Hill at the start of the one-way

road. Good to stay here if you miss the last bus to Kuala Kubu Bahru. Rooms cost around $8 S/D with attached bathroom. All the pricey hotels have restaurants. The most reasonable and best quality is the Merlin. For cheap eats, there's small outdoor Malay restaurants beside the shops. The restaurant at the Golf Club is reasonably priced for snacks, but the best deal in town are the Malay food stalls about half a km from here beside the children's play-grounds. The Gap Resthouse does good strong black coffee and fried noodles, as well as western breakfasts.

Genting Highlands

To get to Malaysia's most kitsch hill resort of high-rise hotels, a casino, and a man-made lake, well-heeled gamblers who can't afford to waste time catch a helicopter from Subang Airport. Buses and share taxis run from Puduraya, and other taxis depart from the Genting stand behind KL Plaza in Bukit Bintang. Genting Highland Tours and Promotion Board, tel: 2613833, 9th floor, Wisma Genting, Jalan Sultan Ismail, run day tours and the price includes gambling chips.

Accomodation and dining

Almost everyone comes here to gamble and it's not a budget travelers scene at all. Like all casino hotels the luxury **Genting Hotel**, tel: 2112345, makes most of its money on the take and the rooms are reasonable at around $60. **The Highland Hotel**, tel: 2112812, has rooms for $32 and the **Pelangi Hotel**, tel: 2113813, is cheaper at $24. All the hotels have restaurants.

WEST OF KL

To get to Petaling Jaya, Shah Alam, or Klang, catch buses from the station in Jalan Sultan Mohamed, just south of Central Market or you can catch the Railbus from the railway station. The KL-Klang bus No.222 stops at Section 8 in Shah Alam and you can walk to the State Mosque and the Agricultural Park from there. Alternatively, charter a taxi from either Puduraya or from Shah Alam itself. From Klang buses go north to Kuala Selangor and south to Banting and Morib. It is easy to get to Jugra, the old royal capital, with your own transport, but quite difficult and slow by public transport.

From Banting you could try hitching to Jugra. Carey Island, where the Mah Meri woodcarvers live is even more difficult without your own car, and before visiting you must get prior permission from the plantation owners Harrison and Crosfield, or from the Department of Orang Asli Affairs, Selangor, tel: 5590375. At Teluk Panglima Garang, 17km (10mi) south of Klang, turn right to Carey Island, then take the right-hand turn across the river to the plantation entrance gates. The guard will give you directions from there.

Perak Practicalities

Includes Ipoh and the Kinta Valley, Cameron Highlands, Pulau Pangkor, Perak River, Kuala Kangsar and Taiping. Prices in US dollars. S=single; D=double; AC=air-conditioned. Telephone code for Perak is 05.

Ipoh and Kinta Valley

GETTING THERE

By air. Malaysian Airlines (MAS) fly daily to Ipoh from Kuala Lumpur ($22), and thrice weekly from Penang ($17), and Johor Bahru ($53). The airport is 5 km (3 mi) from the city. Taxis meet all flights. MAS Office: Lot 108, Bangunan Seri Kinta, Jl. Sultan Idris Shah, Tel: 514155 or 514886. Airport tel: 202459.
By road. From Kuala Lumpur's Pudu Raya taxi stand, share taxis cost $8 for the 3-hr journey. From Kuala Lumpur's Pudu Raya Bus Station express buses run hourly to Ipoh through the day, less frequently at night. Costs $3.50.
By train. Rail travel is the best way to avoid the congested main trunk road north (the expressway will be finished mid '94). It is also the best way to arrive in the city as you alight at the old Moorish Railway Station close to most hotels. Keretapi Tanah Melayu (KTM) run express trains twice daily at 7.30am and 3.00pm. $13-1st AC, $7-2nd AC, $4.5 3rd-non AC.

GETTING AROUND

Walking is the best way to get around Ipoh's old center where most of the historic sights and best eating is. For sights further afield, taxis are inexpensive if shared. Ipoh's main taxi stand is on Jl. Raja Muda. **Taxis** can be chartered for trips to the cave temples ($1 to Perak Tong & Sam Po Kong), Papan, Batu Gajah and Kellie's Castle.

The **local bus** system is slow and cheap, but everywhere is serviced by bus and it's an interesting way to meet the locals. Take the No 66 Kampar bus to Sam Po Kong, and from the city bus station, General Omnibus Co ply to Batu Gajah (45c). Ask the driver to let you off for Papan at the turnoff and walk in. From Batu Gajah take the bus to Gopeng for Kellie's Castle. Make sure you ask when the buses return as it's a long walk to Batu Gajah.

Cars can be hired from the airport and from the major hotels from around $32 per day.

ACCOMMODATION

Rooms range from spacious 5-star luxury to basic lodgings that often double as Chinese-run brothels. The latter are okay for single males and couples, but single women are advised to go for medium-priced hotels which are a better bargain all round.

First Class ($60 and up)

Royal Casuarina Hotel (217 rooms) 18 Jl. Gopeng. Tel: 505555. Ipoh's only luxury hotel. Swimming pool, shopping arcade, car-rental, Italian restaurant, cocktail lounge and good buffet breakfasts. Outside of town near the Turf Club. $88 S and $104 D.

Intermediate ($20-60)

Hotel Excelsior (133 rooms) 43 Jl. Clarke. Tel: 536666. Close to town, popular with Chinese businessmen because of its Chinese restaurant, disco, steambath/sauna and gym. $55-$70 D.
Tambun Inn (100 rooms) 91 Jl. Tambun Tel: 55211. Located 10 km (6.2 mi) from Ipoh on Jl. Tanjung Rambutan amongst limestone hills. Ugly exterior, but inside there's a pool fed by hot springs. Health club. TV, hot-water. AC $30-38 S, AC $35-39 D.
Hotel Lotte (30 rooms) 95 Jl. Dato' Onn Jaafar. Tel: 542215, 542217. Good central location, close to restaurants and fast food centers (Kentucky, A & W), value for money, clean rooms with TV, hot-water, phones, fridge. AC $26 S/D, suites $36-40.
Hotel French (40 rooms) 60-62 Jl. Raja Ikram. Tel: 513455. Close to downtown sights and restaurants. TV, hot-water. AC $28-34 S, $32-34 D, Suites $40.
Station Hotel (34 rooms) Ipoh Railway Station. Tel: 512588. Definitely a nostalgia trip. Renowned old colonial hotel with huge verandah and marvellous city views. Massive rooms and English-sized baths. Original lights, old-style restaurant, and atrocious room decor with clashing colours—a must for kitsch lovers. Undergoing restoration in late 1992. Completion date unsure. Previous prices were $23 S, $28 D, suite $69.

Budget (under $20)

There are dozens of cheap Chinese hotels close to the bus and railway stations. Most offer basic facilities, fans and shared bathrooms, and are usually on busy streets, so try for a rear room. Singles around $5, doubles $7.50.
Winner Hotel, (54 rooms) 32-38 Jl. Ali Pitchay. Tel: 515177. Very clean Chinese hotel with large rooms, attached bathroom with hot-water. AC $13 S $14 D.
Embassy Hotel, (15 rooms) 35 Jl. C.M.Yusof (formerly Jalan Chamberlain. Tel:549496. Clean rooms with attached bath and fan are $7 S, $8.50 D, and $11 D AC.

DINING

Ipoh is famous throughout Malaysia for its Chinese food, notably *kway teow*—flat rice noodles fried with prawns, chicken and greens, and popiah—beanshoots, shredded radish, and pork or prawns in a spring roll. Another local treat is the pomelo, *buah limau bali*, a pendulous-shaped citrus fruit with pink flesh rather like a sweet grapefruit. The fruit thrives in Ipoh's limestone soil especially around Tambun and dozens of fruit stalls line the main road south just past the Sam Po Kong cave temple. The really large variety is sought-after as Chinese altar offerings and although expensive are not as juicy as the smaller ones.

Chinese

There are so many good hawker stalls, often set up in the front of coffee shops, notably around Jalan Leech, and Jalan Sultan Yusof, that diners have merely to look at where the biggest crowds are gathering to ascertain the quality of the food. The Chinese are very fussy eaters and would never patronise a place unless the food is up to their exacting standards. A plate of noodles is rarely over $1.
Kedai Kopi Nam Heong, Jalan Leech, is good for mid-morning curry mee—mee in a moderate curry sauce, and their speciality Ipoh Chicken Kway Teow.
Kedai Kopi Kong Heng, Jalan Leech, another good old-style coffee house is good for kway teow, popiah, and roast chicken and rice.
Hall of Mirrors, Jalan Leech, former barber shop with wall of mirrors, hence its name, specializes in the regular Ipoh mee dishes and a creamy caramel custard.
Restoran Chui Kah, corner of Jalan Pasar and Jalan Leech, have good steamboat—where diners cook their own thinly-sliced meat and seafood in a boiling clear soup. Best for groups, or at a stretch for a couple. More up-market than the coffee shops.
Wooley Food Centre in the outer suburb of Ipoh Garden is also a local favourite with stalls specializing in a wide range of Chinese food. A $1 taxi ride from the town center.

Malay

Pusat Penjaja Padang Kanak Kanak, Jln.Raja Musa Aziz (formerly Jn.Anderson). This food center is set around a small park and is open to the wee hours serving a wide variety of Malay specialities including; satay, chicken-rice, nasi goreng, mee goreng, and local deserts like the shaved-ice treat ABC.
For excellent fresh soya-bean drinks and *chendol*—coconut-milk and jelly drink, try the stall up the road from the Pusat Penjaja, two blocks from Jn.Sultan Iskandar Shah.
Restoran Perwira, 156 Jalan Gopeng, Medan Gopeng. Out of town on the main road south to Ipoh, this restaurant is a good place to dine when returning from Sam Po Kong cave temple. Serves the regular Malay standbys as well as sweet and sour fish, beef with soya sauce. Good for nasi campur at lunch.
Railway Station food stalls, to the left and right

of the station. Not as good a selection as at the Pusat Penjaja, but a good place to hang out while waiting for a train and listen to Malaysian rock on the juke-boxes.

Indian Muslim

Restoran Kader, 71 Jalan Sultan Yusof, in the Indian section of "Chinatown", specializes in nasi kandar—a Penang-style curries and rice, and murtabah—spicy meat pancakes.
Gerai Nasi Kandar Hussein, behind City Hall next to the Clocktower is a food center specializing in nasi kandar and also good for murtabah, roti canai, kaya (coconut jam) on toast. Cheap and centrally located.

Western

FMS Bar, Jn.Sultan Yusof, overlooking the Padang, an original colonial restaurant serves western-style meals and is a good place for drinks in a bar little changed since the days when it was frequented by rubber planters and tin-mining bosses.
Royal Casuarina Coffee House, 18 Jn. Gopeng. Located at Ipoh's only luxury hotel. Serves local and western coffee-house fare, and is good for those craving a good steak and desserts. Prices to match the decor: expensive.
MacDonalds, Jn.Clare. All the usual hamburgers, french fries, but with options of spicy meat fillings to bring in the locals.

NIGHTLIFE

Ipoh's after-dark entertainment centers around a profusion of karaoke lounges, and dimly-lit "lounges" with resident bands that are known as pubs, and often double as pickups for good-time girls. Definitely not your English variety where single women are scarcely noticed, for here it's unusual for unaccompanied women to enter. There are quite discos at the Coliseum on Clare Street and the Royal Casuarina Hotel.

BANKS

Bank Bumiputra Malaysia Berhad, 112 Jn.Sultan Idris Shah. Tel: 542316. Hongkong & Shanghai Banking Corp., 138 Jn.Sultan Yusof. Tel: 511022. Malayan Banking Berhad, 85 Jn.Sultan Idris Shah. Tel: 515433

INFORMATION

Perak Tourist Information Center, Jn.Dewan (behind City Hall). Tel: 532800. Perak Tourist Association, c/o Royal Casuarina Hotel, 18 Jn.Gopeng. Tel: 505555, ext.8123.

Cameron Highlands

GETTING THERE

The **train** only goes to Tapah, but there are plenty of buses and shared taxis from there to the highlands as this is main reason most people get off here. Fares from Kuala Lumpur are

$8 1st AC, $3.50 2nd AC, $2.50.

Ekspress Nasional operates a daily **bus** service to Cameron Highlands (4 hours) which leaves Pudu Raya Bus Terminal at 8.30am. Fares are $6. From Tapah buses leave from the bus station (excellent Indian Muslim restaurants opposite) every hour from 8am to 5pm. The 2-hour journey costs $1.60. From Kuala Lumpur's Pudu Raya taxi stand **share taxis** cost $10 and an entire taxi can be chartered for $40 all the way to the highlands. From Ipoh a seat costs $5 and from Tapah $3.20.

GETTING AROUND

Cameron Highlands is no problem between the two towns of Tanah Rata and Brinchang because local buses ply this route frequently. Buses also run to Kampung Raja at the far end of the highlands road. Taxis can be hired by the hour ($6) for trips to Gunung Brinchang, Boh and Sungai Palas Tea Estates. Or fit travelers can get the bus to the Sungai Palas turn off and walk in past Robertson's Rose Gardens to the tea estate (4 km/2.5 mi).

There are miles of great walking trails around Tanah Rata, ranging from easy to difficult. Walking trail maps with numbered trails are easy to obtain from the shops in Tanah Rata, but these are only a rough guide. Make sure you bring along some food and water and warm clothes on the less-frequented trails.

ACCOMMODATION

Prices tend to match the topography—much higher than the coast. During school holidays (both Malaysia's and Singapore's) prices increase and popular places can be booked out for weeks ahead. However, even at peak periods you can still find a room, especially at the more expensive places.

First Class ($60 and up)

Ye Olde Smokehouse Hotel (19 rooms) By the Golf Course, Tanah Rata. Tel: 941214/5. Tudor-style retreat with English gardens, ivy-covered walls, overstuffed "chintz" lounges by the bar, wood-fires in the evenings, roast-beef, and Devonshire teas. Definitely the best place in Malaysia to have a taste of the colonial life. S/D range from $60 to $152.

The Lakehouse (18 rooms) Lubok Taman, Milestone 30, Ringlet. Tel: 996152. Overlooking a lake (actually a man-made dam) this Tudor-style hotel is good for peace and quiet, but difficult to get around if you have no car as it's far from the towns. Owned, until seven years ago by the eccentric Captain Forster who used to hang a sign reading "No Dogs, No Children and No Asians Allowed", the "Full House" sign was usually displayed even if the hotel was empty. Full of memories, antique furniture, stone fireplaces, vast bathrooms. S/D $72.

Strawberry Park Resort (172 rooms) Jalan Kemunting, Tanah Rata. Tel: 941166. Garish mock-Tudor resort popular with Singaporeans, and package tours, with all mod-cons, good views, squash, tennis, horse-riding. S/D $74, Apartments $88-144.

Intermediate ($20-60)

Merlin Inn Resort (64 rooms) Jn. Tanah Rata, Tanah Rata. Tel:941211. Modern facilities and rooms with views of the golf course. S/D $72.

Intermediate ($20-60)

The Garden Inn (46 rooms), Tanah Rata (opposite playground). Tel: 941911. Nice situation, quiet rooms with wooden floors, attached bathroom with hot water. S/D $28-48.

Kowloon Hotel (24 rooms), 34-35 Brinchang. Tel: 941366. Modern hotel overlooking the square at Brinchang. Warm cosy rooms and downstairs Chinese restaurant. S/D $24.

Budget (under $20)

Bala's Holiday Chalets, Jn. Tanah Rata, Tanah Rata. Tel: 941660. Take the marked turnoff 2 km (1.2 mi) north of Tanah Rata, or just follow the back-packers. Run by the extroverted Bala, who organises cheap tours and bus tickets, this rabbit-warren of rooms is for travelers who love to be around other travelers. Westernised snacks, good views and garden and notice board. Dorms $2, S/D up to $20.

Seah Meng Hotel (11 rooms), 39 Main Rd, Tanah Rata. Tel: 941618. Basic Chinese hotel with clean rooms, very centrally located. S/D $10-18.

Sri Sentosa Hotel (11 rooms), 38 Main Rd, Brinchang. Tel: 941907. Basic rooms with shared bath, and slightly better with own bathroom, overlooking the main square. S/D $8-13.

DINING

Malay foodstalls in the center of Tanah Rata's Main Rd have a good variety of rice and curries—*nasi campur*, fried rice, noodle soups, and western-style meals including sizzling steaks and lamb chops. Cheap and tasty.

Indian-Muslim food is good at **Restoran Kumar,** Main Rd, Tanah Rata. They serve *roti canai*, *murtabah*, and *biryiani*—rice cooked in ghee with spices served with mutton—good for cool evenings. Reasonably priced.

Chinese food-lovers head for **Parkland Hotel,** Main Rd, Brinchang. Serves good steamboat, but best for more than two as the portions are large. $10 for two. **Jasmine Restaurant**, Main Rd, Tanah Rata has good value 4-course set meals for $4.

Ye Old Smokehouse Hotel, serves excellent, but pricey English meals including roast beef and dumplings in the cosy dining room. Less pricey but a treat is their Devonshire teas: scones, strawberry jam and cream (tinned) on the flagstoned terrace. **Lakehouse Hotel,** at Ringlet has expensive, but excellent leg-of-lamb with mint sauce topped off with a cream-caramel dessert. **Chop and Steak House,** Main

Road, Tanah Rata has good western food at reasonable prices and large helpings of apple pie. Bala's do backpackers fare with a set menu at night. Good for those staying at Bala's but hardly worth the journey out from town.

BANKS

Both Malayan Banking and Hong Kong Shanghai have branches in Tanah Rata's Main Road, Standard Chartered is on Jalan Station (near clocktower).

Pulau Pangkor

GETTING THERE

Pelangi Air fly to Sitiawan (12 km/7.5 mi from Lumut) from KL ($25) and Singapore ($78) four times weekly. Taxis meet all flights. Shared taxis from Ipoh to Lumut (83 km/51.5 mi) cost $3 and leave from the bus station at Medan Kidd. From Kuala Lumpur, several daily air-conditioned buses run from Pudu Raya bus station to Lumut, the 6-hour journey costs $5. From Ipoh, buses run at hourly intervals ($1.20), and there's also a daily bus from Cameron Highlands for ($3.20). Cars are left at Lumut overnight at the council car-park west of the jetty, but for longer stays it is safer at the private carparks which provide watchmen. From the main town jetties, ferries ply the half-hour journey from Lumut to Pangkor every 15 minutes between 6.45am to 7.30pm for $1 return. Ferries also service the Pan Pacific Resort (6 times daily), and the Pansea Pangkor Laut (4 times daily) from special jetties at Lumut.

On Pulau Pangkor taxis run from Pangkor to Pasir Bogak (2 km/1.2 mi) for $1.20 and can be chartered for round island and other smaller trips. However, bicycles and motorcycles are a much better mode of transport for exploring the island, and can be hired at both Pangkor and Pasir Bogak for $1.60 a day (bicycle), $10 (motor-cycle). Buses also run from Pangkor to the end of Pasir Bogak Beach at hourly intervals.

ACCOMMODATION

The most luxurious is **Pan Pacific Resort Pangkor** (163 rooms) Golden Sands, Pulau Pangkor. Tel: 951091. Pangkor's prettiest beach is now the private domain of the resort. Day trippers can use it however, with lunch thrown in for $12. Golf course, 5 restaurants, large swimming pool, tennis-courts, aqua-sports center (snorkelling, windsurfing, water-skiing), and a disco. Prices start from $96 S/D, discounts in off-season.
Pansea Pangkor Laut (137 rooms), Pulau Pangkor Laut. Tel: 951320. Private island resort boasts the scenic Emerald Bay, AC "cottages" with bathrooms and verandahs, swimming pool, tennis courts, sauna, jacuzzi, gym and squash. $66 D and upwards. Day-trippers are allowed on the island if they buy lunch at

the resort.
Sea View Hotel (60 rooms), Pasir Bogak. Old-style hotel facing the beach with seaside restaurant. Good value and location—great for sunsets. With bath AC $34 D, AC chalets for $40 all with breakfast included.
Pangkor Anchor, Pasir Bogak. Very clean, mos-quito-proof A-frame huts for $7 in immaculately-kept grounds. The school-mistress proprietor, Mrs.Wong, shows a list of rules before you book in, but it is the cleanest and by far the quietest of all the neighboring establishments.
D'Village Beach Resort, Pasir Bogak. Tents can be rented here for $2.80 per person and there are small chalets for $28 which include breakfast and dinner.

FOOD

All the hotels and "camps" have their own restaurants serving Malaysian food and some basic western fares, but Pangkor is best-known for its Chinese seafood meals—crabs with chilli, baked fish, tiger-prawns in garlic, and lots of other succulent dishes—are best in Pangkor town at the Kedai Kopi (coffee shops) in the main street. At dusk, taxis shuttle customers from the luxury resort to a restaurant where the proprietor pays the drivers a fee for each diner. The shop nearby, the one without all the European diners, serves better food at far cheaper prices. Meal for two (fish, prawns, veges, and rice) costs around $12. The Fisherman's Place, Pasir Bogak, serves good seafood, popular with both locals and tourists and has an extensive breakfast menu.

Along the Perak River

GETTING THERE

This region is best explored by car, rented from either Ipoh or Kuala Lumpur, or it is ideal for bicycling with flat terrain and tiny tarred roads with little traffic. However, travelers can catch local buses for the trip between Teluk Intan and Parit, or alternatively as the locals do, just hail share taxis anywhere along the route. Both express buses and shared taxis run from Kuala Lumpur's Pudu Raya Bus Station and from Ipoh's Bus Station to Teluk Intan ($1.25 bus, $$2.40 taxi).

ACCOMODATION

Rumah Rehat (Resthouse), 858 Jn.Rumah Rehat, Teluk Intan. Tel: 621969. Out of town in a quiet location. Rooms with attached bath-rooms and overhead fans cost $6.50 S and $13 D.
Anson Hotel (51 rooms) Jn.Sekolah, Teluk Intan. Tel:626166. Centrally located, and prob-ably the best of the 10 Chinese-run hotels in Teluk Intan. Air-con rooms around $16.
Rumah Rehat (Resthouse), Jn. Kelab, Parit. Tel: 371311. Wooden traditional-style chalets over-

looking the Perak River. Marvellous setting and good value for $6.50 S and $13 D.

DINING

Restoran Yussofia, Jl. Pasar, Teluk Intan. Turn-of-the-century shophouse with plaster reliefs of Arabic writing and a crescent moon and stars. Their murtabah and roti canai are as memorable as the decor. Malay food stalls in the square in front of the Teluk Intan clock-tower serve up cheap local specialities like gado-gado—bean curd and sprouts in a peanut sauce—and the old stand-bys fried rice, and lots of noodle dishes.

Kuala Kangsar

GETTING THERE

Trains depart from Ipoh at 10.30am, 12.40pm and arrive at 11.26am and 2.04pm. Taxis can be chartered from Ipoh for $8, or less if you can find passengers to share the cost. Reliance Omnibus Co run from the main Ipoh bus stand several times daily.

ACCOMMODATION

Rumah Rehat, Jl. Istana, Kuala Kangsar. Tel:863872. Great value. Upstairs rooms have high ceilings, big windows and fans, while the downstairs rooms have air-con. Great river views from the dining room. Book ahead as it is usually full with civil servants. Fan-cooled $10 D, $12 AC, $20 for a suite.

Mei Lai Hotel, 7F Jl. Raja Chulan. Tel: 861729. Basic Chinese hotel. OK if the resthouse is full. Rooms with bath $6.50.

FOOD

Malay food stalls are clustered around the Railway Station (good for popiah), and down near the Sayong ferry jetty on Jl. Tambang. Restoran Sri Rahmaniah, on Jl. Raja Chulan serves good Muslim Indian curries, murtabah and rojak. There's a Kentucky Fried Chicken on Jl. Kangsar and on the corner of Jl. Sultan Iskandar is the Double Lion Bakery good for hot bread and cakes. Evening meals are best at the Resthouse, which serves Chinese food—try the steamed fish salad for something light. Meals for two with iced lime-juice costs $12. Best place in town for beers.

Taiping

GETTING THERE
Express Sinaran arrives at Taiping Railway Station at 12 noon, departing from Ipoh at 10.30am. The later mail train arrives at 2.04pm. Ipoh-Taiping Express runs buses between these two towns from 6.30am to 6.00pm daily. Fares $1.20. Share taxis from Ipoh's main bus/taxi station cost $2.40 per person. Walking is the best way to get around

town, and the Lake Gardens is only 1 km (0.6 mi) from downtown. Land Rovers run from the base of Bukit Larut to the hill station every hour on the hour from 8am to 6pm. The 40-minute winding route costs $1.20.

ACCOMMODATION

Rumah Rehat Baru (New Resthouse) (27 rooms), Jl. Sultan Mansor, Taman Tasik Taiping. Tel: 822571. Overlooking the Lake Gardens, quiet location with big rooms and balconies. Very popular and often booked out. Phone before making the 1km (0.6mi) trip from downtown. Rooms with fans $12 D, and AC $14.

Hotel Panorama (70 rooms) 61-79 Jl. Kota. Tel: 834111. Top hotel in town, centrally located next to a large supermarket. Rooms have no views, but great bathrooms, huge comfortable beds, Arctic-like air-con so the blankets come in handy. $23 S, $31 D.

Peace Hotel (20 rooms) 30-32 Jl. Iskandar. Tel: 823379. Turn-of-the-century Chinese hotel. Very clean, with stained-glass windows, fans, wooden carvings, Art-Nouveau tiles. $6.50 D.

Bukit Larut Resthouses. Tel: 827241. Bookings can be made in advance, or organized from the Land Rover station. Colonial-style rooms are $7.20 D.

DINING

Taiping is a food freak's dream town and with so few international tourists the food is genuine local cuisine at uninflated prices. Every street corner has a coffee-shop with its own speciality—wan ton mee, chicken rice, curry mee, to name a few. There are two big hawker centers in town—the Malay dominated Pusat Penjaja, and the multi-ethnic food center under the Larut Supermarket, both on Jl. Panggung Wayang. At the latter, Othman's serves up fresh and delicate popiah, Syed Majid is good for satay, and Gerai 14 has rojak sotong—squid salad with peanut sauce and fresh ginger tea. Bismillah Restoran opposite the town market has roti canai breakfast, lunch-time biriyani istemewa (special) is $1.20. The Resthouse has also a good restaurant for those who can't be bothered to walk downtown.

PERAK MUSEUMS

Muzium Perak, Jl. Taming Sari, Taiping. Tel: 822057. Open daily 9.30am to 5pm. Closed between noon and 2.45pm on Fridays and on public holidays. Ethnography and natural history.

Muzium Di Raja, Bukit Chandan, Kuala Kangsar. Tel: 865500. Open daily 9.30am to 5pm. Closed Thursday afternoon, Friday, and public holidays. Royal heirlooms and artifacts.

Geological Survey Museum, Scrivenor Road (off Jl. Sultan Azlan Shah), Ipoh. Tel: 557644. Open Tuesdays, Wednesdays 8am to 4pm. Closed Mondays, Sundays, Saturday afternoon, and between noon and 2.45 on Thursdays and Fridays.

Penang Practicalities

Prices in US dollars. S=single; D=double; AC=air-conditioned. Telephone code for Penang is 04.

The state of Pulau Pinang, or Penang as it is commonly known, consists of the island of Penang ($285km^2/110mi^2$), and Seberang Prai (Province Wellesley) a $759km^2/293mi^2$) strip of land opposite on the mainland which is linked by the 13.5km (8.4mi) Penang Bridge or by ferry from Butterworth, the railhead to Kuala Lumpur and Singapore in the south and Bangkok in the north. Georgetown, the capital, in the northeast of the island, has a population of around half a million and that of the entire state close to one million. Penang has long been the commercial and tourism hub of the northwest and as a result is well set up for travelers with a wide range of accomodation. Visitors either stay in Georgetown or along the northern beaches strip centered around Batu Ferringhi. The island's cuisine is famed throughout the region and is the main reason why many domestic tourists flock there throughout the year.

GETTING THERE

By air

Twice daily flights operate from Singapore (MAS, SIA); daily flights from Bangkok, Haadyai and Phuket (MAS, Thai); regular flights from Medan (Sumatra) and Madras (India) with MAS. Cathay Pacific also have a direct flight from Hong Kong. Malaysian Airlines fly 10 daily domestic flights from Kuala Lumpur, $42 and Langkawi, daily $20. Local Offices: Malaysian Airlines, KOMTAR, Jl. Penang, tel: 620011. Singapore Airlines, Wisma Penang Gardens, Jl. Sultan Ahmad Shah, tel: 363201. Thai Airways International, Wisma Central, 202 Jl. Macalister, tel: 366233. Cathay Pacific, Wisma Hai Tong, 28 Jl.Penang.

Georgetown is one of the best places in Asia for buying cut-price airline tickets, like Aeroflot to Europe, and interesting multi-stop fares including the southern Pacific route to Los Angeles. Shop around, however, as rip-offs have happened. Try and choose a business that's been around for a while to avoid the fly-by-night companies, but generally it's pretty safe. Most agencies are situated along Jl. Penang and Lebuh Chulia.

Taxis run on a fixed-price coupon system from Bayan Lepas International Airport to Georgetown hotels ($7-8.50) and Batu Ferringhi's seaside hotels ($8.50-11). Buses run from the airport to Pengkalan Weld, Georgetown.

By sea

Passenger and vehicular **ferries** operate a 24-hour shuttle service between Butterworth on the mainland and Pengkalan Weld, Georgetown, every 20 minutes and hourly after midnight. The ferry jetty is next to Butterworth railway station.

A five-hour **hydrofoil** service links Penang with Medan (Sumatra) twice-weekly, fare $40. Office in Medan is at Jl. Brigjen Katamso 62A, tel: 061-515562, and next to the TDC Office opposite the clocktower in Georgetown. High-speed ferries also operate from Langkawi. The 800-passenger MV Vignesswara also plys the route between Madras (India) and Penang.

By train

From Butterworth the International Express departs daily to Bangkok, fares are $33-1st AC, $15.50-2nd AC, plus an overnight berth charge $9-1st AC, $5-2nd AC. Express trains from Kuala Lumpur cost $19-1st AC, $8.50-2nd AC, $5.28-3rd non AC. There are additional charges for overnight berths. Reservations can be made at Butterworth station, tel: 347962 or at the Railway Booking Station at the ferry terminal in Georgetown, tel: 610290.

By road

Taxis operate from the railway station at Butterworth and take the long, but interesting route across the Penang Bridge. Fares around $20 to Batu Ferringhi, less to Georgetown.

Long-distance, air-conditioned **buses** operate to and from the bus station beside the railway at Butterworth. However, some budget-travel agencies in Georgetown also offer bargains on bus tickets around Malaysia and these buses operate from Georgetown itself. From Butterworth, fares are as follows; KL-$6, Taiping-$1.20, Ipoh-$2.60, Alor Setar-$1.30. Bus services also run from here to Thailand; Hat Yai-$8, Phuket-$16, Bangkok-$24.

GETTING AROUND

Walking is the best way to get around the old center of Georgetown, but **trishaws** make a good alternative during the hottest part of the day and at night. Negotiate before you get in, but expect to pay $4 per hour. If you arrive late at night the trishaw operators can always find you an empty room. Expect to pay $1.50 from the ferry jetty to the cheap hotel area around Lebuh Chulia.

Penang's taxi-drivers are notorious for never using their meters, even with local customers, so bargain before the ride. From Georgetown to Batu Ferringhi the fare is around $6.

Bicycles can be rented from booths along the main road at Batu Ferringhi, or in Georgetown at the Eng Aun Hotel, 380 Lebuh Chulia for $2. **Motorcycles** are hired at Batu Ferringhi for around $10 per day—shop around for the best price as off season this is negotiable. **Cars** can be hired from all the big hotels. Avis are at the E & O Hotel, tel: 631685, Budget-Town House Hotel, tel: 631240, but there are cheaper car-rental shops at Batu Ferringhi—try Ruhanmas Rent-A-Car, opposite the Golden Sand Hotel, tel: 811023. They charge $28 per day for a Nissan Sunny or $32-Suzuki Jeep.

Buses are the cheapest way to get about the island and the main bus terminus is at Pengkalan Weld. Blue buses (Hin Bus Co.) operate from Georgetown, passing Pulau Tikus, and along the northern beaches to Batu Ferringhi and Teluk Bahang; the Penang Yellow Bus Co., run south of the city to the Snake Temple, on to Balik Pulau and west through the hills to Teluk Bahang; and the green (Lim Seng Seng Bus Co.) ply the Air Hitam route to the Kek Lok Si Temple and the Penang Hill railhead. It's possible to go all around the island in a day for around $1.60, but get an early start as the last bus from Balik Pulau to Teluk Bahang leaves mid-afternoon. City buses operate from Lebuh Victoria, one street away from the Pengkalan Weld terminal: No.7 runs to the Botanic Gardens.

INFORMATION AND TOURS

Tourist Information Centre, Level 3 KOMTAR, tel: 614461. Open 9.30am to 6.30pm, and at Batu Ferringhi outside Eden Seafood Village, tel: 811254, open 11am to 8pm. Tourist Development Corporation (TDC), 10 Jn. Tun Syed Sheh Barakbah (opposite the Clock Tower), tel: 620066. Open office hours. Penang Tourist Association, close by TDC, tel: 366665, open 8am to 4.15pm.

Recommended island and city tours include Tour East, MSL Travel on Lebuh Chulia and Look East Tours and Travel, or check out the sandwich boards outside travel agencies.

ACCOMODATION

Penang is a popular tourist destination all year round but there is an off season from May to August, when the sea gets choppy and dirty from the southwest monsoon, and some hotels, especially at Batu Ferringhi give discount rates. Never accept the first rate quoted and always ask if they have a "discount" price. During the peak times around Christmas it may be difficult to get a room at the popular budget hotels, but Penang has an enormous amount of hotels in all price ranges and there's always empty rooms. On all but budget hotels add on 15 percent for tax and service.

Luxury ($125 and up)

Rasa Sayang Hotel (316 rooms), Batu Ferringhi Beach, tel: 811811, fax: 811984. The original and best luxury hotel along the beachfront. Malay-inspired architecture, beautifully-landscaped lawns with mature tropical trees and coconut palms, huge swimming pool, health club, massage, squash, tennis, watersports, disco and excellent restaurants. $120-144 S, $132-156 D.

Penang Mutuara, teluk Bahang, tel: 812828, fax: 812829. Only five-star resort at Teluk Bahang, west of Batu Ferringhi. Peaceful and quiet and the beach is cleaner than at Batu Ferringhi. $120-150 S, D135-160.

Shangri-La Inn (442 rooms), Jl. Magazine, Georgetown, tel: 622622. Centrally located high-rise has great views across a sea of red-tiled shophouses to the harbor. Swimming pool, health club, Western and Chinese restaurants. $120 upwards.

Parkroyal Penang (333 rooms), Batu Ferringhi, tel: 811133, fax: 812233. Features local, Indian and Japanese cuisine, a European Deli, Art-Deco inspired disco, water sports, gym, flood-lit tennis courts. $114-140 S/D. Suites from $180.

Golden Sands Resort (401 rooms), Batu Ferringhi, tel: 811911, fax: 811880. Beachfront resort boasts the usual facilities, watersports center, swimming pools, 24-hr room service, lawns, beachfront bar and four restaurants incl. Italian. $102-130 S, $114-142 D, Suites from $260, and extra bed $16.

First Class ($75-125)

Equatorial Penang (413 rooms), 1 Jl. Bukit Jambul, tel: 838111, fax: 848000. Really a luxury hotel but rates are low because it is 15km (9mi) from the beaches and Georgetown. Next to the Bukit Jambul Golf Course. Spectacular 41m (135ft) high lobby, tennis, squash, gym, business center, Chinese, Japanese and Western restaurants. $88-120 S, $96-128 D.

Palm Beach Resort (145 rooms), Batu Ferringhi, tel: 811621, fax: 811051. Nestled between the luxury hotels, this reasonable-priced hotel offers good off-season discounts. All rooms have IDD phone, TV, in-house video and refrigerator. Nice shaded beachside restaurant. $62-80 S, $72-90 D.

High Intermediate ($35-75)

E & O (Eastern & Oriental Hotel) (100 rooms), 10 Lebuh Farquhar, Georgetown, tel: 630630, fax: 634833. Renowned colonial hotel built in 1885 has hosted authors Somerset Maugham, Noel Coward and Hollywood greats like Rita Hayworth. Old-world architecture, harborside gardens and pool, central location, good bookshop, and an aura sadly lacking in the new hotels. $42-56 S, $46-72 D, Suites from $78.

Lone Pine Hotel (54 rooms), Batu Ferringhi, tel: 811511, fax: 811282. Best bargain along the beachfront. The rooms are nothing fancy but have TV, IDD telephone and fridge. The old-style beachfront restaurant and gardens shaded by casuarina trees give it a laid-back feeling. Recently refurbished and now has a pool. Management are great with children. "Seaview" rooms are more costly than "hillview". AC $35-40 S/D, huge family rooms AC $48.

Low Intermediate ($15-35)

Bellevue Hotel, Penang Hill, tel: 892256. Only hotel on Penang Hill has bird's eye views of Georgetown. Breakfast amongst the clouds on the garden terrace. Quiet, cool and comfortable rooms are tastefully decorated. Has an aviary of exotic birds—the private collection of the owner, one of Malaysia's foremost architects. AC $32 S/D.

The Merchant Hotel, 55 Jl. Penang, Georgetown, tel: 632828, fax: 625511. One of the many hotels in this price category on Jalan Penang. Competitive prices here mean that rooms in Penang are consistently cheaper than most other Malaysian cities. All rooms with TV, IDD phone, air-con, and there's a 24-hr Coffee House which offers an "all-you-can-eat" buffet supper for $2.60 from 11pm till the wee hours—great for late-arrivals. $35 S/D.

Cathay Hotel, 15 Lebuh Leith, tel: 626271. Close to all the historical and downtown sites, this 70-year-old hotel is in itself an attraction with its tiled and arched foyer, spacious verandahs, and immense lobby. Rooms are massive and spotless. Downstairs rooms have tiled floors, upstairs wooden and the air-con rooms have large bathrooms with very hot water. Guests can also order breakfasts and meals from the restaurant at the back which doubles as a "massage" health club at night. Staff also organize onward travel and are very helpful. Rooms with fans—$16 S, $18.50 D, AC $20S, $23.

Waldorf Hotel, 13 Lebuh Leith, Georgetown, tel: 626140. Just down from the Cathay Hotel, and in a great location for touring the downtown sights—Cheong Fatt Tze Mansion is just opposite. Rather colorless compared to the Cathay, but good value for the rooms have attached hot-water bathrooms for AC $20 S, AC $24 D.

Budget (Under $15)

Ali's Guest House & Restaurant, 53 Batu Ferringhi, tel: 811316. One of the last surviving cheap spots along the beachfront. Turn down the lane to the beach just past the Hotel Parkroyal. The little restaurant in the garden is a favorite hang-out for budget travelers, and the staff are easy-going and helpful. Rooms with fan and shared bathroom are $8 S, $12 D, and rooms with attached bath (due for completion in '93) cost $16.

Shalini's Guest House, 56 Batu Ferringhi, tel: 811859. Just down the road from Ali's, Shalini's is a plain, two-storey house, but has a real Malay family atmosphere. Shalini's Penang/Malay-style cooking (breakfast and evening meal) is what most regulars return for. Shared bath and fan $12 S/D, attached bath and fan $16 and AC and hot-water bath $24.

Swiss Hotel, 431-F Lebuh Chulia, Georgetown, tel: 620133. A favorite backpacker's hotel for at least a decade, this old-style Chinese hotel is set back from the noisy street and is in the middle center of old Georgetown, and adjacent to cheap travel agencies. $5.50 S, $8.50 D for rooms with fan and shared bath.

Eng Aun Hotel, 380 Lebuh Chulia, Georgetown, tel: 612333. Directly opposite from the Swiss Hotel and just as popular. $5.75 S, $7.50 D for large fan-cooled rooms with shared bath.

Tye Ann Hotel, 282 Lebuh Chulia, Georgetown, tel: 614875. Old-style hotel with basic facilities (fan and shared bath). Popular with budget travelers for its ground floor restaurant serving authentic English breakfasts. $6.50 S/D, $2.50 for a dorm bed.

Wan Hai Hotel, 35 Lorong Cinta (Love Lane), Georgetown, tel: 616853. This historic lane of attractive old shophouses is quieter than Lebuh Chulia around the corner. Popular with budget travelers tourists, also has a small roof terrace. All rooms have shared baths and fans for $6.50 S/D, $2.50 for a dorm. bed.

Hang Chow Hotel, 511 Lebuh Chulia, Georgetown, tel: 610810. Close to Jl. Penang's Indian-Muslim restaurants and shopping bazaars. Moneychanger and restaurant on the ground floor. Fan-cooled, shared-bath rooms are $5.75 S, $6.50 D.

Youth Hostel (Asrama Belia), Lebuh Farquhar (next to the E & O Hotel). Go around the back and up to the second floor for the reception office. Must have valid YHA cards and there is a midnight curfew. $2 for a dorm. bed with shared facilities.

YMCA, 211 Jn. Macalister, Georgetown, tel: 362211. Open to both men and women. About 2km (1.25mi) from downtown, but within walking distance of the Thai Embassy on Jl. Tunku Abdul Rahman, and reasonably close to Pulau Tikus town. $M2 is added for non-members but is waived for holders of student or YHA cards. All rooms have attached bathrooms. $12 S, $13 D for rooms with fans, and $14 S, $15 D, for AC.

DINING

Penang is regionally famous for its food and many Malaysians, Singaporeans and Thais come here just for the cuisine. Eating is by far the major leisure occupation of all Penangites and the proliferation of eating stalls, hawker centers and restaurants is testimony to their passion. "*Sudah makan*"—have you eaten? is a popular greeting throughout Malaysia, but in Penang it is universal. Everyone frequents the lowliest of food stalls In a hawker center, if in doubt, just look for the crowded stalls and the food is bound to be good. When Penangites splurge—usually on big family dinners—they go the full hog and flock to the high-priced resort restaurants along Batu Ferringhi.

Mention Penang to most Malaysians and they instantly think of *laksa*—a fish-based soup with flat rice noodles seasoned with lotus flowers and herbs; and nasi kandar—a lunch speciality of various curried meats with rice which was originally carried by hawkers in containers which hung off a *kandar*—a pole supported on their shoulders.

Nonya

The traditional cuisine of the *babas* (Straits-born Chinese), which combines Malay and Southern Chinese cooking styles is widely available in Penang and specialities include *otak-otak*—spicy fish paste steamed in banana-leaf packets, Curry Kapitan—rich chicken curry in coconut cream, and *chendol*—coconut milk with palm sugar and green noodles colored with pandanas leaves. Hawker stalls in the Pulau Tikus area between Jl. Burma and Jl. Kelawei sell *nonya* food as do the following:

Sa Chew Restaurant, 37B Jl. Cantonment, Pulau Tikua, tel: 20552. Good for *otak-otak* and *laksa*, but only open for lunch.

Dragon King Restaurant, 99 Lebuh Bishop, Georgetown, tel: 618035, all *nonya* specialities, open for lunch and dinner.

Malay

Some of the best Malay food in Penang is at tiny food stalls for these are often run by housewives, and home-cooked food is superior to restaurant fare. Pesiaran Gurney (Gurney Drive) foodstalls get into gear after sunset and operate until the wee hours. The first Malay laksa stall from the roundabout (western end) is excellent. Take your plate and sit on the nearby seawall. There's a good soya-bean drink stall next door, and a little further up a sweet corn seller. Malay roadside foodstalls, built onto kampung houses overlooking the seafront at Jl. Tanjung Tokong, serve cheap breakfasts—*nasi lemak* (rice cooked in coconut milk), and *roti canai* with an onion and meat sauce. Further along, in front of the high-rise flat at Tanjung Tokong are stalls selling take-away *nasi campur* (rice and curries).

House of Malay Kampung Food, 387 Batu Ferringhi, tel: 811273. Directly across the road from the Rasa Sayang. Serves delicious beef *rendang*—a dry spicy dish, creamy chicken curries, satay, seafood dishes, and *ulam*—traditional Malay herbal salads.

Indian Muslim

Meat and seafood curries in rich sauces dominate this cuisine which lacks the variety of vegetable dishes found in Malay restaurants. Most establishments also serve *roti canai* (pronounced *chah-nigh*)—a griddle-fried, wheat-flour "pancake" served with *dhall* (lentil curry), and its sister dish *murtabak* which is stuffed with a mixture of spicy ground meat and vegetables. One of the best-known is **Dawood Restoran,** 63 Lebuh Queen, tel: 611633, opposite the Sri Mariamman Temple which serves excellent nasi kandar. **Hameediyah Restaurant** at 164A Lebuh Campbell, and the *original* **Craven Cafe** on Jl. Penang have good *nasi kandar* and *murtabah.*

The lunch-time stall in the Toon Leong Coffee Shop at the corner of Jl. Transfer and Jl. Argyll, and late-night stalls around the **Chowrasta Bazaar** are also good. The nearby **Yasmeen Restaurant,** 177 Jn. Penang is good for roti canai and dhall and murtabah and chicken and mutton biryani is served on Fridays and Sundays. The tiny lane beside the Kapitan Kling Mosque on Lebuh Pitt is also well recommended for nasi kandar. They start early and by 7.30am diners are tucking into massive piles of rice and curries. Tables are set up on the sidewalk and early morning the space is shared with old Chinese women practising tai chi. Another Penang Indian speciality is rojak with deep-fried seafood smothered with peanut sauce. Hawker stalls along Pesiaran Gurney or the Esplanade are renowned for this dish.

Further out of town is the excellent **Restoran Ibrahim** on the main road at Teluk Bahang which is a popular lunch-time stopover for *nasi kandar*, light and delicate *roti canai*, and *murtabah.*

Indian vegetarian restaurants are centered around the "Little India" section roughly bordered by Lebuh Bishop, Lebuh Penang, Lebuh Chulia and Lebuh Pitt. **B.M. Sagars Restaurant** on Lebuh Bishop specializes in North Indian vegetarian, while the best and cheapest place for southern Indian cooking including *masala thosai*—fine, rice-flour pancake filled with potatoes and vegetables—is Krishna Vilas on Lorong Pasar, in the block between Lebuh Queen and Lebuh King. **Kaliaman Restaurant** on Lebuh Penang is renowned for its slightly more up-market food. They do "banana-leaf" lunches—a great mound of rice with curry sauce, meat, vegies, chutney and yoghurt—for around $1.60 per person.

Chinese

A book could easily be written on the Chinese hawker stalls of Penang, so the following is merely the tip of the iceberg. Breakfast is quick and cheap at the outdoor stalls along Lebuh Carnarvon near the Lebuh Chulia end. Good for Hokkien Mee—noodles with bean sprouts and prawns, Wan Tan Mee—egg noodles with sliced pork and dumplings. Other good breakfast spots include the coffee shops along Jl. Penang, Pengkalan Weld, Jl. Burma—up the Pulau Tikus end. For lunch, Sin Kuan Hwa Cafe on the corner of Lebuh Cintra and Lebuh Chulia sells good Hainanese Chicken Rice—rice cooked in chicken stock with sliced chicken.

Many coffee-shops offer a selection of rice with meat and vegetable dishes, for around $1.20. Try **Hsiang Yang Cafe** opposite the Tye Ann Hotel on Lebuh Chulia or the coffee shops along Jl. Penang. Towards evening an entirely different selection of food stalls spring up. Good spots include Lebuh Cintra, the Esplanade, Jl. Macalister (near Jl. Penang), and further west at the all-time favorite Pesiaran

Gurney. At the latter are several large hawker complexes including the **Golden Phoenix** at 104, and the **Golden Dragon Phoenix** at 113. Service starts about 6pm and goes till well after midnight. *Bah kuh teh,* a spicy pork soup served with traditional tea, is popular. Some Chinese restaurants offer no menu (usually the best) and others that do often make the choice confusing by the sheer volume of dishes available—often up to 100.

Try some Penang favorites like "claypot" dishes which are cooked over a charcoal fire, *padi* chicken—frogs legs with chillies, *kai lan*—greens with oyster sauce, *pai kuat wong*—spicy pork ribs, and *ha lok*—deep-fried tiger prawns.

Up-market restaurants always specialize in China's regional cuisines. **The Supertanker,** Komtar Building, tel: 616393 is good for Teochieu cooking—they do an excellent "porridge"—rice gruel with meat and vegetables. Hokkien cooking is good at **Chuan Lock Hooi Restaurant,** 1E-F Jl. Macalister, tel: 26496. Although Georgetown has good seafood restaurants, it always seems fresher by the sea, and some of the best establishments are along the seaboard at Tanjung Tokong. Try **Hai Chu Hooi** at 338 Jl. Tanjung Tokong, tel: 894375 where you can dine on fresh prawns and chilli crabs and watch the sun set over the sea.

On the beachfront, between the luxury hotels at Batu Ferringhi is **Eden Seafood Village**, one of a chain of atrociously, over-decorated restaurants which crop up all over Malaysia. They serve high priced, but extremely popular seafood and western-style dishes. A cheaper alternative, where you don't pay for the decor is **Ferringhi Village Restoran,** 157B Batu Ferringhi, tel: 811211 where a baked grouper with spicy sauce costs $6 and barbecued tiger prawns $4.50.

Western

Many of the Chinese coffee shops around Lebuh Chulia and Lorong Cinta serve westernised snacks and breakfasts, a wise sales technique developed over the years in response to the backpackers who can't stomach Malaysian food early in the morning. Congregated around the cheap hotel area, popular Lebuh Chulia hangouts include: **Tye Ann Hotel** at 282, which serves porridge and toast with marmalade, and similar menus can be found at the **Eng Thai Cafe,** 417, the Sin Hin Cafe, 402, and **Tai Wah Coffee Shop** at 487. At the towering KOMTAR building in Jalan Penang there are a number of fast food outlets, including **McDonalds**, **Kentucky Fried Chicken** and **Pizza Hut.**

Many of the hawker centers also do "western" meals with a colonial Malaysian flavor, including lamb chops, steaks, and "chicken chop"—a deboned, deep-fried chicken steak. A popular spot out of town is the **Medan Selera Mutiara,** a hawker's center off Jalan Tanjung

Bunga, next door to the Mutiara shopping center which also has a great bakery and serves homemade pizza. All these are very popular with expatriates living on the northern beaches.

The **E & O Hotel** on Lebuh Farquhar puts on an excellent buffet lunch and their a la carte menu in the 1885 Grill Room, especially their flambe dishes is superb. All of the luxury hotels along Batu Ferringhi serve western snacks and meals. **Peppino's** at the Golden Sands Hotel is one of Penang's few Italian restaurants. The cheesecake at the **Rasa Sayang's** coffee garden is creamy and delicious and almost too big—$2.80 a slice. Across the road at the **Ferringhi Village Restoran** they serve excellent steaks cheaper than at the luxury hotels. US Rib Eye and Air-Flown Sirloin cost around $10.

NIGHTLIFE

Eating outdoors with a few beers is perhaps the most popular way to enjoy a Penang evening. Bars are not what they are in the west and are usually a "men-only" affair. Interesting spots to meet the locals for a beer are the **Tiger Bar** at 108 Lebuh Muntri, **Sumi's Bar and Restaurant** at 22 Lebuh Pantai, and the **Hong Kong Bar** at 371 Lebuh Chulia. Pubs are usually not your English variety but dark and rather sleazy spots where businessmen usually bring their girlfriends not their wives.

A notable exception is **20 Leith Street,** the pub with the same name as its address, opposite the Cathay Hotel. Housed in an old colonial-style mansion, its walls adorned with scenes by Penang artists and antique clocks, the pub features a beer garden and a cosy bar with darts board.

For sports enthusiasts, **Beers,** at the Parkroyal Hotel in Batu Ferringhi, screen live telecasts of all major sporting events and has a pool table and darts. Lounges (outside of the major hotels) usually have hostesses who sit and chat with the customers and ply them with expensive drinks. All the big hotels have nightclubs or discos. Try **Juliana's** at the Shangri-La Inn and the Cinta Disco at the Rasa Sayang.

MUSEUMS AND ART GALLERIES

Penang Museum and Art Gallery, Lebuh Farquhar, Georgetown, tel: 613144. Displays of historical documents and paintings, Nonya porcelain, Malay kris and handwritten Korans, contemporary paintings, and outside is an old Penang Hill train and a statue of Penang's founder Francis Light. Open 9am to 5pm daily.
Museum and Gallery, Universiti Sains Malaysia, Minden (opposite Penang Bridge), tel: 877888. Contemporary art, traditional shadow-puppet theater, textiles, jewelery and crafts. Open 10am to 5pm Mon to Fri. Closed Sat and Sun pm.
Forestry Museum, teluk Bahang, tel: 811280, arboretum and displays. Open 9am to 5pm daily.
Yahong Art Gallery, Batu Ferringhi, tel: 811251. Arts and handicrafts on display and

for sale including batik paintings by the renowned Chuah Thean Teng.

LIBRARIES AND BOOKSHOPS

Penang Public Library, 1st floor, Dewan Sri Pinang, Lebuh Duke, tel: 622255. Open 9 am-5pm Mondays to Fridays and on Saturday mornings. Other libraries are at the **Universiti Sains Malaysia,** tel: 870230; **British Council Library,** 43 Green Hall, tel: 370330, open Tues-Wed from 10am to 8pm, and Thurs-Fri 10am to 6pm and Sat 10am to 4pm; **Alliance Francaise,** 32 Jl. Kelawei, tel: 366008, open 9.30-12 noon and 3.30-7.30pm weekdays only. **MPH Bookshop** in the lobby of the **E & O Hotel** Lebuh Farquhar has a good range of local interest books as does **Times Bookshop** in Penang Plaza on Jalan Burma. Second-hand books are available in small shops along Lebuh Chulia.

CONSULATES

Britain, Standard Chartered Bank chambers, tel: 625333. Royal Danish, Hongkong Bank chambers, tel: 624886. France, 82 Lebuh Bishop, tel: 629707. Indonesia, 467 Jl. Burma, tel: 374686. Japan, 2 Jl. Biggs, tel: 368222. Royal Norwegian, Standard Chartered Bank chambers, tel: 625333. Sweden, Standard Chartered Bank chambers, tel: 625333. Royal Thai, 1 Jl.Tunku Abdul Rahman, tel: 379484.

COMMUNICATIONS

The GPO is at Lebuh Downing, one block along Lebuh Pantai from the Clock Tower, open Mon to Sat 8.30am to 4.30pm. Another PO is on the ground floor of KOMTAR. Telekom, the center for international calls and faxes, is on Jl. Burma, open 24 hours a day. Calls can be made direct to your home-country operator.

CHANGING MONEY

Major banks are on Lebuh Pantai near the GPO, however they charge stamp duty and a commission on travelers cheques, making it a better proposition to visit the licensed money changers along Jl.Penang, Lebuh Chulia, Lebuh Pitt and Lebuh Pantai.

SHOPPING

Penang lost its duty-free status years ago, but there are still plenty of bargains for the traveler who like feretting around markets and bargaining hard. Department stores are fixed price, but everywhere else haggling for a lower price is very much the done thing.
Antiques and Curios. Lebuh Bishop and Jl. Pintal Tali (Rope Walk) have many interesting and musty old shops selling antique clocks, old bronze and brassware, chinaware, Dutch ceiling lamps, old phonographs, and Chinese embroideries and porcelain. Saw Joo Aun, 139 Jalan Pintal Tali, specializes in antique furniture as do a few dealers on Lebuh Bishop. Chop Hong Seng, 41 Lebuh Carvarvon deals in antique

porcelain. Other knick-knacks are also found in the markets along Jalan Penang.
Arts and Crafts. Seals carved in wood or marble, known as *cap* (pronounced chop), can be made with your own name translated into calligraphy. Some have Chinese lions, or even your own Chinese astrology animal, carved on the tops. Available at Yee Chai Art Gallery, 255 Lebuh Victoria; Tong Bee Trading Company, 319 Lebuh Chulia; and Yahong Gallery, 47 Lebuh Leith and also at Batu Ferringhi. Locally-made mahjong sets are sold at Lim Tan Tin Industries, 108 Lebuh Campbell. Chinese religious paraphenalia is sold along Lebuh Kimberley and Lebuh Carnarvon.
Cassettes and Videos. Copyright laws have slowed down sales in pirate cassettes and videos (not to mention computer software), but some are still available under the counter. These are often poorly-produced, and the legal variety are of much better quality. Cassettes cost around $4.80 and a CD for $16. The larger shopping complexes like KOMTAR in Jl. Penang, and Penang Plaza in Jl. Burma have shops stocking a wide variety of music.
Clothing. At Batu Ferringhi, brightly-colored, hand-painted, batik sarongs and t-shirts are popular souveniros and in the evenings, sidewalk stalls sell fake, but quite good quality, designer t-shirts like Gucci and Benetton. Other good buys are pantsuits and dresses in rayon with printed "batik" designs imported from Indonesia. Tailors make up clothes to your own specifications. It's wise to make a drawing beforehand. Chowrasta Market on Jl, Penang, and Picadilly Bazaar behind Jl. Kuala Kangsar specialize in all kinds of cotton, silk, and man-made fibre cloths. "Little India" near Lebuh Queen and King sell brilliant-colored saris, Indian kurtas, and Punjabi-style pantsuits.
Gold. Chinese goldsmiths are found along Lebuh Campbell, between Jl. Pintal Tali and Lelbuh Carnarvon, and Indian Muslim gold dealers are found along Lebuh Pitt, opposite the Kapitan Kling Mosque. Gold jewellery is an excellent buy in Malaysia as the gold is 22-24 carat and the cost of workmanship is small. Indian shops around Lebuh Queen and King ankle bracelets, nose and toe rings in silver and gold.
Leatherware. Cheap leather sandals and bags are sold in stalls along Jl. Penang particularly around the Chowrasta area, and also in the night market stalls at Batu Ferringhi. Handmade sandals are also available from Medan Capal, 6 Jalan Dato Keramat. Colorfully-painted wooden clogs, known as *terompah,* for the noise they make clomping on a hard surface . Either plain wood, red, or painted with yellow flowers. Make a great gift for less than $2.
Photographic supplies. There are a host of camera and photographic shops in Penang specializing in quick prints and print film, however for good quality slide film go to the dealers in Jl. Penang, just down from KOMTAR.

Kedah Practicalities

Prices in US dollars. S=single; D=double; AC=air-conditioned. Telephone code for Kedah and Perlis is 04.

Alor Setar

GETTING THERE

By air. Malaysian Airlines flies to Alor Setar from Kuala Lumpur, via Penang or Kota Bharu. Mon to Thurs—3 daily flights, Fri to Sun—2 daily flights. Tel: MAS Office 721186/721287, Airport 721106/721462 for flight schedules. The airport is a 20-min north of town. Taxis charge $1 per person to Alor Setar.

By rail. Malaysian Railways run the Langkawi Express which leaves Kuala Lumpur at 9am and arrives in Alor Setar at 4.30pm on Tues, Thurs and Sat. The return service runs on Wed, Fri and Sun, departs Alor Setar at 11.30am and arrives in Kuala Lumpur at 7.00pm. Single fares: 1st AC $26, 2nd AC $13, 3rd non-AC $8. A Day Express also runs from Butterworth and single fares are 1st AC $5, 2nd AC $2, 3rd non AC $1.40.

By road. Express buses depart from Puduraya bus station in Kuala Lumpur throughout the day and night. Fares from KL are $7.20, from Butterworth $1.30. The express bus station is on Jl. Sultan Badlishah. Bus companies in Alor Setar are as follows: Ekspress Nasional, Bas MARA, tel: 734544; Kota Ekspress, Bangunan PAS, Jl. Kota, tel: 720354; Hosni Ekspress, 73 Jn.Langgar, tel: 732389. Ekspress Tunjang, 6 Bangunan Serbanika, Jl. Sultan Badlishah, tel: 723329, run a service from Alor Setar to Hat Yai in southern Thailand for around $4.

Taxis also go to Alor Setar from Butterworth, Bukit Kayu Hitam (Kedah's border town with Thailand), and from Kuala Lumpur's Puduraya taxi station.

Cars can be easily rented from Penang's main hotels or from car hire companies (*see Penang Practicalities, p.245*). Alor Setar's Hotel Royale or Hotel Grand Continental can organize car hire. This is a great way to see the state, especially the southern "Rice Bowl" and Lembah Bujang.

GETTING AROUND

As most of the downtown sights are within a block or two, walking is the best way to get around. There are plenty of trishaws if the heat is getting to you, but fix a fare first. For the Royal Mausoleum at Langgar, and the State Museum take a taxi or a local bus. Both the main taxi stand and the local bus station are on Jl. Langgar in the middle of downtown.

INFORMATION AND TOURS

Brochures and information can be obtained from the State Tourism Department, State Secretariat Office, Wisma Negeri (behind Balai Besar), tel: 722088/722213. Travel and tour arrangements can be organized through Wira Enterprise, 1st floor, Bangunan PAS, Jl. Kota, tel: 714357, or Syarikat Tunjang Enterprise, 147C Jl. Langgar, tel: 713429.

ACCOMMODATION

Intermediate ($20-$60)

Hotel Grand Continental (122 rooms), 134 Jl. Sultan Badlishah, tel: 735917. Alor Setar's fanciest hotel is conveniently situated in the center of the commercial district. All rooms air-con with private bath, TV, IDD phone, coffee house. $38, D $40.

Hotel Samilla (52 rooms), 27 Jl. Kanchut (Jn.Pekan Melayu), tel: 722344. Overlooks downtown historical sights. All rooms have TV and in-house videos, hot-water bathrooms. Coffee house serves Chinese, Malaysian and Western meals. Has a noisy night club on weekends. Otherwise good value. AC $25 S and D.

Hotel Royale, (40 rooms) Jl.Putera, tel: 730922. Spacious rooms with hot-water bathrooms and TV. Laundry and rent-a-car services. Recently refurbished. Excellent value. Their outdoor seafood restaurant overlooking the river is very good. All AC $18.50 S, $23 D, $24 Triple, $3.20 for extra bed.

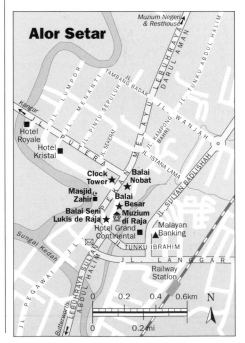

Alor Setar

Kristal Inn, 40 Jl.Kampung Perak, tel: 713333. Good-value with hot-water baths, swimming pool, sauna and coffee house. Easy walking distance to downtown and sights. AC $36 S, $48 D, but ask for discount prices, sometimes up to 50%.

BUDGET (UNDER $20)

Hotel Miramar, 246 Jl.Putra, tel: 738144. Three blocks from the clocktower. All rooms AC with bathrooms, $15 S/D.

There are many old Chinese-style hotels with basic accommodation around the bus and railway station which all offer much the same in terms of value. Typical of these is the Station Hotel, 74 Jl. Langgar, tel: 733855. $6 S or D.

The Resthouse, 75 Pumpong, tel: 722422, is 2km out of town on the Lebuhraya Darulaman. Set beside the Royal Golf Club it is quiet and peaceful, but is inconvenient without your own transport. AC $13 D, AC $9 S, non-AC $6.50.

DINING

The regional favorite is *laksa*—a spicy fish and noodle soup—which is found at dozens of hawker stalls throughout the city, but is best at the two roadside restaurants, Zakariah Laksa, and Din Laksa, 4km from Kuala Kedah. Here diners can enjoy real homemade laksa overlooking the rice-fields.

Further on at Kuala Kedah there are a number of excellent Chinese seafood restaurants on stilts over the river. The **Medan Laut** at Hotel Royale is popular with seafood enthusiasts, but avoid the weekends when it is often booked solid.

One of the town's busiest eating spots is **Hajjah Restoran** on Jl. Tunku Ibrahim which serves Thai-style noodle and rice dishes and a very hot and tasty *tom yam*—chilli and prawn soup. **Restoran Yasmeen** and **Restoran Rose**, within the block just up from Jl. Tunku Ibrahim on Jn.Sultan Badlishah both serve Indian Muslim specialities including *murtabah, roti canai, nasi-kandar* and *rojak.*

The hawker center in **Restoran Empire** on Jl.Tunku Ibrahim serves a wide variety of local dishes including chicken rice, *mee jawa* and Kedah-style curries and rice at lunch. For western dishes the coffee shops at the **Hotel Grand Continental** and the **Samilla Hotel** serve sizzling steaks, lamb chops and soups and salads, but these dishes are not as tasty as the local fare.

For bread, cakes and sandwich fillings, the **City Point** shopping center on Jl. Tunku Ibrahim has a supermarket and an adjoining bakery with tasty sardine rolls, wholewheat bread and a large variety of cakes and pastries.

BANKING AND BUSINESS HOURS

Kedah follows the east coast states and observes the Islamic weekend. Businesses close on Thurs afternoons and all day Fri. Banks open from 10am to 3pm (Sat-Wed) and 9.30am to 11.30am (Thurs). Major banks in Alor Setar include: Bank Bumiputra, Jl. Tunku Ibrahim, tel: 731906; Malayan Banking, Jl. Sultan Badlishah, tel: 723899; Chartered Bank, Jl.Raja, tel: 721715.

Lembah Bujang

Bordered by Gunung Jerai (Kedah Peak) to the north and the Sungai Muda to the south, Malaysia's richest archaeological area, in the southwest of Kedah state, has dozens of Pre-Islamic remains of Buddhist and Hindu temple mounts scattered around the valley floor which date from the 5th to the 14th century. However, many are still unexcavated and far off the beaten track.

Best and easiest to get to are the restored temples of Candi Bukit Batu Pahat and Candi Penkalan Bujang, both within close walking distance from the Muzium Arkeologi (Archaeological Museum) located at the foot of Bukit Batu Pahat, 2km (1.2mi) from the village of Merbok which is 15km (9mi) from Bedong on the main road north of Sungai Petani. Buses run from both Bedong and Sungai Petani to Merbok, but from there visitors must walk as there is still no alternative transport, although it's a pleasant rural stroll up to the museum and the historical park.

Taxis can be chartered from Sungai Petani 26km (16mi) away, but of course nothing beats your own transport as there is no accommodation here.The museum is open daily from 9.30am to 5pm, but is closed on Fridays from 12.15pm to 2.45pm, and on the two major Muslim holidays Hari Raya Puasa and Hari Raya Haji. Entry is free. Guides are available but these should be organized beforehand by phoning the museum on 481236.

Gunung Jerai

Kedah's only hill station is on the peak of Gunung Jerai, a massive limestone outcrop, 1200m (3937ft) high in the southwest of Kedah state. Located 59km (37mi) from Penang and 34km (21mi) south of Alor Setar, access to the mountain is from Gua Chempedak on the main trunk road.

Jeeps ferry visitors up the winding 13km (8mi) road to the top. Private cars are allowed access at their own risk. Rooms cost $19 per night and a chalet to sleep 8 costs $40, tel: 729788. The **Sungai Petani Inn,** tel: 413411 in the town of the same name, also takes bookings for chalets on Gunung Jerai and organizes tours to both the mountain resort and to Lembah Bujang archaeological park.

Perlis

GETTING THERE

By air. Malaysia's smallest state, in the extreme northwest, has no airport, but travelers can fly to Alor Setar and take a taxi from there to Kangar, the state capital, about a 45 minute drive from the airport. Fares are about $1.6 per person for a "share" taxi, or $6.50 for a chartered taxi.

By rail. The Langkawi Express from Kuala Lumpur runs to Arau, Perlis' royal capital, on Tues, Thurs and Sat and departs Arau on Wed, Fri and Sundays. Fares from Kuala Lumpur are 1st class AC $27, 2nd class AC $14, and 3rd class non-AC $8. This train also stops at Alor Setar.

By road. Express buses run daily to Kangar from Kuala Lumpur. Single fares on Ekspress Nasional are $8.40. Ebban Ekspress run from Butterworth to Kangar for $2.40 and Ekspress PPMP ply the Alor Setar route to Kangar for $0.80.

GETTING AROUND

Four local bus companies operate within the state and from the bus station in Kangar run shuttle services to Padang Besar, Arau, Kuala Perlis, Alor Setar (Kedah), Jitra (Kedah), Chuping, Kaki Bukit, and services to all the states other towns. "Share" taxis to the border town of Padang Besar and other major towns are best organized at the taxi stand near the bus station.

Taxis can also be chartered for trips to Gua Kelam at Kaki Bukit, and to other attractions in the state, and prices are reasonable as the distances are small.

ACCOMMODATION

The amount of visitors that Perlis attracts is evidenced by the lack of hotels. Apart from the few hotels in Kangar, there is only one hotel in Kuala Perlis and none in the rest of the state.

Pens Hotel (44 rooms), Jl. Kangar, tel: 760487/760491, is the only "up-market" hotel in Kangar. Relaxed, friendly place, with swimming pool. Restaurant serves Malay and Western cuisine. A larger Pens is being built beside it and will be more luxurious and more expensive. Rates current at the time of writing are AC S $24-52, D $36-60.

Pens Hotel, Kuala Perlis, tel: 754122/754125. A short walk from the Pulau Langkawi jetty. Excellent value when it first opened a few years back, but now standards have dropped. Deluxe rooms have good views. Non AC $14 S, $16 D, AC $22-28 S, $26-32 D.

Federal Hotel (42 rooms), 104 Jl.Kangar, tel: 766288, is a Chinese-style hotel coveniently close to downtown with both fan-cooled and air-conditioned rooms. $14-$25.

Malaysia Hotel (25 rooms), 65 Jl. Jubli Perak,

tel: 761366, is close to banks and shops. Basic rooms from $10. The cheapest place in town is Hotel Ban Cheong, 76 Jalan Besar, tel: 761184, where rooms start from $5.

DINING

Perlis food is basically the same as in Kedah. Breakfast specialities are roti canai and nasi lemak, and the main meal is at lunch when most restaurants serve curries and rice—*nasi campur*. Noodle dishes, including the northern favorite—*laksa*—are often eaten for the evening meal.

Night markets—*pasar malam*—are a great place to sample local delicacies. Kangar's *pasar malam* is on Wed nights, Kuala Perlis on Tues, and Arau on Fri. Food stalls serving cheap food around the bus and taxi station in Kangar's downtown and good Malay food at the Gerai Medan Dato' Jaafar on Jl. Tun Abdul Razak, and Gerai MARA on Jl. Kuala Perlis.

The Federal Hotel has a reasonable Chinese restaurant, and a local favorite for good Chinese noodles is the Soo Guan Restaurant at 96 Jl. Kangar. Thai food, including tom yam is served at Ramlah Restoran, 344 Taman Mutiara, Jl. Pengkalan Asam, and at Sawadee Restoran, 275 Jl. Baru. Diana Fried Chicken, 14 Lorong Seruing, off Jl. Raja Syed Alwi, is good for snacks and fast-food.

Pulau Langkawi

GETTING THERE

By air. Malaysia Airlines flies daily into

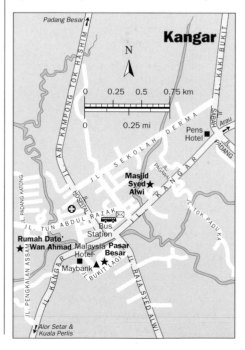

Langkawi from Kuala Lumpur ($54), Penang ($20), and Singapore ($S204). Singapore Airlines also have a flight from Singapore on Mondays, Wednesdays and Saturdays. Langkawi Airport is at Padang Mat Sirat, 20km (12mi) from Kuah, and 14km (9mi) from Pantai Cenang's beach resorts. Taxi fares are fixed price and paid with coupons bought at the airport's taxi counter. Charges are approximately $4 to Kuah and Pantai Cenang, and $5 to Tanjung Rhu and Pantai Kok.

By sea. A variety of high-speed ferries operate from Kuala Perlis hourly to the main jetty about 1km (0.6mi) from Kuah. Different companies operate at different times, but they all offer much the same service—air-conditioning, comfortable seats, and videos with the ubiquitous wrestling matches or sometimes vintage Charlie Chaplin.

The 40-min journey costs $5 one way. A similar ferry service plys from Kuala Kedah, a one-hour journey from Pulau Langkawi, but the service is less frequent than from Kuala Perlis. The high-speed catamaran Selesa Express operates from Penang—the offices are opposite the Clock Tower near the jetty—on Mon, Wed, Thurs, Sat and Sun. During the west coast monsoon season, July to September, services are often cancelled due to rough seas. One-way 1st $16, $14 economy class.

The sea route from Phuket in Thailand via Langkawi to Penang is popular with crusing yachts and some companies run cruises out of Phuket and Penang. For information enquire at the Penang TDC office near the clocktower on Pengkalan Weld in Georgetown.

By rail. Malayan Railway run a special Langkawi Express which leaves from Kuala Lumpur on Tues, Thurs and Sat and returns on Wed, Fri, and Sun. See "Getting There" in the Alor Setar and Perlis section for prices. Taxis and buses meet the trains at both Alor Setar and Arau and connect with the port towns.

GETTING AROUND

At Kuah jetty there are no problems getting a taxi—either a mini-bus or sedan car—to anywhere on the island. As Langkawi is duty-free vehicles are much cheaper here than on the mainland. At peak holiday times there may be a wait but at other times there are no end of taxis to choose from. A **charter taxi** costs $5 to the beach resorts at Pantai Cenang, cheaper if you share.

Returning from Pantai Cenang to Kuah it is easy to wander along the main road and hail a taxi or they can also be booked from most hotels. Some luxury hotels run a shuttle service between the airport and Kuah town. **Local buses** also service the main towns, and leave from the bus station in the center of Kuah opposite the hospital. Fares are very cheap, but the service is often infrequent and buses don't go to many of the more popular smaller beach resorts.

The best way to get around is to hire your own transport. The roads are all paved and many are newly built to cater for the booming tourist trade. **Bikes** can be rented cheaply from bicycle workshops on the main street in Kuah, or more expensively from the larger hotels. Expect to pay around $5 per day for a mountain bike and much less for the standard type. **Motorcycles** are an excellent way to see the island and are hired from shops in Kuah, Pantai Cenang, or organized through hotels. Rates are around $8-12 per day and often no one bothers to check if you have a licence or not.

Car rental is easily organized through taxi drivers, or from locals who hire out their own cars. Rates are around $24 per day, for a newish air-conditioned Nissan sedan, and no one worries about licenses, insurance, or how the fuel gauge reads. Rates are much higher if you rent from the major hotels or car hire offices. Suzuki **jeeps**, non AC, can be hired at higher rates from the Pelangi Beach Resort and from Burau Bay Resort.

Boat trips around the islands can be organized from the beach resorts or ask the boatmen at Pantai Cenang. Burau Bay Resort runs a 3-hour Sunset Cruise for $20, Langkawi Island Resort runs an all-day Robinson Crusoe Cruise to Pulau Beras Basah for a beach barbecue, trekking and snorkeling for $30. Shorter cruises from Pantai Cenang to the offshore islands and to the fresh-water lake on Pulau Dayang Bunting cost from $8.

ACCOMMODATION

Rooms rates vary according to the season and soar during the high season from October to February, especially around Christmas when rooms are often booked out months ahead. However, there are more hotels and chalets being built and even in peak periods you can usually find a room. At all other times, except for major Malaysian public holidays, the island offers ample accommodation, and during the southwest-monsoon off-peak time, the beaches are tranquil and crowd-free.

Luxury ($100 and up)

Pelangi Beach Resort (350 rooms), Pantai Cenang, tel: 911001, fax: 911122. Built in traditional Malay-style using oiled woods, open verandahs, tiled roofs and decorated with wood carvings. Blends beautifully with the scenery and occupies the prime position at the head of the long curving beach. The enormous wood beams and pillars in the Pelangi Lounge are worth a look even if you aren't staying here. Palm-shaded complex includes restaurants, bars, a huge swimming pool, watersports center, tennis and squash courts, gym, and boutiques. Expensive but well worth it. $96-132 S, $104-144 D.

Mutiara Court, Tanjung Rhu, tel: 917091, fax:

917211. High-rise rental condominiums overlook the island-studded bay of Tanjung Rhu. Beautifully-furnished with fully-equipped kitchenette and dining area. One bedroom suites are $132, two-bedroom $180, and larger suites range from $220 upwards.

First Class ($60-100)

Burau Bay Resort, Telok Burau, tel: 911061, fax: 911172. In a picturesque bay backed by rainforested mountains. Cabana-style chalets with fridges, TV and tea-making facilities are scattered around beachside forest. Restaurant, bar, pool and watersports center. AC $$72-84 S, $84-96, family cabanas from $128.

Mutiara Beach Resort, Tanjung Rhu, tel: 916488, fax: 917489. Low-rise, beachside resort in the northeast. Offers fishing trips, and boat excursions to Thailand.$60-88 S and D.

Langkawi Island Resort (220 rooms), Pantai Syed Omar, tel: 788209. Located in the bay to the east of Kuah jetty, Langkawi's original resort has a huge swimming pool and magnificent views, but the beach isn't as good as at Pantai Cenang. $52 upwards.

Intermediate ($20-60)

De Lima Resort (1500 rooms), Kuala Muda, tel: 911801, fax: 911811. Malaysia's largest beach resort. Lacks character, but the rooms are new with all mod cons. Huge pool, tennis courts, shopping mall, hawker center, and karaoke lounge. $44 S and D.

Beach Garden Resort, Pantai Cenang, tel: 911363, fax: 911221. On the beachfront. Thatch-roofed, marble-floored, spotlessly clean. Run by a friendly German couple. Rates include a huge breakfast. Excellent value at $50 S, $58 D, less off season.

Nadias Inn, Pantai Cenang, tel: 911401, fax: 911405. All AC rooms with TV and bathroom, but not on beachfront. Has a good restaurant and hawker center in the evenings. $44 S and D.

Budget (Under $20)

Langkawi Sandy Beach Motel, Pantai Cenang, tel: 911308, fax: 911762. One of the original and now one of the many chalet-style resorts. Still good value. $16 for chalet with bathroom, $12 with share bathroom, and new AC rooms are $40.

Kok Bay Motel, Pantai Kok, tel: 911407. Basic beachside chalets run by friendly Malay family. $12 D with fan.

Resort Southern Cross, Pantai Kok, tel: 911352. Chalets overlooking the beach, clean and basic with small restaurant $20-28 D AC, $12-14 D non-AC.

DINING

Seafood is Langkawi's speciality and the most popular local spot is Restoran Labu Labi which specializes in Thai-style cooking at the **Medan Selera**, the eating stalls in Kuah on the town side of the bridge.

More expensive, but in an unmatched location is the up-market **Sari Seafood Restoran** built on stilts beside the small town jetty and sharing the complex with Kraftangan, the government-run crafts store. Many Chinese restaurants in Kuah and all the big resorts also serve seafood. Malay food is found in dozens of hawker stalls around Kuah, particularly along the main road on the seaward side. Nadias Inn at Pantai Cenang host a nightly hawker complex under the stars with cheap good food. Roti Canai costs 25c, Chicken Rice $1.50, Laksa $1.10. Most of its patrons are from the surrounding luxury resorts. In the adjoining Lada Cafe, western food like beef burgers, steaks, fish and chips are reasonably priced. For western food though, nowhere beats the Beach Garden Resort where the German hostess supervises the kitchen. It's worth the splurge for an evening meal under the palms at sunset. Shark steaks, buttered potatoes, herbed salad, waffles and cream and coffee—a typical meal—although the menu changes nightly—costs around $27 for two. Huge $5 breakfasts—inclusive with room rates—are a main meal with eggs, German sausages, cheese, rye toast, coffee and fresh juice.

SHOPPING

Langkawi is billed as a duty-free shopping paradise, but this is mainly for the locals as there's not much to interest international tourists. However, good buys include liquor and cigarettes, Indonesian batik, air gamak—a traditional "cure-all" medicine made from sea slugs, and cheap T-shirts for souvenirs.

BANKING

Langkawi banks operate to Kedah hours closing on Thursday afternoons and all day Friday. Malayan Banking, tel: 788208 and Bank Rakyat 732860 are both in Kuah town.

Kelantan Practicalities

Includes Pulau Perhentian. All prices in US dollars. S=Single: D=Double: AC=air-conditioning. Telephone code for Kota Bharu is 09.

GETTING THERE

By air. Malaysian Airlines fly daily to Kota Bharu's Sultan Ismail Petra Airport. From Kuala Lumpur ($42), Penang ($35), and Alor Setar ($45). Taxis cost $4 for the 8km (5mi) ride to town, less if you share. MAS office, tel: 747000, is opposite the clocktower on Jalan Gajah Mati.

By rail. Two daily express trains run from Kuala Lumpur and Singapore to Wakaf Bharu, about 7km (4.3mi) from Kota Bharu. The journey from Gemas in Johor is often slow, but the rainforest scenery is balm for the soul. The express departs Kuala Lumpur at 10.21am and arrives at Kota Bharu at 5.30pm the following day, 1st AC $34, 2nd AC $15, 3rd non AC $9. Fares from Singapore (in Singapore dollars) are 1st AC $36, 2nd AC $16 and 3rd non AC $10. Local trains (often slow and full) run from Jerantut and Kuala Lipis in Pahang. Trains also run from Thailand. The station is at Golok, just over the border from Rantau Panjang a 90-min bus ride from Kota Bharu on Bus No 29.

By road. Express **buses** run to Kota Bharu from all major towns and cities. From Singapore's Lavender Street terminal, buses depart at 7.30pm and cost $18. For other times contact Masmara Travel, tel: 02-2947034. From Kuala Lumpur buses depart from Hentian Putra, opposite The Mall on Jalan Putra.

Fares are as follows: from Kuala Lumpur $10, Penang/Butterworth $7, Johor Bahru $12, Alor Setar $7, Grik (at the start of the East/West Highway) $4. Express buses leave Kota Bharu from either the Langgar Bus Station on Jalan Pasir Puteh or the Jalan Hamzah station. **Share taxis** to Kota Bharu cost $18 from Kuala Lumpur and $12 from Penang. For travelers arriving by **car** there are three possible routes. The East West Highway from the West Coast which starts at Grik is 224km (139mi) from Kota Bharu. Grik can be approached from either Kuala Kangsar in Perak (108km/67mi), or Sungai Petani in Kedah (117km/73mi). From Kuala Lumpur take either the highway to Kuantan and then travel up the East Coast Highway (630km/391mi), or a shorter route (474km/294mi) is the new highway which links Kuala Lipis in Pahang with Gua Musang in the south of Kelantan.

GETTING AROUND

Kota Bharu is easy to walk around and alternatively there are plenty of trishaws. Agree on a price before boarding. A 10-min ride shouldn't cost more than $1. **Bicycles** are a great way to see the town, the beaches and the cottage craft areas. They can be rented cheaply from most travelers' hostels. The state-run SKMK runs local **buses** from the Central Bus Station on Jalan Padang Garang. No 10 bus for Pantai Cinta Berahi (30-min) leaves from Central Market or in front of the Kencana Inn at Jalan Padang Garong every 20 minutes. It also runs past the Perdana Resort and returns from HB Village making it feasible to stay out at the beach and cheaply commute to town.

To get to The Reclining Buddha take No 19 or 27 to Cabang Empat and walk 3.5km (1.4mi) to Kampung Jambu, or catch a taxi. For Tumpat and Pantai Seri Tujuh take No 19; for Pantai Irama (Bachok) No 2A or No 2B; for Masjid Kampung Laut at Nilam Puri take No 44 or express No 5. For Pantai Sabak and the Airport take Nos 8 or 9. **Taxis** rates hourly are $6, daily $30. For info. contact Kelantan Malay Drivers Association, Jalan Dato' Pati, tel: 781076 or 785624. For **car rentals** contact Mars Kelantan International Travel, tel: 744737.

INFORMATION AND TOURS

The Tourist Information Center on Jl Sultan Ibrahim, tel: 785534/783543, is open from 8am to 12.45pm and 2pm to 4.30pm, closed Thurs pm and Fri.Cantumas Travel, 2nd floor, above Hanyu Jaya supermarket on Jl Tengku Petra Semerak, tel:787437, run a 3-hour tour for $10.

ACCOMMODATION

Room rates plunge during the annual monsoon,

Kota Bharu

1. Masjid Negeri
2. Istana Balai Besar
3. Istana Jahar
4. Muzium di Raja
5. Handicraft Village
6. Tourist Information Centre
7. Gelanggang Seni
8. Muzium Negeri
9. Central Market
10. Pasar Malam
11. Post Office
12. Hotel Perdana
13. Hotel Temenggong
14. Town Bus Station

N

0   2   4   6 km

0   2 mi

Express Bus Station

Langgar Bus Station

← Tumpat & Pasir Mas

when it can be sunny for days on end, but the rain when it comes can last for weeks and you may find that the only way out is by air. Kota Bharu has no luxury class hotels, but there is ample accommodation from first-class rooms and chalets by the sea, to a competitive range of backpackers' hostels.

First Class (above $50)

Hotel Perdana (136 rooms), Jalan Mahmood, tel: 785000, fax: 747621. Kota Bharu's only "fancy" hotel is close to the Cultural Center, and 1km (0.6mi) from Central Market. Swimming pool, tennis and squash courts, gym. Rooms have mini bar, IDD phones, TV and in-house videos. AC S $64-72, AC D $76-84, suites from $140, extra bed $12.

Perdana Resort (120 rooms), Jalan Kuala Pa'Amat, Pantai Cinta Berahi, tel: 785222, fax: 749980. Resort overlooking the "beach of passionate love". The chalets have verandahs with sea views, private bathrooms, TV, IDD telephones and mini-bars. Excellent restaurant, swimming pool, tennis courts, and watersports center. AC Chalet S/D $48-80, extra bed $12.

Intermediate ($20-50)

Temenggong Hotel, Jalan Tok Hakim, tel: 783481. 5-storey, newish in town center close to all sights. Popular with Malaysians and often full. AC $27 S, AC $30 D all with own bathroom.

Kencana Inn, Jalan Padang Garong, tel: 747944. Close to all sights and buses stop at the door. Cafe, pub and disco. AC S $23-33, AC D $27-37, AC Triple $31-41, extra bed $6, extra mattress $3, all rooms with private bathroom.

Budget (Under $20)

H.B. Village, Pantai Cinta Berahi, tel: 744993. Thatched-roof A-frame chalets and cabins set in a quiet location 1.5km (1mi) from Pantai Cinta Berahi. Town bus stops at the door. Great location for wandering around kampungs and checking out handicrafts. Restaurant has good local food. They also run boat trips and hire bicycles. Dorm $2, non AC chalet S/D $8-12, AC chalet S/D $20, extra mattress $2, TV $2.

Long House Beach Motel & Restaurant, Pantai Cinta Berahi, tel: 740090. Original "beach of passionate love" hostelry. Run-down rooms have clunking air-cons, huge beds, horizontal mirrors at bed level. But the location, right on the sand, and the attached restaurant which serves excellent drinks and Thai-style food helps. Rooms S/D from $15-24.

Rebana Hostel, opposite Istana Kota Lama, up an alley off Jalan Sultanah Zainab close to the silversmith workshops in Kampung Sireh. Malay-style house with friendly hosts 1km (0.6mi) from downtown. Dorm $1.6, S $2.5, chalets and garden rooms $4-6.

Ideal Traveller's Guest House, off Jalan Pintu Pong, tel: 7442246. Popular and often full, centrally-located with nice garden. Dorm $1.6,

rooms with bath $5.

Rainbow Inn Guest House, near Royal Thai Consulate on Jalan Pengkalan Chepa, and Mummy's Hitec Hostel opposite, are both old traveler's favorites with gardens and interesting hosts. Dorm $1.6, rooms from $3.

DINING

Kota Bharu is one of the best towns in Malaysia for cheap street cuisine. At breakfast, coffee shops serve various types of rice with accompaniments wrapped in banana-leaf packages. The favorite is *nasi dagang*—"trader's rice"—an unbleached rice with a sweet curry sauce (50 cents), and is best at **Kedai Kopi White House** opposite the State Mosque on Jalan Sultanah Zainab. Other coffee shops, including Razak Restoran on the corner of Jalan Datok Pati and Jalan Padang Garong, serve Indian Muslim breakfasts of *roti canai, murtabah,* and even an Indian favorite toast and *kaya*—coconut jam. For lunch, upstairs at **Central Market** there are dozens of stalls. At dusk the night stalls opposite Central Market provide probably the best eating in Malaysia.

Pulau Perhentian

GETTING THERE

Take a SKMK bus from Kota Bharu to Pasir Puteh, then change for Kuala Besut via Jertih. Share taxis from Kota Bharu cost $2, from Pasir Puteh 80 cents. From Kuala Besut, the 2-hr boat trip to the islands costs $6 one way. Organize the boatman to pick you up for the return trip if it's off season.

ACCOMMODATION

In Kuala Besut there is only the **Primula Besut Beach Resort,** tel: 976322, on the quiet beachfront with swimming pool and restaurant, S $36, D $44, Suites from $56. On Pulau Perhentian Besar the top-priced, and only accommodation other than rock-bottom budget-style is the **Perhentian Island Resort,** tel: 333910, to the right of the jetty. Comfortable chalets cost $13, bungalows $21 with attached bath and AC, and dorm $5. All the budget accomodation is north of the jetty. Boats will either drop you at the beach—you'll have to wade in—or it's a 20-min walk from the main jetty. **Abdul's Chalets,** the first from the jetty have large rooms with verandahs for $4, further on Coco Hut's A-frames are $4; **Rosli Chalet's** dorms are $2, rooms $6; and **Hamid's** rooms are $4. All have basic facilities, washing from wells, and no electricity. Kerosene lamps are provided. Food is the main problem, there are places but there's little variety. **Isabella Coffee Shop** at the jetty is good for *mee goreng,* fresh squid and drinks. Tiny, **Coral Cave Cafe** on the beach has good food, and a marvellous ambiance, but incredibly slow service.

Terengannu Practicalities

All prices in US dollars. S=Single: D=Double: AC=Air-conditioning. Telephone code for Kuala Terengganu and all Terengganu state is 09.

KUALA TERENGGANU

Getting there. Sultan Mahmud Airport, 18km (11 mi) north of Kuala Terengganu, has daily Malaysian Airlines flights from Kuala Lumpur ($41), Penang ($32), and Johor Bahru ($60). MAS office, 13 Jalan Sultan Omar, tel: 621415. Taxi to downtown costs $5. Express buses from Kuala Lumpur's Henrian Putra, opposite The Mall on Jalan Putra, cost $8. From Kota Bharu the fare is $3; and from Singapore's Lavender Street terminus $9. Long-distance share taxis from Kota Bharu cost $5, from Kuantan $6, from Penang $24 and Kuala Lumpur $14. All buses, both local and express, operate from the Central Bus Station on Jalan Masjid Abidin.

Getting Around

The best time for sight-seeing is early morning and late afternoon when it is pleasant to walk around. Trishaws are still extremely popular, and at the annual Terengganu Fest there is a decorated trishaw competition—for the town was once known as Malaysia's Trishaw Capital. Cheap ferries ply across the river to Pulau Duyung, they can also be hired for river trips. The Tourist Information Office is in Wisma MCIS, 2243 Jalan Sultan Zainal Abidin, tel: 621433.

Accommodation

Like most places along the East Coast, prices drop substantially during the annual monsoon season (Oct-Feb). The only luxury hotel is the **Pantai Primula Beach Resort** (264 rooms), Jalan Persinggahan, tel: 622100, fax: 633360, which overlooks Batu Buruk Beach, 1km (0.6 mi) from town. Great sea views, a landscaped swimming pool, grillroom by a waterfall, tennis courts, car rental, island and waterfall excursions. S $83, D $90, Suites from $140, extra bed $12. The second best is **Motel Desa** (20 rooms), Bukit Pak Apil, tel: 623033, on top of a hill overlooking town. Good views, swimming pool, and large well-appointed rooms, but is difficult to get to without a car. S/D $52.

The cheap and intermediate-priced hotels are downtown. **Warisan Hotel** (16 rooms), 65 Jalan Sultan Ismail, tel: 622688, has large, but run-down rooms, but is centrally located. AC S $22, D $27. Two other similarly-priced hotels on the same street are the Seri Hoover at No. 49, tel: 624655, and the **Sri Terengganu Hotel,** at No. 120, tel: 634622. Seri Indah Resort, 898 Jalan Haji Busu, at Batu Buruk Beach, tel: 621564, is rather expensive, but the chalet-type rooms are clean with AC, TV, hot shower, phone. Quiet location on the beach and close to good foodstalls. S $28, D $32, triple $40.

The most popular place for budget-travelers is **Ping Anchorage**, 77A Jalan Dato Isaac, just past Jalan Tok Lam, tel: 620851, with clean rooms, rooftop restaurant and bar. They also organize island and inland tours. Rooms are all non AC. Dorms $2, S/D $4-$5 with shared bath, $6 with bathroom. There are plenty of other cheap hotels around this area, but for peace and quiet at a budget price, **Awi's Yellow House,** across the river on Pulau Duyung is a great alternative. Dorm beds cost $2 and rooms are slightly more. Close to the boat builders' workshops. Cooking facilities and tea and coffee are free.

Dining

For a good cheap breakfast walk east on Jalan Sultan Zainal Abidin to a stall set back from the road on the right with a red and white picket fence. Other good cheap stalls are upstairs at the market. For lunch, nowhere beats **Sofinaz Restoran,** 38 Jalan Masjid Abidin, opposite the mosque, which specializes in *nasi padang Sumatra.* For Chinese food, **Restoran Cheng Cheng,** 224 Jalan Bandar, has a cheap buffet of rice and noodle dishes. **Restoran Golden Dragon** on the same street serves delicious chicken rice and roast duck. Batu Buruk Beach, east of town, has outdoor restaurants, excellent for reasonably-priced Malay seafood dishes.

MERANG AND NORTH

Getting there. Four daily local buses, and a mini-van service run from the bus station on Jalan Masjid Abidin along the coastal road via Merang to Penarik. For travelers coming from Kota Bharu, get off at Permaisuri on the main East Coast highway and catch a local bus to Penarik. Share taxis from Kuala Terengganu also ply this route. Hitching is also quite feasible.

Accommodation

At Batu Rakit, 24km (15 mi) from Kuala Terengganu, Pantai Batu Rakit Guest House has rooms for $10. Beside the beautiful beach at Merang is the Merang Beach Resort with A-frames with shared bathrooms for $10, and rooms with attached bath in the hilltop guesthouse cost $16. Breakfast and lunch are provided for an extra $4. Man's Homestay, 500 m past Merang, is not on the beach and is very basic, but the English-speaking host is amiable and it's a great place for travelers wanting a real kampung experience. $4 for a bed and all meals, more for a chalet. There's also other homestays and chalets being built along this coast which are expected to open in '93.

PULAU REDANG

Passenger boats leave from the jetty in Kuala Terengganu or the Chendering Fisheries Complex south of town, but it's often a long wait. Boat charters are upwards of $100, so the best way to get to the island is with a tour. Dahlan, tel: 627050, organizes **dive trips** and runs Dahlan Beach Chalets on Pulau Redang's Pasir Panjang beach. A chalet costs $8 or less for a bed in a tent. Man's Homestays in Merang also organizes boat and camping tours to both Pulau Redang and Pulau Lang Tengahfor groups of six or more. Tour groups which specialize in island trips are WLO Holidays in Kuala Terengganu, tel: 635844; and Kuala Lumpur based Camping Holiday, tel: 03-7178925; Mayflower Acme Tours, tel: 03-6267011; and Scenic Holidays 03-2424522.

MARANG AND SOUTH

Getting there. Local buses from Kuala Terengganu cost 40 cents, chartered taxis $4, and share taxis $1 per person for the 15km (9km) journey to Marang. The main highway runs through the back of town, but all the accommodation, eating places, jetty, and markets are a short walk from here.

Accommodation

There's basic budget accomodation for $2 a dorm bed, and $4 a room at the **Marang Inn,** tel: 681878, and at **Hotel California** for similar prices, located in the old shophouses in the main street. Heading north of town, overlooking the lagoon, is **Island View Resort,** tel: 682006 which charges $2 a dorm bed, $6 a chalet, and offers free bicycles. Just past here, at similar prices, is **Kamal's, is** the original and best-known budget resort. At the top of the hill behind Kamal's is the **Marang Guesthouse** which has it's own restaurant, and good views. $2 dorm, $5 S/D with shared bath, and $6 with own bath. South of town, across the river on the beachfront at Kampung Rhu Muda is the **Beach House,** tel: 682403, a friendly, long-running resort run by the patriarch Hajee and his extended family. Chalets are priced from $10 for the basics, up to $32 for AC and attached bathroom. There's a good restaurant and the resort runs day trips to Pulau Kapas. Just north along the beach is the Mare Nostrum, tel: 681433, which has pokey, cheap chalets with no views ($6) or large rooms with verandahs and beach views for $25.

Dining

The cheapest food is at the foodstalls beside the market. Most guesthouses have their own restaurants and Marang Inn is well-known for its tasty fare.

PULAU KAPAS

Getting There. Wooden passenger boats make the 6-km crossing from Marang jetty for $3 one way. Boats are easy to organize from the guest-houses or the boat offices in the main road.

Accommodation and food

Primula Kapas Island Beach Resort, tel: 633360, is comfortable although expensive, with swimming pool, restaurant, bar, and facilities for snorkeling, scuba-diving, wind-surfing and fishing. Traditional Malay-style chalets with AC and attached bath cost $56 S, $64 D, and family bungalows are $112. The best of basic chalets is **Zaki Beach Chalet,** tel: 811475 where clean A-frames with shared bathroom are $6 and chalets with bathroom and fan $10. Order food in advance if you dislike slow service, and bring snacks and fruit from the mainland.

SEKAYU WATERFALLS AND KENYIR DAM

Local buses and share taxis run from Kuala Terengganu to Kuala Berang. It is 15km further to the waterfalls and the same distance in the other direction to the dam. Hire a taxi for around $8 for either trip. For accomodation at Sekayu resthouse and chalets, $12-16 per room, make reservations through Kuala Berang District Office, tel: 811259. Tours are also organized from the Primula Beach Resort in Kuala Terengganu which has overnight houseboats on the lake, Ping Anchorage run trekking trips and ask at the TDC office on Jalan Sultan Zainal Abidin.

RANTAU ABANG

Local buses from Kuala Terengganu's main bus station cost $1.20, chartered taxis are $10 or $2.50 per seat for the 58km (23 mi) journey south. The bus stop is at the Turtle Information Center which is open daily except for Fridays, during the season (May to September).

Accommodation and dining

Rantau Abang Visitor Centre, 8th mile, tel: 842653, 1km (0.6 mi) north of the information center, has traditional-style wooden houses overlooking a lagoon. The large rooms sleep six, have overhead fans and attached bathrooms. Peak season (June-Aug) $44, fringe season (Apr.May, Sept) $40, off season (Oct-Mar) $24. If there's a turtle sighted, the managment wake you and take you to where it's nesting. The nearest food is at the Malay restaurants near the information center.

Cheap accommodation close to the information center includes the **Awang's,** tel: 842236, with a restaurant and chalets on the beach for $5, and neighbouring Ismael's with similar prices. **Dahimah's,** 1km (0.6 mi) south on the highway, is another popular budget hostelry with a good restaurant. **Tanjung Jara Beach Hotel** (100 rooms), tel: 841801, fax: 842653, is 9km (5.6 mi) south of Rantau Abang, at the 8th Mile, Dungun. This Malay-style resort is a great place to unwind. They also organize turtle-watching. Rooms all AC with TV, phone, hot showers, S $80, D $92.

Pahang Practicalities

All prices in US dollars. S=single: D=double: AC=air-conditioning. Telephone code for Kuantan and all eastern Pahang is 09.

KUANTAN

Getting there. Malaysian Airlines fly direct from Kuala Lumpur and Singapore to Kuantan Airport which is 15km west of downtown on the main road to Kuala Lumpur. Taxis meet all flights and charge around $4 for the trip to town. Several daily express buses run from Kuala Lumpur's Putra Bus Station, opposite The Mall in Jalan Putra for $4.50; from Kota Bharu for $6; from Kuala Terengganu for $2.8; and from Singapore $7. Share taxis are also prolific from Kuala Lumpur $10, Kuala Terengganu $7, Kota Bharu $9, and Johor Bahru $8.

Getting around. All the downtown hotels, restaurants, sights, post-office, banks, etc., are within a few blocks of each other and are an easy walk. Tourist information is in the 22-storey Kompleks Terantum at the southern end of Jalan Mahkota. Hertz Rent-A-Car is beside the Samudra Hotel on Jalan Besar and Avis are at 102 Jalan Teluk Sisek.

Accommodation

Kuantan's most luxurious hotel is out at Teluk Chempedak, but the fanciest lodging downtown is the **Samudra Hotel River View** (75 rooms), Jalan Besar, tel: 522707, comfortable rooms with TV, AC, hot showers. $32 S, $50 D. Another mid-price hotel close by is the **Classic Hotel** (33 rooms), Jalan Besar, tel: 554599, recently renovated. All rooms have AC, TV, IDD phones, hot-water baths. $26-$34 S, $30-38 D, family $44. The cheapest lodgings in town are at **Hotel On Heng,** 22/24 Jalan Mahkota, tel: 504885, with swing doors, wooden floors and an arched verandah which hasn't changed in decades. $4 S, $4.5 D, $5.50 triple.

Dining

The Taman Selera foodstalls on Jalan Mahkota just north of Jalan Masjid have good Chinese food and beer. Opposite there is an open-air fruit market. There are also stalls along the riverbank walkway south of the Samudra River View Hotel which serve excellent seafood.

TELUK CHEMPEDAK

Getting there. Taxis ply the 5km (3mi) to Teluk Chempedak, Kuantan's closest seaside beach, or take bus No 39 from the main bus station on Jalan Besar or the stand near the corner of Jalan Mahkota and Jalan Masjid.

Accommodation

The beachside **Hyatt Kuantan** (185 rooms), Teluk Chempedak, tel: 501234, fax: 507577, has luxurious rooms, restaurants, a disco, boutiques, tennis courts, water sports center, and swimming pool. $84-128 S/D, suites from $200, extra bed $12. **The Merlin Inn Resort,** at the end of the beach, tel: 522300, has first-

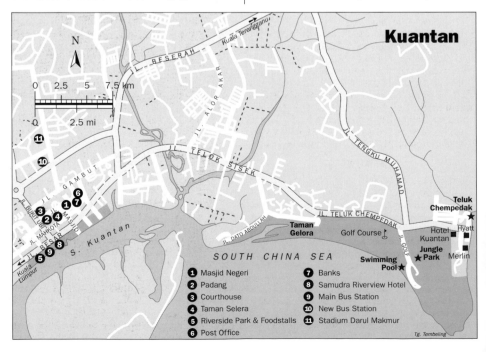

Kuantan

0   2.5   5   7.5 km

0   2.5 mi

SOUTH CHINA SEA

Teluk Chempedak

Taman Gelora   Golf Course

Swimming Pool
Jungle Park
Hotel Kuantan   Hyatt
Merlin

① Masjid Negeri
② Padang
③ Courthouse
④ Taman Selera
⑤ Riverside Park & Foodstalls
⑥ Post Office
⑦ Banks
⑧ Samudra Riverview Hotel
⑨ Main Bus Station
⑩ New Bus Station
⑪ Stadium Darul Makmur

Tg. Tembeling

class rooms from $50 upwards but lacks the style and the facilities of the Hyatt. The best value at the bay is the **Hotel Kuantan**, tel: 554980, opposite the Hyatt, an impeccably-clean, 60s style, 2-storey hotel. $15 non AC with bath, $22-30 S/D AC and bath, $35-40 family. The cheapest lodgings, popular with backpackers is **Asrama Bendahara**, on the way to the Merlin, tel: 525930, has outdoor restaurant and nice atmosphere. Dorm beds $3, $6 S, $7 D. There is more reasonable accommodation in the street behind the restaurant strip.

Dining

Everyone from Kuantan goes to Teluk Chempedak for a night out. The **Hyatt** has a varied, but expensive buffet, good for a splurge, and **Hugo's**, the region's only gourmet restaurant. The **Pattaya**, an outdoor restaurant on the promenade is popular for seafood, as is the **Katong Seafood Restaurant** on the main road which specializes in fishhead curry. **Nisha's** nearby serves good North Indian. The cheapest food is at the food stalls at the end of the promenade.

BESERAH

Getting There. From Kuantan's Jalan Besar bus station, take a Balok bus No 30, Sungai Karang No 28 or Kemaman No 27 which all stop on the main highway at Beserah, 10km (6mi) north of Kuantan, or alternatively flag down a share taxi.

Accommodation

Beserah Beach Resthouse, tel: 587492, a wooden, colonial-style house overlooking the beach, is in a quiet kampung area, has a marvellous verandah, and friendly hosts. $12 S, $14 D, with fan and bath. On Jalan Pantai, halfway between the highway and the beach, is **Belia Perkasa Hotel**, tel: 522355/526540, a newly-built low-cost hostel with clean, fan-cooled dorms for $3, and 4-bed rooms for $20. Cooking facilities cost $3 per day. One km (1.6mi) north of Beserah, the **Gloria Maris Resort**, tel: 587788 has attractive wooden chalets by the beach, a restaurant serving home-style Thai, Western and Malaysian food and wholemeal bread. $20-24 S/D AC with bath.

Dining

There's foodstalls along the highway serving Malay food including rabbit satay at the first place from Kuantan on the left. The Beserah Beach Resthouse has a small restaurant serving breakfasts and local fare, and there's an excellent stall, just down from Belia Perkasa Hotel towards the beach which opens early.

CHERATING

Getting there. From the main Kuantan bus station take a Kemaman No 27 bus for the one-hour journey, and then walk the short distance to the beach from the road, or get a share taxi from Jalan Besar.

Accommodation

There is no problem with cheap accommodation here—at least a dozen choices of thatched-roof chalets and homestays, and more are springing up all the time. Favorites are **Mak Long Teh's** and **Mak De's** homestays, next to the bus stop on the highway where full board (3 meals) is $7, and $6 (2 meals). On the south end of the beach is the good-value **Kampung Inn** with chalets for $6-10, dorms for $2; and the **Coconut Inn** is clean with A-frames for $4-6 and chalets with bath $7. Heading up the beach, there's **Hussaien's Bungalows** where large, but old rooms cost $4; and further north is the newer and cleaner **Oni Motel**, with AC rooms for $14 and chalets $10. More up-market accomodation is found further south along the coast.

PEKAN

Buses run from the main bus stand several times daily or get a share taxi from Jalan Besar for the 44km (27 0) journey. The town is small and easy to walk around. At the Sultan Abu Bakar Museum pick up the brochure which has an excellent map with all the sights marked. To get to the Silk Weaving Center and Tun Razak's Birthplace take a taxi from the stand in front of the market on Jalan Sultan Ahmad. There's a couple of old Chinese hotels in the downtown with basic rooms for $4, but the only place to stay with atmosphere, albeit rather rundown, is the **Pekan Resthouse** on Jalan Sultan Abu Bakar where huge rooms cost $6. You can book Malay style meals here, or alternatively there's a good variety of foodstalls beside the market.

TASEK CINI

Getting there. Travelers with their own car can drive to Chini, an oil-palm plantation town accessible from the Kuantan/Segamat highway and then follow the road 8km (5mi) to the Lake Cini Resort. No 121 Cini buses leave from Kuantan's main bus station, three times daily, for the 2-hour trip. From Chini you'll have to organize a lift on a motorbike to the resort. The best way to get to Tasek Chini is by boat from Kampung Belimbing on the Sungai Pahang. To get there take a Maran bus along the main Kuala Lumpur highway and get off at the turnoff 56km (35mi) from Kuantan. Then you'll have to hitch a ride to the riverside kampung. Return day trips from here by 4-seater wooden longboat cost $16 per boat, and overnight trips $28. There are parking areas for cars here. The only place to stay is the **Lake Chini Resort**, tel: 2433890, a quiet wooden place amongst the rainforest. Chalets S/D $22-26, dorms $6. There are camp sites for 80 cents per person and the hire of a 3-person tent costs $2. The restaurant serves good local food. Alternatively daytrips are organized by the Tourist Information Office, Kuantan hotels, and chalet-owners in Cherating which cost from around $14.

Rainforest Practicalities

All prices in US dollars. S=single: D=double: AC=air-conditioning. Covers Taman Negara, Kuala Lipis, Kenong Rimba, and Endau Rompin.

PREPARATION

All rainforest areas are difficult to reach during the annual Nov-Jan monsoon season when the rivers get dangerously high. Taman Negara is closed from 15 Nov-15 Jan. Except for early-mornings and evenings, or at high altitudes, the rainforest is a hot and humid, so loose cotton clothing is best. If you plan on hiking make sure you have good hiking boots, or jogging shoes—but canvas shoes dry out the quickest. Long pants and sleeves protect against sharp rattans, and from the sun on river trips. Leeches can be a real problem; if you're really squeamish about them don't bother to do any hiking. Keep your trousers tucked into your socks and boots laced tight. Calico "leech socks" can be purchased from the Malayan Nature Society (MNS), 485 Jalan 5/53, Petaling Jaya, tel: (03)7912185, for $3. Poncho-style raincoats, water bottles, first-aid kits, and a torch are helpful. Carry everything in plastic as glass is not permitted in the park.

TAMAN NEGARA

Getting there. Jerantut, the jump-off town for Taman Negara, 194km (120mi) northeast of KL, is reached by either road or rail. Share taxis leave from KL's Puduraya station. Oriental Bus Co buses depart from Perhentian Pekeliling on Jalan Tun Razak 9am, 1.30pm, and 5.30pm. The 3-hr trip costs $3.40.

Travelers coming from Singapore should take the train: it stops not only at Jerantut, but at Tembeling Halt, a half-hour walk to the boat jetty for Taman Negara. Make arrangements in advance for the train to stop at this station. A night train leaves Singapore at 10pm and arrives at Tembeling Halt at 7.57am the next morning.

From the north, the train leaves Tumpat in Kelantan at 10am and reaches Jerantut at 7.30pm. A local bus and taxi service ply the 16-km (10mi) stretch between Jerantut and Kuala Tembeling. The only way from Kuala Tembeling to Kuala Tahan, the headquarters base at Taman Negara, is by boat. For bookings tel: (09) 262284. Boats leave at 9am and 2pm daily and return from the park at the same time. Depending on the river level the boat journey takes 3-4 hours and costs $12.

Information

Park permits must be purchased by every visitor and cost 40 cents at the reception center.

Fishing permits $4, camera $2. Guides, porters, accommodation at overnight hides and fishing lodges, boat trips within the park, are all paid for and organized here. For further information and bookings contact Department of Wildlife and National Parks, Km 10, Jalan Cheras, KL, tel: (03) 905287, fax: (03) 9052873.

Accommodation and food

All accommodation (except for the hides and fishing lodges) is now run by Pernas International. Tel: (03) 2610393, fax: (03) 2610615 for all bookings including the return boat journey. Also check with the tourist information center (MATIC), Jl. Ampang, KL, tel: (03)2423929. A deposit of 50% must be made when booking. You can also arrive at the park and organize everything from there. Hostel rooms with shared bathroom and cooking facilities cost $4 per bed. Chalets with own bathroom and hot shower cost $36 S/D non AC, $48 S/D AC, and deluxe AC rooms $76. Campsites at Kuala Tahan are 40 cents per night. Elswhere, camping is free. two-man tents cost $2.40 per night. All hides, except for Bumbun Tahan have sleeping facilities for 6-8 people, and a bathroom. There are no cooking facilities and it is advisable to bring in pre-cooked food to maximize your chances of spotting wildlife. If you must cook, do it away from the hides. There are visitor lodges at Kuala Terenggan and Kuala Kenyam with beds, bedding, eating utensils, kerosene stove, and water. The Fishing Lodges at Lata Berkoh and Kuala Perkai have beds and mattresses but bedding and cooking equipment must be brought in. All camping and hiking gear

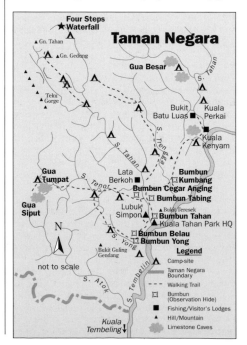

Taman Negara

★ Four Steps Waterfall
▲ Gn. Tahan
▲ Gn. Gedung
Gua Besar ▲
S. Tahan
Teku Gorge
Bukit Batu Luas ■ Kuala Perkai
Kuala Kenyam
S. Trengga

Gua Tumpat
Lata Berkoh ■
S. Tenor
Bumbun Kumbang
Bumbun Cegar Anging
Bumbun Tabing
Gua Siput
Lubuk Simpon ▲ Bukit Teresek
Bumbun Tahan
Kuala Tahan Park HQ
N
Bumbun Belau
S. Yong
Bumbun Yong
Bukit Guling Gendang

not to scale

S. Atok
S. Tembeling

Kuala Tembeling ↓

Legend
▲ Camp-site
— Taman Negara Boundary
- - - Walking Trail
⌂ Bumbun (Observation Hide)
■ Fishing/Visitor's Lodges
▲ Hill/Mountain
Limestone Caves

can be rented from the reception center. At the expensive hotel restaurant buffet-style breakfast costs $7, lunch $10, dinner $12. The restaurant near the reception center has cheaper local fare and they also pack take-away meals for treks. A small shop sells tinned food and basics like batteries and insect repellent.

Hikes and boat trips

Guides are a good idea for long treks. They cost $30 per day and are organized through the reception center where you can pick up a good booklet outlining all the trails, boat trips, fishing, etc., with trail maps. Trails are signposted with approximate walking times. Organized daily hikes with lunch included cost $16. The first goes to Bukit Teresek and Tabing Hide, then by boat to the rapids at Lata Berkoh and hike back to HQ. The second goes to Bukit Indah, then by boat through the rapids to Kuala Trenggan and then hike back. Boat trips to Lata Berkoh, Kuala Trenggan, and further afield to Kuala Kenyam and Kuala Perkai are cheaper if the four-seater boat is full. Expect to pay around $24 per boat for the shorter journeys.

KUALA LIPIS AND KENONG RIMBA

Getting there

Kuala Lipis, the former capital of Pahang, in the northeast of the state is 171km (106mi) from Kuala Lumpur. By road take the KL/Kuantan highway to Bentung, then turn off via Raub and Benta. Buses run four daily services from Putra Bus Station, KL, or twice-daily from Kuantan and Kota Bharu. Share taxis also run from these towns. Kuala Lipis is on the east coast railway line and is a good stopover for travelers enroute to Kota Bharu. The Singapore mail train leaves at 8.30pm daily and reaches Kuala Lipis at 7am on the following day. From Tumpat (Kota Bharu) a southbound train leaves at 10 am and arrives at 6pm. To get to Kenong Rimba take the early-morning local train from Kuala Lipis to Batu Sembilan. From the nearby jetty, motorized longboats (20-min trip) run to Kenong Rimba. Some cheap hotels organize trips into the park, but the most reliable is run by Hassan Tuah, at Tuah Travel & Tours, No.2 Jl. Lipis-Benta, Kuala Lipis, tel: (09)312144.

Accommodation and food

There are a few wooden chalets inside the park at Gunung Keson, take your own bedding. If you go with a tour this is taken care of. Past here, hikers must bring their own tents. A tiny store at Kampung Dusun beside the park sells basic foodstuffs but past here travelers have to bring in all their own foodstuffs and cooking equipment. The best place to stay in Kuala Lipis is the hilltop **Resthouse,** on Bukit Residen, 1km (0.6mi) south of town, tel: (09)312599. It has an in-house museum, great views, and the restaurant serves excellent Malay-style food.

Rooms cost $14-20 S/D and have bathrooms and AC. Most backpackers stay in the cheap downtown hotels. In the main street, the **Hotel Paris** and **Hotel Central** have basic rooms for $5.

ENDAU-ROMPIN

As this proposed state or national park is only being developed at the present there is no organized transport system into Endau Rompin and only very basic accommodation at Kuala Jasin, however more is being planned. For up to date information contact the Malaysian Tourism Promotion Board, Ground Floor, KOMTAR, Jalan Wong Ah Fook, Johor Bahru, tel: 07-223590, fax: 07-235502. Travelers must either have their own 4-wheel drive vehicle or join a package camping trip. There are two routes to Endau-Rompin, but there are no signs, and it is best to have someone on board who knows the way. To get to the park facilities at Kuala Jasin on the Johor side, turn off at Air Hitam, 94km north of Johor Bahru on Route 1, then on to Kahang via Kluang on the Mersing road. One km (0.6mi) from Kahang, turn left onto a plantation road which ends up at Kampung Peta. Boatman can take you up to Kuala Jasin from here. Access from the Pahang side starts 10km (6mi) north of Rompin, goes via Seladang Felda then to Kampung Mok and the logging trail leads to Kuala Jasin. The easiest way to get to Endau Rompin is with a fully-organized camping trip. Wilderness Experience, 6-B Jalan SS 21/39, Damansara Utama, Petaling Jaya, tel: (03) 7178221, run a 4-5 day trip from Kuala Lumpur for $200, inclusive of food, camping equipment, travel, and guides.

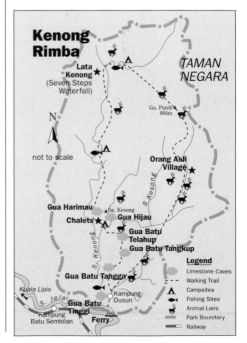

Melaka Practicalities

All prices in US dollars. S=single: D=double: AC=air-conditioning. Telephone code for both Negeri Sembilan and Melaka is 06.

Melaka

GETTING THERE

By air. Pelangi Air runs three weekly flights from Singapore ($44), and Ipoh ($40). There are also Friday flights from Pekan Baru, Sumatra ($58). The airport is at Batu Berendam, 9.5km from town and taxis meet all flights. Contact Pelancongan Kota Malacca, tel: 247728, or Atlas Travel, tel: 220777.

By boat. An express ferry runs between Melaka and Dumai, Sumatra, on F, Sa, M, and W. It takes 4 hrs and leaves Melaka at 10am. Departs Dumai 2pm. $32 single, $60 return.

By road. The fastest way from Kuala Lumpur is by share taxi from Puduraya taxi station for $5. Share taxis from Johor Bahru cost $7. AC express buses, Jebat Express, tel: 249940, and Melaka/KL Express, tel: 222503) run frequently from Puduraya for $2.50; Ekpres Nasional, tel: 220687 from Ipoh ($5), Butterworth ($9); Malacca/Singapore Express, tel: (02) 2935915, from Singapore ($4.50); Barat Express, tel: 233462, ply the coastal route from Klang through Port Dickson to Melaka for $3.

By train. Nearest train station to Melaka is at Tampin, 38km north of town. For train schedules phone Melaka Railway Office, tel: 223091, or Tamping Railway Station, tel: 411034.

GETTING AROUND

Walking is by far the best way to see Melaka, as many of the town's attractions are centered within the heart of old downtown.

Trishaws are the second-best mode of transport and are excellent for getting to slightly out-of-the-way places like St.John's Fort, and the Portuguese Settlement. **Buses** are cheaper than trishaws, although not as pleasant. The bus station is at Jalan Tun Mamat, off Jalan Hang Tuah in the north end of town, but there are convenient bus stops throughout the downtown area. Bus No 17 goes to the Portuguese Settlement, and close to St.John's Fort (get out at the jail). Bus No 19, goes past the new State Mosque to the recreation area at Ayer Keroh where Mini Malaysia, the jungle recreation park and other theme parks are located.

For the seaside drive northwest, past Klebang to Pantai Kundor, take a Pat Hup Bus No 51. To get to Umbai for boats to Pulau Besar, and also for Merlimau and Muar, take an Aziz Co bus from the central terminal. From Umbai, walk to Pengkalan Pernu (or the bus may go inside) for ferries to Pulau Besar. One-way fare is $1.60, but this is for a full boat load of 12 persons. To charter a boat costs something around $16.

Riverboat cruises up the Melaka River start from both sides of the river near the Melaka River Bridge and cost around $2 for a 45-min trip, $4 for a 90-min trip. Sea Safari (Melaka) Sdn Bhd, tel: 235882, do coastline cruises, and run boats to Pulau Besar from the jetty opposite the Majestic Hotel in Jalan Bunga Raya.

Melaka is a beautiful state to **drive** around and there are many picturesque villages with outstanding examples of traditional architecture which are not easily accessible by bus. Car rentals can be organised at Sintat Rent-a-Car, Ramada Renaissance Hotel, Jl. Bendahara, tel: 248888, ext.327. Avis Rent-a-Car are at 27 Jl. Laksamana, tel: 235626.

INFORMATION AND BANKING

Melaka Tourist Information Centre, is in the Town Square, tel: 236538. Banks are open 5 days a week and halfday on Saturdays. Hongkong and Shanghai Bank is on Jl. Kota and next door is Bank Bumiputra. Overseas-Chinese Banking Co is on Jl. Hang Jebat. There is a money changer on Jl, Munshi Abdullah.

ACCOMMODATION

Melaka is a popular tourist destination all year round, and has a wide variety of lodgings ranging from luxury hotels to cheap dorms. Accomodation is always available, but at public holidays up-market hotels are often full.

First Class ($60 upwards)

Ramada Renaissance (295 rms), Jl. Bendahara, tel: 248888, fax: 249269. The premier downtown hotel. Centrally located, good views of Melaka River and the Malay village. Luxurious, well-appointed, comfortable rooms, restaurants, sauna, swimming pool, disco. $60 S, $65 D and upwards.

Melaka Village Resort (146 chalets), Ayer Keroh, tel: 323600, fax: 325955. 10km (6mi) from downtown in the new recreational area. Traditional Malay-style wooden architecture, beautifully-landscaped grounds, swimming pools, tennis courts, horse-riding, Malay, Western and Japanese restaurants. S/D chalets from $60-120.

Intermediate ($25-$50)

Shah's Beach Resort (50 rms), Tanjung Keling, tel: 511120. Overlooking the straits, 10km (6mi) north of town, this wooden motel-style resort has character, cane chairs on the verandahs, bamboo blinds, a Malay/Western cuisine restaurant, small swimming pool and tennis

court. AC rms with bath S/D $32 upwards.
The Emperor Hotel (225 rms), 123 Jl. Munshi Abdullah, tel: 240777. Central and comfortable. $40 S/D includes breakfast.
The City Bayview (182 rms), 20 Jl. Tun Sri Lanang, tel: 239888. Good views. Near St.Peter's Church and town attractions. Pool, TV, inhouse videos, restaurants, S/D $40 upwards.
Ayer Keroh Country Resort (47 rms), Ayer Keroh, tel: 323600. Next door to Mini Malaysia. Quiet location with jungle trees, pool, restaurant. $40 S/D AC with own bathroom, TV.
Tanjung Bidara Beach Resort (45 rms), Tanjung Bidara, tel: 542990. Beside the Strait's best swimming beach, but hard to get to without own transport. $40 S/D AC with own bathroom, TV.

Low Intermediate ($10-25)

Majestic Hotel, 188 Jl. Bunga Raya, tel: 222367. Old colonial era hotel with high ceilings and fans. Located beside the Melaka River. Non AC $10S, $12 D, AC with bath $15 S, $18 D.
May Chiang Hotel, 52 Jl. Munshi Abdullah, tel: 222101. Very clean, centrally located. Non AC with bath $10 S, $12 D, AC $14.
Westernhay Hotel, Batu 4, Klebang Besar, tel: 353196. Old seafront Baba mansion (6km/4mi) north of town. Clean and old fashioned. $9 S/D non AC, $12 S/D with AC and bath.

Budget (under $10)

Chong Hoe Hotel, 26 Jl. Tukang Emas, tel: 226102. In the heart of Chinatown, opposite Kampung Keling Mosque. Clean and basic. $6 S, $7 D non-AC with shared bath, $11 with AC and attached bathroom.
Kancil Guest House, 177 Jl. Parameswara. In an interesting old shophouse area about 1km from town. Quiet, clean, safe, cooking facilities, bicycle hire. $2 dorm beds, $3.50 S, $4 D.
Paradise Hostel, 4 Jl. Tengkera, tel: 230821. Centrally located near Chinatown. Clean and friendly. $2 dorm bed, $3.50 S, $4 D with shared bath, $5 S, $6 D with own bath.
There are also guesthouses in Taman Melaka Raya, a characterless suburb built on reclaimed land south of Jl. Parameswara. Those recommended are **Trilogy Homestay,** 223B Taman Melaka Raya, tel: 245319—they rent out mountain bikes; **Shirah's Guest House,** 229-230B; **Cowboy Lim's Travellers House,** at 269; and **Travellers' Lodge,** 214B. All dorm beds are around $2, and S $4-5, D $6-8.

DINING

Melaka is well-known regionally for its cheap, tasty food, and the majority of famous food spots are unnamed hawkers' stalls.

Chinese

Chinese food freaks start with a dim sum breakfast—steamed delicacies served with Chinese tea—at the coffee shop opposite **Masjid Kampung Keling** on Jl. Tukang Emas. Around mid-morning to lunch, a tiny shop at 4 Jl. Hang Jebat (just near the bridge) is famous for its chicken rice with the rice shaped in billiard-size balls, and home-made barley drink. Further up Jl. Hang Jebat, on the corner of Jl.

Lekir, a satay seller makes Melaka's best pork satay throughout the afternoon.

For refreshing *chendol*—a coconut-milk based drink—try shop on the corner of Jl. Hang Jebat and Jalan Hang Kasturi. Roast pork or roast red-skin duck is good at the stall opposite the Kong Wah Hotel in Jl. Bunga Raya. For dinner, **Madame Fatso's** at Glutton's Corner, the hawker stalls along Jl. Merdeka, serves baked crab and Chinese-style steamboat. Nonya food, or Straits Chinese cuisine, a blend of Chinese and Malay, is good at **Ole Sayang Restaurant,** 198/199 Taman Melaka Jaya, tel: 231966; and at the **Peranakan Restaurant,** in a restored Baba villa at 317 Klebang Besar, tel: 354436. **Jonkers Melaka Restoran,** in a revamped Baba townhouse on Jl. Hang Jebat, does a set nonya-style lunch.

Malay

Malay food is best at **M. Annuar Catering,** tel:229413, a small shop next to the food stalls on Jl. Taman facing the Padang. Their delicious *nasi biryani*—spicy rice with chicken or mutton—comes with tasty *rojak* and pickles. The stalls either side serve cheap nasi campur—rice with curries at lunch—and Malay-style soups and noodle dishes. Out of town, and well worth the trip to Klebang Besar, 8km (5mi) north, are a group of outdoor restaurants overlooking the Melaka Straits which specialize in satay, and baked fish—*ikan bakar*. Another popular downtown eatery is the **Melaka Pandan Restoran** behind the tourist office at the back of the town square.

Portuguese cuisine, which is similar to Malay, but slightly more Mediterranean, is good at the square in the Portuguese Settlement. Recommended places include **Restoran De Lisbon,** tel: 248067, **Restoran De Portugis,** tel: 243156; and the San Pedro opposite the square. Their baked fish and"devil" curry is good, and the small deep-fried fish, known as gading gading, are delicious as a snack with beer.

Indian

Indian food shops are centered around the Jl. Temenggong and Jl. Bendahara. Sri Lakshmi Vilas Restaurant in Jl. Bendahara and Restoran Veni in Jl. Temenggong serve delicious South-Indian pancakes—delicate *dosai* with curry sauces. Also in this area are plenty of coffee shops selling *roti canai* and *murtabah*.

Western

Western food is best and expensive at Summerfield's Coffee Shop in the Ramada Renaissance Hotel, Jl. Bendahara. Their cheesecake is delicious. Other major hotels and resorts also serve western cuisine. The small restaurant in the Majestic Hotel, Jl. Bunga Raya does reasonably-priced steak and lamb chops. On Jl. Laksamana, Restoran Kim Swee Huat, serves"travelers" food—porridge

and muesli breakfasts—and is popular with backpackers. The Tai Chong Hygienic Ice Cafe on Jl. Bunga Raya has a large menu of drinks and desserts including peaches and ice-cream.

Negeri Sembilan

SEREMBAN

GETTING THERE

Seremban, is 64km (40mi) south of Kuala Lumpur, a 45-min drive on the North/South Expressway (Lebuhraya Selatan Utara). Frequent buses from Kuala Lumpur run from Puduraya terminal, and share taxis can be hired upstairs. Trains, although much more infrequent than the buses, also stop at Seremban's old colonial-style railway station, fares from Kuala Lumpur are $1.60 AC, and from Singapore $10 AC.

GETTING AROUND

Seremban's attractions are easily seen by foot, however to get to the Cultural Park & State Museum, which is out of town on the link road to the expressway, catch a taxi from the bus and taxi station at Jl. Sungai Ujong. It is also feasible to hire a car from Kuala Lumpur, where the rates are more competitive, and make a 2-day trip to Seremban and Sri Menanti, and then take the coast road via Port Dickson to Melaka.

ACCOMMODATION

Seremban's only up-market hotel is the **Tasek Hotel** (42 rms), tel: 730994, overlooking the

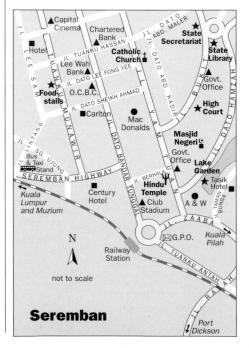

Seremban

Lake Gardens on Jl. Tetamu off Jl. Za'aba. Motel-style rooms overlook the pool. Quiet and comfortable. $36 S AC, $44 D AC.

Low Intermediate ($10-25)

Hotel Carlton (38 rms), 47 Jl. Tuan Sheikh, tel: 725336, AC rms with bathroom are $10-$20.

Budget (under $10)

There are a host of cheap Chinese hotels which all offer very basic facilities.
The Oriental Hotel (18 rms), 11 Jl. Tuanku Munawir, tel: 730119 costs $5.
Wang Sang Hotel, 111 Jl. Dato' Bandar Tunggal, tel: 725669 is $4.

DINING

Negeri Sembilan food follows the traditions of the Minangkabau from Sumatra and the cuisine is tasty, but very hot and spicy. The cheapest and best place in town is the hawker center on Jl. Tuanku Munawir. More up-market Malay cuisine is served at **Flamingo Inn,** 1A Jl. Za'aba. Indian Muslim food—curries, and roti canai, and murtabah—are good at **Bilal Restaurant,** 100 Jl. Dato' Bandar Tunggal. Recommended Chinese restaurants include **Suntori Restaurant,** 10/11 Jl. Dato' Sheikh Ahmad, and the **Happy Restaurant,** 1 Jl. Dato' Bandar Tunggal. Tasty banana-leaf curries cooked in the South Indian style are a lunchtime speciality at **Samy Restaurant,** 120 Jl. Yam Tuan. There is an **A & W Restaurant** on Jl. Yam Tuan near the lake, and a **McDonalds** two blocks north.

SRI MENANTI AND KUALA PILAH

Getting there. Catch share taxis to the royal town of Sri Menanti, 33km (20mi) west, and to Kuala Pilah from the Seremban bus and taxi station in Jl. Sungai Ujung for $1.60. Local buses run every two hours.

Accommodation. There is no hotel in Sri Menanti, but Kuala Pilah, 6km (4mi) further northwest, has a hilltop Resthouse (Rumah Rehat Kerajaan) on Jl. Seremban. $6-18. The Minangkabau food here is more authentic than in the capital. The hawker center at the corner of the roads to Seremban and Tampin has a good variety of dishes. There are also a number of cheap Chinese and Indian coffee shops in town.

PORT DICKSON

GETTING THERE

By car take the Port Dickson exit on the North/South Expressway and then follow the main access road from Seremban. Share taxis from Kuala Lumpur's Puduraya station cost $4, from Melaka $3.50, and from Seremban $1.20. Bestu Sdn. Bhd run express buses from Kuala Lumpur (Puduraya) for $1.80 and frequent local buses depart from Seremban for 65

cents. To get around the Port Dickson region hail a share taxi anywhere along the beachfront road, or catch local buses to Blue Lagoon (walk in to Tanjung Tuan), or to the megaliths at Pengkalan Kempas.

ACCOMMODATION AND FOOD

Ming Court Beach Hotel (164 rms), Batu 7 Jl. Pantai, tel: 405244. Top range beachfront hotel. Comfortable rooms, TV, IDD phones, swimming pool, tennis courts, restaurants. Weekdays are cheaper $40 D (country view), $50 (poolview). Weekends, $55-$64.
On the same beach stretch is the mid-priced **Si Rusa Inn,** Batu 7 Jl. Pantai, tel: 405233, a 1960s-style "motel" where AC rooms with bath cost $20 D to $36 family. There are a number of cheap, Chinese-run guesthouses which get very noisy on weekends, but are quiet through the week, including the **Coastal Inn,** Batu 4, Jl. Pantai, tel: 473388, $12 AC S, $14 AC D.; **Pantai Hotel,** Batu 9, Jl. Pantai, tel: 405265, $16 AC S, $20 AC D; **Lido Hotel,** Batu 8, Jl. Pantai, tel: 405273, $10 S, $12 D. There are good seafood restaurants, Malay-style, with economical prices, on the beachfront at Pantai Bagan Pinang, and at Teluk Kemang. Beside the information center at the former there is a small food center which serves excellent Malay-style breakfasts. For a splurge, the buffet at the poolside coffee shop in the **Ming Court Hotel,** is excellent. They also serve western cuisine, and snacks and cakes throughout the day.

Johor Practicalities

All prices in US dollars. S=single: D=double: AC=air-conditioning. Telephone code for Johor is 07.

Johor Bahru

GETTING THERE

Malaysia's southernmost major town is usually visited either coming or going to Singapore, 1km (0.6mi) across the Causeway, a half-hour drive from downtown. AC express buses shuttle from Singapore's Rochor Road. terminus ($S1), or the regular bus No 170 from Queen St. stops along the way. Share and charter taxis also depart from Queen St. for $4 a seat.

Johor Bahru has a much better range of express bus and long-distance taxi services than Singapore, and many travelers to Malaysia merely get across the border and make onward travel arrangements from Johor Bahru. The taxi station is on Jl. Wong Ah Fook, and the bus station on Jl. Gertak Merah.

The Kuala Lumpur/Singapore train passes through Johor Bahru.

Malaysian Airlines fly to Johor Bahru's airport, 15km (9mi) from town, from Kuala

Lumpur ($37), Kuala Terengganu ($60), Kuantan ($35), Kota Kinabalu ($347), and Kuching ($169) and there are direct flights to and from Hong Kong. Malaysian Airlines, Orchid Plaza, Jl. Wong Ah Fook, tel: 220888, and airport, tel: 594737. Most downtown attractions can easily be seen on foot, or taxis can be hailed from the roadside. Contact M. G. Travel, tel: 244533, for car rentals..

Accommodation

Hotels are more expensive in Johor Bahru than in most other Malaysian towns, mainly because of the demand by Singaporeans, and decent rooms are hard to find on weekends.

Puteri Pan Pacific Hotel, Jl. Salim, tel: 233333, is the top luxury hotel. Beside Kota Raya shopping complex in the heart of downtown with silver-service restaurants, swimming pool, fitness and business centers. $104-$136 S/D

Hotel Straits View, 10 Jl. Skudai, tel: 241400. Out of town overlooking the straits. Huge beds, hot showers, TV, IDD phone, and renowned seafood restaurant. $40 S/D.

Fortuna Hotel, 29A Jl. Meldrum, tel: 238671, is cheap and clean for $20 S/D AC.

Hotel JB, 80A Jl. Wong Ah Fook, tel: 2247888. Basic with fan, shared bath for $12 S/D, $20 with own bath and AC.

The Holiday Inn, Jl. Dato Sulaiman, Century Gardens, tel: 323800. 2km (1.2mi) north of town. Swimming pool, health club, and restaurants, S/D $75.

Dining

Johor Bahru is well known for its excellent and cheap food. For the best Johor-Malay cuisine, head for **Tepian Tebrau food center,** Jl. Abu Bakar, for seafood steamboat, Nasi Beriani—spiced rice with mutton or chicken, Ikan Bakar—fish grilled in banana leaf.

Another favorite with locals is **Capati Corner,** which serves home-made capati—Indian bread, and curries, on Jl. Kolam Air (parallel to Jl. Skudai).

Good up-market restaurants include **Rang Mahal,** 68 Jl. Padi Satu, Bandar Baru Uda (a new suburb on the main road north), tel: 360888, which specialises in North Indian cooking good for naan and Tandoori chicken. **Manhattan Grill,** Lot 110, Level 5, Plaza Kotaraya, tel: 246846, does prime ribs, stews, steaks, salads and mouth-watering desserts. **Restoran Tokugawa,** the town's best Japananese restaurants and puts on a set lunch or dinner for around $8 per head.

Recommended seafood restaurants include Jaws 5, at the **Straits View Hotel,** Jl. Skudai, which has delicious tiger prawns. **Midland Garden,** 11 Jl. Skudai, tel: 228136, does excellent grilled fish dishes, "drunken" prawns and shark's fin soup.

Muar

From Melaka to Muar, 45km (28mi) south, take a share taxi or bus from the main bus station. From Johor Bahru, taxis depart from Jl. Wong Ah Fook or buses from Jl. Terus. Car hire can be organised in Melaka or from Johor Bahru.

Accommodation

Muar has an old-world **Resthouse** on Jl. Sultan, Tanjung Mas, tel: 922306, close to the river-mouth. S AC $11, D AC $12 with own bathrooms. More upmarket is the **Hotel Sri Pelangi,** 79 Jalan Sisi, tel:918088. Overlooks the river. Comfortable rms with TV, IDD phones.S/D AC $25. There are plenty of basic, cheap, Chinese hotels like the **Lee Wa Hotel,** 44 Jl. Ali, tel: 921604. $7.

Dining

The town speciality is rojak petis—fruit salad with peanut sauce—at Tanjung foodstalls on the riverside. Cheap Chinese restaurants are found in Chinatown (downtown). Malay food is good at the riverside stalls in town.

Catch a local bus, or a share taxi from Johor Bahru (126km/78mi), Melaka (98km/61mi), or Muar (53km/33mi). Buses and taxis can also be stopped anywhere along the Muar/Batu Pahat road.

Batu Pahat

Catch a local bus, or a share taxi from Johor Bahru (126km/78mi), Melaka (98km/61mi), or Muar (53km/33mi). Buses and taxis can also be stopped anywhere along the Muar/Batu Pahat road.

Accommodation

Hotel Carnival, 2 Jl. Fatimah, tel: 415122. Classiest hotel in town. Comfortable rooms. $25 upwards. Near the roundabout where **Route 5** goes to Pontian, is the **Resthouse,** 80 Jl. Tasek, tel: 441181, with large rooms for $13 with own baths and a good restaurant. Cheaper rooms can be found in the old-style Chinese hotels like the **Fairyland Hotel,** Jl. Rahmat, tel: 441777. $7.

Dining

Batu Pahat has a great variety of eating spots and some of the tastiest and cheapest eating on the peninsula. For Chinese food, especially pork satay and oyster omelletes, try **Glutton's** Corner beside the river at the end of Jl. Rahmat. West along the riverbank are Malay satay and grilled fish stalls.

Opposite the Immigration Department on the Pontian road is the best fried bananas in Malaysia—served with a hot soya-sauce sambal. The food center north of the bridge on the Muar road, serves delicious Malay curries and rice.

Pontian/Kukup

No one really stays in Pontian—they just drive through on the way to Kukup, or further south to Tanjung Piai, to eat seafood. But it's an interesting town if you want to stay overnight at the Resthouse overlooking the Melaka Straits on the Pontian seafront close to foodstalls. Tel: 878937. $20. To get to Pontian, take a share taxi or local bus from Johor Bahru (61km/38mi), or Batu Pahat (73km/45mi). Most visitors to Kukup either come by tour bus from Johor Bahru or Singapore or drive their own cars. However, you can catch a local bus from Pontian (19km/12mi) or hail a share taxi. Kukup has a wide variety of seafood restaurants, but the best for atmosphere are those with large dining areas built out over the water. The best-known is **Restoran Makanan Laut** Kukup—great for prawns and crabs; also well-known is **Restoran Tong San**—good for grilled fish and **Restoran Zaiton Hussin**—good for Malay-style seafood. At Tanjung Piai, the tip of the Asian mainland (hard to get to without your own transport) is **Atan Seafood Restaurant**—atmospheric cheap eating with marvellous views. restaurant.

Kota Tinggi

Local buses and share taxis ply the 42km (26mi) from Johor Bahru to Kota Tinggi. To get to Lombong Waterfalls take a No 23 bus. At the waterfalls, chalets set amongst the rainforest with cooking facilities and fridges, cost from $19 to $28, tel: 241957.

In town there is only basic, old-style hotels. The best is **Hotel Bunga Raya,** opposite the bus station, for $8 D. To get to Johor Lama is difficult without your own transport, but you can hire a taxi in Kota Tinggi.

Desaru

Catch a bus or share taxi from Kota Tinggi, or alternatively from Singapore a ferry service plys between Changi Point and Penggerang and from there you can catch a taxi north to Desaru.

There is no cheap accommodation at Desaru as it is all run by a private resort company. The three hotels are all along the same stretch of beach. **Desaru View Hotel,** tel: 821221, is the top-priced from $76 to $115; **Desaru Golf Hotel,** tel: 821101, $46-$112, and **Desaru Holiday Resort,** tel: 821240 has chalets from $35.

There are a few foodstalls here, only open in the day, and for most meals guests rely on the pricey hotel restaurants. Further south there are newly-built chalets along the seafront at Sungai Musuh, but you must have your own transport, and there's also a few Chinese hotels in Sungai Rengit, and good seafood restaurants at the latter.

Mersing

The jump-off port for all the islands, Mersing is located 186km (115mi) south of Kuantan, and 137km (85mi) north of Johor Bahru. Buses and taxis connect from both towns and the local station is on Jl. Sulaiman, beside the river. Share taxis cost $4.50 from Johor Bahru, and $6 from Kuantan.

Accommodation

Mersing is a pleasant town with an interesting riverside and if you have to wait overnight for a boat to the islands there is plenty of accomodation and restaurants. The top-priced hotel is the **Mersing Merlin Inn**, tel: 791312, 2km (1.2mi) north on the Kuantan road. $36 S, $40 D, all AC with pool. The nicest place to stay is the **Mersing Rest House**, tel: 791101, about 1km (0.6mi) from downwtown on the seafront. Huge rooms overlook the sea and distant islands. Book ahead as it is always popular. $14 S/D. **The Hotel Embassy**, Jl. Ismail, tel: 791301, is central and clean. $6 S and $8 D. Dorm beds for $2 are upstairs from Sheikh Tourist Agency, tel: 793767, on Jl. Abu Bakar (opp. PO).

Dining

Western breakfasts, lunch and dinners are good at the **Mersing Rest House.** They also put on good lunches and dinners. The seafood is tasty at the **Hotel Embassy** downtown. Malay food is cheap and good at the foodstalls next to the bridge particularly the satay in the evening. Sri Mersing Cafe on Jl. Sulaiman is good for tea and cakes and the Taj Mahal Restoran on Jl. Abu Bakar has delicious North Indian food.

Information and Banking

Most island resorts have offices close to the jetty where you can enquire about boats, prices and accomodation. and there's always plenty of touts and boatmen around that are knowledgeable and easy to talk to about island information. **Bank Bumiputra** in Jl. Ismail changes travelers' cheques, and you can change money at the goldsmith's on Jl. Abu Bakar.

Pulau Tioman

GETTING THERE

Pelangi Air have daily flights from Singapore and Kuala Lumpur on Tu and F, Su from Kuantan. **Silk Air** also fly from Singapore. The airport is at Tekek. Jeeps from the Tioman Island Resort meet all flights. To book a flight out go to Bukharie Services, just south of Tekek.

There are a variety of **boats** serving the island. The "slow" boats—revamped fishing trawlers—are the most reliable, but slowest. Most boats leave in the morning, trips take 4-5

hours, cost $6 one way, to either Tekek or Ayer Batang. For boats to Mukut (south), Teluk Nipah and Kg. Genting (southwest), ask around as these are much more infrequent. Faster "slow" boats—about an hour faster—cost $8, and express boats which take around two hours (they advertise 90 mins) cost $10 although these only stop at Tekek and the resort. Tioman Island Resort also has its own boat which costs $12. Other express boats, and hydrofoils come and go, they often operate for one season and are under repair the next. The shallow harbor often forces them to leave later than most of the slow boats and as they don't service the popular beaches north of Tekek you often end up arriving at much the same time. Passenger boats also run from Singapore to Pulau Tioman, enquire at the tourist information office in Singapore.

Getting around

Walking is the only way to get about on the land. A path runs from Tekek north to the end of Ayer Batang. The only road goes from the airport to just south of the resort. The cross-land walk from Tekek to Juara takes 3 hrs. Sea Bus boats make 8 daily trips between Tekek, Tioman Island Resort, Ayer Batang and Salang; twice-daily service operates to Juara for $6; and a daily round-the-island trip, including a stopover at the Kampung Asah waterfall, costs $12.

For boat trips to the other beaches ask the agents to get the boat to stopover. Many resorts also organise boat trips to Pulau Tulai (Coral Island) the best diving spot.

Accommodation and food

During June-August the most popular places are often booked out and the main beaches are quite crowded. The island is practically deserted during the annual monsoon (Nov-Jan), but the water isn't clear and boat services are highly irregular. The shoulder months, particularly from August to November when the seas are clear are often the best time to visit.

Travelers have an incredible range of budget accomodation to choose from, but practically nothing in the mid-price range and only one luxury resort. **Tioman Island Resort** (185 rooms), tel: 445445, south of Tekek, has one of the island's best beaches. Comfortable chalets, pool, a watersports center for scuba gear and windsurfers, a golf course, tennis-courts and horse-riding. AC rooms and chalets from $50 to $114. The restaurant serves good, but highly-priced western and Malaysian cuisine.

There's dozens of small chalet-type resorts with restaurants, all along the beachfront at Tekek,. and further north at Ayer Batang. At the south end of Tekek beach, is the **Swiss Cottages,** $27 for comfortable chalets with bath. Babura, nearby has good value rooms with bath and fans, $12. Past the jetty, near the track to Juara, is popular **Railey's Villa** with dorm beds $2, rooms $4. At the north end, set amongst the jungle is **Ramli's**, A-frames $4, chalets $10. Quiet, **Mango Grove** at the far end with restaurant and batik shop, huts $4.

Over the headland is popular **Ayer Batang. Nazri's,** the Tioman pioneers, at the south end, has the best beach, an amiable host, and a good restaurant. A-frames $4, rms with bath and fan $12. Further north is **CT's Cottages,** chalets with bath in a nice garden $12. There's at least a dozen more places to stay between here and **ABC**, the backpacker's favorite at the end of the beach. Prices are the same as at Nazri's but his chalets are better value.

Further north from ABC is isolated **Penuba Bay Cafe,** huts cost $4. Other recommended places to stay at the less popular beaches include **Salang Sayang,** at Sayang, huts $6; **Happy Cafe** at Juara, clean rms $4; **Mutiara's** at Juara with chalets and bath $5; **Desa Nipah** at Teluk Nipah, chalets $10, a good restaurant and dorm beds $4.

Pulau Rawa

The island is owned and run by Rawa Safaris Island Resort, tel: 791204, who have an office at the Mersing jetty and run their own boat for $6.50 round trip. Comfortable, shaded, bungalows with thatched attap roofs cost $20 and rooms from $25. There is an excellent restaurant and bar and watersports facilities.

Pulau Babi Besar
(Pulau Besar)

Most of the resorts here have offices near the jetty at Mersing that can advise of boat times, and accomodation availability. This island is popular with weekend trippers as it's only one hour by boat from Mersing, $7 return.

Through the week it is often deserted. **Radin's,** tel: 793124, just north of the jetty have basic A-frames for $12, but most of the other resorts including **Whitsand Beach Resort,** tel: 314511 and **Pulau Besar Village Resort,** tel: 791205 are slightly more expensive. Hill Side Chalets, tel: 236603, has chalets with great views overlooking the sea, but the beach is rocky at low tide and not as good as those in the south. Chalets are $24 upwards.

Pulau Tengah

Boats are rather infrequent here, although it is only one hour from Mersing. Enquire at the jetty for boat times. Pirate Bay, run by an Italian and his Malaysian wife, tel: 241911 is the sole resort here and the restaurant serves good western and Malaysian cuisine.

Pulau Tinggi

Enquire at the Mersing jetty for boat times which are irregular. The recently-built Smailing Island Resort, with its private beach, swimming pool, and restaurant with live entertainment, karaoke bar, and comfortable air-conditioned chalets has transformed this formerly sleepy island. Chalets start from $25.

Pulau Sibu

This is another favorite island with backpackers for there is a good range of accomodation and restaurants, the beaches are clean and quiet, and there is also a nice kampung atmosphere. Boats run from the jetty at Mersing for $8 return. Booking for resorts at Sibu can be made at the jetty office, tel: 793125. **Sea Gypsy Village Resort,** the original establishment has wooden chalets with attached bathroom for $14, and a popular and reasonably-priced restaurant and bar.

The cheapest island accomodation is **O & H Kampung Huts** where chalets cost $5-6. Further along the coast is the Sibu Island Cabanas, tel: 317216 where the restaurant serves Chinese, Western and Malaysian cuisine and comfortable bungalows and chalets cost from $20-36.

Singapore Practicalities

All prices in US dollars unless noted: Singapore telephone code is 02. S=single: D=double: AC=air-conditioning.

Singapore is one of the most readily accessible tourist destinations worldwide. Island tours can be booked at any travel agent or major hotel. But it is more fun to simply explore on your own; 2 or 3 days are sufficient to see most everything.

If arriving from a northern climate, remember it takes time to adapt to the tropical heat. An entire day spent poking around can be exhausting, so plan early morning outings. The early afternoon, when the weather is hottest, is best spent in an air conditioned restaurant or at the poolside. Late afternoon and early evening are pleasant for shopping, and most stores in Singapore's Orchard Road shopping district stay open until 9pm, though they open late, after 10 am.

ARRIVAL/DEPARTURE

By Air

Arriving in Singapore by air is an immensely positive travel experience. Changi International Airport was voted the world's best airport for the third successive year in 1990 in a survey by Business Traveller. In November 1990, Changi's second terminal opened, doubling passenger handling capacity to 24 million a year, the largest capacity of any Asian airport. It houses 100 shops, 20 restaurants, 75 dayrooms, two business centers, two fitness centers and a number of other service centers.

The airport is linked to 111 cities in 53 countries by 52 airlines operating 1,900 scheduled flights weekly. A few of the airlines operating from Changi include United Airlines, Delta Airlines, Thai Airways, Qantas Airways, Cathay Pacific Airways, British Airways, Air India, Air Canada, Garuda Indonesia, Japan Airlines, Malaysian Airlines Systems and Air France.

Singapore Airlines, consistently the world's most profitable carrier, has long-term equity arrangements with Delta Air Lines and Swissair providing a route network with more than 300 destinations in 80 countries. Singapore Airlines has daily flights to and from Montreal, Toronto, Auckland, London, Los Angeles, San Francisco, and New York. Additionally, Singapore Airlines and Malaysian Airlines Systems jointly operate a regular shuttle between Changi Airport and Kuala Lumpur's Subang Airport with 12 flights daily, at a third cheaper than scheduled flights. Taxis ply to 20 to 30-min journey to town for $8 to most hotels. There is also an AC city bus

No.390 from Changi to Orchard Rd. Many hotels also operate mini bus and limousine services; check at the reservation counters at the terminal or with your travel agent. Singapore Airlines is at SIA Building, 77 Robinson Rd, (2238888, 2297270, 2297271), and ticket sales counters are at Mandarin Hotel, 333 Orchard Rd; Raffles City Shopping Centre, 252 North Bridge Rd; and Winsland House, 01-03 Kiliney Rd. Travel agents give cheaper fares than airline offices and are easily found in shopping arcades.

By Sea

Singapore is the busiest port in the world in terms of shipping tonnage and there can be as many as 700 cargo ships in port at any one time. All passenger cruise ships arrive and depart at the World Trade Centre terminal, 10-min taxi ride from downtown. This fantastic port can be viewed from luxurious catamarans, or the traditional wooden junk or "tongkang," restored and reconditioned. Either can be hired at Clifford Pier. A Cruise Development Department opened in late 1988 to develop and promote Singapore as a center for cruising in Southeast Asia. Further information on cruises can be obtained from the department at Raffles City Tower #37-00, 250 North Bridge Road, Tel. 3396622 and 3300372) or any travel agent.

The following ships call on Singapore at regular intervals: Sea Princess/Pacific Princess/Royal Princess, depart from Sydney, London and Los Angeles, respectively, once a year. Sagafjord, from Port Everglades once a year. Canberra, from London once a year. Coral Princess, from Hong Kong and Singapore in Nov and Dec. Orient Princess, from Singapore from Jan to Dec. Pearl of Scandinavia, from Bangkok, Singapore and Hong Kong from Jan through April. Queen Elizabeth II, from London on its annual round the world cruise between Jan and April. Rotterdam, from Los Angeles once a year. Royal Viking Star, from Hong Kong in Nov and March.

By Train

Singapore Railway Station on Keppel Road, 5-mins taxi ride from most hotels takes travelers from Singapore to Bangkok, Thailand, through Kuala Lumpur and Butterworth, Malaysia and vice versa. Customs and immigration are on the premises. Singapore to Bangkok, S$175.60 (1st AC), S$80.30 (2nd AC). To Butterworth (Penang), S$119 (1st AC), S$54 (2nd AC). To Kuala Lumpur S$64 (1st AC) and S$31 (2nd AC).

By Bus

A number of buses also arrive at Singapore from Malaysia. Customs and immigration points are at the joint border. From Johor Baru to Rochor Road Terminus costs S$1. All the following buses arrive at New Bridge Road Terminus: Mersing S$11, Melaka S$11, Kuala Lumpur S$17, Butterworth S$30, Kuantan S$16.

ACCOMMODATION

Singapore boasts a string of major award-winning hotels whose special character reflects the island republic's unique Asian appeal. Visitors can choose from a wide range of accommodations either luxuriously upscale or the more moderate roof-over-your-head variety for a student's budget. Room rates are for single occupancy standard rooms, and do not include the 10% service charge or 4% government tax. Booking hotels through a travel agent is usually cheaper than walking in off the street.

Luxury ($200 and up)

Shangri-La Hotel Singapore (750 rooms, 60 suites), 22 Orange Grove Road, Singapore 1025. Tel: 7373644. Fax: 7337220/1029. Routinely voted among the world's top 10 hotels. 5 mins minutes from Orchard Road, among lush landscaped greenery.$200.
Raffles Hotel (104 suites), 1 Beach Road, Singapore 0718. Tel: 3371886. Fax: 3397650. Conveniently located in the heart of the business and historic district, Raffles reopened in September 1991 amidst much fanfare. All suites have a spacious parlor, bedroom, dressing room and bath. $400.
Goodwood Park Hotel (192 rooms, 43 suites), 22 Scotts Road, Singapore 0922. Tel: 7377411. Fax: 7328558. One of the most unique hotels in Singapore, set in lush gardens in the fashionable Scotts Road district. $220.
The Oriental Singapore (518 rooms, 62 suites) Tel: 3380066. Fax: 3399537. 5 mins from the business center, located in Marina Square, Southeast Asia's largest shopping and hotel complex. Full exercise facilities, meeting and convention rooms. $220.
Omni Marco Polo Hotel (603 rooms, 60 suites) 247 Tanglin Road, Singapore 1024. Tel: 4747141. Fax: 4710521. 5 mins from the Orchard Road shops and adjacent to the Botanic Gardens. Renowned for top quality food and service. $222.

First Class ($150-$200)

Hilton International Singapore (406 rooms, 29 suites) 581 Orchard Road, Singapore 0923. Tel: 7372233. Fax: 7322917. Rooftop pool with an incredible view. Health club with a gymnasium. $160.
Dynasty Hotel (379 rooms, 21 suites) 320 Orchard Road, Singapore 0923. In the heart of the shopping district. Tel: 7349900. Fax: 7335251. $165.
Mandarin Singapore (1,200 rooms, 59 suites) 333 Orchard Road, Singapore 0923. Tel: 7374411. Fax: 7322361. Classic Chinese decor with a rooftop revolving restaurant. $170.
Westin Plaza (796 rooms, 47 suites) 2 Stamford Road, Singapore 0617. Tel: 3388585. Fax: 3382862. World's tallest hotel surrounded by a shopping complex which hous-

es 60 stores. $175.
Royal Holiday Inn Crowne Plaza (493 rooms, 30 suites) 25 Scotts Road, Singapore 0922. Tel: 7377966. Fax: 7376646. Beautiful landscaped garden terrace and an excellent business center. $165.
The Regent of Singapore (441 rooms, 47 suites)1 Cuscaden Road, Singapore 1024. Tel: 7338888. Fax: 7328838. Breathtaking atrium lobby; located just five minutes from Orchard Road. $195.

High Intermediate ($100-150)

Hotel Imperial Singapore (561 rooms, 39 suites) 1 Jalan Rumbia, Singapore 0923. Tel: 7371666. Fax: 7374761. 5 mins to Orchard Road and 25-min drive to airport. $140.
Plaza Hotel Singapore (350 rooms, 2 suites) 7500A Beach Road, Singapore 0719. Tel: 2980011. Fax: 2963600. Minutes away by bus from Marina shopping district. $135.
Orchard Hotel Singapore (350 rooms, 6 suites) 442 Orchard Road, Singapore 0923. Tel: 7347766. Fax: 7335482. Rooftop pool and sundeck. $135.
Concorde Hotel (497 rooms, 18 suites) 317 Outram Road, Singapore 0316. Located near the Singapore River. $105.
The Boulevard Hotel (500 roms, 20 suites) 200 Orchard Boulevard, Singapore 1024. Tel: 7372911. Fax: 7378449. $145.
Hotel Furama Singapore (355 rooms, 19 suites) 60 Eu Tong Sen Street, Singapore 0105. Tel: 5333888. Fax: 5341489. 24-hr room service and free shuttle service available. $120.

Low Intermediate ($50-$100)

Hotel Phoenix Singapore (300 rooms, 18 suites) 277 Orchard Road, Singapore 0923. Tel: 7378666. Fax: 7322024. $87.
Cockpit Hotel (176 rooms) 6/7 Oxley Rise, Singapore 0923. Tel: 7379111. Fax: 7373105. Nestled on the fringe of the Orchard Road shopping area. $85.
Hotel Supreme (86 rooms) 15 Kramat Road, Singapore 0922. Tel: 7378333. Fax: 7337404. $52.
Ladyhill Hotel (174 rooms, 1 suite) 1 Ladyhill Road, Singapore 1025. Tel: 7372111. Fax: 7374606. Lovely poolside coffee shop. One of the best-kept secrets in Singapore. $95.
Hotel Premier (28 rooms, 1 suite) 22 Nassim Hill, Singapore 1025. Tel: 7339811. Fax: 7335595. Wonderful atmosphere; an excellent bargain. $67.

Budget ($4-$50)

Singapore's budget hotels aren't so cheap by international standards due largely to the strength of the Singapore currency. The **YMCA International** House at 1 Orchard Road in the central tourist district goes for $40 a night, with comfortable AC rooms, own bathroom and TV.

The **YWCA** at 6/8 Fort Canning Road is $25 a night, for AC rooms with communal bathrooms. **The Pasir Panjang Guest House** near the University of Singapore on 404 Pasir Panjang Road comes with attached bath and AC $42 a night.

Other good bargains include the **New 7th Storey Hotel** at 229 Rochor Road for $45 a night, and the **Mayfair City Hotel** at 40/44 Armenian Street at $30 a night.

There used to be dozens of old Chinese-style hotels around Bencoolen St., but now there's only a few left, and they are usually full. The **San Wah**, at No 36, has great character, and rooms with AC and communal bath for $27. Further up at No 81 is the **Kian Hua,** another old villa with cheaper rooms with fans.

The only real cheap accommodation is at the slightly illegal "crash pads" which have sprung up in residential and office high rises in the downtown in response to the growing need for cheap rooms. Most have no signs, are crowded, with tiny rooms or dormitories, but are clean and basic. Some of those recommended are **Peony Mansions**, 6th flr, 50E, 46-52 Bencoolen St. (entrance at rear of shops) $4 dorm bed, $12 S/D; **Bencoolen House,** opposite, 7th flr with similar prices and AC S/D $27; Hong Guan Bldg, 173-175 Bencoolen St., has **Hawaii Guest House** on 2nd flr, **Goh's Homestay** on 6th, both at similar prices. The popular **Why Not Homestay,** 127 Bencoolen St., has a good Indian restuarant downstairs.

GETTING AROUND

Walking. Generally a sweaty experience over 100 meters. Best to walk only in early morning or after 5:00 p.m.

Buses. Singapore has a superb city bus network. All major places of interest and residential areas are accessible by bus. Singapore Bus Service, operates 207 routes, and Trans-Island Bus Service, plys 32 routes. Other smaller operators include the City Shuttle Service and Schemes A and B services. Regular buses run between 6am and 11.30pm with fares starting at 50 cents (S) to S$1.20. The Singapore Explorer ticket provides the traveler with unlimited local bus use for one day (S$5) or three days (S$12). Timetables are sold at bookshops and all bus terminals.

Trishaws. A fascinating way to view the downtown area. Most Trishaw rides are organized by tour groups though individuals can hire one after agreeing on the destination and fare. Allowing the tour operator to negotiate is strongly advised.

Mass Rapid Transit. The Singapore MRT is quite simply the most advanced system in the world. Fully completed in early 1990, three MRT routes cover nearly the entire island, with fares ranging from 60 cents (S) to S$1.20. The squeaky clean polished marble stations, complete with works by local artists, are tourist attractions in themselves. The system operates between 6am and 11.40pm and is simple and easy to use. Warning: **Fines** exist for littering and smoking (S$500), as well as eating and drinking (S$200). A Transitlink fare card (minimum S$12) will pay for your fares on both bus and MRT train.

Taxis. The easiest and coolest way to see Singapore is to take one of the 12,000 taxis that are all over the island. Readily available and reasonably cheap, they offer among the most courteous and helpful drivers anywhere in the world. Fares recorded on the meter are S$2.20 for the first 1.5km, and 10 cents (S) for every additional 300 meters and 10 cents for every 45 seconds of time spent waiting in traffic. Additional charges not recorded on the meter include S$3 for every trip from the airport; a Central Business District surcharge of S$1 for taking a taxi inside the designated restricted zone at peak hours; 50 cents for each passenger in excess of two; S$1 for each piece of luggage; and a surcharge of 50% of the metered fare between midnight and 6:00 a.m. Radio cabs cost S$2 extra on-call and S$3 for an advance booking.

Car Rentals. International companies are prevalent in Singapore but rates are high, about $100 a day. Most of the country's six taxi services rent vehicles with a driver for an hourly and daily rate. A few of the many rental agencies include: Avis Rent A Car, Tel. 7379477; Ace Tours & Car Rentals, Tel. 2353755/2354433; Happy Car Rentals & Tours, Tel. 2359902; City Car Rentals & Tours, Tel. 7332145; Blue Star Car Rentals & Tours, Tel. 2534643/2534661; Friendly Tour Corporation, Tel. 3732292; Negara Tourist Service, Tel. 7372080; San's Tours and Car Rentals, Tel. 7349922; Orchard Motors, Tel. 4759466/4748897; Z-Car Rental & Travel Service, Tel. 3386901/3388122. Rates for chauffeur-driven cars start at S$40 an hour, with a 3-hr minimum, and a daily rate of between S$220 and S$400. Rates for self-driven cars are between S$75 and S$225 a day and between S$360 and S$1,200 a week with a mileage charge of 60(S) cents perkm.

Central Business District. An important thing to remember is the Area Licence Scheme, which is designed to alleviate traffic congestion during peak hours (7.30am to 10.15 am, Mon-Sat, and 4pm-6.30pm, Mon-Fri). Under the scheme a S$3 sticker must be purchased and displayed.

TOURS AND TRAVEL

Most travel agents and hotels offer air-conditioned coach tours of Singapore's major sights. Tour operators pick up at all hotels and the cost for an 8-hr day tour is about $15 for an adult and $10 for a child under 12. The coach passes Elizabeth Walk, Supreme Court, City Hall, the Singapore River and Merlion Park; proceeds towards Chinatown where it stops at the Sri Mariamman Temple; then continues on to Haw Par Villa and stops for the Instant Asia Cultural Show; then drives past the Queenstown Housing Estate and proceeds to the Botanical Gardens where the tour ends.

The operators of the tour are Singapore Sightseeing, Tel. 4736900; Siakson Coach Tours, Tel. 3360288; RMG Tours, Tel. 3373377; and Tour East International, Tel: 2202200. Other major tour operators include Holiday Tours and Travel, Tel. 7347091 and Elpin Tours and Limousine Service, Tel. 2353111. All of the mentioned operators offer more specific packages to all of Singapore's tourist destinations at the same day rate.

There are daily tours of Sentosa, the most developed and organized of Singapore's offshore islands, organized by Tour East, RMG, Siakson and Singapore Sightseeing.

FOOD

Located at the crossroads of Asia, Singapore is a melting pot of cuisines of every conceivable kind. A dizzying array of affordable cuisines are available from the casual, open-air hawker center to Cantonese "dim sum" and exquisite French. All major hotels offer several specialty restaurants as well as a coffeeshop with both international fare and Asian delicacies. All hotels levy a 10% service charge and a 4% government tax.

Chinese

House of Blossoms, Marina Mandarin Hotel, 6 Raffles Boulevard, Marina Square. A beautifully decorated Cantonese restaurant renowned for its lunchtime "dim sum." A moderately priced set menu is available for groups between four and ten.

Mooi Chin Palace Restaurant, 01-05 Funan Centre, 109 North Bridge Road. Located in a modern shopping complex near the Central Business District, it serves Hainanese cuisine and is especially noted for its spicy hot Sambal Pomfret fish

The Pine Court, Mandarin Hotel Singapore, 333 Orchard Road, a plush restaurant in the heart of the shopping district serving Peking cuisine. Exquisite Peking Duck.

Ming Jiang, Goodwood Park Hotel, 22 Scotts Road. Elegant Szechuan restaurant in one of Singapore's most stylish old hotels.

Happy Realm Restaurant, Pearl's Centre, next to People's Park complex. The very best Chinese vegetarian fare in Singapore at cheap prices.

Malay/Indonesian

Aziza's Restaurant, 36 Emerald Hill Road, Singapore's most stylish Malay restaurant well known for its spicy Beef Rendang.

Arumanis Indonesian, Far East Plaza, 14 Scotts Road. Reasonably priced with a snazzy decor in the heart of the shopping district.

Sabar Menanti, 62 Kandahar Street, Adjacent to the old Arab Street region, this authentic coffee shop is as close as you'll get to pre-War Singapore. Serves authentic Malay and Indonesia Padang at cheap prices.

The Rendezvous, 3rd Floor, Raffles City Complex, 2 Stamford Road. Excellent Indonesian Padang food served cafeteria style at reasonable prices. Located in one of Singapore's swankiest shopping centers.

Japanese

Inagiku Japanese Restaurant, Westin Stamford Hotel, 2 Stamford Road. An old Japanese chain expanded into Singapore, the Inagiku is renowned for its tempura.

Hoshigaoka, #03-45/46 Centrepoint, 175-180 Orchard Road. Right in the middle of an Orchard Road shopping center, Japanese fare at reasonable prices.

Restaurant Kobe, #04-06/07 Tanglin Shopping Centre, 19 Tanglin Road. Lovely decor, specializes in "shabu shabu," or food simmered in fondue.

Nadaman Japanese Restaurant, Shangri-La Hotel, 22 Orange Grove Road. Probably the best, most authentic Japanese restaurant in Singapore, but you pay for it. Excellent food.

Seafood

UDMC Seafood Centre, East Coast Parkway. Eight large restaurants in one enormous complex by the sea offering moderately priced seafood.

Whee Heng Seafood Restaurant, 893 Ponggol Road. At the end of Ponggol Point by the seaside, this is one of Singapore's most famous restaurants and one can easily see why. Excellent and cheap family cooked food. A terrific experience.

Garden Seafood Restaurant, Goodwood Park Hotel, 22 Scotts Road. Just off Orchard Road. Cantonese style seafood in an attractive atmosphere.

Ocean Spray, 31 Marina Park. An enormous restaurant designed as a Viking ship. Fairly expensive but worth the experience.

Indian

Muthu's Curry, 76/77 Racecourse Road. A functional, air-conditioned southern Indian restaurant with spicy hot food served on banana leaves. Not for the faint-hearted.

The Kurry Korner, 74 Thomson Road. A stall inside a coffeeshop serving excellent Indian Muslim food cheap.

Mayarani Restaurant, 01-09/13 Amara Hotel Shopping Centre, 165 Tanjong Pagar Road. Specializing in Tandoori food, features live Indian music for dinner.

Rang Mahal, Imperial Hotel, 1 Jalan Rumbia. North Indian food in an elegant atmosphere. Floor show at night.

Komala Vilas Restaurant, 76/78 Serangoon Road. Southern Indian vegetarian, very cheap, very good. Located in the heart of "Little India."

French

La Brasserie, Omni Marco Polo Hotel, 247 Tanglin Road. Elegant French brasserie with superb food.

Restaurant Latour, Shangri-La Hotel, 22 Orange Grove Road. Impeccable atmosphere and impressive menu featuring such dishes as pan-fried venison and sauteed deep-sea scallops.

Cafe Bonjour, Marina Village, 31 Marina Park. A Parisian-styled sidewalk cafe moderately priced.

Palm Grill, Westin Plaza Hotel, 2 Stamford Road. Interesting cross of Oriental ingredients in French dishes.

Italian

Prego, Westin Stamford Hotel, 2 Stamford Road. A large range of pastas, moderately priced, in a cheerful atmosphere.

Da Paolo, 66 Tanjong Pagar Road. Cosy, authentic restaurant with wonderful food and excellent wine list.

Rocky's Central, 9 Emerald Hill Road. Pizza and pasta at cheap prices in an informal environment.

Ristorante Bologna, Marina Mandarin Hotel, Marina Square, 6 Raffles Boulevard. Gourmet Italian cuisine in a refined environment overlooking one of the world's most spectacular atrium lobbies.

American

Ponderosa Steakhouse, Plaza Singapura Shopping Centre and Raffles City Shopping Complex, steaks and Mexican food.

Steeples Deli, #02-05 Tanglin Shopping Centre, 19 Tanglin Road. New York deli favorites in a bright atmosphere.

New Orleans, Holiday Inn Park View, 11 Cavenagh Road. Creole food and southern fried chicken with wild rice. Live jazz music during the evenings.

Thai

Thanying Restaurant, Amara Hotel, 65 Tanjong Pagar Road. Features a chef imported from a Thai royal household. Sophisticated Thai cuisine in a casual atmosphere.

Tunk-ka of Thailand, #02-200 Marina Square, 6 Raffles Boulevard. Gorgeous woodcarvings in a classic Thai setting with excellent food at reasonable prices.

Klongtan Ping Restaurant, 46 Lorong Mambong. Located in fashionable Holland Village, high quality Thai/Chinese seafood but a fairly limited menu.

Street Food

Eating at a hawker center is one of the highlights of any visit to Singapore. Unlike many other Asian countries cleanliness is not a problem as stringent health regulations are strictly enforced. Hawkers are conveniently housed in centers attached to fresh produce markets. All types of local food — from Malay Muslim through the entire spectrums of Chinese and Indian — are represented. Over the past few years many have moved upmarket into shopping complexes and are attractively designed and air-conditioned, though not as authentic.

Free seating is the norm, so you are never obligated to order from any one particular stall. Order from several stalls and pay for the food as it arrives. (No tipping, please).Hawker centers to try include:

Newton Circus, the largest and most famous hawker center in Singapore. Exceptional quality food with a wide range and specializing in seafood. While some stalls are open in the morning, it doesn't really get rolling until the early evening and goes through the night.

Bugis Square, Foch Road (off Lavender Street). Noted for its Chinese food. Also busiest at night.

Telok Ayer Market. Right in the heart of the Central Business District, this recently renovated masterpiece serves the entire range of Singapore food and remains open from early morning until the wee hours.

Satay Club, Connaught Drive. The place to go for satay and other Malay cuisine at night. Telok Blangah. If you're at the World Trade Centre en route to Sentosa, just across the street is one of Singapore's finest. Serves the entire gamut of Singapore food from lunch to midnight.

Hill Street Centre, 64 Hill Street. Good cheap food, open from morning till dinnertime.

SHOPPING

If ever there was a shopper's paradise, it has to be Singapore. Because of its location at the crossroads of Asia and duty-free status, prices are often cheaper than in their country of origin. The shopping centers along Orchard Road are among the most modern in the world. Unlike many other Asian countries, bargaining is discouraged in most places. There is a fantastic range of goods to be found, from Japanese consumer electronics, to American computers and compact discs to gems from Sri Lanka and silk from Thailand and China. The Good Retailers Scheme established by the Singapore Tourist Promotion Board ensures high quality goods and service in shops displaying the red Merlion symbol, which are all over the island.

One-Stop Gift Shopping. Orchard Road and the immediate outlying area are riddled with air-conditioned, ultra-modern shopping centers. Here is just a sampling: **Tang's Department Store,** the corner of Orchard and Scotts Roads. Five floors stuffed with a variety of household goods, fashion and electronics. Has an excellent souvenir shop. **Lucky Plaza,** Orchard Road. Four floors of specialty shops offering a wide range of goods with the modern Metro Grand Department Store on the fifth floor. **Marina Square**, 6 Raffles Boulevard. The largest shopping center in Singapore, it is the size of seven football fields and has three floors of shops with two department stores, Metro and Tokyu. **Liang Court**, between River Valley Road and the Singapore River. This attractive retail complex is home to the Japanese Daimaru department store as well as scores of small specialist shops and bookstores.

Antiques. **Tanglin Shopping Centre**, 19 Tanglin Road. With four floors of valuable antiques shops, it houses Singapore's only specialist in antique maps and the renowned Hassan's Carpets.

Just behind the Centrepoint Shopping Centre on Cuppage Road is a row of antique shops, **Babazar Design Market** and **Cuppage Terrace** for the complete range of Oriental antique knickknacks.

Other areas replete with antique shops include Smith and Temple Streets in Chinatown and Holland Village. **Peter Wee's Katong Antique House** on East Coast Road also has bargains. **Chinese Cloisonne-Ware Centre** in Raffles City, 2 Stamford Road, offers a complete selection of cloisonne-ware pots, vases and decorative items.

Jewelry. At the top of Arab Street near North Bridge Road are goldsmiths and jewellers in tiny shops selling sets of gold worn by Malay brides. Similar items can be found in the Geylang Serai area of town. Precious gems can be found at virtually all of the many shopping centers. **C.T. Woo** at Tanglin Shopping Centre, and **Colombo Jewellery** at Far East Plaza make items to order. **Larry's Jeweller's** in Orchard Towers on Orchard Road, opposite the Hilton Hotel, offer some unique designs.

Arts and Crafts. Local art can be found in galleries such as Sun Craft, Tanglin Shopping Centre; Decor Arts, Wisma Atria; or at Orchard Gallery in Orchard Point. For arts and crafts with true ethnic character, Arab Street and the nearby streets is the ultimate. Tiny shops abound carrying basketry, camel skin bags, Indonesian and Malaysian textiles and batik. Jothi Palayakat Co., 42 Arab St. B & K Textiles at No 42, Habib Handicraft No 18, and Aljunied Brothers at No. 91 are all excellent.

Tailoring. Delivery is generally fast and the price reasonable. Tailors are in nearly every shopping center and most hotels with an excellent selection of fabrics. Recommended men's tailors and women's dressmakers include Mode O Day, Tanglin Shopping Centre; Couples, Far East Plaza.

Electronics. Sim Lim Tower and Sim Lim Centre, on Jl. Besar offer the best deals for consumer electronics. Always bargain, test the equipment purchased and insist on a receipt. Cost Plus in the basement of Scotts Shopping Centre, on Scotts Rd. is also cheap and reputable. The ground floor of Orchard Yaohan in Plaza Singapura, Orchard Rd. also has some bargains.

Computers. Funan Centre, 109 North Bridge Rd. Good for personal and notebook computers, printers, accessories and software. Also good is Peninsular Plaza, North Bridge Rd.

PHOTOGRAPHY

One-hour processing is the norm, and shops can be found all over Orchard Road and many other places. Camera shops offer excellent deals in such places as Albert Photo in Orchard Towers, A&P Photo in Lucky Plaza and Cost Plus in Scotts Shopping Centre.

NIGHTLIFE

Singapore is a 24-hour city. Nightclubs, discos and bars get going at around 10pm and continue till the wee hours. The vast majority of nightlife centers on or around Orchard Road, but there are also pockets outside the district.

Prices vary widely depending on the entertainment offered. Most bars and lounges do not impose a cover charge, but the fee for entering a disco is about $30, inclusive of the first drink. Like restaurants, many establishments charge 10% for service and 4% tax. Dress is almost always informal, but you will feel out of place in many establishments in jeans and t-shirt, so smart casual is recommended.

Bars

Brannigan's, Hyatt Regency Singapore, 10-12 Scotts Rd. Classic singles bar with good jazz-fusion music. Cheers, Novotel Orchid Inn, 214 Dunearn Rd. Reasonably priced, with 30% off all drinks from 5pm to 8pm. Club 392, #01-21 Orchard Towers, 400 Orchard Rd. The most densely packed place in Singapore between 11pm and 1.45 am. Wall-to-wall cigarette smoke with scores of bar girls on offer.

Elvis' Place, 1A Duxton Hill. A nostalgic tribute to Elvis, with a DJ spinning discs from the 50's and 60's. Anywhere, #04-07 Tanglin Shopping Centre, 19 Tanglin Rd. The resident band, Tania, is a Singapore institution and are part-owners of the bar. Well worth the experience.

Bierstube, Marina Village, 31 Marina Park. Rustic German bar offering Guinness Stout on tap.

Music Clubs

Saxophone, 23 Cuppage Road. Wonderful local Jazz and Blues bands with other musicians sitting in. Somerset's Bar, Westin Plaza Hotel, 2 Stamford Rd. International bands play Jazz and Chicago blues. The best spot for live music. **Ginivy,** #02-11 Orchard Towers, 400 Orchard Rd. Authentic Honky Tonk bar featuring Texas swing and country music.

Peacock Bar, Shangri-La Hotel, 2 Orange Grove Rd. Home of Matthew Tan, legendary

Singaporean C & W singer.

Hard Rock Cafe, Cuscaden Rd. Original Rock 'N' Roll memorabilia lines the walls of this hard-driving club. Excellent American food is also served.

Discos

Scandals, Westin Plaza Hotel, 2 Stamford Rd. Highly posh surroundings and frequented by the younger crowd.

Xanadu, Shangri-La Hotel. Hi-tech hangout with laser displays and pop videos. **Zouk,** 17-21 Jiak Kim St. incorporates a disco, restaurant, bar and cafe. A fountain in the middle of the dance floor modeled after a moorish home set the tone.

Top Ten, #04-35 Orchard Towers, 400 Orchard Rd. A converted cinema, with live band and DJ. Khameleon, Marina Village, 31 Marina Park. Tastefully decorated like a Roman villa. International artists occasionally perform here. **Floating Disco,** on board the Equator Dream, Clifford Pier, Collyer Quay. After a cruise around the harbor, this catamaran moors alongside Clifford Pier for discoing till 2 am.

Nightclubs

Neptune Theater Restaurant, #07-00 50 Collyer Quay. Occasionally risque supper club.

Lido Palace Nite-Club, #05-01 Glass Hotel Shopping Centre, 317 Outram Road. Chinese banquet cuisine in plush atmosphere with beautiful Chinese hostesses and flashy dance floor.

Dallas Theater Lounge and Nite Club, #05-01 Amara Hotel, 165 Tanjong Pagar Road. Spectacular night-club floor show featuring Chinese pop stars.

CULTURAL EVENTS

Singapore is an astonishing contrast of racial and cultural roots and there is much to see and do.

At Tang Dynasty Village, Jurong, go back to 7th Century China at Asia's largest cultural and historical theme park. Visitors can see replicas of the Silk Road and the Great Wall, as well as take in cultural films at any of the three film studio blocks. Haw Par Villa, on Pasir Panjang Road, is world famous for its colorful statues and the Spirits of the Orient Theater.

Plays are staged at the Drama Centre, at Fort Canning and at the Victoria Theater, Empress Place. Chinese street opera takes place all over the island during the Festival of the Hungry Ghosts, usually August or September.

Multi-cultural and multi-religious Singapore celebrates festivals and holidays throughout the year and they are always colorful events with food and mystique.

Starting with the Christian New Year on Jan. 1, the southern Indian festival Thaipusam follows in Jan/Feb, and then Chinese New Year, fixed on the lunar calendar, is held in late Jan or Feb. Twice a year, in Feb and Oct, Chinese mediums in trance celebrate the Birthday of the Monkey God. The Muslim fasting month of Ramadan falls in Mar or April, with believers consuming nothing during daylight hours until the feasting day of Hari Raya Puasa on April 16. Vesak Day on May 28 commemorates the Buddha's birthday. The annual Dragon Boat Festival, June 16, honors ancient Chinese poet and statesman Qu Yuan. The Chinese Hungry Ghosts Month falls between Aug and Sep, while the Chinese Mooncake Festival is held Sep/Oct. In Oct Hindu temples offer classical dances during the Festival of Navrathri. Fire walking to celebrate the Hindu Thimithi Festival takes place on Oct. 27.

The Festival of the Nine Emperor Gods is celebrated between Oct. 8-16 and the Hindu holiday Deepavali is held Nov 5. Singapore then finishes the year off with impressive illuminations and decorative displays during Christmas, Dec. 25.

MUSEUMS

The National Museum and Art Gallery, Stamford Rd. Houses a fascinating display of artifacts and ethnology tracing Singapore's development, together with a wide array of Southeast Asian treasures. Displays include the Haw Par jade collection, one of the world's largest; the History of Singapore Gallery, with its ornate history and artifacts. Admission S$1.50.

Empress Place Museum, next to Cavenagh Bridge, is Singapore's newest museum. A newly-renovated neo-classical building that used to house government offices, the building is now a world-class museum and exhibition center. A changing program of archaeological treasures from China is being featured until 1993.

MEDICAL SERVICES

Singapore's healthcare facilities are the best in Southeast Asia and nearly of Western standard. Pharmaceuticals are readily available. Most hotels have their own doctor on 24-hour call. Other doctors are listed under Medical Practitioners in the Yellow Pages. The Tanglin Medical Clinic, #05-28 Tanglin Shopping Centre, has an excellent reputation for competent, reasonably priced service.

There are nine government facilities and several private hospitals. Singapore General Hospital on Outram Road is very efficient and competent. However, be ready with identification and cash or credit cards, as a foreigner you will likely be asked for money upfront before admission. For an ambulance, dial 911.

POST & TELEPHONE

Singapore has the best telecommunications system in the world. Virtually all hotels have fax machines and International Direct Dialing.

Public pay phones are all over the island and cost 10 cents (S) for 3 mins. Public phones designated for international calls are clearly marked and operate using special phone cards costing S$2-S$50 purchased at post offices and some shops..

The Singapore postal system is quick and efficient. The PO at Comcentre Bldg., Exeter Rd, close to Orchard Rd is open 24-hrs a day, and most hotels provide postal service.

VISA FORMALITIES

With just a few exceptions, a valid visa, onward travel reservations and adequate finance are all the traveler needs to enter Singapore. However, citizens of China, India and the Organization of Independent States are required to produce a visa. You will automatically be given a 14-day tourist visa upon entering Singapore, though 30-day visas are readily available upon request.

CUSTOMS

Singapore is essentially a free port; however, some consumable items are dutiable. These include alcoholic beverages and tobacco products. Chocolates, sweets, cakes and biscuits are also dutiable (5% of the value). Each incoming traveler is allowed one liter of spirits, one liter of wine, and 200 cigarettes, or 50 cigars.

The penalty for drug trafficking (defined by the quantity of drugs carried, including "soft" drugs like marijuana) is death. Any traveler possessing pharmaceuticals must have a valid prescription.

LANGUAGES

Although Chinese Singaporeans have traditionally spoken their own dialects, generally the southern Chinese dialects, such as Hokkien and Teochew, the government actively encourages the use of Mandarin. There are 4 official languages—Mandarin, Malay, Tamil, and English. The latter is the language of business and administration and is widely spoken and understood. Most Singaporeans speak English as well as their mother tongue.

TIPS & SERVICE CHARGE

Tipping is not expected. It is prohibited at the airport and discouraged in hotels and restaurants that have a 10% service charge.

AIRPORT TAX

Airport tax is S$12 for all destinations, with the exceptions of Malaysia and Brunei when the tax is S$5.

TIME

Singapore is 8hrs ahead of Greenwich Mean Time, 12hrs ahead of New York and 8hrs ahead of Tokyo. Bangkok and Jakarta are 1hr ahead, and Hong Kong, Kuala Lumpur, Bali, Manila and Perth are in the same time-zone.

ELECTRICITY

The electrical supply in Singapore is extremely reliable and is on the 220-240 volt, 40 Hz system. Most hotels have transformers for 10-120 volt, 60 Hz appliances.

OFFICE HOURS

Business hours at all government departments and international agencies are from 9am to 5pm, and from 9am to 1pm on Saturdays. Banks are open from 10am to 3pm on weekdays, and from 9 to 11.30am on Saturdays. Closed Sundays.

EMBASSIES & CONSULATES

Australia, 25 Napier Rd. (7379311). **Belgium,** 10 Anson Rd. #09-24 International Plaza (2207677). **Britain,** Tanglin Rd. (4739333). **Burma,** 15 St. Martins Drive (2358704). **Canada,** 80 Anson Rd. IBM Towers (2256363). **Denmark,** 101 Thomson Rd. #13-01/02 United Square (2503383). **France,** 5 Gallop Rd.(4664866). **Germany,** 545 Orchard Rd. #14-01 Far East Shopping Centre, (7371355). **India,** 31 Grange Rd. (7376777). **Indonesia,** 7 Chatsworth Rd. (7377422). **Ireland,** 541 Orchard Rd. #08-02 Liat Towers, (7323430). **Italy,** 101 Thomson Rd. #27-02/03 United Square, (2506022); **Japan,** 16 Nassim Rd. (2358855). **Malaysia,** 301 Jervois Rd. (2350011). **Netherlands,** 541 Orchard Towers, #13-01 Liat Towers, (7371155). **New Zealand,** 13 Nassim Rd. (2359966). **Norway,** 16 Raffles Quay, #44-01 Hong Leong Bldg. (2207122). **Spain,** 15 Scotts Rd. #05-08/09 Thong Teck Bldg. **Sweden,** 111 Somerset, #05-08 PUB Bldg., (7342771). **Switzerland,** 1 Swiss Club Link, (685788). **Thailand,** 370 Orchard Rd. (7372644). **USA,** 30 Hill St. (3380251);

BANKS

Algemene Bank Nederland, 18 Church Street (5355511). **Banque Nationale de Paris,** 20 Collyer Quay, #01-01 Tung Centre (2240211). **Bangkok Bank,** 180 Cecil St. Bangkok Bank Bldg. (2219400). **Bank Negara Indonesia,** 158 Cecil St. (2257755). **Bank of America,** 78 Shenton Way, Ong Bldg. (2236688). **Bank of China,** 4 Battery Rd. (5352411). **Bank of India,** 108 Robinson Rd. (2220011). **Bank of Tokyo,** 16 Raffles Quay, #01-06 Hong Leong Bldg. (2208111). **Chase Manhattan,** 50 Raffles Place, Shell Tower (5304111). **Citibank,** 1 Shenton Way, Robina House (2255225). **Hong Kong & Shanghai Banking Corp.,** 10 Collyer Quay, #01-01 Ocean Bldg. (5305000). **Malayan Banking,** 2 Battery Rd. Malayan Bank Chambers (5352266). **Oversea-Chinese Banking Corp.,** 65 Chulia St. OCBC Centre (5352266). **Societe Generale,** 105 Cecil St #20-01/04 The Octagon, (5338686). **Standard Chartered,** 6 Battery Rd. (2258888).

Further Readings

This selection is intended to provide an introduction to Peninsular Malaysia and Singapore and the books listed below are both readable and informative. Many books were written in English during the British colonial days, and some have been reprinted by Oxford University Press in Singapore and Kuala Lumpur available at Times and MPH bookshops. Select Books in the Tanglin Shopping Complex, Singapore, specializes in books on the Southeast Asian region. Many of the best journals on history and culture were written and published through the Malayan Branch of the Royal Asiatic Society, referred to as JMBRAS. Reprints are available at selected bookstores.

HISTORY

Andaya, Barbara Watson, Leonard Y. (1982) *A History of Malaysia*. Excellent and readable, with a non-colonial contemporary viewpoint similar to current local interpretations. The best book in the field for a comprehensive, unbiased coverage.

Bellwood, Peter (1985) *Pre-history of the Indo Malaysian Archipelago*. A revolutionary view of where the region's first inhabitants came from. Detailed and fascinating reading.

Brown, C.C. (Translator) (1953) *Sejarah Melayu* or "Malay Annals", JMBRAS. The finest Malay literary work which traces the geneology of the Melakan Sultanate. Vivid narrative, and superb story-telling of the Malay's 15th-century "Golden Age".

Butcher, J.G. (1979) *The British in Malaya, 1880-1941. The Social History of a European Community in Colonial South-East Asia*. Interesting, and written in a lively style.

Coates, Austin (1968) *The Commerce in Rubber: The First 250 Years*. The definitive work on the crop that changed the face of Malaya. Starting with its discovery in Brazil, then its growth, booms and slumps in Southeast Asia.

Gullick, J.M. (1987) *Malay Society in the Late Nineteenth Century, The Beginnings of Change*. An indepth look at how this traditional Islamic society adapted to a different world.

Linehan, W. (1936) *A History of Pahang* MBRAS. Scholarly, and sometimes difficult going, but nonetheless a fascinating look at the historical development of the Peninsula's largest state.

Wheatley, Paul (1964) *Impressions of the Malay Peninsula in Ancient Times*. An absorbing look at pre-16th century history according to Chinese, Indian and Arab sources. This is the synthesized version of his more scholarly tome *The Golden Khersonese* (1961).

Windstedt, R.O. (1935, reprint 1982) *A History of Malaya*. Rather dated colonial viewpoint, but is well written and easy to read.

BIOGRAPHIES & REMINISCENCES

Chapman, Frederick Spencer (1949, reprint 1983) *The Jungle is Neutral*. A true tale of the author's three and a half years spent hiding from the Japanese in the Malayan jungle. One of the classic tales of World War II.

Coope, A.E. (Translator) (1967) *The Voyages of Adbullah*. A journey up the little-known East Coast in the early 19th-century by Abdullah bin Abdul Kadir, former scribe to Raffles.

Hill, A.H. (Translator) (1955) *The Hikayat Abdullah* JMBRAS. Abdullah bin Abdul Kadir's autobiographical tale of 19th-century Melaka and Singapore. Tells of the coming of Raffles, and many other first-hand reminiscences.

THE ARTS

Couillard, Marie-Andree (1980) *Tradition In Tension: Carving in a Jah Hut Community*. A look at these indigenous wood sculptors and their work.

Edwards, Norman and Keys, Peter. (1988) *Singapore - A Guide to Buildings, Streets, Places*. Not a travel guide, but an intensive street-by-street compilation of Singapore's architecture. A must for architecture buffs.

Lim Jee Yuan (1987) *The Malay House*. Profusely illustrated, large-format work on the indigenous Malay house. Contains house-building styles, regional variations, and an interesting look at the economic reasons behind the demise of the traditional home.

Werner, Roland (1973) *Mah Meri, Art and Culture*. The only authoritative book on sculptures and lifestyle of this west coast Orang Asli group.

CULTURE & RELIGION

Carey Iskandar (1975) *Orang Asli: the Aboriginal Tribes of Peninsular Malaysia*. Good introduction to the peninsular's indigenous people.

Khoo Kay Kim (1992) *Malay Society: Transformation and Democratisation*. A stimulating and discerning study of the evolution of Malay society from the time of the Melakan Sultanate to the present by the nation's leading authority.

Lat. *Kampung Boy, Town Boy, Mat Som, Best of Lat*. Malaysia's best-known cartoonist gives his humorous and highly-accurate account of contemporary life and politics.

Mahathir bin Mohamad (1970) *The Malay Dilemma*. A controversial, but interesting theory by Malaysia's Prime Minister on the background behind the nation's racially-dominated economy.

Schebesta, Paul (1928, reprint 1973) *Among the Forest Dwarfs of Malaya*. This classical work on the so-called Negrito peoples of the Malay Peninsula has an introduction by Geoffrey Benjamin.

Winstedt, Richard (1947, revised 1981) *The Malays - A Cultural History*. The pre-history is outdated, but it is a good introduction to the beliefs, religion, and the political, social, legal and economic systems of the Malays.

LANGUAGE

Coope, A.E. *Macmillan's Malay-English, English-Malay Dictionary*. Pocket-sized and concise, revised in the new Malay spelling.

Hamilton, A.W. (reprinted 1985) *Malay Made Easy*. Lives up to its title, but its colonial-style phrases are incredibly dated, albiet amusing. There are commands for ironing collars correctly, and getting the syce to exercise your horse, among others.

Sulaiman, Othman (1990) *Malay for Everyone: Mastering Malay Through English*. Probably the most up to date, teach-yourself book. Set out in a series of lessons and good for anyone wanting a thorough grounding of the language.

LITERATURE

Fauconnier, Henri. *Soul of Malaya* (1931, Oxford reprint 1965). Evocative, semi-autobiographical novel written by a French rubber planter. This sensitive portrayal of the Malays won the Prix Goncourt in 1930.

Han Su-yin (1956) *And the Rain My Drink*. A novel about life in the Emergency—the communist-terrorist uprising—set in a New Village.

Maugham, W. Somerset (1933, reprint 1986) *Maugham's Malaysian Stories*, and *Ah King and Other Stories*. Short stories by the master English novelist which brings to life the colonial era. Many tales were of true characters and events, thinly-disguised, which scandalised Malaya's early expatriate society.

Theroux, Paul (1977) *The Consul's File*. A collection of short-stories set in a small Malayan town. Amusing, and cynical, but not very accurate.

Winstedt, Richard (revised 1992) *A History of Classical Malay Literature*. A collection of the best works. Excellently compiled.

NATURE

Cubitt, Gerald, and Payne, Junaidi (1991) *Wild Malaysia*. Large-format book profusely illustrated with high-quality photographs.

Glenister, A.G. (1951) *The Birds of the Malay Pensinula, Singapore and Penang*. Good compilation but not enough color plates for identification.

King, Ben, Woodcock, Martin and Dickinson, E.C. (1975) *Birds of South-East Asia*. The definitive guidebook for all birdwatchers. Profusely illustrated.

Morrel, R. (1960) *Common Malayan Butterflies*. Well-illustrated guide for both laymen and lepidopterists.

Shuttleworth, Charles (1981) *Malaysia's Green and Timeless World*. An aborbing account, and excellent introduction to the flora, fauna, and indigenous peoples of the rainforests.

Tweedie, M.W.F. and Harrison, J.L. (1981) *Malayan Animal Life*. Well-illustrated introduction to the Peninsula's diverse fauna.

GUIDES AND TRAVELOGUES

Bird, Isabella L. (1967) *The Golden Chersonese, Travels in Malaya in 1879*. This intrepid Victorian adventuress give a perceptive and beautifully-descriptive account of her travels through Singapore and the peninsular west coast in the days when the British were just starting their push into the interior.

Falcon Press (Publisher) *Petronas Heritage Mapbook of Peninsular Malaysia*. Easy to follow guide for motorists in a mapbook form. Covers many off-the-beaten-track attractions.

Harrison, Cuthbert Woodville (1923, reprint 1985) *An Illustrated Guide to the Federated Malay States*. The first real guidebook to the Peninsula covers "Notes for Travellers", "Hints for Motorists", and section on big-game shooting, museums, mining, and an informative appendix. Although very dated some of his countryside scenes are still the same and the British colonial-style writing makes for a great read.

Lloyd, R.Ian and Moore Wendy. (1987) *To Know Malaysia*. Large-format book with informative essays. Superbly photographed by one of the region's top photographers.

Wheeler, Tony, etc. *Malaysia, Singapore and Brunei*. Lonely Planet's travel survival kit is good for getting around and budget accomodation. Take the opinionated comments with a grain of salt, however, as these are often biased taxi-driver's tales.

About the Authors

Barbara Watson Andaya has a Ph.D from Cornell University and is currently Lecturer with the Department of History, University of Auckland, New Zealand. Her research focuses on the Malay-Indonesian archipelago.

Hashim Awang A.R. holds a Ph.D in medical anthropology from University of Hawaii-Manoa, and is an Associate Professor at the Department of Malay Studies, University of Malaya. His major research is in Malay medicine and he has published many articles on this subject.

Peter Bellwood is a Reader in Prehistory at The Australian National University, specializing in Southeast Asian and Pacific prehistory. His books include *Man's Conquest of the Pacific* , *Prehistory of the Indo-Malaysian Archipelago* and *The Polynesians*.

Geoffrey Benjamin studied at Cambridge but has spent most of his adult life in Singapore, where he is Associate Professor in Sociology at the National University. Since the 1960s he has been studying the Temiars and other Orang Asli.

Shane Callahan, is a regular contributor to regional magazines and writes on culture, travel and food. As a Eurasian Singaporean his unique background,gives him the advantage of a multi-cultural insight.

Geoffrey Davison is a biologist who received his Ph.D from the University of Malaya and has lived and worked in the country ever since. He now works for WWF Malaysia. His particular interests include animal behavior.

Mohd. Kassim bin Haji Ali was born in Melaka, and first joined the Museums Department in 1962. During his museum tenure he has held various posts including Curator of Ethnology and is is currently the Senior Assistant Director for Education and Exhibitions. Kassim has written several catalogues and reference books.

Yahaya Ismail has written over 30 books on politics, culture, literary criticism, fiction and tourism and has been appointed the royal biographer to the present King of Malaysia. In his varied career, he has been a teacher, research officer, lecturer, and chief editor of a newspaper.

Kiew Bong Heang is a well-known Malaysian naturalist currently lecturing at the Department of Zoology, University of Malaya. He has over 20 years of field experience and has been involved with numerous expeditions. He regularly contributes to a number of publications.

Ku Zam Zam Ku Idris is an Associate Professor at the Department of Malay Studies, University of Malaya, lecturing on ethnomusicology and Malay culture. Her numerous articles in English and Bahasa Malaysia, on traditional Malay jusic, culture and expressive arts can be found in several academic journals and books.

Lee Kam Hing obtained his M.A. from the University of Malaya and his Ph.D from Monash University, Melbourne. He currently holds the post of Associate Professor in the History Department, University of Malaya, where he teaches Southeast Asian history, but researches mainly in Indonesian and Malaysian history.

Zuraina Majid, a Professor at Universiti Sains Malaysia in Penang, obtained her Ph. D from Yale. Archaeology is her main research area and among the major sites she has excavated are the Niah caves, Sarawak, and Kota Tampan in Perak. She has written several books and articles based on her research.

Wendy Moore, a freelance writer and editor, born in Sydney, Australia, has traveled extensively. In 1984 she was based in Singapore, then moved to Malaysia in 1986 where she has lived and worked ever since. She is a frequent contributor to many publications and has written a number of travel-related books.

Fiona Nichols, a travel writer and photographer, has been based in Singapore fo r the last 10 years. Her worlk has been published in Asia, Europe and Africa and includes the first photographic book on Phuket, and photography fro a book on the Taj Mahal.

Said Halim Said Nong is a lecturer at the Language Center, University of Malaya. To date he has published books on television drama, literary text analyses, a collection of folk tales and children's stories.

Ilsa Sharp is a British-born freelance writer who has lived in Singapore for the past 25 years. A Chinese studies graduate, and for 12 years a business editor with the Straits Times newpaper group, she has also worked for the *Far Eastern Economic Review*. She currently specializes in the environment and wildlife, as well as Southeast Asia.

Morten Strange, a Danish national who has lived in Singapore since 1980, retired from his career as a petroleum engineer in 1986 to pursue a lifelong interest in birds. He has birdwatched and photographed all over Asia, in particular Peninsular Malaysia. In 1992 he wrote and photographed a guide to birds of Peninsular Malaysia and Singapore.

Yeow Mei Sin is a Singaporean freelance writer specializing in travel and culture. She has contributed articles to many regional magazines.

Index

Bold entries indicate a section or article on the subject, *italics* donote a picture.

MAPS